# LABOUR IN POWER?

# Labour in power?

a study of the Labour Government
1974–1979

*David Coates*

*Longman*
London and New York

**Longman Group Limited** London

*Associated companies, branches and representatives
throughout the world*

*Published in the United States of America
by Longman Inc., New York*

© Longman Group Limited 1980

*First published 1980*

**British Library Cataloguing in Publication Data**

Coates, David
  Labour in power?
  1. Great Britain – Politics and government
  – 1974.
  I. Title
  354'.41'0009    JN309     79-42850

  ISBN 0 582 29536 X
  ISBN 0 582 29535 1 Pbk

Set in 10/12 pt V-I-P Bembo
Printed in Great Britain by
Richard Clay (The Chaucer Press) Ltd, Bungay, Suffolk

# Contents

# *Preface*

The debate within and beyond the Labour Party on the reasons for the recent electoral defeat of the Labour Government is only just beginning, and this study should be seen as one contribution to that debate. At least two things will be at a premium in the years to come if that debate is to be as informed and productive as it needs to be. The first is a full and accurate account of what actually happened between 1974 and 1979. The second is a clear statement of why the Party was unable to live up to the radical ambitions expressed by leading Party figures in 1973 and 1974. In the study that follows I have attempted to meet both these requirements. In Part One I have recorded the development of Labour Government policy in the crucial areas of finance, labour and industry, in the hope that this will provide a reliable (and hence relatively uncontroversial) source to which participants in the debate can turn for a record of the events whose significance they are disputing. The second part is more openly partisan. It contains one particular explanation of why the Labour Government's performance was so unimpressive, and why neither the trade union leadership nor the Labour Left were able in the end to prevent it from being so. The final chapter seeks to draw the lessons of this period of Labour Government, and argues the necessity for a socialist transformation that goes beyond the politics even of the Labour Left, if the objectives which the Labour Party espoused in 1973 are ever to be realised.

I do not imagine that what follows will always be particularly easy to read and digest, though I have attempted to make it so. Particularly in the second part of the study I have attempted to present the relatively complex arguments of other Marxists about the workings of a capitalist economy (and its political and social implications) in language which is intelligible to the concerned layman. Yet at times the argument is

unavoidably technical and its presentation dense; and at those points I
suggest that the reader turns to the references at the end of the book, in
the hope that the presentation of similar arguments by other writers
may prove to be easier to understand and to assess. Even where I have
managed to make my argument clear, I may have been defeated by a
problem that seems to be endemic to this kind of analysis – namely that
of establishing a proper relationship between the parts of the analysis
and the whole. Ideally, a study of this kind should establish its central
thesis in its opening pages, the better to illuminate the detail of the
argument that follows; and yet I have found no satisfactory way of
laying out my central thesis except through a detailed examination of its
complementary parts. This means that at times the explanation has had
to be delayed, in order to establish the complexity of the underlying
detail, but I hope the reader will find the subject matter sufficiently
important to justify the slow buildup of the argument, and will move
with me from the specific to the general as I try to show how a particular
understanding of what has happened to this Labour Government can
and should be related to a wider body of economic and social analysis
and to a more international pattern of working-class political struggle.

Perhaps it will help if I make clear in some detail how the argument
that follows is built. In Part One there are three detailed narratives: on
the Labour Government's overall economic strategy, on its policy on
incomes and employment, and on its industrial strategy (including here
both its relationships with the private and public sectors, and its attitude
to industrial democracy – to the shift of class power within industry).
At points in the narrative, notably early in Chapter 1 and at the ends of
Chapters 2 and 3, I discuss more generally the nature of this Labour
Government and its problems, as a way of beginning to link the
narrative to the more openly explanatory analysis in Part Two. There
(in Chapter 4 in particular) I trace the constraints on the Labour
Government, moving from a discussion of the most obvious and
pressing constraint – its lack for a long period of a parliamentary
majority – through to an assessment of the impact of world capitalism
on its agenda of action and on its effectiveness. In Chapters 5 and 6 these
constraints are used to explain why trade union pressure became more
moderate and less effective over time, and why the Labour Left was so
unsuccessful. Chapter 6 widens to include a critique of the Labour Left's
programme; and this leads, in Chapter 7, to a more detailed discussion
of the lessons of this Labour Government for socialist politics in the
1980s.

I hope that the subject matter of this study will be of interest to
anyone concerned with developments in British politics and society in

the last quarter of the twentieth century, but it is addressed also to a more specific body of people. It seems inevitable that what follows will alienate those who think that programmes and manifestoes are documents that are as short as they are unimportant, and that *the* test of the 'virility' of a government, particularly one containing a left-wing element, is to be measured by how far it departs from its promises, rather than by how far it implements them; and that for all these reasons it is inappropriate to use election promises as a benchmark against which to measure a government's performance. I remain unconvinced by such arguments. This study begins with a discussion of the election promises of the Labour Government, and it does so for two distinct reasons. One is that, for the Labour Party at least, the policy-making process in Opposition still provides the initial framework for the subsequent development of policy, and is therefore not to be regarded as simply dismissible whenever Labour returns to office. The second is that my argument is addressed to a particular and very important body of men and women who take party manifestoes very seriously indeed – namely those on the left wing of the Labour Party. For them, the 1973 Labour Party Programme (and the election manifestoes that it inspired in 1974) were, and remain, important victories; and for this reason, if for no other, it is important to consider the nature and cause of their fate.

So in general the argument that follows should be of interest primarily to those people who still believe that the search for a more socially just and equal society has something to do with the question of socialism. It is true that any critique of the policies and analyses of those on the left of the Labour Party, of the kind that follows here, can be attractive to those on the right and centre of British politics who pride themselves on their 'realism', and for whom public ownership, State planning and extensive welfare provision are major causes of Britain's economic malaise. But to them I would argue strongly that their faith in the wonders of a self-regulating private economy is even more misplaced than is the faith in parliamentary socialism which inspires the Tribunite Left. It is to men and women of this latter persuasion that what follows is primarily addressed. It is with their thinking, rather than with the perspectives of the social democratic wing of the Labour Party coalition, or of the Party centre, that I have been concerned; and the current thinking on the Labour Left is criticised here not because I reject their aspirations but because I share them. I hope that those on the left of the Labour Party will be generous enough to react to this argument in the fraternal spirit in which it is offered, and use it as a base on which to clarify the strengths and weaknesses of the alternative routes to that democratic socialist society to which we all aspire.

As the footnotes to the text (pp. 285–296) should make clear, very little of what follows is in any sense original. In building the analysis, I have drawn heavily on the recent renaissance of Marxist scholarship in the English-speaking world, and have relied unashamedly on the expertise of others in the fields of political economy, sociology, Marxist political science and industrial relations. I have interpreted my task as one of synthesising important work done by others in these fields, the better to apply their findings to a specific and important case. Though I am sure that many of the people on whose work I have relied so heavily will not share the conclusions to which their analyses have been put, I think it only proper to record my political and intellectual debt to them. Like many Marxists working in higher education, I have been the beneficiary of the long academic debate on the role of the State in a capitalist society that was initially revived by the exchanges between Ralph Miliband and Nicos Poulantzas, and of the recent 'rediscovery' of Marxist economics, not least in the Conference of Socialist Economists. I would like to record my debt in particular to the writings of Ben Fine, Andrew Gamble, Andrew Glyn, Ian Gough, Lawrence Harris, Richard Hyman, Bob Jessop, Ernesto Laclau, Ernest Mandel, Paul Mattick, Ralph Miliband, Lewis Minkin, Leo Panitch, Nicos Poulantzas, Henrietta Resler, Bob Sutcliffe, Paul Walton, John Westergaard and David Yaffe. If nothing else, I hope that the study will make references to their work familiar to a wider audience, and encourage the serious student of British politics and labour movements to make use of the suggestions for further reading given in the bibliography at the end. I realise only too well that in drawing on so many fields of academic expertise I have overstretched my own area of competence, and that as a result some at least of what follows will have to be amended in the light of reactions from those with more expert knowledge and greater theoretical sophistication. But I am also sure that the *detail* of the argument, though important, is less vital than its *range*. If the Left is ever to persuade a mass audience of the need to transcend capitalism, it must first understand that capitalism in all its complexity; and that means that socialists have to become competent – indeed very competent – in at least the fields of political economy, sociology, and industrial relations as well as in political science and labour history. We have to be able to circumvent the fragmentation of scholarship that goes on even at university level, and build a total analysis of the capitalist universe against which our politics must struggle. This study will have achieved its aim if it acts as a catalyst to the building and refining of that analysis; and to the degree that it acts in this way, it will in my view have a value, even if its substantive content is an early casualty of that theoretical development.

## Preface

A number of my friends and colleagues have discussed the Labour Government with me and have commented on earlier drafts of what follows. These include Raymond Bush, Lionel Cliffe, David Hay, Gordon Johnston, Robert Looker, Keith Nathan, Leo Panitch and David Skidmore. I have learned many things, and continue to learn many things, from each of them, and I am particularly grateful for their help. In addition, colleagues at York and Leeds were generous with time and assistance at crucial moments in the manuscript's preparation, and I would like to thank them for that. But I should also add that by far my greatest and continuing debt is to Joan. It is one of the pleasures of writing to be able to record in so public a place the existence of so great an affection and support.

D. C.
*Leeds*
*July 1979*

# List of abbreviations

ACAS   Advisory Conciliation and Arbitration Service
ASLEF   Associated Society of Locomotive Engineers and Firemen
ASTMS   Association of Scientific, Technical and Managerial Staffs
AUEW   Amalgamated Union of Engineering Workers
BALPA   British Air Line Pilots Association
BL   British Leyland
BLMC   British Leyland Motor Company
CBI   Confederation of British Industry
CIS   Counter-Information Service
EEC   European Economic Community
EETPU   Electrical, Electronic and Telecommunications and
   Plumbing Union
GEC   General Electric Company
GLC   Greater London Council
GMWU   General and Municipal Workers' Union
IMF   International Monetary Fund
IRC   Industrial Reorganisation Corporation
JRC   Joint Representation Committee
MSC   Manpower Services Commission
NEB   National Enterprise Board
NEC   National Executive Committee
NEDC   National Economic Development Council
NUJ   National Union of Journalists
NUM   National Union of Mineworkers
NUPE   National Union of Public Employees
NUR   National Union of Railwaymen
OECD   Organisation for Economic Cooperation and
   Development

## List of abbreviations

OPEC    Organisation of Petroleum Exporting Countries
SNP    Scottish National Party
TGWU    Transport and General Workers Union
TUC    Trades Union Congress
UCATT    Union of Construction, Allied Trades and Technicians
USDAW    Union of Shop, Distributive and Allied Workers

# PART ONE

# *The record of Labour in power*

CHAPTER ONE
# The Government's economic performance

The Labour Party entered office in 1974 with a series of clear policy commitments more radical in tone and in aspiration than any that the Party had endorsed since 1945. The new Labour Government also possessed a degree of support from the leading figures of the trade union movement that contrasted sharply with the strained relationships between Labour Cabinet and TUC General Council that marked the last years of the previous Wilson Government. Indeed the shift to the left in language and programme after 1970 was on a scale last seen in the Labour Party as long ago as 1931, though in one important respect at least the two periods differed significantly. When the Labour Party lost office in 1931, the subsequent realignment of policy was accompanied by a change in the leadership of the Party in Parliament. This did not happen in 1970. The parliamentary leadership of the Party throughout the years of opposition remained almost entirely in the hands of the men and women who had formed the last Wilson Cabinet of 1970. But these parliamentarians faced a TUC General Council whose leading members were now keen to play an active role in the shaping of future Labour Government policy. The parliamentarians also had to come to terms, after 1970, both with their own electoral defeat and with the Conservative Government's controversial and bitterly resisted attempt to consolidate its new Industrial Relations Act. Though the labour movement continued to be divided on the other major political issue of the 1970–74 period – namely entry into the Common Market – the unions' confrontation with the Government of Edward Heath helped to bring leading trade unionists and the Labour Shadow Cabinet back together after 1970, and the memory of the traumatic events that had preceded Edward Heath's return to power gave the left of the Party a brief period of dominance.

In the light of subsequent events, much of the debate in those years of opposition already seems quaint and anachronistic, and any recapitulation of the policy-making process within the Labour Party between 1970 and 1974 must begin by admitting that the 'rediscovery' by many leading parliamentarians that what Britain required was nothing short of 'a fundamental and irreversible shift in the balance of power and wealth in favour of working people and their families'[1] was visibly only skin deep – a set of rhetorical concessions to the prevailing mood and language of Labour Party conferences. There are many examples of this conference rhetoric, which have to be guarded against and discounted. Denis Healey's promise of tax changes that would produce 'howls of anguish from the . . . rich'[2] and Harold Wilson's defence of industrial militancy[3] sat uneasily against the political record of these men between 1964 and 1970, and proved in the end to have been as temporary a conversion to political radicalism as they were then expedient. Yet beneath the rhetoric, solid plans and agreements were laid, which alone hold the key to the subsequent development of policy, and which also marked the high point of recent left-wing influence on Labour Party thinking. For both these reasons the policy commitments and agreements of the years of opposition are worth recording in detail, as a basis on which to assess the performance of the Labour Government that they were supposed to inspire.

# I

At the heart of the new radicalism of the Labour Party in opposition was a series of agreements between the National Executive Committee of the Labour Party, the Parliamentary leadership and the General Council of the TUC, meeting together as a TUC/Labour Party Liaison Committee. As early as the Labour Party conference of 1971 Hugh Scanlon of the AUEW (Amalgamated Union of Engineering Workers) was reported as insisting that no trade union support for Labour Party planning documents should be given 'unless a public assurance was made from the platform that the policy would involve no incomes policy, voluntary or otherwise, and no restraint on free collective bargaining'. For the NEC (National Executive Committee) Roy Jenkins was reported as assuring the AUEW and the TGWU (Transport and General Workers Union) that there would be no return to the incomes policies of 1966 and 1967, but that future policy would need 'a much closer mutual understanding between the unions at all levels and the political leaders'.[4] The first fruits of that 'closer mutual understanding' came in July 1972, when the Liaison Committee agreed that a future Labour Government would immediately replace the Conservatives' Industrial Relations Act with an Act establishing a Conciliation and Arbitration Service, and with legislation setting up a new series of legal rights for workers and trade unions. These were to include the right to belong to a trade union, protection against unfair dismissal, and the establishment of a procedure by which unions seeking recognition from reluctant employers could obtain arbitration on their case. With these immediate preoccupations of the trade union leadership resolved, it was then possible for the Liaison Committee to turn to the negotiation of a wider set of agreements between the unions and the parliamentary leadership, under which union cooperation with a future Labour Government would be guaranteed by Government policy in a number of economic and social fields. The text of that agreement (a joint TUC – Labour Party Liaison Committee *Statement on Economic Policy and the Cost of Living*) was published in February 1973. While remaining significantly quiet on the question of incomes policy, it committed the next Labour Government to:

(a) what it termed 'a wide ranging and permanent system of price controls', particularly on food;

(b) a new approach to housing and rent that would include the repeal of the 1972 Housing Finance Act, the long-run municipalisation of private rented property, the public ownership of required building land, and the building of at least 400,000 houses a year;

(c) the strengthening of public transport, and experiments with free public transport in major conurbations;

(d) a large-scale redistribution of income and wealth, by wealth taxes, gift taxes, and steeply progressive direct taxation;

(e) the end of prescription charges, and an immediate rise in pensions, with pensions thereafter to be annually updated in line with average earnings;

(f) the expansion of investment and the control of capital by further public ownership, by the extension of state supervision of private investment, and by new measures of control to prevent excessive investment overseas;

(g) the extension of industrial democracy, by bringing investment policy and closure policy into the scope of collective bargaining.[5]

This set of agreements between the trade unions and the Labour leadership came to be known as the 'social contract', and it is significant that from the beginning it was given different emphases by different labour leaders. James Callaghan, at the 1972 Labour Party conference, saw the emerging social contract 'as a basis for beginning talks with the TUC on a voluntary incomes policy'.[6] Jack Jones saw it as creating 'basic standards which no worker (or pensioner either) can be below, but which offers the right of negotiation about the whole complex range of subjects – including productivity – which are central to the lives of individual workers'. For him, the agreement between the two wings of the labour movement had 'above all . . . place[d] Industrial Democracy . . . into the centre of Party thinking and policy', 'such that a future Labour Government can be elected on the basis that millions of workers will be given a new status in influencing the control of their firms and industries'.[7] Harold Wilson presented the social contract as the key to national economic recovery. As he told the 1972 Labour Party conference, 'there can be no road to national agreement, national unity, on a policy adequate for dealing with inflation and unemployment except on the basis of social justice'.[8] But though the emphasis differed, the content of the Government's part of any future 'social contract' was clear – radical and innovatory policy in the fields of industrial relations, housing, prices, social benefits, investment and industrial democracy.

The strategy of reforms built round the social contract did not restrict its focus simply to the rights of trade unions and workers. The social contract was part of a wider set of policies that the Party in opposition adopted on the control of economic activity in total by a future Labour Government. The speeches of major parliamentary figures, and the draft Programmes presented to Labour Party conferences in 1972 and 1973, contained a rudimentary but consistent analysis of the causes of inflation and unemployment in the British economy, an analysis which laid heavy emphasis on the impact on economic performance of class privilege and private industrial and financial power. There seemed to be general agreement that inflation and unemployment were the key problems of policy to be tackled, and that their cause lay not in the level of industrial earnings but in the persistence of poverty, in the paucity of manufacturing investment, in the disproportionate power of a small number of large companies, and in the excessively dominant role of what the 1972 Programme called 'irresponsible private hands, crude market forces'. The Labour Party's answer was to propose direct government intervention into the private economy to strengthen its investment record and manufacturing base, and to establish public control. The 1973 Programme talked of 'three major pillars – each one of which is essential' to future Labour Government success:

(a) the extension of public ownership, and the creation of a State holding company;

(b) the setting up of a system of planning agreements with major companies;

(c) the passing of a new Industry Act.

The 1973 conference was dominated by the (eventually successful) attempt by the Labour leadership to avoid a commitment to the public ownership of the twenty-five largest companies. But the whole leadership agreed to the nationalisation of North Sea oil and gas, registered and unregistered ports, shipbuilding and ancillary services, aircraft production, and 'identifiable sections or individual firms within the pharmaceutical, machine tool, construction, and road haulage industries'.[9] In addition 'all land required for development, redevelopment and improvement' was to come into public ownership. Harold Wilson also spoke speculatively of the creation of a State merchant bank, and a National Housing Finance Corporation, to act as a publicly owned building society. This massive extension of the public sector was to be carried still further by the creation of a National Enterprise Board (NEB) – 'a central instrument in our industrial policy' as Harold Wilson called it in the same conference speech – to take over and manage existing State assets, to 'socialise' existing public industries by establishing real industrial democracy there, and to buy 'a controlling interest in relevant companies in profitable manufacturing industries'.[10] Major companies left in the private sector would be obliged to sign planning agreements with the Government, both as a way of making them accountable to Parliament, and as a means of facilitating government planning and the direction of government aid. All these innovations were to be consolidated in a strengthened Industry Act, giving a future Labour Government greater powers to gather information, direct investment policy, control prices and profits, and even to buy outright individual companies whose entry into the public sector was deemed to be 'in the national interest'. And in addition, of course, as part of the agreements already made with the TUC, the private sector under a future Labour Government would have to operate within a system of price controls designed to minimise prices and profits commensurate only with the maintenance of an adequate rate of investment, and to cooperate in the consideration of industrial democracy, with a view to its eventual extension throughout British industry. As Harold Wilson put it, *Labour's Programme for Britain* is directed to the assertion of democratic control over the industrial decisions which determined the lives of every individual within our democracy. It is democratic and relevant.'[11] It was also, according to Michael Foot at least, 'the finest Socialist Programme I have seen in my lifetime'.[12]

It was this battery of proposals that formed the basis of the Labour Party's manifesto in February 1974: a twin strategy of a social contract with the trade unions and their members (to guarantee a set of basic rights, steadily improving real incomes, jobs, welfare benefits, social equality and industrial democracy in return for income restraint), and a tight government control over industrial activity. The Party also proposed to renegotiate the terms of entry into the Common Market, and to make significant increases in the provision of health care, education and consumer protection, and in the establishment of sexual equality. Both the programmes and the manifesto admitted the severity of the problems likely to be faced by an incoming Labour Government, and of the time and energy that would be required to remove them. 'The longer the Conservative Government survives,' the manifesto declared, 'the more desperate a situation a Labour Government will inherit. The British people will understand if we are then compelled to give so absolute a priority to rebuilding the economic fabric of the nation that some of our expenditure will have to be delayed.' But the claim of the Labour leadership as they approached the February election was clear. If the problems facing the British economy 'cut so deep . . . the solutions must cut deep also'.[13] That depth would involve the creation of a climate of social justice, and the re-establishment of political, public control over market, private forces. It would involve, in other words, the return of a Labour Government.

## II

That Labour Government was elected in February 1974, as the single largest party in Parliament, but without a majority over all the Opposition parties combined. Not until the second election, in October that year, did the Party gain that overall majority, and even then it was to be a slender one (an effective majority even in October of only three votes) which was to slip away in Scottish party schisms and by-election defeats over the next two and a half years. From February to October 1974, and especially after April 1977, the Labour Government survived by the tolerance of the Liberals or the other minority parties, a beneficiary of their reluctance to test their own popularity at the polls. This political weakness, and the absence of majority electoral support in either election, weakened the Labour Government's capacity to tackle both the immediate problems it faced on taking office, and its longer term plans for fundamental reform. The day it took office, the

Organisation for Economic Cooperation and Development (OECD) estimated that the economy's balance of payments deficit for 1974 would be at least £3350 million.[14] Wage rates were rising at an annual rate of between 15 and 20 per cent. So too were prices; and with the Conservative Government's dispute with the miners still unresolved, the economy was on a three-day week. The Government could hardly have been given a more difficult beginning.

But it was hard to tell, in those opening months, that this was a minority Government, poised for political defeat. The Cabinet acted decisively to settle with the miners, and to return the economy to five-day working. There then followed a series of consultative documents, White Papers and pieces of legislation that augured well for the full implementation of the Party's manifesto and programmes. There was an immediate change in the public relationship between the Cabinet and the national trade union leadership. Harold Wilson's first meeting as Prime Minister was with the TUC General Council; and from then on, with Michael Foot at the Department of Employment, relationships between Labour Ministers and national trade union leaders were regular, visible and cooperative. As agreed in 1972 the Government announced its intention of establishing the Conciliation and Arbitration Service in an Act which, as became clear in a draft Bill published in May 1974, was also to strengthen the legal right of peaceful picketing, and to extend the procedures already laid down in the 1971 Act to prevent unfair dismissal. At the same time, the Government announced its intention of introducing later a more comprehensive set of legal protections for workers – the Employment Protection Act – and a consultative document was published on this in September.

In line with the agreements reached in opposition with the TUC General Council, the incoming Labour Government imposed an immediate freeze on rents in both the private and council house sectors until the end of the year, began the repeal of the Housing Finance Act, and (in a White Paper published in September 1974) announced its intention of bringing land required for development into public ownership. Harold Wilson created a new Ministry of Prices, Consumer Protection and Fair Trading, with a seat in the Cabinet; and Shirley Williams, as that Minister, promised tougher price controls and selective food subsidies 'in weeks rather than months' at her first press conference early in March. Food subsidies on bread, milk and butter followed in Denis Healey's first budget; and by the end of March 1974 the Government was proposing a rigorous system of price controls under which the onus of proof in the justification of price increases was placed on firms themselves, and by which the Government would take to itself the power to block price increases on a wide range of consumer goods. Though Shirley Williams later agreed not to legislate for these powers immediately, she did win from the Retailers Consortium an agreement to concentrate price cutting in a narrow range of essential food stuffs, including bread, cheese, butter, fruit, vegetables and meat. At the same time the renegotiation of the terms of entry into the European Economic Community (EEC: Common Market) was begun and pensions were increased, as promised. A White Paper in the autumn undertook to keep pensions in line with the general level of earnings in the economy as a whole; and this followed the publication in the summer of a consultative document in which the Government proposed to bring in an annual wealth tax on assets over £100,000, and a capital transfer tax on gifts of over £15,000. A White Paper on legislative changes to guarantee equality for women came in September 1974, to complete the list of social reforms foreshadowed in the February manifesto. It was on this basis that the Labour Government began negotiations with the TUC on what, in the Queen's speech, was euphemistically referred to as an 'orderly growth of incomes on a voluntary basis'.[15]

The leading members of the left wing of the Party – Tony Benn and Eric Heffer – were sent to a new Industry Department, charged with the implementation of the 'three pillars' of the economic strategy outlined in Labour's 1973 Programme. Tony Benn's White Paper, *The Regeneration of British Industry*, came out in August; and though significantly muted in both content and presentation after lengthy disputes in Cabinet, it still reflected the Labour Government's commitment to extensive State activity and ownership in the industrial sector. Plans for public ownership were announced for the docks, and for the aircraft construction industry; and the Government announced its intention of taking a majority stake in the exploration and extraction of North Sea oil. A National Enterprise Board was to be created, and the Government was to give itself new powers of intervention and control in a strengthened Industry Act. Later a Committee of Inquiry was established, with tightly specified terms of reference, to explore the extension of industrial democracy; and a number of worker cooperatives received financial assistance from the Government in its first fifteen months of office. Indeed it was a measure of the degree of radicalism that Government policy towards industry was thought to contain in those early months that Tony Benn became the subject of a major press and business campaign of criticism, scaremongering and denigration. There was then some justice in the Labour Party's claim, in its October manifesto, that 'despite its minority position the Labour

Government have made a good start' and that what was required now was 'the return of a Labour Government with a working majority . . . that . . . can continue to tackle the great problems facing Britain'; or, as Jack Jones is reported to have put it to the Trades Union Congress in September, that a vote for Labour would 'help to build the new Jerusalem'.[16]

In fact this was not to be. In spite of the October manifesto's claim that 'as at the last election we are not making any promises that we cannot keep', the promise of industrial regeneration and social justice was in the end renegued. With the election over, and in the face of persistent inflation, low rates of investment, heavy foreign debts and periodic currency crises, the Labour Government slipped imperceptibly but steadily away from what the left of the Party had held to be the radical promise of the opposition years. The changes in the renegotiated terms of Common Market entry proved to be cosmetic rather than real, and the result of the subsequent referendum seriously weakened the Left within the Cabinet. The emphasis, within the dialogue of the social contract, changed from social reform to incomes control, so that by July 1975 the Government was back into that by now almost traditional summer practice of young Labour Governments – handling sterling crises by winning voluntary pay restraint. However it should not be thought that the willingness of the Labour Government to support official trade unionism before the courts, or to strengthen the legal rights and procedural powers of trade unionists, was also a summer casualty. There was, at least, no return to the anti-union tirades of the 1966–69 period. Nor did the 'visibility' of trade union leaders (and the associated myth of their excessive political power) decline with the pound. But the function and political significance of that visibility did alter, and did so quickly, to become an index of the trade union movement's lack of political leverage on the critical questions of living standards and employment. Under this Government, trade union leaders gained not so much power as a new role: that of increasingly hard-pressed guarantors of pay restraint and overseers of falling real wages in the face of sustained inflation and intolerably high levels of unemployment that both they, and seemingly the Government, could only regret but not prevent.

The plans for a wealth tax were abandoned, and the real value of welfare benefits continued to be eroded by a price inflation on foodstuffs and rent which by the end of 1976 had forced the Cabinet to negotiate a major loan with the International Monetary Fund (IMF), at the cost of substantial cuts in public spending (and hence in the social wage). New men took over the Industry Department after the referendum on the Common Market and presided over the emasculation of the new interventionist powers and institutions that the Tony Benn White Paper had promised to establish. The NEB in particular became virtually indistinguishable from any other major institutional investor in private manufacturing industry, except that its portfolio and investment became swamped (as theirs presumably were not) by the problems of an ailing car industry that had to be sustained by State funds in its period of crisis. There was a steady and significant shift in the whole emphasis of government policy to industry after the October election: a shift from intervention and control to more conventional patterns of exhortation and support, as the Government attempted to win economic growth by reassuring private industry and by restricting its own use of financial and material resources to 'leave space' for private industrial investment. As a part of this changing attitude to private incentives and managerial power, the Government's early enthusiasm for industrial democracy at boardroom level as a key to economic recovery gave way to prevarication on the Bullock Report[17] in the face of a major public campaign against radical reform from senior managerial personnel in both the public and the private sectors.

So by the end, as in 1970, the high hopes of a radical and reforming Labour Government petered out, and the economic transformation promised in opposition failed to materialise. There was no fundamental and irreversible shift in the balance of power and wealth in favour of working people and their families. There was not even an end to inflation, nor a lowering of unemployment. There was simply a renaissance of Conservative political strength, and a further step towards the tight integration of the State and the private capitalist economy. It is this decline from initial purpose and radical pretensions which has to be charted and explained.

III

As has been the common experience of Labour Governments, the conditions that Ministers faced on entering office were severe. Over and above the immediate issue of the miners' dispute and the resulting three-day week, the Government faced an economy in which retail prices were rising at an annual rate of 15 per cent, and in which the index of average earnings (linked as these were to the retail price index under the threshold agreements of the previous Government's incomes policy), once the three-day week was over, rose 17.7 per cent from July 1973 to July 1974. Indeed in the Labour Government's first year of office price inflation and the rate of increase of earnings both quickened significantly. By December 1974 the general level of wholesale prices in the economy was 28 per cent higher than it had been twelve months before; and by the summer of 1975, at the first peak of the inflation rate under this Government, the retail price index was rising at an annual rate of just over 30 per cent (and as such, was higher than in any of the other main industrial nations). In the same period, and at the beginning of Phase I of voluntary wage restraint in July 1975, the annual rate of growth in the average level of earnings was 27.4 per cent. Moreover this price and wage inflation was occurring in an economy which ended 1974 with a record deficit in its balance of payments of £3323 million, and in which the Gross Domestic Product (GDP) *fell* between the second half of 1974 and the first half of 1975 by 2.5 per cent. By October 1975 the British economy was producing less than at any time (except for major strikes) since 1970; and unemployment had risen steadily to cross the one million mark (as an adjusted total – the crude total was even higher) by October 1975, for the first time since the 1940s.

These indicators give some impression both of the severity of the economic situation faced by the Labour Government on entering office and of the failure of its early policy to redress the balance. If it was any consolation to the growing numbers of the unemployed, the Labour Party had warned in its manifesto that the country should expect no overnight cures, and that – in the language much favoured by politicians since the mid 1960s – 'we faced a long slow haul', and 'two or three years of hard slog'. As the October 1974 manifesto put it, 'the regeneration of our economy is not going to be easy, even with a Labour Government. The next two or three years are going to be difficult for us all. There will be no easy times and no easy pickings for anyone.'[18]

So it proved to be. The freedom of manoeuvre enjoyed by the Chancellor of the Exchequer and his Cabinet colleagues was very limited, and Denis Healey's speeches in budget after budget (there were fourteen between March 1974 and June 1978) give some clue to the nature of the problems as the Labour Government came to see them. The country faced, he said in his first budget, 'what even before the onset of the three-day week was generally regarded as the gravest situation Britain has faced since the war'.[19] The rise in oil prices alone, he estimated, would add £2000 million to the import bill for oil in 1974. The balance of payments had to be financed, and eventually corrected. Inflation had to be curtailed if the economy's export competitiveness was not to be eroded still further. There was the ever present danger of a sterling crisis, which would add further to the rate of inflation and to the deficit on the balance of payments. And there were the threshold wage agreements, signed under the Heath Government's incomes policy, to add an extra twist to the inflationary spiral.

The Chancellor's strategy emerged quickly, and remained set. The immediate deficit on the balance of payments was to be financed by international borrowing. This was preferable, and less likely to be counterproductive in the long run, Denis Healey maintained, than the alternative strategy of reducing the import bill by massive deflation. The loans ('the largest . . . ever raised in the international capital markets'[20]) were a temporary solution, bringing with them the additional burden of interest (and later capital) repayments. Their role was to provide yet another breathing space within which the Government could tackle the internal economic problems that it faced. These it took to be rates of price and wage inflation significantly higher than those faced by Britain's major industrial competitors, an insufficiently successful export sector, and the absence of any growth in the output of the economy as a whole. At the same time the Government began a systematic search for a growth in world trade which was eventually to make it a major initiator of great power economic summits and of international banking and monetary reforms.

Initially the key to the solution of these problems seems, in the Government's view, to have been the creation of an atmosphere (and the underlying reality) of social justice, through the development and sustenance of the strategy of the social contract. Harold Wilson's introduction to the October election manifesto stressed this. So did Denis Healey's first budget speech. To quote the Prime Minister in October 1974:

What we as democratic socialists maintain is that when the going is toughest it is more than ever necessary to base our policies on social justice, to protect the weak, the poor, the disabled, to help those least able to help themselves, and to maintain and improve our living standards. Other parties which do not believe in fair shares deny themselves the right to call for equal sacrifices. Injustice is the enemy of national unity.[21]

These sentiments found their way directly into the design and explanation of the Labour Government's first budget. Denis Healey was at pains to stress that, though government expenditure could not increase greatly in the immediate period because of the constraints imposed by the economic situation, the Government would concentrate, as promised, on pension increases, food subsidies, and controls on the cost of rented property. To pay for these, the balance of taxation was to be shifted on to the rich, in order to lessen the relative tax burden on the average worker and the average family. A wealth tax and a gift tax were to come. There was, he claimed, no tension between the needs of economic management and those of social justice. On the contrary, and in particular, speaking of his predecessor's propensity to give tax concessions to the better off, the Chancellor said:

I believe that Britain cannot acquire the national unity required to surmount the problems ahead unless that process is now reversed. This is an area where the needs of economic management coincide with the needs of social justice. It is essential that we should fully cover the demand effects of the increases in expenditure to which the Government has committed itself. . . . I hope I shall carry with me those many [Conservative MPs] who complained about the excessive size of the public sector deficit in recent years when I put the major part of the new taxation this year on the better off.[22]

It was in this spirit that the Chancellor anticipated the acceptance by the trade union movement of a voluntary process of wage restraint, and in which he looked to British industry to invest in manufacturing plant and equipment as the long-term solution, as the Government saw it, to both inflation and the balance of payments deficit. Indeed, in relation to the private manufacturing sector, Denis Healey's first budget was a strange mixture: on the one hand, an exhortation to invest, with the Government's blessing ('the best assurance that businessmen can be given as a basis for their investment decisions is that it is the aim of government policy to maintain output at a high and sustainable level. I hope that this can now be seen to be my aim.'[23]), yet at the same time the private manufacturing sector faced, as a result of this first budget, heavier corporation tax, higher national insurance contributions, increases in the prices charged to them by the nationalised industries, and a tough set of price controls.

In spite of these apparent inconsistencies, the Chancellor's claim for his budgetary strategy was considerable. Even allowing for political rhetoric and every Chancellor's need to end his speech on a high note, the closing words of that first budget speech are worth recording, for they are typical of the sense of confidence and urgency of Labour Ministers in those early months: that this time things were going to be different, and radically so.

Britain today, [Denis Healey concluded] is face to face with a crisis which is no less challenging because it has come on us slowly – almost imperceptibly – over the years. A fundamental change of course is long overdue. I believe that the action which the Government has taken in the last few weeks can mark the turning point in our people's postwar history. A new spirit of confidence and cooperation is already abroad.[24]

In fact the optimism about the harmony of economic management and social justice, and about the political impact of a Labour Government, proved to be misplaced. As became very rapidly apparent the Government's basic dilemma was that it did not, and could not, control the origins and determinants of the processes that it sought to handle, and which it *had* to handle if policy promises were to be realised. It just was not as easy as the Party's manifestoes implied to bring inflation, unemployment and economic stagnation under rapid government control; and it certainly was not possible to tackle these – Labour's own chosen targets of action – while pursuing an ambitious and effective programme of social reform. Far from social reform being the prerequisite of economic success, it became once again one of its earliest casualties. I shall discuss the reasons for this, and their political consequences, at length in later chapters; and my main concern here is to record the impact of that discovery on the day-to-day development of the Government's policy. But even so it is necessary, if only to give shape to what is to follow, to say a little about the dilemmas facing the Chancellor, before tracing his reactions to them.

The difficulties Denis Healey faced in seeking to master inflation, unemployment and stagnation reflected in part the dependence of the Government on others – on workers, trade unionists, businessmen, financiers and civil servants, all of whom were actors in the political drama, to be cajoled, negotiated with and won over. It should be said that from the beginning the Government was aware of this, and made it a major theme of its speeches: that no government could solve Britain's problems alone, and that only a Labour Government could mobilise enough sections of the community behind it even to attempt the task. Yet the development of Government policy also reflected the fact that not all of these actors were equally significantly placed, and that some, and only some, were in particularly important positions within the economy, able by their actions to shape the world that the Government faced. The men who invested short-term funds in sterling were one such group, the negotiators in the social contract were another, and I shall examine later their relative political strengths. All we have to grasp for the moment is that the Government had no monopoly of economic power. On the contrary, Ministers had to mobilise and shape the self-interest of private power groupings, or appeal to their sense of patriotism, loyalty or duty, in their search for price stability, economic growth and full employment.

We have to note too that for the British economy in the 1970s so many of those key groupings were external to the domestic political scene. They were oil sheikhs, international bankers and foreign governments. The Labour Government might be able to 'deliver' the British trade union movement, at least for a while. Its capacity to 'deliver' oil sheikhs, or to prevent what Denis Healey once called a 'massive wave of imported inflation'[25] was altogether less marked. In this regard, it should be noted that the Government's commitment to social reform was predicated on this recognition that only a common effort of all significantly placed private groupings would 'solve' Britain's inflation and unemployment, and that the creation of a climate of social justice (not least by massive public spending on welfare provision) was likely to be the most effective way of winning that voluntary common effort. The Government's tragedy was to discover how incompatible the search for social justice was to be with the requirements of significantly placed groupings both inside and outside Britain; and how in consequence the persistence of inflationary pressures and unemployment would eat away at even the trade union leadership's willingness to pursue the strategy of the social contract indefinitely.

This is not to say that the radicalism of British social democracy was strangled by the avarice and conservatism of foreign investors, any more than it was by the greed and irresponsibility of the average British trade unionist. This has to be stressed, because each version of the conspiracy theory has its adherents. What has also to be grasped is that these private groupings were not in control of their situation either. The impression that the Labour Government was 'in the grip of the trade union leaders', or 'dictated to by the IMF' is a profoundly misleading one – at best only half true. It is true that trade union leaders played a significant role in critical negotiations, and that the IMF loans in 1976 were given only in return for quite clear (and unpalatable) policy commitments; but even so the general impression of external dictation should be resisted, especially when that is accompanied by the usual implication that these trade union leaders and international bankers were themselves free agents. On the contrary, they were not. They too were subject to the very processes which the Government attempted to control – processes at work in the world economy which neither trade unionists nor bankers could individually (or indeed collectively) control, but which shaped their interests, and to which their actions gave expression. Denis Healey said in his 1975 budget speech that 'we in Britain must keep control of our own policy. We must keep ahead of events. It would be disastrous if we were forced, as sometimes in the past, into running desperately after events which we could not control.'[26] Yet what is significant about the entire Labour Government experience is the degree to which every section of the political élite, from trade union leaders through Cabinet Ministers to bankers and industrialists, throughout the Western world were 'running after events' in the 1970s, were trying with greater or less degrees of desperation to cope with an agenda of problems – inflation, unemployment, stagnation, balance of payments deficits – common to them all but which no one of them either initiated or desired. Well might Michael Foot speak to the 1975 Labour Party conference of the 'typhoon' within which the Labour Government was forced to govern. In later chapters I argue that the world recession to which he referred was here only throwing into relief the overriding feature of the world that the Labour Government faced, a world that was anarchic at its core because it was capitalist in its essence. But again for the moment it is enough to recognise merely what followed from that, namely the intractability of the problems with which the Labour Government had to struggle, and the degree to which they appeared immune from the control of any of the élite groups, no matter how well-intentioned those élites were. 'I am not here to throw people out of work,' Denis Healey told the 1974 Labour Party conference; and yet the numbers of the unemployed grew and grew.

There are as many explanations of why this was the case as there are analysts, and the careful reader will do well to consider them all. In Chapter 4 I argue that the problems with which the Labour Government struggled were themselves only consequences of a deeper crisis within the international capitalist system, and as such beyond the control of any one national government, particularly of one like the Labour Government in Britain, which had no comprehension of the imperatives of international capitalism as a whole. That is, associated with the lack of control over events was the absence from the Labour Government of a theory which could adequately explain why those events occurred in the sequence and at the time that they did, and why they were so difficult to control. The Labour Government defined its problem not as a national consequence of an international capitalist crisis, but as a set of national economic difficulties intensified by world recession – and that difference of definition is crucial. In the speeches of Labour Ministers, the problem was the familiar one of a failure to export enough, too high a rate of inflation by international standards, low productivity in the manufacturing sector, and so on; and indeed these were (and remain) features of the British experience of international capitalism which impinge directly on us all. At that level of analysis, Ministers became increasingly sophisticated in their understanding of the relationship between inflation, the exchange rate of sterling, and economic stagnation. In their growing sophistication they became increasingly aware of how difficult it was for an economy such as they had inherited to strengthen its international position or to reverse its long-established vulnerability to 'deindustrialisation – the steady loss of jobs and factory capacity year by year'[27] as the Chancellor put it. But they remained seriously deficient in their understanding of *why* that process was going on, and of what the underlying capitalist forces were that were responsible for the problems with which they struggled; and as a result, by couching their analysis time and again in terms of the *surface* phenomena of the capitalist crisis (in terms of 'Britain's problem', in terms of 'inflation' and so on) they misled themselves and us all.

But this is to carry us farther than for the moment we need to go. It is enough for the purpose of establishing the record to recognise that the Labour Government faced a world capitalist economy dogged by inflation and recession, and inherited a British economy that was a weak link in the entire capitalist chain. The Government found very quickly that the severity of the world recession compounded the difficulties which any British Government would have faced in attempting to restructure British capitalism out of its competitive weakness. It found too that the changing relationship between the State and the economy had already progressed to such a degree that its own freedom of manoeuvre was seriously curtailed; and that in particular its own spending (and its own welfare programme) was a major contributory factor to the very inflation which it sought to contain. The Labour Government found itself, that is, hemmed in by constraints so tight that policy had to be amended, and yet constraints so paradoxical and mutually incompatible that no matter how hard it tried it seemed incapable of satisfying any one of the groups that pressed it.

Initially, until North Sea oil and an ailing American dollar eased the situation, the most immediate and pressing constraint on the Labour Government came from the enormous deficit in the economy's balance of payments. As Denis Healey told the House of Commons in April 1975, 'we entered 1974 with a balance of payments deficit already running at a rate equivalent to 3 per cent of our Gross National Product. But the cost of the oil we imported (in 1974) was about £2900 million more than the year before, and this left us with a current deficit . . . of £3800 million – equivalent to more than 5 per cent of our Gross National Product.'[28] This deficit was made worse by the increased cost of oil after 1973, but it was not caused by the oil producers: in the words of the Prime Minister, 'it was already the grimmest [balance of payments] on record before a single oil producer had raised his price or turned off his tap'.[29] This deficit constrained the Government at every turn and its removal was an early stated objective of policy. In the short run, the deficit could only be handled by the raising of vast international loans, whose servicing (in the form of interest payments and later capital payments) became immediately a growing part of government spending, and which in the end brought with them tight externally dictated limits on public sector borrowing, and hence on the social wage. Indeed when those constraints on government spending came, the fact that massive debt repayments had been accumulated (which could not themselves be cut) made the size of cuts that were found to be necessary in social expenditure doubly severe. This provided the Government with the first of many paradoxes: foreign loans raised to prevent immediate and draconian cuts in the social wage in the end (by the burden that their repayments place on government spending in total) became one cause of the severity of the cuts in social expenditure that had to be imposed.

The balance of payments deficit, and the differentially high rate of inflation that underlay it, also left confidence in the pound weak, and obliged the Government in its early years to hold interest rates higher than it might otherwise have preferred in order to attract foreign currency to strengthen the reserves. The pound declined dramatically in its exchange value under this Labour Government, and at certain critical junctures dominated policy-making. To the degree that this devaluation reflected the continuation of a higher rate of internal inflation in Britain than elsewhere in the OECD countries, the fall in exchange rate was to be expected, even desired, by a Labour Government seeking export-led growth. Exports, after all, had not to lose their competitive edge; and the Government had to strike a balance between allowing the pound to fall in order to stimulate export sales, and preventing its fall in order to stop too great an increase (caused by the extra cost of imports) in the internal rate of inflation. But before December 1976 the balance of payments deficit was too great, and the reserves of foreign currency too small, to give the Labour Government this degree of control; and at times the Chancellor was literally helpless in the face of speculative moves against sterling, whose very weakness inspired the speculation which made it weaker still. A point came in the life of this Government when speculation against the pound seemed to have a logic of its own. The foreign holders of sterling, noting the persistence of inflation and fearing the pound's continued devaluation, sold their holdings of sterling, and its exchange price fell, as they had feared. And if the Bank of England acted to support the pound, this stood a good chance of actually inspiring more selling, as any remaining holders of sterling took a heaven-sent opportunity to move into another currency before the pound declined yet further.

Each fall in the pound added to domestic inflation, strained the social contract, and militated against the increase in industrial investment on which the Government depended for the generation of wealth with which to pay off foreign debts and on which to move into an external surplus. The general effect of the pound's depreciation on private industry was disadvantageous: helping by making exporting a highly profitable venture, but eating away at the capacity to export by the inflation it generated and the high rates of interest it sustained. Here then was a second paradox faced by the Labour Government: namely that the international indebtedness of the economy made the pound weak, and yet at the same time the falling value of the pound worked against the restructuring of industry which that indebtedness required. All the Government could do was to build ever more complex sets of standby credits and accumulate still more international debt while it waited for the arrival of North Sea oil to improve its balance of payments and strengthen sterling; and at the same time act internally to reduce inflation and stimulate exports within the considerable constraint imposed on investment by the internationally high rates of interest in the London money markets which the weakness of the pound necessitated, and by the high rate of internal inflation which the falling pound sustained.

In the early years of the Government's period in office, the pressure of the balance of payments was so great that the Chancellor felt himself to have no freedom of manoeuvre at all on the general strategy of his policy. As he told the House of Commons in 1975, the balance of payments deficit necessitated

a strategy which will enable us to achieve a very substantial improvement in our current account deficit in the next two years, and to eliminate the deficit entirely as rapidly as possible thereafter. We have to set more of our national resources aside for export. *This is not a question of choice or of political decision. It is a fact of the world we live in* – a fact which I must budget for now. Our overseas deficit must be removed – and the world must know that it will be removed.[30]

The removal of that deficit, as Denis Healey never tired of pointing out in the first ten minutes of budget speech after budget speech, required a major revival in world trade and therefore in the growth of the world economy as a whole. The Government had obviously no direct leverage on this. All it could do was to encourage the creation of more international liquidity, and the recycling of the Arab petrodollar surpluses, to prevent any deepening of the world recession, while urging the world's stronger economies to reflate. At times this strategy brought temporary diplomatic victories. The London summit in May 1977 brought a paper commitment from the leaders of all the major capitalist powers to pursue policies that would bring down levels of unemployment. But in practice few tangible results came from all this summitry. Economic activity in the world economy did revive in the first half of 1977 (it slackened everywhere in the second half of 1977, only to revive slightly in 1978); but this hesitant and uneven recovery was insufficient to reabsorb the unemployed. For the Labour Government had no effective answer to the fear of rising inflation that checked the expansionist propensities of the stronger capitalist powers. Ironically, from 1974 to 1978 its own rate of inflation, which it looked to greater world trade to ease, stood as a warning against any significant reflation by those stronger economies. The Labour Government found itself, that is, in a bad internal position from which to urge reflation on others, and yet the very nature of its internal position made that reflation all the more essential.

Faced with a world recession, all the Government could do was to attempt to capture a greater share of a stagnant world market, while working to prevent this stagnation in world trade sliding into a major world slump of 1930s proportions. That is, the Government was driven back to the pursuit of precisely the policy that each national government in the OECD was pursuing: shifting unemployment on to some other country's working class by strengthening the international competitiveness of the economy's export sector. Both the Government's industrial strategy and its wages policy were crucial here; but neither separately nor together did they prove to be enough. To the degree that each national government within the OECD had a similar preoccupation, some countries were bound to lose; and the weaker economies were more likely to be confirmed in their weakness than to be transformed by the fierce international competition for export-led economic growth. To strengthen the international competitiveness of British exports required major industrial investment, and this was not easy to generate. The economy which the Labour Government inherited had a long history of low rates of investment in manufacturing plant and equipment; indeed this was one cause of the competitive weakness which the Government sought to rectify. But the very weakness of the economy meant that investment abroad continued to be more attractive, and the export of capital went on at a great pace through the 1970s, beyond the effective control of a Labour Government too constricted by a weak pound and international indebtedness to start interfering in the international movement of money. Here was yet another vicious circle within which the Government had to operate: that the competitive weakness of the British economy which had resulted from low rates of investment in the past, acted as a barrier to investment in the present, and so seemed to guarantee even greater degrees of competitive weakness in the future.

Meanwhile, investment by and in the industrial sector at home continued to be undermined by price inflation (industry was particularly badly hit by rising oil prices) and in the first eighteen months of the Labour Government, by high rates of growth of earnings also. In an attempt to cope with inflation in his first budget, Denis Healey added to the tax burden of the industrial sector; but soon found that, in the face of limited demand in both internal and external markets, companies under this kind of pressure were unable to ride out these tax increases by adding to the volume of their turnover. Far from investing in new plant and equipment, as the Chancellor hoped, the industrial sector reacted by economising on stock levels (to a really quite remarkable degree, as he later admitted[31]), by laying off employees and cutting back on investment plans. The Government's own survey of business intentions in late 1974 suggested anything between a 7 and a 10 per cent *fall* in investment in 1975[32]; and the bulk of the economic forecasts available in December 1974 suggested that the GDP would rise by at most only 1 per cent over the next twelve-month period; for in spite of its heady rhetoric, the Labour Government could give manufacturing companies very little immediate relief. True, Ministers had ambitious schemes for long-term structural reform, but in the crucial immediate period, total demand could not be increased without intensifying inflationary pressures, nor the cost of borrowing reduced rapidly without underminding the reserves or crippling the Government's own spending programmes. Inflationary pressures kept industrial costs high and product demand low, and so squeezed the rate of return on investment at the very time when the cost of borrowing was so high that only the most profitable ventures could generate the rate of return required to cover the borrowing costs involved. So low demand and high rates of interest conspired together to prevent the recovery of investment to which the Government looked as a long-term solution to the economy's inflationary pressures. The policy consequences of inflation, that is, precluded policies which might enable industrial investment to bring inflation down; and the Government was in a very real sense trapped between a weak currency and an internal inflation that it could only hope to remove by economic growth, and an economic growth that it could not create because of inflation and a weak currency.

Though the Labour Government periodically assured the business sector of its commitment to a healthy and vigorous private sector, and repeatedly asserted its belief that such 'vigour' required a healthy return on private capital invested, the Government remained hampered in its aid to private industry by the other constraints operating on it. The amount of money it could make available to aid investment directly (through the Industry Act and the NEB) was difficult to insulate from the general pressure to curb public spending which a weak pound and a high rate of inflation necessitated, as the July 1976 cuts made clear. Nor could Ministers easily bring down very high interest rates (by, say, even larger reductions in public sector borrowing), or even remove the price controls which, with high interest rates, so hampered private capital accumulation, because of their need to win from the trade union movement voluntary restraint over rates of wages and earnings. Here then was another contradiction for the Labour Government: that its search for economic growth, as the long-term cure for inflation, required the very easing of interest rates and price controls which, in the short run, would threaten the wage settlements on which the Government depended to slow the rate of inflation in the immediate period. It was not surprising then that the Chancellor repeatedly found himself trapped between incompatible and unpalatable policy options: 'between rapid monetary expansion, industrially ruinous interest rates and politically daunting expenditure cuts'.[33]

It was not simply the need to protect the reserves which kept rates of interest, and therefore the costs of borrowing for industrial investment, so high until 1977 as to prohibit all but the most profitable investment programmes. High rates of interest also reflected competition for funds from the public sector, as the public sector borrowing requirement continued to soar. Yet high public sector spending was an intimate part of the Labour Government's third area of constraints: those that arose from its relationship with the trade union movement. We have already seen that the Government placed its hope for the regeneration of British industry in the creation of a climate of social justice, through the consolidation of the social contract. The contract was initially consolidated on the basis of the social reforms of the Government's first twelve months in office, but it proved ever more difficult to sustain as time went on, as it became clear that the economic growth which the social contract was supposed to release could only be achieved (if it could be achieved at all) by a shift of resources away from the higher personal consumption and greater social wage on which the contract had initially been constructed.

In fact, as inflation persisted and rapid economic growth failed to materialise, the Government had greater and greater difficulty in maintaining its part of the bargain. It soon became obvious that the heady optimism about the social contract in the years of opposition had rested on an inadequate recognition of the degree to which the determinants of rates of inflation, levels of employment and standards of living lay beyond the control of the Government and the trade unions acting together. As James Callaghan put it to the 1976 Labour Party conference: 'We used to think that you could spend your way out of a recession and increase employment by cutting taxes and boosting government spending.'[34] That option no longer existed; and the difficulty of generating economic growth meant that from the beginning the Labour Government had to hold its social contract 'in a situation in which there was no prospect of any general increase in living standards'[35], and in which internal rates of inflation were sustained by factors external to the trade union movement: by rising world commodity prices in 1973–74, and by the declining rate of the pound thereafter. In such a situation the Government had to squeeze extra expenditure on social reform from a static gross national product (GNP), and from an electorate already pressed by inflation and heavy taxation. At the same time the static nature of the GNP drove the Government on to spending more and more money funding industry, and added to the cost of social security benefits for the rising number of the unemployed. Even before the Government began spending more on social reform, inflation and stagnation were already forcing the total level of government expenditure up and up.

The Government's problem was that it had no easy way of financing its growing social expenditure. As the *Guardian* once put it, 'popular expectations about improvements in welfare programmes and public services have not been matched by the growth in national output, or by [any] willingness to give up improvements in living standards in favour of those programmes'.[36] As a result, the Government could not easily finance new public spending by additional taxation without either adding to the cost of living and hence to the rate of inflation, or without adding still further to the tax burden on incomes. In either way it stood a fair chance of alienating the very trade union members whose voluntary agreement to limit wage increases was vital if industrial costs were not to rise still further and if confidence in the pound was not to be further reduced. There were limits, too, to how far social reforms could be funded by cutting other areas of Government expenditure. The defence budget could not be cut indefinitely: in the end there would be no soldiers left. This left the Government with the choice of either cutting expenditure programmes or continuing to borrow heavily. Neither option was attractive, or without its problems. To cut government programmes was likely to have a serious immediate effect on employment in the private as well as in the public sector, and also to undermine morale in the Party and erode trade union loyalty to the social contract – a loyalty that was in any case ever more strained by the rigidities of the wage norm, by the persistence of inflation, by heavy taxation and by rising unemployment. But to borrow heavily to finance government programmes that were uncut was equally likely to make the achievements of government targets for inflation, growth and employment difficult to attain. Uncontrolled government borrowing would add significantly to the growth rate of the money supply; and the Chancellor came to believe that this was both inflationary (this seemed to be the lesson of the 1970–73 period) and damaging to foreign confidence in sterling. He also came to realise that a government under foreign pressure to control the growth rate of the money supply could not at the same time continue to borrow heavily to finance its own programmes without running the risk, in the period of economic recovery it sought to create, that government borrowing would squeeze out all but the most profitable industrial investment, as competition for funds from government and industry caused interest rates to rise. Government borrowing, that is, ran the risk of either stimulating inflation or reducing confidence in sterling by causing the money supply to rise rapidly; or if the money supply was controlled by high interest rates or limits on bank lending, ran the risk of preventing the upturn in private investment on which long-term economic growth depended. Here then was another paradox for the Labour Government to handle: that the existence of a public sector deficit was vital to the maintenance of existing levels of output and employment in the economy, but its financing militated against the strengthening of those levels in the next period.

The Government found itself then in its usual dilemma: needing working-class industrial discipline to strengthen exports and to prevent a disastrous, inflation-generating run on the pound; and yet unable to stimulate the growth in the economy which would fund government spending without greater taxation or borrowing, and so forced to cut back on programmes vital to the sustenance of trade union and working-class industrial discipline. Indeed, given the constraints under which it operated, the Labour Government after 1975 performed little short of a political miracle – winning trade union support for wage cuts and unemployment, and ending abruptly the highest level of industrial militancy since 1926. Even by the standards of earlier Labour

Governments, its position was extraordinarily difficult.* All that it could do was try and squeeze greater investment and economic growth out of a hard-pressed company sector by turning the social contract into a wage freeze that cut living standards as well as industrial costs, and by letting unemployment rise steadily, in the hope that these would only be temporary features of political life, rendered unnecessary eventually by falling rates of inflation and growing industrial production that would produce the surplus from which greater amounts of social reform could be funded. The Chancellor came to recognise very rapidly that the constraints operating on him made public sector spending cuts inevitable, and that foreign creditors could if they wished impose immediate draconian cuts by withdrawing the loans on which the deficit was temporarily financed, or by moving in great numbers out of sterling. The Chancellor found himself, not with the option of deciding where to spend more, but of seeking a way of cutting back on government spending at so controlled a rate that political and social upheaval did not immediately ensue. Indeed, the need to cut slowly and carefully 'if our democratic institutions were to survive' must have been his one major bargaining ploy in the face of international pressure for public retrenchment, just as the argument that 'little' cuts now would prevent bigger ones later became his major defence against backbench Labour pressure to defend public spending at all costs.

It was the Government's belief from the beginning that a recovery of world trade and the arrival of North Sea oil would enventually ease the constraints under which they operated; and the Chancellor's determination to shift resources into investment and exports grew from his desire 'to ensure that our economy can take full advantage of the strong recovery in world trade'[37] that was perennially expected. In fact, those constraints eased only slightly over the years. In part this was because world trade did not recover on the scale and with the speed which the Government required. In part it was because the inflationary pressures continued well into 1977, even with an effective incomes policy, under the impact of repeated sterling crises before which the Government was helpless. And of course the Government did not find a way of significantly increasing the rate of investment in manufacturing

---

* This was recognised by serious commentators from the very beginning. Peter Jay had this to say of Denis Healey's November 1974 budget: 'The hope must be that he will be able to keep his balance on the high wire, having done enough to ward off immediate financial collapse with galloping monetary inflation, but not so much as to alienate organized labour to the point of abrogating the social contract. The fear of the more seasoned observers of many previous acrobats is that the wire is itself an illusion – a middle way that does not exist, an impossible compromise between incompatibles' (*The Times*, 13 Nov. 1974, p. 16).

plant and equipment, for all the publicity surrounding its industrial strategy. I examine why these constraints persisted in Chapter 4; for the moment we should note that the short-term concessions squeezed from the trade union movement (on delayed social reforms, on living standards and on employment) became long-term and permanent; and the Labour Government was left to soldier on in a universe it did not control, electorally unpopular, presiding over cuts in social services, watching unemployment remain high and the rate of inflation only slowly begin to fall.

## IV

Not all these constraints were immediately obvious either to Ministers or to commentators. The White Papers of the summer of 1974 were dominated by Labour plans to regenerate British industry by establishing close liaison between major firms and government departments, and by injecting public money into private sector investment programmes after the creation of the National Enterprise Board. The Chancellor spent the late summer of 1974 claiming that he was getting to grips with the root causes of inflation, and on one famous occasion he even suggested that the inflation rate was already down to 8.4 per cent. His second budget in July 1974 was mildly reflationary, adding £800 million to purchasing power by cuts in VAT and increases in the regional employment premium, food subsidies and rate relief. Yet it was significant for what was to follow that even in this mildly reflationary move the Chancellor felt it necessary to attempt to offset any resulting speculation against the pound by announcing a new set of foreign credits – $1200 million to be lent over three years by the Iranian Government to the nationalised industries.

By November, and Denis Healey's third budget, the constraints on policy were obvious. Even in July he had indicated his dependence on world trade, and hence on the policies of other governments.

Britain is part of the world economy, heavily dependent on the activities and attitudes of the parties in world trade. . . . The shape and content of the autumn budget. . . now depends on the extent to which international action to head off a world recession can be agreed by the major economic powers. So far [he told the Commons], the governments of most of the advanced economies are far more frightened about inflation than about unemployment and are taking measures to cut rather than to expand economic activity.[38]

They still were by November, but by then the constraints the

Government faced were not simply external ones. By November the cash position of many major manufacturing companies was serious. *The Times* estimated that the company sector's financial deficit in the second quarter of 1974 was almost as large as in 1970, which had itself been a record year for company liquidity problems.[39] Far from stimulating a revival in private investment, the tax changes of Denis Healey's first budget had added to the pressures of rising import costs and threshold-protected wage agreements on companies who were already restricted in their pricing policy by the Government's own tight price controls. By November, after only six months of office, the Labour Government was visibly trapped between a stagnant world economy and the danger of major redundancies in its shrinking manufacturing base.

It was against this background that the Chancellor laid out the economic strategy that he was to follow thereafter. At the level of the international economy, his overriding fear was that the existing 'stagflation' would turn into a major world recession as the unintended consequence of separate national attempts to solve commonly experienced problems of trade deficits and inflation by domestic retrenchment. Denis Healey committed himself to preventing this by arranging for the recycling of the oil surpluses (that is, by borrowing back large amounts of Middle Eastern oil revenues to maintain levels of aggregate demand in the Western economies), and by pressing the governments of the United States and West Germany to reflate. Meanwhile on the domestic front he announced four preoccupations: to improve the balance of payments, to avoid unemployment, to shift resources towards exports and investment, and to cut inflation by avoiding any excessive growth in the money supply and by pulling earnings into line with the TUC's July guidelines. The language of these priorities was bland and uncontroversial, and beyond the mention of the money supply could have come from the mouths of any of a dozen postwar Chancellors; but in making them his priorities Denis Healey announced, in effect, that he was to be an orthodox Chancellor, following orthodox budgetary targets because he was unable to do otherwise – and in the process, though few of us recognised it at the time, blocking off that 'fundamental and irreversible shift in the balance of power and wealth in favour of working people and their families' which the 1973 Labour Party Programme and the February 1974 election manifesto had so loudly proclaimed.

This should be clear if we examine the specific proposals in the November 1974 budget, which foreshadowed much that was to come. In an attempt to avoid mass unemployment, the Government began its retreat from the subsidies and price controls promised in the social contract, and from the tight discipline over private firms anticipated in the debates in opposition. For the moment the shifts were slight, but the general drift of the Chancellor's remarks was sufficiently distinct to warrant the claim (from watching journalists and the Labour Left) that it constituted a 'U turn' from the budgets of March and July. 'A Bosses Budget', the *Socialist Worker* called it. It was hardly that, but it marked a change nonetheless in the Government's relationship with the business sector, and the CBI, though not satisfied with the Chancellor's decisions, made clear its sense of relief at the greater 'realism' that the budget contained. That 'realism' led Denis Healey to ease price controls, to make changes in the payments of corporation tax, to urge the banks to give priority to loan requests from manufacturing firms, and to announce plans to cut the subsidies to public sector industries. Together these changes amounted to an injection of £1500 million of extra liquidity into a hard-pressed company sector. The Government's need of trade union support in the establishment of effective wage control prevented any further easing of the price code at this time, but the drift of policy was set. If the Government wanted a mixed economy in which, as Denis Healey put it, 'the private sector was vigorous, alert and prosperous', they had to create the conditions in which private enterprise could flourish. Indeed, since the Labour Government believed (with what degree of validity we shall have to discuss later) that only a regenerated private industrial sector could guarantee full employment, inevitably the provision of the conditions under which private enterprise could flourish became the essential part of employment policy. It was in this way, that, in the end, the logic of the Labour Government's search for full employment through a regenerated private sector drained away the distinctive features of the Party's early radicalism.

This was also the budget in which the Chancellor made clear the Government's intention 'to give priority to investment and the balance of payments over both public expenditure and private consumption' by making 'the shift in resources into exports and investment (his) first priority in economic management'.[40] Again, in November 1974 the full consequences of that policy decision were not obvious. For the moment the public sector borrowing requirement continued to grow, and to remain at what Denis Healey significantly believed to be 'a disturbingly large figure which one would never accept under normal circumstances'.[41] The Government was well aware that an immediate and drastic reduction in public sector expenditure could only bring a large fall in output and employment in its wake. But Ministers had at least succumbed to the view that public sector spending had to be curbed, no matter what the Labour Party in opposition had believed, and the November 1974 budget made a series of small beginnings. One was the decision to phase out subsidies on public sector prices, subsidies which in November 1974 were running at £550 million a year higher than had been anticipated in Denis Healey's first budget, and which were now to be abolished, particularly in the energy industries. High prices for coal, electricity and gas inevitably followed. Beyond this, the main immediate consequence of the decision to curtail public sector spending was the Chancellor's instruction to local authorities 'to limit the rise in their expenditure to what is absolutely inescapable'.[42] Again the language of the announcement was innocuous, and the whole instruction was easily lost from view amid the mass of detailed tax changes in the entire budget speech. But in effect that single phrase began the cutbacks in the quality and scale of provision of crucial social services (and hence in the social wage) which were later to be intensified as a result of financial crises and their consequent IMF loans, and which in the end seriously undermined the Labour Government's claim to be able to deliver its side of the social contract of government social reform and trade union wage restraint.

To this shift from control to exhortation in the Labour Government's relationship with the private sector, and to the erosion of the social wage by limits on government spending, the November 1974 budget added a third and later much more significant development in policy: the beginning of the respecification of the social contract as an agreement pre-eminently concerned with controlling the rate of increase of earnings. In the fight against inflation, the November budget made clear, the Government would seek wage controls. This was a difficult area for the Government, and Denis Healey proceeded with caution. His budget had already added to the tax burden of the employed, and eaten away at the real purchasing power of industrial earnings by its easing of the price code and its planned abolition of private sector subsidies. Indeed the Chancellor made some attempt to insulate the poorer sections of the working class from these budgetary changes by bringing forward increases in social security benefits, by increasing family allowances and by introducing new tax allowances for the elderly. But he was also adamant that the Labour Government was determined to contain increases in the rate of earnings within the guidelines already published by the TUC; and in saying this he made his opening move in the long campaign which was to culminate in the voluntary £6 pay policy of July 1975.

All that the TUC could take as comfort from the budget was the

Chancellor's assertion that 'deliberately to adopt a strategy which requires mass unemployment would be no less an economic than a moral crime'.[43] Time alone was to tell how much that was worth as unemployment continued to rise. Indeed Denis Healey conceded the emptiness of his words as he told the Commons that the rise in unemployment resulting from his measures would 'be modest, and its level will remain well below a million'[44] – a figure which, as he had previously conceded in a television interview, would be tolerated by the Government in its search for price stability.[45] So the strategy of the Labour Government from November 1974 was not simply to retreat from the control of private industry, and to cut planned public expenditure, it was also to search for wage restraint and tolerate rising unemployment. The language of politicians could briefly mislead the unwary. The Chancellor could, in the one breath, admit that 20,000 extra people would be made redundant because of the cuts that he planned in public expenditure, while in the next he could declare in the House that 'the effect of the Budget on employment had given [him] great concern, since [he] absolutely reject[ed] the use of mass unemployment as an instrument of policy'.[46] Apparently an extra 20,000 people out of work did not constitute 'a mass' on this argument. Unemployment levels from now on were to be repeatedly described by Labour Ministers as 'intolerable' and 'unacceptable', but tolerated and accepted they continued to be, and in rare moments of candour Ministers would admit their impotence in the face of the growing social misery that rising unemployment entailed.[47] By January 1975 678,000 people were out of work in Great Britain. By December 1975 that figure had risen to 1,129,000; and by December 1976 to 1,273,000. By then, after nearly three years of Labour government, one potentially employed worker in twenty was without a job, and unemployment rates were running as high as 10 per cent in Northern Ireland, and over 6 per cent in the North, North West, South West, Wales and Scotland.

Presumably Ministers could have taken some comfort from these figures if they had at least looked temporary, the short-term price for eventual success in other areas of government policy. But success continued to elude this Labour Government in its attempt to eradicate inflation and to achieve a high rate of economic growth. The Retail Price Index, which had been rising at an average annual rate of 15 per cent as the Labour Government entered office, rose steadily for the first fifteen months of the Government's existence, to touch 30 per cent in May 1975. Inflation then eased, in line with revised government targets, to just under 14 per cent by June 1976. But instead of falling further, the rate stabilised for the rest of 1976, and rose again to 17.5 per cent by

31

April 1977. On the third anniversary of the Conservative Government's defeat, the Prices Secretary found himself having to explain a rate of increase, over three months, which if it had persisted would have pushed retail prices up by 21.8 per cent in the course of a year.[48] Not until January 1978 did the retail price index start to grow at less than 10 per cent per annum, so that the first four years of the Labour Government were dominated by an uphill struggle against double-figure inflation, the fear of whose return haunted it to the end.

Only in the fields of wages and earnings did the Labour Government's policy of containment see some initial success. Average earnings in July 1975 were 27.4 per cent higher than in July 1974, but thereafter earnings rose more slowly and at less than the rate of increase of prices: by 13.9 per cent between August 1975 and July 1976, and by 9 per cent under Stage 2 of the counter-inflation policy. Stage 3 was less successful from the Government's point of view. Earnings rose faster than prices in that year, at 14.2 per cent overall; and that rate of increase was maintained in Stage 4, after August 1978, although this time it was accompanied by bitter and prolonged strikes in both the public and the private sector which cost the Government large amounts of public support. Yet there was no significant increase in industrial output until 1978. As Denis Healey prepared his November 1974 budget, both the gross domestic product and the index of industrial production were poised to fall dramatically, to the extent that neither was to have recovered its November 1974 level even by the first quarter of 1977. The pound meanwhile fell heavily and persistently against the dollar. At its lowest point, in November 1976, its exchange rate with the dollar was 1.646, where two years before it had been over 2.3; and though it improved against an ailing dollar in 1977 and 1978 (it reached $2 again in the second half of 1978) its exchange rate against the other major currencies showed little commensurate improvement, beyond a slight strengthening in 1979 caused by the adverse effect of oil price increases on the currencies of even the strong non-oil-producing economies.

## V

Under this pressure, Labour Government policy began to 'run behind events'. The April 1975 budget was an austerity one, which cut personal consumption, eased the price code in an attempt to facilitate private investment, and made £100 million of public funds available to assist firms beginning new capital projects in 1975. Public expenditure plans for 1976–77 were also cut by £900 million at the cost of an estimated 20,000 jobs. Yet this of itself could not prevent a major fall in the exchange rate for sterling between April and July, nor avoid the rate of inflation reaching 30 per cent in May. Amid growing press and media reports of sterling's crisis and of the Government's lack of control of inflation, the Labour Government transformed its social contract into a full-scale incomes policy. In July 1975 the TUC, under heavy ministerial pressure, gave its support to a policy which set £6 as the maximum weekly wage rise allowable between August 1975 and July 1976. In return the Cabinet agreed to reduce slightly its planned cuts in food and housing subsidies. Within fifteen months of taking office, the Labour Government was back to explicitly cutting the living standards of its electorate by at least 2½ per cent over the year, on the Government's own figures. The nature of the pay settlement with the TUC had its egalitarian elements (in that at least it departed from the previous practice of setting a percentage wage norm), and this brought some solace to the Government's more radical supporters. But the fact that living standards would fall could not be hidden. Instead, Harold Wilson made a virtue of necessity, and appealed for 'a year for Britain', a year of 'sacrifice', 'toil and sweat' in which to begin to tackle 'problems which have developed in Britain over the years'. In the speech to the nation which he made to consolidate public support for the policy, Harold Wilson listed those problems, and his list was indicative of the shift of emphasis in policy that was occurring, moving this Government back towards the unbridled managerialism of the 1964–70 Wilson governments. As unemployment soared and strike figures slumped, he could still say that, in addition to 'lack of investment', the causes of Britain's abnormally high rate of inflation were to be found in 'acquiescence in chronic overmanning in essential industries, endemic problems of industrial relations in individual industries and individual plants'. It was essential to overcome these, he said, if the Government's targets were to be met: of bringing inflation down to 10 per cent by the third quarter of 1976 and to single figures by the end of 1976, and to keep it in line with 'the inflation rates of our major competitors' thereafter.[49]

The degree of acquiescence by the rank and file of the labour movement in that voluntary policy was considerable. Denis Healey could tell the House of Commons in April 1976 that 'with only a few months of the current wage round left to run, we know of no instance where wages are being paid in breach of the £6 pay limit'.[50] Average earnings rose only 13.9 per cent in the period of the policy, while unemployment grew from 956,000 to 1,242,000 and the rate of inflation hovered around 14 per cent. But the pound remained weak and investment low; and the Government found itself obliged to seek another twelve months of restraint and 'sacrifice'. The second round of incomes policy was more difficult to negotiate, but again, once the norm was settled (at 4½ per cent) the degree of general acquiescence in the policy was impressive. Earnings grew only by 9 per cent over the year, while the rate of inflation remained well above 14 per cent. But the spring of 1977 was marked by growing industrial unrest, as opposition to unemployment, falling living standards and dwindling differentials ate away at the union leaders' ability to support publicly a third year of restraint. As a result, the third year of the Labour Government's incomes policy was less tight, and earnings rose at a significantly higher rate. Yet the Government's achievement here was still a considerable one. It had persuaded over 24 million working people to accept a dwindling standard of personal consumption for more than two years, in its attempt to create the conditions in which the private manufacturing sector of British industry could grow. The tragedy for the Labour Government, of course, was that that growth was very slow to come, in spite of the working-class restraint that Labour Ministers repeatedly managed to orchestrate.

This Labour Government, no less than its 1964–70 predecessor, found it extremely difficult, not to say impossible, to transform the economy's manufacturing sector into the high investment, high growth, high wage international competitor that its policies required. The strategy that the Government pursued, and its relationship with private industry, altered significantly after November 1974. In the wake of the EEC referendum defeat for the anti-marketeers, Tony Benn was moved from the Industry Department and the legislation creating the NEB was toned down during its passage through the Commons. These moves can be seen as part of the Government's increasing concern to reassure private industry about its commitment to a healthy private sector, and about its willingness to subordinate its social programme to the gaining of greater industrial production. Verbal gymnastics were at a premium here, as the social contract with the trade union movement had also to be sustained. The common preoccupation with unemployment proved to be the key. Time and again we find Ministers approaching the problem circumspectly, by arguing to the TUC that jobs had to be saved (and therefore industry helped) even at the cost of delaying some aspects of the Government's programme of social reforms. To industrialists, the Government often spoke more directly and explicitly of its need for a healthy private sector. As James Callaghan told the Lord Mayor's Banquet in November 1976: 'we must make a success of the mixed economy by adhering to an industrial strategy worked out and agreed by both the TUC and the CBI, which aimed at giving abolute priority to industrial needs ahead of even our social objectives.[51]

The industrial strategy to which the Prime Minister referred came to replace the Labour Government's earlier promise of considerable State interference and public control. The Government fell back rapidly into a more traditional relationship with private manufacturing industry: on to an attempt to create the conditions in which private investment could flourish by the tripartite development of industry-by-industry growth targets via the NEDC, supplemented by direct State funding where required. Yet after eighteen months of office the Labour Government was still only 'launching' its strategy in November 1975 – a strategy that might one day 'transform a declining economy into a high-output, high earnings economy based, as it must be, on full employment',[52] to quote Harold Wilson at the launching ceremony. In the long term this initiative by the Labour Government will doubtless mark an important stage in the growing intimacy of government departments and private manufacturing industry, and in the creation of procedures by which government funding will come to play an ever greater part in industrial investment. But for the bulk of the Labour Government's period of office it brought no tangible short-term improvements in the levels of investment, output, sales or employment, and remained what Sir Charles Villiers of British Steel called 'a paper chase', a procedure for generating documents rather than investment.[53] At least the industrial strategy provided the Labour Government with yet another opportunity to reassure private industry that it realised the necessity of earning 'a reasonable return on capital if it was to flourish' and to gain official trade union support for this. But the assertion of a recognition was not enough to produce that return, and investment and output remained persistently low. So though the Labour Government had set great store in 1974 in its ability to regenerate British industry in time to take advantage of the revival in world trade when that came, that regeneration still remained to be achieved as the Government left office in 1979.

Nor had the much awaited revival in world trade really happened by then, in spite of the role which the Labour Government played in a series of international initiatives to end the world recession. In November 1975 the heads of the governments of France, West Germany, Italy, Japan, the United States and the United Kingdom met in the Château de Rambouillet to announce their common commitment to the pursuit of policies which would bring economic growth and full employment without 'unleashing additional inflationary forces' into the world economy. The May 1977 summit in London, of a slightly wider gathering, made the same set of public pronouncements, though with less emphasis on the fear of inflation. That fear of renewed inflation continued, however, to block the revival in world trade and economic activity on which the Labour Government had set such store. In fact the world boom of 1972–73 ended abruptly as the Labour Government fought its two 1974 elections. In the first half of 1975 the gross national product of the eight largest OECD countries *fell* by an annual rate of 5 per cent and world trade fell at an even steeper rate (14%). The growth in the world economy thereafter was patchy and uneven, with an average rate of about 3½ per cent.

This compares with the 4% needed just to maintain the level of capacity use and unemployment at a stable level, and the 5½% or so which is the official target that Western countries adopted in 1976 as their strategy to move back towards full employment.[54]

Even at the May 1977 summit the German, Japanese and United States governments were still unprepared to expand at the rate for which the 'weaker' capitalist powers, and Great Britain in particular, pressed. And no amount of international summitry, internal reforms or public statements by American presidents could prevent unemployment in the OECD countries reaching 15 million by the end of 1976 and 17 million two years later. Nor could they prevent at least 20 per cent of existing productive capacity standing idle in the OECD area as a whole by the beginning of 1977.[55] World leaders publicly acknowledged their previous failures when they met for a third time in Bonn in July 1978, and both the West German and American governments did reflate their economies slightly in the second half of 1978, to give an OECD growth rate of 4½ per cent by early 1979. But this 'boom rate was still below the growth rates achieved in an *average* year of the 1960s', and left more than 5 per cent of the total OECD labour force unemployed throughout 1979.[56]

If this was not bad enough, the Labour Government also had to govern, as we have seen, against the background of a weak currency. Within a fortnight of the announcement of the £6 pay norm in July 1975, fresh speculation against the pound (which had already fallen a record 29 per cent below its December 1971 parity with the dollar, by the end of June) led the Bank of England to put its minimum lending rate up to 11 per cent (3¼% higher than the interest rates ruling in New York) in an attempt to persuade foreign holders of sterling – and in particular, the goverments of the Organisation of Petroleum Exporting

Countries (OPEC) – to keep their reserves in sterling. Here again monetary policy to defend sterling ran counter to the Government's much publicised search for new private investment, economic growth and falling unemployment. In the summer of 1975 jobs were being destroyed at the rate of 30,000 a month, a situation to which the Government responded with what was to be the first of a number of injections of public money into job saving schemes. In September 1975 the Government released £175 million in an attempt to save 100,000 jobs by the end of 1976. The Chancellor said then, and would repeat, that the main cause of unemployment continued to be the world recession, and that the Labour Government was doing well to keep the numbers of the unemployed so low. This was doubtless true, but in the immediate period the fact that a greater percentage of people were unemployed in other OECD countries could have been small comfort to the rising numbers of the British redundant.

Whatever the Government might claim about the long-term consequences of its policies, in the short term unemployment was not eased by the attempts made to cut back the rate of growth of public spending. From November 1974 the Government was adamant – and Denis Healey was explicit even to his severest critics at the 1975 Labour Party conference – that the release of funds to private investment had to take priority over greater public borrowing, and that this meant either higher taxation or reductions in government expenditure. It also meant that the bulk of any such reductions would have to fall on the sensitive areas of social provision – on education, housing, health, even social security benefits – as the Government sought to insulate public spending on investment in both publicly and privately owned industry from any retrenchment in public spending in general.

The cuts fell initially on the local authorities. 'The party is over,' the Secretary of State for the Environment told them in a much publicised exchange in 1975, and thereafter both the quality and scale of services provided by local authorities began to decline. At national level the Government concentrated its energies initially on scaling down its own expenditure *plans*. The February 1976 White Paper on public expenditure pruned the previous year's totals drastically: education lost £618 million off its planned budget for 1978–79, transport lost £506 million, defence £198 million, health £150 million, food subsidies were to be phased out more quickly to save £290 million, and £365 million was to be saved in the general area of housing. But ironically even when only attempting to reduce future expenditure plans, public sector expenditure in total proved difficult to control, and even the strict imposition of cash limits on spending Departments could not prevent the February 1976 White Paper from increasing government spending in total. In spite of the economies, politically so painful for a reforming Labour Government, two areas of government spending continued to grow: investment in industry and the servicing of the public sector debt. As Peter Jay said, 'one wonders how Ministers will feel when they realise that all their labours of the summer, autumn and winter have merely led to a gigantic redistribution of priorities in favour of the rentier owners of gilt-edged securities'.[57] The growing indebtedness of the economy added £3300 million to the provisions for debt interest in the February 1976 White Paper, and this more than cancelled out planned expenditure cuts elsewhere.

Meanwhile the failure of either the industrial strategy or the £6 pay norm to produce any immediate transformation in the economy's competitiveness, the severity of the world recession and the weakness of the pound combined to force the Government to borrow yet more foreign currency, this time from the IMF in December 1975. Even this did not prevent the pound falling steeply against the dollar through the spring of 1976. Its exchange rate fell below $2 for the first time in its history on 6 March. The 4 per cent decline in the external value of sterling in March 1976 added 4.75 per cent to the cost of raw materials imported by industry during that month, and this was the largest single monthly increase since the big rise in oil prices in January 1974. In spite of heavy Bank of England spending to support sterling, the pound continued to lose value at an alarming rate in April and May. The Labour Government used up $1250 million of foreign currency in March alone, trying in vain to stem the collapse, and a further $1500 million was consumed in April. In the process the entire loan from the IMF that had been added to the reserves in January was used up. Further enormous standby credits were announced in June (of $5000 million, to last until December). The Minimum Lending Rate went up again in May, in an attempt to attract foreign short-term investors in to London and the nationalised industries were encouraged by the Treasury to borrow heavily in Euro-currencies, to boost the reserves. At the peak of the first major run against sterling, in June, the pound lost ten cents against the dollar in just thirteen working days, and was effectively devalued by 15 per cent in three months. It became clear later that the Bank of England drew heavily on the foreign currency raised by the European borrowing of the nationalised industries, and used $1000 million of the June standby credit, in a vain attempt to stop the rot; but by midsummer the Labour Government had been forced to recognise that the Bank of England could not go on supporting the pound indefinitely in this way. To do so would have drained the reserves, and would have consumed vast quantities of foreign borrowing (which had eventually to be repaid) merely to maintain the exchange rate. Yet to let the pound fall indefinitely at the rate of the first half of 1976 would have been to abandon entirely any hope of achieving single-figure inflation by the end of the year. So, in order to restore foreign confidence in the exchange rate, the Government turned reluctantly to the question of public expenditure cuts.

Under heavy pressure from international sources (from the American Government and the Bank of International Settlements among others[58]) the Government announced a set of public sector spending cuts in July. Denis Healey maintained throughout that there was 'no economic justification for the fall which has taken place in recent weeks. It goes beyond anything required to make good past differences in the rate of inflation. . . . Those who have sold sterling have done so in disregard of the basic facts of our economic situation'.[59] Still, he was forced to take £1012 million off planned public expenditure, and this time government aid to industry suffered as heavily as the rest. The resources planned to be available to assist private investment and to stimulate employment were cut by £150 million, the capital investment programme of the nationalised industries was cut by £157 million, and even private employers had to pay an extra 2 per cent National Insurance contribution for their employees. Planned defence expenditure took another £100 million cut, education and health expenditure plans were pruned still further, and the removal of food subsidies was accelerated. By taking £1700 million off the public sector borrowing requirement for 1977–78 the Labour Government strained its relationship with the trade union movement, and ate away at the recovery of the industrial sector, because of the prior external pressure that a weak pound represented. The Chancellor continued to insist both that the pound was undervalued and that cuts could not be avoided. As he said, 'the foreign exchange market has not so far taken that view [of the pound's undervaluation] and the Government must live with the judgements of that market, whether they like them or not'[60]. Here was a clear admission of Government impotence.

The July package, like so much of Government policy, was an attempt to balance incompatibles: the social contract, the attempt to stimulate investment, and the strengthening of the pound; and seen as a compromise, it failed to restore sterling's stability in the international money markets. By September the Government's reserves of foreign currency stood at their lowest level since 1971, and the Government was forced to go back to the IMF for a second time. This second loan brought with it an IMF investigation and the eventual indignity of yet more cuts in public expenditure as a condition of the loan.

This vetting was only the public manifestation of the weakness of the Labour Government. Beneath it lay the continuing decline in the exchange rate of sterling to which the IMF loan was a reluctantly adopted response, and which would have necessitated cuts in public expenditure even if the IMF had miraculously vanished. It was the pound, not the IMF, that constrained government policy. The run against the pound built up again from September and after 8 September the Bank of England let the exchange rate fall, taking no action to support it. The point of no return appeared to have been passed, and there was no way in which the Bank of England alone could stem the flow. As David Blake wrote at the time, 'so great is the desire now to get out of sterling that any attempt by the Bank of England to hold the rate steady would merely lead to massive liquidation by foreign holders of sterling assets keen to sell up before their value is eroded by what seems to be an inexorable deterioration'.[61] The pound fell below $1.70 on 27 September. By 13 October it stood 13 per cent lower than in April. By 26 October it stood below $1.60 for the first time.

The week of the Labour Party conference in 1976 was particularly difficult for sterling. The Chancellor delayed his departure to an international conference as the pound slipped from $1.68 on Monday to $1.64 on Tuesday morning. He went instead to the Labour Party conference, arriving 'not with a Treasury view but straight from the battlefield' as he put it somewhat melodramatically to a hostile audience.[62] Nerves were very frayed at the Treasury that week. 'An unwise resolution,' Denis Healey told the delegates, 'an ill-judged statement, can knock £200 million off the reserves in a minute or add 20p to the price of goods in your shopping bag.' And so it seemed. The fall in sterling's external value was only slowed by the news that the Labour Government had asked the IMF for permission to borrow the maximum permitted loan of $3900 million, and by the progress announced in the Government's attempts to replace the sterling balances. With the money supply (M3) growing at an annual rate of 20 per cent by the autumn, the Chancellor found that the IMF's loan would be conditional on his ability to restrict that growth in money supply to nearer his own target (announced in July) of 12 per cent; and that in turn would require cuts in company borrowing and reductions in the public sector borrowing requirement. So the Minimum Lending Rate went up to 13 per cent in September (adding, according to the CBI, over £1 million a day to the costs of borrowing by the industrial sector); and was raised still further, to 15 per cent, a month later.

In December, after lengthy battles in Cabinet, further cuts in public expenditure were announced. £3000 million was to be saved on planned expenditure over two years, with savings in all the usual areas of the social contract. Savings on food subsidies were to be £160 million in the first year, and £60 million in the second. Expenditure on roads and schools was to be £270 million less than planned in 1977–78, and £300 million less in 1978–79. Public funds for housing and land acquisition were cut, and the regional employment premium ended. Defence expenditure was reduced again, and finance to the nationalised industries scaled down; and though the main social security benefits again remained unaltered, Denis Healey did announce that it was his intention to end the indexing of certain public sector pensions. The only beneficiary of the cuts seems to have been the NEB, to whom extra resources were directed, as the Government reduced the public sector borrowing requirement by £2000 million in 1977–78 and by £3000 million in 1978–79. The general effect of all this, if the February 1977 White Paper on government expenditure is a guide, was the first actual reduction in the levels of public spending since 1970. To satisfy the IMF, the Labour Government had gone beyond the scaling down of targets actually to halt (at least for the moment) the hitherto inexorable rise in total public expenditure. The February 1977 White Paper proposed to spend 3 per cent less in 1977–78 than the February 1976 White Paper had planned for that financial year, and 1.7 per cent less than was actually spent in 1976–77.

December 1976 provides a good vantage point from which to assess the performance of the Labour Government in its early years. As Denis Healey told the IMF in his *Letter of Intent* that accompanied the loan, the Labour Government was still pursuing, as it had been 'since the summer of 1975 . . . a medium-term strategy whose objective is to reduce the rate of inflation and to achieve a sustainable growth in output, employment and living standards based on a strong expansion in net exports and productive investment'.[63] Yet success continued to elude it, and Government targets were continually recast and postponed. 'The next two or three years' which 'are going to be difficult for us all' in the October 1974 manifesto ended in December 1976 with the Prime Minister still talking of 'a long road to prosperity' (with the clear implication that we were still only at the beginning of it) and with the Chancellor still telling the IMF that it would take a further 'three-year programme . . . [to] fully establish the recovery of the nation's economy'.[64] Every year, and not just 1975–76, became 'a year for Britain', 'a difficult year of transition'[65] always a foundation for future prosperity and never the real thing. Indeed the Labour Government was forced by its situation to make almost a virtue of 'straight talking' about the inevitability of falling living standards. After its protection of living standards in 1974 (by government spending, pension rises, cuts in VAT and extensive subsidies) stoked the rate of inflation and weakened the pound, the line changed. 'In the fight against inflation living standards will have to fall' became a familiar theme. Harold Wilson said it in October 1974. So did Denis Healey in his austerity budget in April 1975. He said then that sacrifice now would 'place British industry in a position to take advantage of any improvement in the world economy next year'[66] with the clear implication that any sacrifice would only be shortlived. It was not. The heavy fall in living standards in the first half of 1975 was matched by a 3.3 per cent drop in personal disposable income in the fourth quarter of 1976.

The rate of inflation, which the Government had aimed to reduce to single figures by December 1976, stayed well above that until 1978. In spite of two years of highly disciplined wage restraint, prices were still rising by 14–15 per cent by the end of 1976, and that was the rate at which they were rising when the Labour Government took office. So if the Labour Government could claim (as the Chancellor did in his *Letter of Intent*) that it had reduced the rate of inflation, even halved it, it had done so only by comparison with the 30 per cent rate over which it had itself presided by the end of the first year of office. Nor had the Labour Government by December 1976 managed to stimulate large amounts of investment and economic growth. On the contrary, 1975 had seen an unprecedentedly sharp fall in the volume of capital spending in industry, and a further fall in 1976 had brought investment levels in manufacturing, distribution, shipping and services to their lowest level since 1969. Even the Treasury was only forecasting a 2 per cent increase in GNP in 1977, and unemployment was expected to rise. Indeed over the entire Labour Government period unemployment remained at a level that would have been inconceivable (and politically disastrous) only a decade before. By December 1976 the Government had not shaken itself free of that old bogey of Labour Governments down the years: financial crises and public spending cuts. It was true that Ministers had managed to protect social security benefits from the worst effects of retrenchment, and had avoided the worst fears of Michael Foot that they would end up 'pulling down our hospitals brick by brick with our bare hands';[67] but still the Government had been forced to preside over a period of falling living standards, rising unemployment and cuts in the social wage that stands in marked contrast to the aspirations of their manifesto. As the numbers of the poor were swelled by the rising tide of the unemployed, the Labour

Government's early promise to achieve 'a fundamental and irreversible shift in the balance of power and wealth in favour of working people and their families' began to look empty indeed.


## VI

Throughout 1977 the Labour Government lived under close IMF scrutiny. There were regular visits by teams of IMF inspectors. Policy had constantly to be assessed against the monetary targets specified in the *Letter of Intent,* * and the need to meet deadlines for debt repayment had to be kept firmly in mind. Indeed the acceptance of a specified monetary target could have proved particularly embarrassing if the recession had suddenly worsened, for then the combination of falling tax receipts and growing unemployment benefits would have pushed the public sector borrowing requirement still higher, and forced the Government to intensify the recession by still more public spending cuts. In fact this did not occur, and the Government lived out its last two years in a remarkably improved financial position. Unexpectedly, December 1976 marked the nadir of the Government's financial dilemmas, and part of the IMF loan was actually repaid earlier than anticipated, so marked was the change in the Government's fortunes. In 1977 and 1978 the pound stabilised, the balance of payments improved and inflation rates eventually fell; and it was for these reasons that Labour Ministers were able to go to the country claiming that the corner had been turned and that better times were ahead. The underlying industrial weakness of the economy remained unaltered, to give the lie to the more ambitious of such claims; but the financial constraints on the British State eased after December 1976, and with them the visibility of Government impotence eased also.

The unexpected strength of sterling after December 1976 was partly a result of the Labour Government's capacity to control its working-class supporters. There was no major industrial opposition to the December 1976 cuts, to falling living standards, or to rising unemployment. Stage 2 of the incomes policy achieved a record 8 per cent gap between prices and earnings, and though this fall in real wages was reversed under Stage 3, tacit TUC support for further wage restraint and the lack of any effective unofficial militancy kept wage costs under control at least until

* That the public sector borrowing requirement be kept to £8,700 million in 1977–78, and to £8,500 million in 1978–79, with Domestic Credit Expansion held within a ceiling of £6,000 million.

the 1978 Ford workers' strike. Only in the last winter of the Government's life did working-class militancy against wage restraint erupt again, to weaken confidence in sterling once more; and by then foreign holders of British currency were able to take heart from the patent resolve of the Labour Cabinet to match any rise in money wages with parallel reductions in the provision of real public sector services. For the pound stabilised too because of the cut backs in government spending, and a consequent reduction in the rate of growth of the public sector borrowing requirement, that followed the December 1976 agreement with the IMF. The borrowing requirement, which had exceeded £10,000 million in the financial year 1975–76, and reached £7300 million the year after, remained easily within the ceilings set in the *Letter of Intent* (at £5580 million for 1977–78); and future Government plans for public expenditure still restricted its growth to 2.2 per cent in 1978–79 and to 2.0 per cent thereafter.[68] Again, sterling strengthened as it became obvious that the Treasury calculations on future public sector borrowing on which the December 1976 negotiations had occurred had been 'wildly inaccurate'[69], and that the problem of public expenditure was as much that of *underspending* against targets as of any lack of Treasury control over cash limits in the public sector. Only two sections out of 136 in the government service proved to have exceeded their budgets in the financial year 1976–77, and this kept government spending £1600 million down on the levels that had been projected – a degree of underspending of about the same scale as the cuts made so publicly and painfully in July and December 1976.[70] This level of underspending continued in 1977–78, to keep central and local government expenditure £1000 million lower than had been intended.

The arrival of North Sea oil also had a dramatic effect on sterling and the balance of payments. Money began to flow into London in large amounts. The United Kingdom's reserves of foreign currency rose from $7196 million to $20,557 million in 1977, as the balance of payments went into surplus for the first time for six years. The surplus that year, of £7363 million, replaced a deficit of £3628 million the year before, and was the economy's largest ever. But its size was a product almost entirely of a reduced foreign oil bill (North Sea oil improved the visible trade balance by an estimated £2400 million in 1977) and of considerable movements of foreign capital into the London money markets. The economy's visible trade still remained in deficit over the year as a whole (apart from oil its trade deficit was estimated by one commentator as possibly still £2000 million in the middle of 1977[71]), and even invisible earnings were reduced in 1977 by the outflow of interest payments to foreign sources of capital temporarily lodged in London. Indeed the international movement of capital into London in 1977 brought almost as many difficulties as had its equally sudden departure in the year before. The strengthening balance of payments enabled the Government to cut interest rates steadily until November 1977. They were reduced twenty-one times after December 1976, to bring the Minimum Lending Rate down to 5 per cent in November 1977. But the generalised belief in the money markets that the exchange rate of the pound was now *too low* against the weakening dollar set the logic of speculation running the other way. Money flowed into London, in spite of falling interest rates, enlarging the money supply and forcing the Government both to push interest rates up again (to 10 per cent by June 1978) to slow down the rate of domestic credit expansion, and to allow the exchange rate of sterling to rise. In an ironic reversal of fortunes, the Labour Government spent the first half of 1977 selling sterling, to keep its rate down in line with the promise to the IMF to keep British export prices competitive, only to have to abandon this in July because of the potentially inflationary consequences of the resulting inflow of speculative funds. Once again, when facing the money markets, the more the Government acted the more it had to act. As Caroline Atkinson observed at the time,

The more determined the Government seems to be to keep its money targets, the greater the chance for the dealer to make a profit on an appreciation. For this implies that if the crunch comes between the external objective of a stable pound and the internal objective of money growth between 9 and 13 per cent the first will be the one to go. Hence the money rushes in and speculation is self-fulfilling.[72]

'As so often in the past, the lesson of the failure of this policy [was] that the power of markets is such that governments just do not have the staying power to outlast those speculating against them':[73] and as a result the pound crept backwards towards a $2 parity. On 31 October 1977 alone, twelve months after the sterling crisis was at its height, the pound *rose* six cents against the dollar. As this persisted, it altered the balance of advantage on costs against British exporters and in favour of foreign producers once more, so that the volume of imported manufactures also increased steadily through 1978 to prevent the visible trade balance from showing the unambiguous strengthening that the arrival of North Sea oil might otherwise have occasioned. But so long as North Sea oil continued to flow the continuing weakness of Britain's trading position would be a long-term, not a short-term problem; and the cumulative impact of this financial transformation was that the annual rate of inflation fell at long last to less than 10 per cent in January 1978 and stayed at or around that figure through to the election.

As David Blake noted at the end of 1977, the twelve months that followed the sterling crisis had not only seen 'a most remarkable turn-round in Britain's financial position', it had also witnessed 'a steady deterioration in the country's underlying economic base'[74]. What satisfied the financial houses was not nearly so much to the liking of the industrial sector of British capitalism. World trade made only the weakest of recoveries from the 1974–75 recession, and unemployment continued to rise throughout the OECD economies as a whole, as we have seen. The competitive position of British manufactures amid that world recession continued to decline, once the immediate advantage of the 1976 sterling depreciation had come and gone. According to IMF calculations in 1978, British manufacturers 'witnessed a more rapid deterioration in their relative cost position during the fourth quarter of 1977 than in any other single quarter since at least 1970';[75] and this clearly persisted into the first quarter of 1978, as sterling continued to gain value on the foreign exchange markets[76]. Moreover, as Stage 3 of the incomes policy weakened, Treasury calculations (if these can be trusted) suggested that wage costs in manufacturing began to rise more rapidly in the United Kingdom than in its six leading industrial competitors; and that when all this was seen in conjunction with an only slowly rising rate of growth in output per worker, it left British manufacturing 'less competitive internationally than it [had] been for about two years'.[77] Not surprisingly then, unemployment did not begin to fall until October 1977 (its peak in September of that year was 1.38 million in Great Britain, 1.609 million if Northern Ireland is included); and the fall thereafter still left more than 1.3 million people officially unemployed in December 1978. The index of industrial production at the end of 1977 still stood lower than it had during the three-day week in 1974. The index for the last quarter of 1977, at 110.2, was only 0.1 higher than twelve months before; and though production did then begin to rise, the volume of output from the manufacturing sector in the first quarter of 1978 was still 2.25 per cent *lower* than in the same period four years earlier, when the three-day week had been in full swing. The result was a fall in consumer spending throughout 1977 that contrasted sharply with the degree of financial stability so gratuitously placed in the Labour Government's lap by the movement of foreign capital and by the arrival of North Sea oil. Levels of real personal disposable income in the second quarter of 1977 were 6 per cent lower than in the late summer of 1976, before the sterling crisis, and were at their lowest for four years; and it was this gap between the 'real' and the 'financial' economy which Denis Healey attempted to bridge in 1977 and 1978 by a degree of controlled reflation.

In his March 1977 budget the Chancellor announced tax concessions worth £1290 million (by raising the thresholds of tax and by taking almost a million low paid workers out of the tax net altogether) with the promise of an extra £960 million of tax relief (by a 2p reduction in the standard rate of income tax) if and when the union leadership agreed the details of a third stage of incomes restraint. In July 1977, and in spite of the TUC's inability formally to agree a Stage 3 pay norm, Denis Healey increased child benefits and made further tax concessions (of a penny off the standard rate of tax, plus changes in petrol duty and personal allowances forced on him in the committee stage of his Finance Bill by Liberal MPs and Labour left-wingers). That package was followed by a clear statement that Ministers would hold a 10 per cent Stage 3 pay norm in spite of union opposition, and that they would insist on maintaining a twelve-month gap between major pay settlements. As they prepared (successfully as it transpired) to resist the Fire Brigade Union in defence of Stage 3, Denis Healey announced in the autumn of 1977 yet another round of tax cuts: increasing personal allowances, giving £10 to each old age pensioner, £400 million to the construction industry and extra aid for small businesses. This was followed in April 1978 by the injection of an extra £2500 million into the economy, by increasing child benefits still further, by increasing personal allowances and altering certain tax bands, and by providing extra (if tiny) amounts of money for hospitals, small firms and farmers. The result was a long overdue consumer boom during 1978 that brought retail sales in the first six months of the year to a level 3.5 per cent higher than the year before. These tax cuts, plus the way in which average earnings under Stage 3 rose by 15.4 per cent, gave living standards a boost of 6–7 per cent between August 1977 and August 1978.

Under this degree of government-inspired reflation, industrial production at long last began, if only briefly, to revive. The precise scale of the revival was difficult to chart from official figures, as the Government's decision to alter the base year of its indices from 1970 to 1975 (and as a result to alter the weight given to North Sea oil in the averages), boosted the growth statistics by at least 1 per cent. Yet it is clear that oil production continued to be the major growth sector in the British economy, and that the manufacturing sector remained relatively stagnant. The volume of production of oil and associated products grew 9.1 per cent in the three months to July 1978, whilst manufacturing output grew by only 1 per cent. So whilst industrial output in total rose by 4 per cent between August 1977 and August

1978, the output of the manufacturing sector (which accounts for 70 per cent of all industrial output) grew at only half that rate.[78] Yet this was enough to give an annual rate of growth for industrial production as a whole of more than 3 per cent in 1978, and to reduce the total of the unemployed slightly but steadily through the year (by 90,000 in total, to 1.32 million). This rate of growth stood in sharp contrast to the industrial stagnation of the first three years of the Labour Government; but even so was disappointingly slow, and effectively ground to a halt in the last half of 1978. By December 1978 the index of industrial production, at 110.0, stood 5 per cent higher than it had twelve months before, but down slightly on its peak in the third quarter of 1978.* This rate of improvement in the level of industrial output came as some relief to a Government long used to total industrial stagnation, but was hardly enough to sustain the reductions in unemployment and the expansion in social services which Labour Ministers required for their own electoral survival. As Denis Healey said in August 1978, 'we are not where we want to be, and we need another term of office at least before that point is reached'.[79]

Yet time was not the crucial factor, as Denis Healey's remark implied. What barred the way to sustained and high economic growth were the contradictory forces to which government policies were subject, and which repeatedly obliged the Government itself to dampen down economic recovery before it could become sustained. This was very evident by November 1978, when the Government had to raise MLR again, from 10 per cent to 12.5 per cent, and was underlined in February 1979, when the rate was increased still further (to 14%; it fell back to 13% a month later, and to 12% in the run up to the general election). Such rates of interest were bound to discourage further investment by a company sector whose financial deficit was already approaching the crisis levels of 1974.[80] Treasury Ministers felt themselves to have very little choice, not least because of the fear of a new sterling crisis. By the autumn of 1978 UK reserves were already threatened by rising interest rates in New York, inspired by a United States administration that was equally beset by the weak currency and large balance of payments deficit of an internationally uncompetitive economy. In addition, the 'sucking in' of foreign-manufactured consumer goods during the brief consumer boom of 1978 was already affecting the economy's non-oil trade balance. International capital movements throughout 1978 turned the £7363 million balance of

---

* The non-oil figures were similar in their movement but even less impressive in their levels: 103.4 in December 1978, as against 101.8 in December 1977 but 104.9 in the third quarter of 1978.

payments surplus of 1977 into a deficit of £1130 million twelve months later and capital was only attracted back in the spring of 1979 by holding interest rates on long-dated government stock 4 and 6 points higher than in the United States and West Germany respectively.

This is not to say that the Labour Government left office amid another sterling crisis. Sterling remained strong, and the reserves relatively healthy, in the last twelve months of the Government's life because North Sea oil continued to lessen the dependence of the UK economy on foreign oil. This became particularly important in 1979, as the UK's achievement of net self-sufficiency in oil coincided with OPEC's decision to increase oil prices substantially. What forced interest rates up was much more the fear that such a sterling crisis *could* develop unless the Government made clear its determination to control the money supply and to contain inflation; and it had to make this determination plain again because of growing industrial unrest amongst its own working-class industrial base, and because of an associated rise in the public sector borrowing requirement which threatened to exceed the Government's own chosen target of £8.5 billion for the financial year 1978–79. The decision to hold interest rates high was, in fact, a statement by the Labour Cabinet that it would match wage increases with parallel cuts in industrial output, in employment and in public sector services; and the fact that it was still having to make these choices in 1979 was a measure both of how little it had achieved in five years of office, and of just how conservative it had grown in the process.

Denis Healey approached his last budget in 1979 surrounded by just the set of dilemmas which had beset him in 1974. His own tax cuts had created the situation in which government borrowing was already growing rapidly again (it had reached £6620 million in the first nine months of the financial year 1978–79, as against £5480 million for the entire financial year that preceded it). The Government's incomes policy was under very heavy pressure from predominantly public sector industrial militancy, in a situation in which every 1 per cent increase in earnings across the public sector as a whole added £300 million to the Government's wage bill. Yet at the same time the rate of inflation was quickening again (moving once more towards double figures), interest rates and unemployment were already abnormally high, and British industrial output and the entire world economy were sliding into yet another recession. With certain world commodity prices (and particularly oil) once more on the increase, and with business confidence, investment and profits low, the Chancellor faced his perennial dilemma: how to boost investment (and therefore, he hoped, long-run employment levels) when this required cuts in interest rates, wages control, and reductions in public sector expenditure that, at one and the same time, threatened the stability of sterling (and hence eroded price stability) and jeopardised jobs and trade union support in the build up to a closely fought general election. But unlike 1974, the Chancellor this time could not lay the blame on his predecessors. Instead he faced an electorate whose real living standards by the end of 1978 were, at best, little better than they had been in 1973, even after his brief consumer boom. With unemployment significantly higher than in March 1974, with industrial production in 1979 unlikely to rise by more than 1–2 per cent, and with an electorate who still required an estimated 14.5 per cent increase in their money income merely to keep pace with rising inflation and taxation,[81] it was not surprising that the only relief the Chancellor was given was his own Government's electoral defeat – and this, of course, only left a new Government and a new Chancellor to continue the same impossible juggling act, with doubtless the same long-term electoral consequences.

# VII

Denis Healey claimed in the House of Commons in June 1978 that Labour had 'brought Britain through the severest crisis' and that 'the rewards were there for all to see in falling inflation, falling unemployment and rising living standards'.[82] Yet though much had certainly changed from the crisis days of 1976, the claims were deceptive, and the mood distinctly electioneering. For in all its years of office, the Labour Government had found itself trapped in a set of appalling dilemmas which in the end it could not escape. On the one side, it had inherited an internationally high rate of inflation and balance of payments deficit, which was then accentuated by the high wage settlements and falling exchange rates which these produced. On the other side, the Government found its manufacturing sector in crisis, shrinking yearly in its contribution to the GNP, facing the most serious world recession since the 1930s, with unemployment rising steeply. The long-term solution which the Labour Government understandably sought was that which any British government in this situation would presumably have followed: the search for a strengthened manufacturing base, providing greater employment, a stronger balance of payments, and a larger set of goods and services on which rising real living standards and stable prices could be built.

Yet the Government was blocked at every turn in its pursuit of this objective. Private investment was deterred by the levels of inflation prevailing, and by the competitive pressures on industrial profits which that inflation intensified. The control of that rate of inflation required a strong pound sterling, yet the pound's weakness for much of the Labour Government's early period in office necessitated a level of interest rates that helped to deter large-scale capital investment. Wage restraint was vital to strengthen the pound, and to remove one major indigenous pressure on export costs; but the maintenance of incomes policy over a long period required the achievement of a level of employment, personal disposable income and price stability that proved incompatible with the maintenance of the level of public spending on which the social contract had been built. The financing of government spending by taxation threatened wage controls directly, while its financing by borrowing did so just as effectively in an indirect way, either by stimulating inflation by generating a rapid growth in the money supply; or by threatening the recovery of private investment in the upswing of the business cycle by squeezing out company borrowing from a money supply whose growth had to be severely restricted if inflation was to be slowed. Yet unemployment levels could not come down significantly without that recovery in private investment; and indeed, to the degree that investment was labour-saving, could not fall without a level of investment and economic activity of truly enormous proportions. But how was the Labour Government to bring unemployment down if, by cutting public expenditure, it added to the loss of jobs in the public sector, and if by not cutting public expenditure it added (either by higher personal taxation and lower private demand, or by government borrowing, high rates of interest and low private investment) to the slow rate of recovery of employment in the private sector?

Not surprisingly, the Labour Government was offered no easy answers to this set of dilemmas by the economic advisers to whom it turned. Conventional economics in the 1970s was as much in crisis as was the world economy it sought to analyse, as the Keynesian orthodoxies of the postwar years of stability and growth struggled to cope with the new problems of inflation and unemployment. Among conventional economists the Labour Government could find no agreement on the causes of the sudden spurt in inflation throughout the world system, but only a limited degree of consensus on what kinds of policy would accentuate rising prices and greater unemployment. It could not opt for the 'expansionism and protection' that its left wing argued, for fear of international retaliation and soaring inflation. It could not opt for the monetarist call for massive cuts in public expenditure for fear of the immediate deflationary consequences on levels of employment. Nor could neo-Keynesians offer the Labour Government more than a slow amelioration of inflation and unemployment, and only then if the Government could deliver and continue to deliver superhuman loyalty from the trade union movement, as Ministers and union leaders waited for a revival of world trade that in practice never came. What came instead was persistent industrial stagnation and a growing tension between the Labour Government and sections of its own working-class electoral base. Five years of Labour Government produced, not economic growth and social justice, but the return of a Conservative Government who were the electoral beneficiaries of the failure of leading Labour politicians to turn their special relationship with the trade union movement into a solid foundation for economic prosperity and Labour Party electoral strength. It is to the changing nature of that relationship in the 1970s that we must now turn.

# CHAPTER TWO

# The Labour Government and the trade unions

## I

It is impossible to understand fully the nature and development of the relationship between this Labour Government and the major trade union leaders without recognising the strong historical, institutional, ideological and personal connections that unite them. The Labour Party, after all, was the creation (in 1900) of an already established trade union movement, and the nature of the Party's creation has given a particular character to its internal politics ever since. The main organisational legacies of the Party's early years remain as the formal subordination of Party leaders (including parliamentarians) to democratic control through the annual conference, on conventional trade union lines, and the dominant position, within that extra-parliamentary structure of control, which the trade unions themselves enjoy. Trade union bloc votes at annual conference far outweigh even the collective voting power of the constituency parties; and between conferences, when the National Executive Committee (NEC) of the Party is charged with the implementation of conference decisions, trade unions directly nominate twelve of the Committee's twenty-nine members and, via their voting strength at conference, in effect dictate the choice of the five women members and the Party Treasurer. Between 40 per cent and 70 per cent of the Labour Party's funds come from affiliation fees paid by individual trade unions; and in addition the unions have sponsored never less than 30 per cent of the entire Parliamentary Labour Party since the war, and on occasions that figure has been as high as 40 per cent. It is facts like these that give credence to the repeated Conservative claim that the Labour Party in office is the creature of trade union control.

In fact the relationship between the Labour Party and the organised trade union movement (and especially between Labour Ministers and national trade union officers) is infinitely more complex and subtle than such an assertion would allow. The divisions that have come to predominate within the Labour Party have rarely divided parliamentarians from trade unionists as two distinct and internally united blocs. Rather, in each period of the Party's history a section of the parliamentary party and a number of trade union leaders have found themselves in minority positions on the question of conference sovereignty and on the associated drift of party policy. The majority view, in each generation of the Party, has been that the parliamentarians should enjoy considerable freedom of manoeuvre from extra-parliamentary control, in spite of the formal specification of conference domination. As early as 1907 the parliamentarians began to establish their autonomy from conference (and hence from the dominance of the trade union bloc vote), an autonomy which the trade union leadership has, in the main, been only too happy to sustain. There have been periods of left-wing ascendancy within the Party, most notably in the early 1930s and after 1970, when conference sovereignty has been reasserted, and the political leaders have been obliged as a result to formally adopt policies they might otherwise have chosen to ignore. So to this important degree at least, leading Labour Party politicans have had to operate, and continue to have to operate, with a sensitivity to the views and requirements of party activists and trade union leaders outside Parliament that has no parallel in the other major parties. But significantly such periods of Left ascendancy have been rare and shortlived. More normally trade union leaders have used their constitutional position within the Labour Party's internal decision-making processes to buttress the leadership and autonomy of relatively moderate parliamentary leaderships, if need be *against* left-wing demands for greater conference and NEC control; and have preferred to exercise their influence over Labour Governments through direct negotiations with Ministers and their officials, rather than by relying exclusively (or even mainly) on any position of privilege they enjoy within the Party itself.

What the close involvement of trade unions in Labour Party decision-making and finance has sustained is a similar set of political perspectives in the minds of leading Labour parliamentarians and trade union officials, a propensity to share broadly similar definitions of long-term policy aspirations and short-term practicalities. It has also served to sustain a powerful sense of loyalty to Labour Governments and to their policies among trade union leaders which, at critical moments in the Party's history, has lessened the degree of trade union resistance to government encroachment on union freedom of action and on working-class living standards and job security. If, in the periods of opposition, trade union influence on policy-making has been enhanced by the unions' position within the Party structure, in periods of Labour Government that structural connection between the two 'wings' of the Labour movement has invariably worked to the advantage of the Government itself, as a mixture of strong organisational loyalty, close personal connections and shared political perspectives has led trade union leaders to subordinate their aspirations (and those of their members) to the changing specifications of Labour Government policy.

The rapprochement that was established between leading Labour parliamentarians and trade union leaders in the postwar period appears, in retrospect, to have rested on a common agreement on relative spheres of autonomy, on what Lewis Minkin has referred to as the trade unions' 'closure' of certain areas of policy-making to parliamentary action.[1] The willingness of major trade union figures to leave the parliamentarians to initiate policy in the majority of areas through the 1950s had as its corollary the willingness of those parliamentarians to avoid any political trespassing on matters close to the daily preoccupations of union officials, namely wage settlements and industrial relations reform. That concordat was easy to maintain while the Party was in opposition, and while British capitalism did not impose the need for incomes control on its political élite. But this division between industry and politics, which had been challenged briefly by Sir Stafford Cripps's incomes policy in the late 1940s, could not easily be sustained after 1961, as governments of both parties found it imperative to widen the scope of their policy to include the national control of wage settlements and the lowering of industrial costs. The resulting development of incomes policies, productivity bargaining and industrial relations legislation by the Labour Government between 1964 and 1970 proved a traumatic experience for the whole labour movement, and brought relationships between the Labour Cabinet and the TUC to a bitter and low ebb over *In Place of Strife* in 1969.[2] The reassertion of trade union influence on policy-making within the Labour Party after 1970, and the left-wing sympathies of key trade union officials that shaped the direction of that policy-making, seems to have been a direct reaction to the events of the 1966–70 period, as a new generation of union leaders emerged who were prepared to play a more positive role within the Labour Party in an attempt to avoid any repetition of the 1969 'attack' on trade unionism and to re-establish the electoral domination of Labour.

The internal balance of forces within the Labour Party after 1970 was unparalleled since the 1930s. At leadership level in both the industrial and political wings of the movement a strong determination to avoid any repetition of *In Place of Strife* acted as a powerful barrier to any clear statements of difference, and precluded any set of policies that threatened to impose tight legal constraints on trade union industrial action. The bitter Government–union confrontations of the Heath years re-established the Labour Party's claim, somewhat tarnished by the events of 1969, to be *the* Party capable of articulating and defending the political interests of organised labour; and the more radical trade union leaders elected by the groundswell of rank and file resentment against the incomes policies of the 1960s gave the Left of the Party a unique degree of support from the major trade union bloc votes at the critical party conferences in the years of opposition.[3] For 'the new trade union leadership had a significant impact on the Party', and some, 'Jones in particular, became more closely involved in policy-making through the new joint liaison committee'.[4] From that committee, as we have seen, a whole series of radical policy commitments emerged: on the repeal of the Industrial Relations Act, on new rights for trade unionists and other employees, on price controls and government intervention in industry, on welfare payments and on industrial democracy. But on the question of incomes control, the new accord between the two wings of the labour movement was either silent or ambiguous. Both agreed that there would be no return to a statutory incomes policy, but whether that meant free collective bargaining or voluntary pay restraint seemed to vary with the speaker and the audience as the general election of 1974 approached. Even those who, like Jack Jones, were later to play so important a role in shaping Labour Government incomes policies, were hard to pin down on this question in the years of opposition. As John Elliott later reported of the 1971 Labour Party Conference:

Drawn into a discussion on an incomes policy, Mr Jones said 'If we have to make some form of sacrifice involving incomes then we have to decide how it can be done equally. It cannot be done as it was tried under the last Labour Government. It is impossible to put a ceiling on wages while one man works for another man's profit.' Pressed further, he said it was impossible to talk about incomes without thinking in terms of prices. 'If you can find a way of keeping down retail prices and rents, you will get a reaction from the unions, but it needs thinking out.'[5]

Certainly by 1973, if there was a general consensus throughout the Party, it seemed to be that incomes control would be voluntary, and would come only as a *response* to the prior establishment of price stability and social justice in the context of an expanding economy.

Lewis Minkin has argued convincingly that, with the Labour Government in power, even this new generation of more radical trade union leaders exercised considerable restraint in their dealings with Labour Ministers. The novelty of the social contract should not be allowed to obscure the limits of trade union influence: that, with the 'exception of old age pensions, rents and (belatedly) child benefits', trade union leaders 'exercised little pressure on the Government's social, educational and housing policies', and they restricted their influence on foreign policy to 'economic sanctions on trade with Spain, Chile, South Africa and Bolivia'.[6] As we have seen, the drift of economic policy ran counter to their expectations and preferences, and yet in general – and with the exception of specific unions, like the National Union of Public Employees (NUPE), which waged a strong inner-party campaign against public spending cuts – union leaders did not use their position inside the Party to embarrass the Cabinet, even on issues directly related to the living standards and job security of their members; nor, with very rare and quickly withdrawn exceptions, did they even apply pressure on their sponsored MPs. Rather, the majority of union leaders came to play a very important subordinate supporting role to this Labour Government, acting for as long as they could as allies in the development of policies that involved the control of incomes and the toleration of rising unemployment, and eroded the living standards and job security of trade union members. It is this process, and its resulting tensions, rather than any excess of trade union power, which has to be documented and explained.

## II

One very important reason for this abnormal degree of loyalty lay in the parallel commitment of this Labour Government to official trade unionism. There can be no doubt that the Government stood closer to (and identified itself more publicly with) trade unions and their aspirations than had its 1964–70 predecessor. There was to be no return to *In Place of Strife*. Instead, Ministers repeatedly showed the genuineness of their concern for official trade unionism by public statements and policy initiatives that were motivated by more than the simple desire to 'keep the unions happy' within the social contract. Trade union leaders were consulted often, regularly, and at an early stage in the development of policy. Major government decisions, even its budgetary changes, were made conditional at times on union support, and leading trade unionists were allowed to shape (and to police) the detail of the early stages of incomes policy in a way that blurred the public's sense of whose responsibility that policy was. The legislative programme of the Labour Government included substantial concessions to trade union demands. The Industrial Relations Act was repealed; so too was the Housing Finance Act; a new Trade Union Act and an Employment Protection Act followed; so did Acts on equal pay and sexual equality. Interventionist agencies in the labour market were established: the Manpower Services Commission, the Advisory Conciliation and Arbitration Service, and the Health and Safety Commission, and leading trade union figures played a prominent part in the design and running of each.

In general the trade unions found Cabinet Ministers willing to defend union rights publicly, on a scale and with a regularity that has no recent parallel in British political history. Ministers defended the right of trade unionists to boycott South African mail, against critics in the judiciary and in Parliament.[7] Ministers stood on picket lines in support of rank and file trade unionists seeking the right to negotiate with their employer.[8] And Ministers resisted the campaign to remove trade union representation from the boards of trustees of the newly proposed occupational pension funds.[9] Even the Bullock Commission on industrial democracy was given the terms of reference which leading trade union figures required.[10] The Queen's Speech at the beginning of the 1977–78 parliamentary session announced the Government's willingness to grant the right to strike to postal workers; and only two rebel backbench MPs prevented an earlier session of the same Parliament implementing the Dock Labour Bill for which the Transport and General Workers Union had fought so hard. In the last Queen's Speech of the 1974–79 Parliament, the Labour Government proposed to introduce a permanent statutory scheme to provide better benefits for workers placed on short-time working. In all these ways this Labour Government, unlike its predecessors, left trade unionists with a new set of legal rights and gave trade union leaders a new status as participants in the formation of national economic policy.* It also, by doing so, sustained a new and misleading popular image of excessive trade union power.

This image was misleading because it ignored the changing substance

* This is not to say that the new set of labour laws was without its problems. The dispute at Grunwick's was the most glaring example of loopholes in the law (in this instance, of union recognition) which remain to be remedied. Patterns of sexual and racial discrimination remain firmly entrenched; and the courts remain all too willing to interpret the new Acts in a manner which restricts their coverage in certain crucial areas, not least that of picketing.

of union–Government relations after February 1974. In the opening days, the Labour Government did not constrict its trade union allies. The miners' dispute was resolved on terms that were highly favourable to the miners. High pay settlements were tolerated and a dramatic drop in the strike figures was achieved as evidence of how different the new Government was. But as time progressed, trade union influence on policy waned. More powerful forces and processes came into play. Trade union leaders could resist particular details, could block and negotiate, and (where their members' direct cooperation was required) could exercise some kind of veto on particular policy options. But they could not define the agenda of proposals that the Government put before them, nor the context within which policy had to be formulated; and so in the end they proved unable to prevent the transformation of the social contract from its initial character (of a set of concrete and immediate legislative proposals that favoured the working class), into its later form (as a vehicle of wage restraint, buttressed by general statements of aspiration and vague long-term commitments to social change). The drift to incomes policy, the rise in unemployment, and the Government's resistance to the TUC's expansionist economic policy stand as major pieces of evidence against the thesis of excessive trade union power, and make clear that the visibility of trade union leaders in the process of policy-making was less an index of their power than of their subordination. The story of the relationship between this Labour Government and the trade union movement after 1974 is one of the transformation of the national trade union leadership into vital junior allies of the Cabinet in the implementation of incomes control – policemen in their own arena of action, visibly pursuing policies with which they were uneasy within limits set only by the sporadic degree of rank and file protest to which they were subject.

This is clear if we watch the development of incomes policy from 1974. As the Labour Government returned to power it was in no position to build on the statutory incomes policy inherited from the Heath Government. Nor was there any political will to do so. On the contrary, for at least a number of leading Cabinet members such a retreat from statutory wage control was near to being a defining element of their political faith. So the Pay Board was abolished, as promised, and there was no Stage 4 to replace the Stage 3 of the Conservatives' incomes policy when that expired in July 1974. Instead the miners were given a generous pay settlement, and this set the pace for the pay agreements to follow. As the Labour Government entered office railwaymen, engineering workers, Ford manual workers, merchant seamen and local government white-collar staff were all in the process of negotiating 'substantial' pay awards; and by November 1974 the average level of wage settlements stood 25 per cent higher than it had twelve months before. The Prime Minister was adamant that the social contract was not a policy of wage restraint in another guise; and the rate of increase in earnings bore out only too well the accuracy of his assertion. Between the two elections in 1974, the Government chose to take the longer view, and persisted in its belief that wage demands would moderate as the implementation of its side of the social contract was felt at shop floor level.

The early indicators were that the major figures in the TUC shared that optimism, and senior trade union officials soon dropped into what was to be their customary role, at least until 1978, as advocates of wage restraint on behalf of the Labour Government. In March 1974 the TUC let it be known that 'in response to the policies of the new government it will be possible to influence the size of claims and settlements achieved'[11]. But this did not mean that any but a minority of trade union leaders wanted a resuscitation of the TUC's own vetting machinery, last used in the 1960s. Rather, men like Jack Jones of the TGWU saw wage restraint as a natural product of government policy, a long-term consequence of Labour radicalism. As he put it,

The idea is to try and encourage a climate where, because of social improvements like increased pensions, controlling prices and redistributing wealth so that more people can get their fair share, we shall also improve our industrial relations. . . . I think the base is there all right. Providing we get Government action on things like prices, rents and so on . . . then there will be a reaction at the grass roots level.[12]

It was with this in mind that trade union leaders greeted Denis Healey's first budget with such enthusiasm. It provided them with evidence of the Government's intention to push for social justice, such that, in Len Murray's words, 'the Chancellor will be able to count on a good response from the mass of working people in combating the effects of worldwide inflation'[13]. As Jack Jones made clear, when he welcomed 'a very good socialist budget' with the confident prediction that the Government 'could expect 1.7 million T & G members to react in a responsible way',[14] the bulk of the trade union leadership was not opposed to the moderation of wage demands. Their opposition in 1974 was to the *imposition* of such moderation by government decree. Their hope was that moderation would come of itself; and if it did not, that it should be engineered from within the trade union movement. For all the insistence by Ministers and trade unionists that the social contract was not a wages policy, few among the national trade union élite were prepared to deny the need for such a policy. Even in 1974 all that was at stake was its authorship, its severity and the mechanisms for its achievement.

So by the summer of 1974 the pattern of future developments was already being foreshadowed, as Ministers talked the language of 'shared responsibilities' and the TUC urged moderation and restraint. TUC language was, at this stage, very guarded, but its significance was clear. 'The TUC faced a test of its own credibility,' Len Murray told a union conference in April 1974, in delivering its response to the Labour Government's radical policy initiatives. For 'it would be the shop floor [that] determined the success or failure of the social contract' and therefore it fell to the TUC 'to convince its 10 million members of the reasonable policies now being adopted by the Government'[15]. It was up to the TUC, Murray insisted, to establish its priorities 'lest Whitehall decide to impose its own';[16] and that is what the TUC set out to do. As early as April 1974 its leading figures were reassuring Ministers that they would help to achieve 'realistic wage-claims and fewer strikes'.[17] As Jack Jones put it to his union delegation to the Scottish TUC,

It is up to us to ensure that every working man and woman supports this Government. That is not to say that within our movement we should not be free to criticise. . . . The social contract does not mean control of wages, but it does mean a realistic approach to which we in the trade union movement are already responding, and so are the Government.[18]

The Government, for its part, backed such calls for wage moderation with appeals of its own. Michael Foot made one to the National Committee of the AUEW in April, who obliged by calling off their work-to-rule and deferring their next national pay claim for twelve months. At a number of successive trade union conferences, Michael Foot made clear his concern lest the end of Stage 3 be followed by a 'wages explosion' that could lose the Labour Government its next election. 'One of the difficulties of the statutory control of wages,' he said, 'is bringing it to an end, because so many expectations have been built up. There is likely to be an explosion. When such an explosion occurs it can upset the economic policy of any Government.' It was for this reason, he told the Association of Scientific Technical and Managerial Staffs (ASTMS) conference in May, that 'the Government was anxious for a smooth return to free collective bargaining, so that its own policies were not upset'.[19]

The first document to result from the shared concerns of the Labour Government and the TUC with wage restraint came in June 1974 and was ratified by Congress in September as *Collective Bargaining and the Social Contract*. This was a TUC document, laying out guidelines to unions for wage negotiations after Stage 3, and giving TUC support for the policy of the Labour Government. Negotiators were told to press for a low pay minimum of £30 per week, and to give priority to agreements 'which will have beneficial effects on unit costs and efficiency, to reforming pay structures and to improving job security'. But they were also to recognise that 'the scope for real increases in consumption is limited' and that as a result the 'central negotiating objective will be to ensure that real incomes are maintained', and that a smooth transition to free collective bargaining is achieved by the observation of a twelve-month interval between major increases.[20] This policy was not without its critics. Major white-collar unions resented the TUC's new role. Divisions in the National Union of Mineworkers (NUM) also ran deep on incomes control, and its conference in 1974 managed both to reject any form of wage control and to avoid a left-wing call for pay rises of up to £20 a week by November. The AUEW President let his lack of enthusiasm for wage restraint be known again in June, and only withdrew his motion of opposition to the TUC document in September after heavy pressure from other leading union figures.

The TUC's debate on its own document in September 1974 was particularly illuminating. The justification for trade union moderation in wage demands given by supporters of the social contract was the *radicalism* of the Labour Government programme, and the *short term nature* of the restraint proposed. As the document put it, 'the current circumstances . . . impose limits on what can be achieved at this time, though these circumstances are not permanent and indeed the aim of the Government's industrial and economic policy is to create the conditions for an early resumption of increased living standards'.[21] Indeed the AUEW delegation felt able to withdraw its opposition not simply out of a desire to create unity in the build up to the general election, but also because its eight-point demands (on price controls and wealth redistribution) were subsumed into TUC policy. Both Len Murray and Lawrence Daly publicly urged 'some kind of incomes policy' (Daly) that this time was to be of a new order. As Len Murray said 'do not confuse the sort of wage restraint we are asking unions to accept temporarily now with the sort of restraint governments tried to impose on unions in previous periods. The purpose is different and the policy context different.'[22] More radical trade union leaders were not so sure. As Ken Gill put it in reply; 'It appears we are saying that we hate restraint under Heath but we welcome it under Wilson. . . . Instead of the employers refusing, we don't ask.'[23]

The degree of self deception in Len Murray's assertion of the novelty of the policy became clearer when the election was over. In the last quarter of 1974 the total volume of economic production fell sharply. Gross Domestic Product (GDP), measured in output, fell by 1.5 per cent on its level in the same quarter of 1973, and the total figure obscured greater falls in the volume of exports (of 5 per cent) and of manufacturing and construction levels (of 4 per cent). As we have seen, the resulting massive balance of payments deficit weakened the pound, which had depreciated by over 20 per cent in three years by the end of 1974. The run on sterling after the November trade figures took one-eighth of the Government's reserves of foreign currency, and reintroduced the fear of international financial insolvency into Government thinking. At the same time the retail price index in December 1974 was 19 per cent higher than the Christmas before, and underlying rate of price acceleration was still increasing. Average earnings stood 25.3 per cent higher in November 1974 than in the same month in 1973; and the pattern of settlements in the public sector in early 1975 was higher still. In April 1975 500,000 civil servants negotiated an extra 32 per cent and 100,000 power workers 31 per cent, to match the miners' 31 per cent in March 1975 and to follow the postal workers' 24 per cent and the gas manual workers' 34 per cent earlier in the year. Settlements like this raised the rate of growth of average earnings to twice the rate of growth of retail prices between the middle of 1974 and the middle of 1975, and brought ministerial demands for wage restraint to a new pitch.

Harold Wilson played an important part in the new Government campaign for restraint. In the first of his post-election television addresses, he singled out trade union power for oblique criticism, saying that the country 'could not afford the big battalion philosophy, with power groups, whoever they are, trying to seize more than their share of what is available';[24] and he repeated this attack on trade union militancy to the Labour Party conference in November. James Callaghan gave a similar stern warning to the conference on the adverse effects on jobs and prices of any trade unionists 'opting out', as he put it, of the social contract; and by January the Chancellor was being even blunter: 'Britain must now accept lower average wages or face mounting unemployment'.[25] Significantly Michael Foot publicly supported the Healey position by early 1975, a position laid out in some detail by Denis Healey in his April 1975 budget speech. Indeed the continuing high level of public sector wage settlements brought Cabinet divisions into the open, with Reg Prentice, then Anthony Crosland, and finally the Prime Minister himself letting it be known that they feared for the continuation of the social contract, and that the time was ripe for a Government stand against a major public sector wage demand. The dubious honour of being the next public sector union to put in a major wage demand fell to the National Union of Railwaymen (NUR), and it was on them that the toughening of policy was in fact to fall.

Not that the TUC had been entirely inactive as wage settlements and inflation had grown in the winter of 1974–75. In November 1974 the General Council issued a further circular to its constituent unions, reminding them of the guidelines already issued, and stressing the importance of the twelve-month gap between settlements and the need to aim only to maintain existing real standards of living. The November circular also made clear the TUC's preference for a negotiating strategy that achieved such a maintenance of real living standards by 'gradually [getting] prices to rise more slowly, with money wages correspondingly not going up so fast, [rather] than have prices and wages equating with each other at a higher and higher level'.[26] This view was reflected in Len Murray's reactions to a number of important wage claims that winter. The miners were told that 'the Government had the right to demand that they did not mount a pay claim which was outside the social contract guidelines';[27] and in January unions were told by the General Secretary not to base their claims on anticipated price increases or on attempts to protect their members against higher income tax.[28] A month later the TUC made clear its opposition to settlements outside the guidelines that were justified by artificial and unnecessary wage restructurings; and by May the TUC was publicly discussing Jack Jones's proposal that the union movement as a whole should accept a flat rate increase on basic pay rates. By then the case for incomes control had been conceded, and the TUC was discussing not *whether* but *how* it should be implemented. All that was required to establish the policy was the conventional financial crisis, and that came in June and July.

The build up to the adoption of the Government's counter-inflation policy followed a by now recognisable pattern. The long sequence of government warnings, each tougher than the last, culminated in the decision to make a stand over the next claim to be made, which happened to be that of the NUR. And behind the specific dispute, a run on sterling and talk of national insolvency acted to complete a scenario in which Ministers could make sharp reversals of policy, call for national wage restraint and promise a return to 'normal' after twelve months or two years of 'sacrifice for Britain'. In early June 1975 the NUR was resisting an arbitration offer of 27 per cent as it sought its 35 per cent claim, to which the Government would not agree. At the same time the national press were making known what Joe Haines's memoirs later confirmed, that the Treasurey was pushing for the introduction of an incomes policy of a statutory kind. On 30 June the pound fell 5 cents against the dollar, and reports from the City suggested that the withdrawal of large amounts of sterling by the Governments of Kuwait and Saudi Arabia was imminent. In this atmosphere of panic, the NUR were 'beer and sandwiched' at No. 10, and settled for 30 per cent. The Treasury pressure for statutory controls on wages was resisted, though only at the eleventh hour if Joe Haines's report is correct. Instead the Government, committed by the explicit nature of its opposition to statutory wage control, looked to the TUC to police a 'voluntary' agreement, and drafted legislation, which in the end it held in reserve, to give that agreement possible statutory effect by fines on employers – a sleight of hand to avoid legal sactions on trade unionists which could not mask the sharp reversal of policy which July 1975 brought. On 1 July the Chancellor committed the Labour Government to holding 'the increase in wages and salaries during the next pay round . . . to 10 per cent'[29] and this was confirmed when the counter-inflation policy was publicly launched on 11 July. Amid clear indications from senior Ministers that incomes control was to be a semi-permanent feature of political life, the Government announced its intention to reduce inflation to less than 10 per cent by the late summer of 1976, by restricting pay settlements to an overriding limit of £6 a week during the next twelve-month period.

   This was very much in line with the kind of policy emerging from the TUC as the financial crisis intensified. A paper submitted to the TUC by Jack Jones in mid June suggested the setting of a price target for late 1976, the acceptance of a flat rate increase for all, a freeze on higher incomes, a reduction in unemployment and tighter price controls. The £6 limit was lower than union leaders were reported as suggesting (the TUC document was reported as naming the maintenance of real incomes as still 'the central TUC guideline'[30]), and the counter-inflation white paper explicitly rejected tighter price controls. Nor in the event did unemployment fall. But higher incomes were frozen entirely, trade unionists were not to be jailed for breach of the policy, and the flat rate principle was accepted; and all this was enough to win explicit TUC support for the very income restraint they had rejected in 1974. Union leaders were clearly impressed by the 'depth and gravity of the crisis',[31] and by the danger that hyperinflation would force sweeping public expenditure cuts and drive the Labour Government out of office. Union leaders were subject in addition to heavy pressure from Labour Ministers to 'make it a year for Britain', as Harold Wilson put it to the

NUM conference, and to accept voluntary restraint now to avoid compulsory restraint later. TUC resistance was restricted to Len Murray's insistence that the £6 was not a maximum, but a rise which all should get (and in pursuit of which industrial action would be legitimate). Otherwise TUC support was total, and was confirmed by a massive majority at the Congress in September. The Government, for its part, was well aware of the degree of TUC compliance, and the significance of the TUC's new role. As Denis Healey said,

the most impressive thing has been the speed with which members of the General Council [of the TUC] have themselves reached a voluntary agreement on a limit to pay which falls considerably short of full compensation for the increase in the cost of living over the past twelve months, and which will mean some reduction in real take home pay for the majority, though by no means all of its members.

I do not think there has been any previous occasion in the history of this country, nor maybe any other country, in which the trade union movement of its own will has not only agreed to such a policy but has agreed it in very great detail.[32]

Though a few unions objected, their objections were publicly countered by Len Murray. 'Some people,' he told a TUC regional council in Bristol, 'seem to think you can get instant socialism to solve our problems at a stroke.' He accepted that the policy cut living standards, but he could see no alternative. 'Those who challenge the policy,' he said, 'as distinct from those who just don't like it – and I don't like it – have really got an obligation of putting forward an alternative and telling us very clearly what they would do if they reject the policy.'[33] In the event, no powerful alternative was forthcoming, and the policy held, without resort to legal sanctions. The overall increase in earnings fell to 13.9 per cent in the twelve months of the policy and, with TUC monitoring, was subject to no major challenge throughout its entire course.

The Chancellor had said in July 1975 that the restrictions on incomes would last for several years, and so in 1976 the exercise was repeated again. As before, financial crisis hovered in the background, unemployment was higher, at 1.2 million, and public sector spending plans had already been scaled down once, in February 1976. So with the rate of inflation still remaining at around 14 per cent, the negotiations proved more difficult and were more protracted. In February the Chancellor made clear that he was prepared to cut income tax if the trade union movement would accept a pay limit lower than £6 in the next round; and in his budget in April, he suggested a figure of 3 per cent. That was rejected as too low by a series of major trade union leaders, and Jack Jones continued to press for a flat rate system. But his was becoming a lone voice on this within his own union and within the trade union hierarchy, and the Government itself preferred a percentage settlement that would help middle management and skilled workers by maintaining differentials. By May the TUC and the Government had agreed a Stage 2 limit of 4.5 per cent. Negotiations were delayed slightly by initially vigorous TUC opposition to the proposed scaling down of government expenditure plans, and to the ending of food subsidies. But this opposition petered out in a joint declaration of support for the Labour Government by Hugh Scanlon, Jack Jones and David Basnett (respectively President of the AUEW and General Secretaries of the TGWU and GMWU), as they publicly dissociated the country's three largest unions from the campaign of the Tribune group of MPs against these clear signs of the Government's retreat on its previous commitments on social expenditure. The 4.5 per cent pay increase ceiling for Stage 2 was then ratified by an overwhelming majority at a special congress in June 1976, and was successfully implemented after August 1976, again, without a single *official* trade union challenge. As a result, the rate of increase in wage rates in the second year of the policy was held to 8.8 per cent, as prices continued to soar.

These two years of successful pay restraint stand as clear evidence of the loyalty of trade union leaders to this Labour Government, and their willingness to subordinate their wider policy aspirations to Government pressure. They stand too as evidence of the trade union leaders' hold on the loyalty of their own membership and of the weakness of any rank-and-file movement of protest against pay restraint and trade union incorporation. Not even the left-wing union leaders most hostile to what they saw as TUC capitulation to bankrupt Treasury orthodoxy could galvanise mass support against policies which explicitly cut living standards, failed to prevent price rises, and allowed unemployment to grow. By August 1977 the Labour Government could legitimately claim that it had achieved a degree of working class cooperation over a long period that no Conservative Government could match, and had in the process cut back significantly the pressure of wages on industrial costs.

III

Yet even as the second stage of the pay policy was being accepted by the trade union leadership in May 1976, the signs of the policy's internal decay were already looming. The processes which ate away at the loyalty of trade union officialdom, and undermined their credibility and role as advocates and enforcers of pay restraint, were the rising tide of the working-class unemployed and the persistent fall in living standards that accompanied this. In 1975 union leaders had seen wage restraint as an alternative to mass unemployment – that the choice they faced was between rising real wages or jobs for all. But as the choice became more clearly one between rising unemployment *and* wage restraint on the one side, and the threat of even greater unemployment on the other, their willingness and ability to preside over further cuts in their members' living standards began to erode.

The concern with unemployment was there from the beginning, and was shared by leading Labour Ministers. When the £6 limit was accepted by the TUC in July 1975, union leaders called for a temporary employment subsidy and selective import controls to reduce the loss of jobs. 'Our problems could not be solved,' Len Murray told the 1975 Trades Union Congress, 'by deliberately allowing unemployment to rise';[34] and though many union leaders accepted that a general immediate reflation was impossible, they were determined that the impact of the world recession should be cushioned by aid to the construction industry, and by active State participation in medium-term economic planning.[35] In all this they echoed the words of Michael Foot, that 'unemployment at the present level was totally unacceptable to the Labour Movement', reflecting as it did 'a crisis of capitalism of a most fundamental character'.[36]

Yet unemployment *was* accepted and tolerated by union leaders and Cabinet members. Trade union pressure on unemployment (and indeed press treatment of union affairs) soon settled into a distinctive pattern. Between April and July, the question of the next round of pay settlements dominated public discussion, with unemployment as a side issue, part of the TUC's response to calls for wage restraint. With the policy established, agitation for a reduction in unemployment returned to centre-stage, with TUC calls for greater Government action. In September 1975 the TUC repeated its call for mild reflation, job subsidies, and selective import controls. In January 1976, with unemployment at over 5 per cent, the TUC again pressed the Government, implying clearly that the successful negotiation of a second round of pay restraint would be conditional on government action in five areas: a doubling of the temporary employment subsidy, extra money to the Manpower Services Commission both to create jobs and to add to the number of training places, the provision of extra money to the NEB to speed investment and stock building, and selective import controls for particular industries. In August 1976 TUC leaders were back again, 'seeking urgent talks with Mr Callaghan'[37] before the September Congress, with a seven-point programme. 'Watch it,' Len Murray was reported as saying to Ministers on that occasion – the unions could not tolerate unemployment running at its then level of more than a million and a half; and he urged the Government to adopt the TUC's emergency measures (on job creation, particularly for the young) and to plan the 'expansion of the economy so that we can use the nation's resources to the full'.[38] By January 1977 the official trade union tone was even harder. The Government's record 'does not constitute a satisfactory picture' (Murray) and is 'deplorable' (Daly). 'The Government need to be reminded,' David Basnett said, 'that the success of government economic policy for trade unionists is not measured by the rate of sterling or the diminishing size of the trade balance, but by whether or not the Government can reduce the appalling levels of unemployment and reverse the upward trend in prices.'[39]

But the bulk of the TUC leadership was not prepared to go beyond public condemnation of unemployment, and the constitutionally sanctioned pressure group practice of submitting alternative economic proposals. They refused to support the 'Right to Work Campaign' initiated by the Socialist Workers' Party, and for two years did not push their opposition to rising unemployment to the point of refusing to sign and administer the policies of voluntary wage restraint. In this, TUC leaders were sustained by the Government's willingness repeatedly to introduce tiny (and inadequate) packages of measures to alleviate elements of the unemployment situation. In September and December 1975, and again in February and April 1976, the Chancellor brought forward sets of selective measures which stimulated employment either directly, through the introduction and improvement of the temporary employment subsidy, or indirectly, through funds to industry or for industrial training. So, as an example, in September 1975 the Chancellor extended the temporary employment subsidy to the entire country, gave £30 million to the Manpower Services Commission to create new jobs, gave a £5 a head payment to all companies recruiting the young unemployed, gave £20 million for extra industrial training and provided £100 million for more industrial investment and factory construction. The total package cost £125 million, and was presented as likely to provide eventually an additional 100,000 jobs (a claim which, it should be said, was quickly challenged by serious commentators[40]). These monies were supplemented in December, a further £200 million was released for job creation in February 1976, and a special £160 million a year scheme to reduce youth unemployment was introduced in June 1977.*

All these initiatives were welcomed by the TUC as going some way towards their demand for Government action in this critical area. But as Ministers repeatedly made clear, the rise in unemployment was a consequence that they were prepared to accept in the pursuit of price stability, a *deliberate* part of Government policy, and a direct result of the Government's refusal to reflate the economy on TUC lines. For if the small print of TUC employment policy found a direct echo in the Chancellor's tiny packages of selective measures, the full force of the TUC's alternative strategy (of reflation and selective import controls) was consistently rejected by Government Ministers. The regularity of TUC protests is a measure of the way in which policy drifted against them; and the resigned nature of their regular acceptance of cuts in government spending could not mask the growing sense of frustration with the Government's general economic policy in wider and wider sections of the trade union leadership. This was the TUC's real area of failure on unemployment, their inability to persuade the Government to accept the kind of reflationary programmes that the TUC's *Economic Review* annually suggested. The fact that the TUC now drew up and published an alternative economic strategy was a measure of its growing role in Government circles. But Government policy did not follow TUC specifications, for all their publicity; and when it is also realised that the TUC's own set of demands as late as February 1977 left unemployment at over a million by the end of 1978, the limits on TUC power become clear. Union leaders accepted as *targets* levels of unemployment that would have been politically inconceivable only a decade ago, and yet they could not win even the policy to achieve that from the Labour Government with whom they claimed such a close and special relationship. So that when reflation came, after November 1977, it came because of the easing of other constraints on the Labour Government. It was no consequence of TUC power, but a byproduct of a strengthening of sterling and of cutbacks in government spending, to the last of which at least the TUC had always offered ambiguous but undeniable opposition. TUC leaders could claim with some justice that unemployment would have been higher, and public spending cuts more severe, but for their pressure; but this *defensive* rearguard action

---

* Critics were sceptical: 'None of these measures make any contribution to the longer term number of jobs and are short-term palliatives. The Job Release and Youth Employment schemes are just methods of redistributing jobs from older to younger workers' (P. Townsend, 'The problem, an over-view', in Michael Barratt Brown, ed., *Full Employment: priority* Nottingham, Spokesman Books, 1978, p. 12).

was quite different in kind and impact from the *positive* aspirations of
TUC – Labour Government liaison embodied in the earlier stages of the
social contract.

In spite of TUC protests and Government mini-packages,
unemployment remained high. It grew inexorably until September
1977, when the seasonally adjusted figure for Great Britain reached 1.37
million (6 per cent of the work force), eased slightly over the next
eighteen months, but was still well over 1.3 million by the general
election. Indeed between the autumn of 1973 and the autumn of 1977
male unemployment rose nearly two and a half times. Female
unemployment rose more than fivefold.[41] Unemployment was
particularly severe among the young. Frank Field estimated that
800,000 people under the age of twenty-five were unemployed at some
time in 1976, when they constituted 40 per cent of the total
unemployed;[42] and the Manpower Services Commission's most
optimistic projection still had 100,000 young people out of work in
1981.[43] On rare occasions Ministers admitted their helplessness. Shirley
Williams told the 'Youth Charter Towards 2000' conference in
February 1977: 'We are seeing the increase in unemployment
throughout the industrial world, and it is a problem for which we still
have no real answer'.[44] The intractability of the world recession made
the rapid achievement of high rates of economic growth a near
impossibility, and rising productivity cut the number of jobs which any
economic expansion would bring. Yet demographic changes (the high
birth rate of the late 1950s and early 1960s, and the low birth rate of the
1914–18 generation coming to retirement), plus the growing number of
married women returning to employment, gave a potential working
population that was rising by between 150,000 and 160,000 each year in
the mid 1970s. Trapped between a growing labour force and a stagnant
economy, even a modest reduction in unemployment (say to 800,000)
by 1981 required the creation of an extra 1.3 million jobs (or a growth
rate of 5 per cent between 1978 and 1981) which was quite beyond the
capacity of the Labour Government to deliver or the TUC to force. So
official aspirations, even in trade union circles, were repeatedly scaled
down, 'target reductions' in unemployment were reduced and the time
scale lengthened, as unemployment grew and trade union dissatisfaction intensified.*

* The contradiction facing the Labour Government was well put by Peter Jay: 'That
contradiction lies between the maximum amount of unemployment that is politically
practical in a democracy and the minimum amount of unemployment that is apparently
involved in containing the long-term acceleration of inflation – it being assumed that the
alternative of indefinitely accelerating inflation is also irreconcilable with the political
imperatives of democracy as well as with the stability of the present type of political
economy' (*The Times*, 2 Sept. 1975, p. 1).

IV

It was against this background that official trade union support for tight incomes control began to erode. Ministers were aware of their growing difficulties even before Stage 2 was signed in May 1976, and the Chancellor let it be known that he foresaw 'a gradual return to more normal wage bargaining'[45] after July 1977. In this he was echoing Jack Jones, who was by now the key supporter of Government pay policy in the General Council of the TUC. Even he was calling (by June 1976) for 'a return to free collective bargaining towards the end of next year'.[46] Both were clearly in step with the general sentiments expressed at the TUC Special Congress which ratified Stage 2, that this was the last time that this kind of agreement would be forthcoming. It was not only amongst those unions opposing Stage 2 (including ASLEF, ASTMS, BALPA and the NUJ*) that the desire for free collective bargaining was growing. The wider failure of the social contract was eroding the commitment of other union leaders too.

By mid-1976 the familiar tensions of rigorous income control were becoming all too obvious. The simple and general rules which characterised Stage 1 and 2 clearly helped to sell the policy and 'to establish rough justice' between wage earners, as Harold Wilson claimed when the £6 limit was introduced. But they brought with them rigidities, injustices and anomalies which, as they persisted, exacerbated industrial tension. The sense of diminishing differentials between the skilled and the unskilled which the £6 limit accentuated was the most obvious case of this, and trade union leaders were aware of growing rank and file dissatisfaction in the unions of the skilled.[47] Nor could the industrially strong exploit their advantages, and this was bound eventually to generate tension between rank and file members and any trade union leaders who were prepared to go on acting as an unpaid substitute for the Government's own vetting machinery. These tensions could perhaps have been handled if the early claims for wage restraint had been met. But industrial stagnation continued well into 1978, unemployment, as we have seen, continued to grow, and the cut in real living standards that had been asserted as temporary showed no sign of abating as Stage 2 progressed. Far from bringing inflation down to single figures, prices were still rising at 17.1 per cent by the end of May 1977, and this gave a gap of 8 per cent between the movement of prices and real earnings which each working family felt directly and

---

* Associated Society of Locomotive Engineers and Firemen; Association of Scientific, Technical and Managerial Staffs; British Air Line Pilots' Association; National Union of Journalists.

persistently as a financial pressure and as a curtailment of previous standards of consumption and leisure. This 8 per cent gap was the largest ever recorded between prices and earnings since the information on both was first published in the early 1960s, and it brought an inevitable working-class response.

The Government began its attempt to win a third round of pay restraint even earlier in the yearly cycle than before. In late November the Chancellor let it be known that if a satisfactory third stage was signed, income tax could be reduced in the spring, and that without such an agreement, the country would face 'catastrophe'.[48] In March the unions were told that a limit of 4–5 per cent would have to apply to wage rates under Stage 3, if the Government's revised inflation targets were to be met in 1978. From all sides of the Cabinet came repeated public warnings of the dangers of wage explosion: from Michael Foot and Tony Benn no less than from David Ennals and the Prime Minister himself. The Chancellor repeated in April that his forecast of 13 per cent inflation by the end of 1977 was based on the assumption that earnings would not rise into double figures under Stage 3,[49] and through the summer of 1977 there was no easing in the Government's campaign for a third round of restraint that would keep increases in basic rates of wages to around 5 per cent.

This time union leaders fell into line less easily. The Trades Union Congress at Brighton in September 1976 voted overwhelmingly for 'an orderly return to free collective bargaining' at the end of Stage 2. Though the ambiguity of the term 'orderly' kept alive in official circles the hope of a third year of agreement, it was clear that a much looser form of pay policy was generally desired by delegates to the Congress. Len Murray told the Government in December that TUC leaders were prepared to contemplate a third year of pay restraint, if Government policy on prices and jobs was acceptable. But the unions' requirements on wider economic policy were not in line with Government thinking. As Jack Jones said, 'we need import deposits or controls, a measure of reflation, a prices freeze and very substantial increases in old age pensions. We need an alternative economic policy, and it is not coming.'[50] As this became clear, union support for a third round dwindled. Some union leaders and union conferences continued to argue for restraint, out of a fear of the consequences (for inflation, employment, the low paid and the survival of the Labour Government) that a 'free for all' on wages would bring after two years of pent up rank and file frustration. Tom Jackson of the Union of Post Office Workers urged his conference to back a Stage 3. So did David Basnett of the General and Municipal Workers' Union (GMWU). But hopes of an effective settlement were destroyed by the clear votes of the AUEW, TGWU and NUM conferences to oppose any third year of restraint, and in this they were supported by many other union conferences in the spring and summer of 1977. Even Jack Jones, who had argued through the winter and spring for some kind of agreement with the Government as a stage in the return to free collective bargaining, found himself defeated by his own union conference's refusal to support further voluntary pay restraint, or even to underwrite their executive's acceptance of Stage 2.

The pattern of official voting in the governing bodies of the major trade unions ran counter to the often expressed preferences of the majority of national trade union general secretaries and presidents (including Jack Jones and Hugh Scanlon no less than David Basnett and Len Murray) for some kind of third year of pay restraint. But discontent with falling living standards and dwindling differentials had to find expression through the union movement or erupt into unofficial action: 1975 and 1976 had been unusual for the low level of industrial militancy and the generalised acceptance of temporary pay restraint, but in 1977 the degree of unofficial action against pay policy and its associated anomalies grew significantly. Skilled workers often played a crucial role in this wave of sporadic protest. In March and April 1977 skilled workers in Leyland cars struck for eight weeks in an attempt to win a separate negotiating structure through which to restore differentials, and there were parallel strikes by skilled men at British Steel's Port Talbot works and at Ford's. At Heathrow in the spring of 1977 4000 engineers defied both employers and their union in a similar demand for better shift pay and separate negotiating rights. More than 1700 shop stewards met in Birmingham in April to reject any third year of restraint for workers in the industries which they represented: these included car plants, mines, docks, engineering works, offices and building sites.[51] It is not surprising then that in the first two months of the year alone, over one million days were 'lost' through strikes involving 198,500 workers in 445 stoppages,[52] nor that a public opinion survey commissioned by *New Society* in April 1977 showed a significant fall in the degree of public support for income restraint. Though the shop stewards at Leyland had their call for an all out strike for a £31 pay claim rejected by their constituents in August, union leaders were left in no doubt by the summer of 1977 that a pay deal of the Stage 1 or Stage 2 type could not be delivered, and that if a Stage 3 policy was to be followed, the Government would have to implement it alone.

The Government persisted in its negotiations with the TUC on a possible Stage 3 through April and May. But with union leaders under growing rank and file pressure, and in the face of Government unwillingness to follow TUC policy on reflation, price controls, food subsidies and unemployment, those talks proved sterile. Union leaders had gone to the talks hoping for a more flexible set of guidelines to steer the labour movement back to free collective bargaining in an 'orderly' way that would avoid 'aggro, bother and a punch up' as Len Murray put it.[53] They were not prepared to see a global total set by the Government for pay rises within every plant or company – the so called 'kitty bargaining' which certain Ministers favoured – and in the end no agreement was reached. All that the TUC was prepared to give, by way of assurance that the end of Stage 2 would not generate a major wage explosion, was an insistence that there be a twelve-month gap between wage settlements for any one group of workers, that those settlements due before 31 July should not be deferred but should continue to operate within the Stage 2 limits, and that now was not the time to increase the unions' low pay target from £30 a week to £50. All this was carried by a surprisingly large majority (7.1 million to 4 million on the twelve-month rule) at the September Congress, and in the event Stage 3 of the Labour Government's incomes policy received considerable tacit TUC support. Indeed the willingness of the majority of trade union leaders to respect the twelve-month rule was alone responsible for delaying large numbers of major pay claims into the spring and summer of 1978, by which time the TUC's own failure to help the firemen had consolidated the very wage norm against which they officially committed themselves at the end of Stage 2.

However this was not initially clear, and in the summer of 1977 the Government was obliged to initiate and police its Stage 3 policy alone. Ministers confirmed their intention to hold public sector pay rises to 10 per cent, to maintain the twelve-month rule, to prevent unions negotiating settlements that recouped the loss of real earnings by their members since 1975, and to introduce sanctions against private companies settling with their workers at a higher figure or on a more regular basis. The Prime Minister made clear the Government's willingness to face strikes in order to maintain the policy, and the Chancellor let it be known that spurious productivity deals would not be tolerated as a way of avoiding industrial confrontation.[54] Instead Ministers set out on what James Callaghan called 'a gigantic essay in persuasion' to defuse rank and file industrial unrest,[55] and (the firemen apart) it is clear that opposition to a further round of pay restraint waned in the face of unemployment, more stable prices and Government intransigence. It is true that Ministers had at times to use their sanctions. By May 1978 thirty firms had apparently been blacklisted in

Government circles for settling with employees above the pay norm. By August that figure stood at seventy-four.[56] But in general pay settlements did cluster around the 10 per cent level. This was partly because of the residual TUC backing already mentioned, in particular because of the General Council's insistence that 'the approach of securing very large increases in order to make up ground lost over the past three years would be self-defeating'.[57] It was partly because the rate of inflation did, at last, begin to fall. It was also partly a consequence of the big unions' willingness to settle within or at the 10 per cent limit, and in particular of the NUM's eventual abandonment of its 90 per cent pay claim in favour of a 10 per cent settlement supplemented by the self-financing pit-based incentive schemes which a secret ballot of NUM members had initially rejected. Productivity agreements proved a way round the 10 per cent limit which many unions took, as 12 million workers settled pay claims within the Stage 3 guidelines in the first thirty-six weeks of the policy alone. And of course the policy held because the Government was willing to blacklist firms, and because the firemen were defeated.

Stage 3 was challenged by *one* official national strike, called by the Fire Brigades Union in November. For eight weeks firemen struck in support of a 30 per cent pay claim, in spite of a refusal by the TUC to mobilise other unions in a public campaign against the 10 per cent policy. The TUC's new role of unofficial assistant to the Labour Government was very evident here; and the General Council's reason for its inactivity, 'that the Government is not likely to be deflected from its present course of action',[58] is an amazing and self-fulfilling admission of union impotence in the face of ministerial resolve. The firemen were forced eventually to settle within Stage 3 guidelines in return for exemption from pay policy norms in a settlement to come. Similar two-stage agreements followed for other public sector groups: for policemen, doctors, the armed forces, university teachers, and at the end of Stage 3, the high paid. Indeed the Government's sympathetic and very rapid response to the report of the Boyle Committee on the plight of the high paid stands in stark contrast to its determined resistance to the militancy of the firemen. Though both were officially handled 'within the Stage 3 guidelines' there is no escaping the fact that a Labour Government supposedly committed to greater social equality refused firemen with eleven years service a £900 a year increase in their basic wage of £3000 a year, in spite of eight weeks of official industrial militancy, only later to give the head of the British Steel Corporation an extra £3000 on his £30,000 a year (with more to come), and to do so voluntarily, without overt industrial pressure, and in response to the logic of market forces that might otherwise tempt Sir Charles Villiers back into the private sector. It is clear too that certain private sector settlements (most noticeably at Ford's) did exceed the pay norms, and that not all the self-financing productivity deals were as genuine as their authors claimed, in spite of Government vetting. The result was a rate of increase in earnings under Stage 3 of 14.2 per cent – a rate of growth which, at 6.4 per cent higher than the rate of growth of prices during the same period, combined with cuts in personal taxation to increase the personal disposable income of the employed by between 6 and 7 per cent.

The gap between Government aspiration and working-class response which had begun to emerge under Stage 3 came fully into the open in the fourth year of the Labour Government's incomes policy. Wage settlements in the fourth year returned to the levels which had characterised the first twelve months of the Government's life, but did so this time *in spite* of explicit ministerial determination to hold wage settlements to an even tighter, 5 per cent norm. For by the middle of 1978, Labour Ministers had travelled far from their opposition preoccupation with free collective bargaining. As Stage 3 ended, senior Ministers stressed the need for a *permanent* procedure for specifying national income norms. As Denis Healey put it in December 1977, 'the Government has the duty to give the country some idea of the aggregate increase in earnings compatible with growth and keeping inflation under control',[59] particularly when the absence of a general policy covering both public and private sector employees could not remove the necessity for a public sector wage policy, and so introduce the danger of systematic differences in treatment unless the Government acted. Far from retreating from incomes policy, the Labour Government *toughened* its wages control in Stage 4. The new norm was 5 per cent (with greater flexibility for the very low paid), and this was to herald a more permanent policy. As the White Paper put it in July 1978,

it is the Government's view that the country should aim at a long-term approach in which collective bargaining is based each year on a broad agreement between Government, unions and employers about the maximum level of earnings which is compatible with keeping inflation under control in the following twelve months. The policy for next year has been shaped so as to permit a transition to such longer term arrangements.[60]

Ministers persisted in their defence of 5 per cent through the autumn. James Callaghan argued for it to the TUC in September, and to the Labour Party conference a month later; and both in the debate on the

Queen's Speech and at the EEC summit in Bonn, he made public the Government's determination to hold the norm, no matter what degree of industrial militancy resulted. Secret directives to the local authorities insisted that any settlement in excess of 10 per cent in Stage 3 should be compensated by a lower than 5 per cent settlement in Stage 4, and sanctions were prepared for use against private sector firms exceeding the new limit. According to a confidential guidance document issued by the Department of Employment in September 1978, only British Leyland was to be allowed to waive the twelve-month rule, and employers and government departments were to discourage the notion of 'special cases' which had so eroded the tightness of the Stage 3 norm.

Yet all this was to no avail. The Callaghan Government, like the Heath Government before it, was forced to retreat as industrial militancy grew. Within the official institutions of the labour movement, the Government's 5 per cent was repeatedly rejected. The TUC explicitly turned down 'arbitrary pay limits', and called for a return to free collective bargaining. Union bloc votes brought the same result at the Labour Party conference in October. In each case, the rejection of wages policy was linked to a demand for economic expansion, greater state investment in industry, a shorter working week, tight price controls and the redistribution of wealth; and the size of the defeats prompted the Labour Cabinet to offer renewed talks to the TUC on pay policy and economic strategy. Yet the Government was unable to bring even these discussions with the TUC to a successful conclusion, as the General Council of the TUC narrowly refused to support its negotiators' willingness to publish jointly with the Government a vacuous document calling for 'responsible' collective bargaining aimed at keeping inflation in single figures.[61] This third failure, following as it did the defeat for Government policy at the autumn conferences, showed just how widespread was the sense of frustration within the labour movement. Here was a Labour Government, with a much-vaunted 'special relationship' with the trade unions that no other political party possessed, still unable to win union support for an empty show of words that would not have affected the level of wage settlements to any significant degree, but which might have improved Labour's election chances.

However it should not be thought that Stage 4 of the Labour Government's incomes policy was destroyed by the activities of union leaders or by the non-signing of bits of paper. The immobility of union leaders reflected grass roots industrial pressure that they could no longer restrain. Early in the pay round, there had been evidence that some groups of workers were settling around 5 per cent, but this did not survive the successful strike by workers at Ford's. This strike was a prolonged one, partly because the threat of sanctions against the multinational by the Government helped initially to toughen managerial resolve in the face of a £20 a week pay claim and a demand for a thirty-five-hour working week. But after nine weeks of total shut down by militant Ford workers, Ford's management settled for 17 per cent, and in so doing successfully called the Government's bluff on sanctions. The Ford settlement provided a target and an inspiration for a whole set of subsequent pay negotiations, and as a result the early months of 1979 were dominated by a series of prolonged strikes against the Government's incomes policy that were particularly concentrated among the Government's own employees. The distribution of food, fuel and raw materials to industry was disrupted by strikes, first by tanker drivers, then by lorry drivers (with their secondary picketing) and finally by a series of one-day strikes by ASLEF, the train drivers' union. The work of government agencies was disrupted by a series of strikes by strategically placed groups acting for 700,000 civil servants, and by a one-day token stoppage by civil servants in the run up to the general election; and public utilities were seriously affected by a prolonged campaign by 1,500,000 low-paid workers in the public sector that added strikes and work-to-rules by water and sewage workers, local government manual workers, school caretakers, ambulancemen and health service ancillary staff to difficulties of work and travel already created by the severest winter weather since 1963. So if the backcloth to the Labour Government's arrival in office in 1974 had been the successful miners' strike against the incomes policies of Edward Heath, the backcloth to the Government's departure in 1979 was a pay revolt of even greater scale. The number of workers involved in strikes in January 1979 was the largest for any month since May 1968, and the number of working days lost the greatest since February 1974, at the height of the three-day week.

The result was a level of wage settlements that was significantly in excess of the Government's 5 per cent target. The lorry drivers' 22 per cent proved to be the exception rather than the rule, but even so public sector settlements probably averaged over 10 per cent and contained the promise of comparability increases later that made them more valuable still. The Government's policy was not entirely without its successes. The Cabinet won from the TUC the 'concordat' that had escaped it so narrowly in November, as it traded tougher price controls, machinery through which to allow comparability studies of private and public sector pay, and a slight reduction in the restrictions on increases for the low paid, in return for a TUC agreement to bring pay rises down to 5 per cent by 1982, to participate in an annual national assessment before Easter each year, and to issue tighter guidelines to encourage strike ballots, more flexibility in the closed shop, and more controlled picketing. Moreover, Ministers were reportedly satisfied with a miners' settlement that turned a 20–40 per cent claim into an agreement worth 9–11 per cent on paper, and perhaps 16 per cent in practice; and many private sector settlements even after the Ford strike averaged nearer to 10 per cent than to 17 per cent, held down by the fear of redundancy and the intensification of international competition. Indeed overall the rate of increase of earnings under Stage 4 did not exceed significantly that under Stage 3 in spite of the industrial unrest that accompanied it. But nonetheless the cost of Stage 4 to the Labour Government was enormous, turning as it did the possibility of a closely run election in the autumn of 1978 into the near certainty of a Conservative victory in the spring of 1979. Four years of wage restraint may have given British capitalism a breathing space on industrial costs, but they gave the Labour Government in the end industrial unrest and electoral defeat.

Indeed the events of 1978–79 threw a number of features of this Labour Government into sharper relief. They certainly revealed how limited was the commitment of many right and centre Labour Cabinet Ministers to greater trade union political power, and showed with what ease such men could drop back into the kind of anti-trade union strictures last heard from Labour Ministers like Ray Gunter and Harold Wilson in the 1960s. With opinion polls showing that support in the country was moving away from the Government as the strikes intensified (the Conservative Party had a 19 per cent lead in the opinion polls early in 1979) some Labour Ministers began to show that other face of Labour Government – union relations. This can be seen not only in William Rodgers's call for a wages freeze (which was perhaps to be expected from a man openly on the right of the Party) but also in Lord Peart's decision to suspend civil servants whose only 'crime' was their refusal to do the work of colleagues on strike, and in David Ennals's reluctantly taken decision to allow hospital authorities to enlist volunteers to do the work of striking ancillary staff. Even the Prime Minister, who had resisted the worst anti-trade union excesses of *In Place of Strife* in 1969, joined in this time, urging trade unionists to cross picket lines during the lorry drivers' dispute, and speaking of the 'limit to the nation's patience' in the face of the industrial unrest that his own Government's policies had provoked. The Chancellor joined him in repeatedly lecturing the unions on the evils of secondary picketing, and on the dangers which high wage settlements would bring for price stability, for employment, for public sector spending and for the survival of the Labour Government. The feature of secondary picketing which seemed to anger the Government was that it succeeded – it actually shifted power away from managements and governments towards striking workers; and this was incompatible with a Labour Government's firm intention to hold wages down for a fourth year in the name of a wider national interest that seemed, year by year, to require unemployment, cuts in public spending, persistent income inequality and restrictions on the real purchasing power of the employed, even including the low paid. When the electoral chips were down, Labour Ministers were quite prepared to add their pressures to those of employers and Conservative politicians and to encourage the TUC to curb those manifestations of working–class power that eroded the State's capacity to control its labour force; and this contrasted sharply with the Party's promise in 1974 to do just the reverse, and to achieve a fundamental and irreversible shift in the balance of power and wealth in favour of working people and their families as a first step towards the creation of a democratic and socialist Britain.

Yet the industrial disputes of early 1979 did more than show Labour Ministers in their true colours. They also eroded the capacity of Labour politicans to claim with any conviction that their special relationship with the trade union movement would bring a degree of industrial peace and national unity that was beyond the capacity of any Conservative Government. The scale of industrial dislocation in the winter of 1978–79 was simply too reminiscent of the last months of the Heath Government to permit that claim any credibility that it might have enjoyed prior to the Ford workers' strike. Nor, as a result, and this was yet more vital for the electoral fortunes of this and future Labour Governments, could the parliamentarians properly claim that Labour's new policies in the 1970s were capable of avoiding the alienation of significant sections of the Party's electoral base that some commentators had seen as a feature of earlier Labour Governments. On the contrary, the industrial and electoral fortunes of the Labour Government in 1979 demonstrated all too clearly the very tension between government policy and working-class interests that had brought the Labour Government of 1964–70 to electoral defeat, and which had helped to demoralise the Attlee Government twenty years earlier. Though the fear of the Conservative alternative kept most trade union leaders loyal and active in the build up to the 1979 general election – the signing of the 'concordat' is proof enough of that – the reality of the Labour Government's incomes policies and economic retrenchment over five years proved to be an electoral liability which even the Party's industrial and political élites acting together could not overcome. The first and most immediate cause of the Labour Government's electoral defeat in 1979 lies quite distinctly here: in the widespread disillusionment caused among traditional Labour voters by four years of pay restraint, and in the revival of Conservative electoral support amongst the floating and undecided voters to which the resulting industrial unrest gave rise.

## V

The single most striking feature of the relationship between the Labour Party and the trade unions in this period is the gap between the public *image* of trade union power and the private *reality* of waning trade union influence over public policy. Rank-and-file militancy could act to veto policy in the specific area of pay, but union leadership could find no way of turning that class power into a general control of economic policy in total. Many of the indicators of government performance stand as evidence of this. The unemployment figures, the limited nature of the recent reflation, the persistence of poverty, the threatened living standards of those union members avoiding unemployment – all these can and must be taken as signs of the failure of the trade union movement to dictate the general shape of government strategy or to control the market forces to which both government and unions were subject. This is nowhere clearer than in the changing status of the 'social contract' itself. Wage restraint, a hidden and undiscussed element in the documents establishing the contract in the years of opposition, became its centrepiece from July 1975. The first set of documents contained a specific series of policy proposals for the next Labour Government: industrial relations reform, price controls, food subsidies, and State control of industry. Later versions of the contract measured the demise of certain of these (particularly subsidies on food and housing, planning agreements and effective price controls) whilst replacing specific policy proposals with vague commitments to future social reform. As the NUPE report on the original nineteen commitments contained in the first social contract concluded:

It is true that there has been some progress in some areas, but in others the promised advances made in the early months of the Government have been reversed and in yet other areas there has been no progress. The Government's policies have been at variance with the letter and spirit of the original Social contract. . . . the Social Contract has been transformed, in the eyes of trade unionists, from an agreement about economic and social priorities into a vehicle for implementing a policy of wage restraint – and nothing more.[62]

So *The Next Three Years and the Problem of Priorities*, adopted in July 1976, concentrated on job creation in the immediate period, reasserted the need for price controls, and then returned to the vaguer areas of possible wealth taxes, urban renewal and integrated transport services. It still talked of a target for full employment. It still called for the use of planning agreements with the top 100 companies to achieve this, and it still proposed that an investment reserve fund be created to stimulate investment and smooth out cyclical fluctuations: but the gap between the assertion of policy and its actual implementation remained. As Eric Varley conceded when the unions and the Government met to revise the contract later, 'voluntary planning agreements with individual firms had so far been unsuccessful and . . . more should be done to encourage their implementation. But it appears that he stopped short of suggesting legislative action to bring about statutory enforcement.'[63] Little wonder then that the third version of the social contract, *The Next Three Years and into the Eighties*, agreed in July 1977, was even more vacuous. The wealth tax was again promised, but postponed until after the general election. The same calls for investment, greater output, selected import controls and full employment were repeated, and the failure of the earlier versions of the social contract was underlined by the document's repetition of the call for a stronger National Enterprise Board and for planning agreements, as yet unsigned.

The fourth version of the social contract followed in July 1978, and with a general election looming which the Labour Government seemed likely to lose, there was renewed publicity for a 'radical economic contract' between unions and Government. Promises toughened slightly. In *Into the Eighties: an Agreement* the Liaison Committee promised the return of free collective bargaining (in the very week in which the Labour Cabinet's Stage 4 White Paper had proposed annual pay consultations), the strengthening of the economy's manufacturing base, the use of 'pressure' to spread planning agreements, a wealth tax, and speedy reductions in unemployment. It also committed a re-elected Labour Government to give 'high priority to a real expansion of house building and improvement, the health service, education, and other social services'.[64] But by then few people were listening, for the substantive impact of the social contract on immediate Government policy had long gone. By 1977 and 1978 the specification of targets had replaced the adoption of policy.

So, under this Labour Government, in spite of the 'special relationship' with the trade union movement, poverty persisted and intensified, and major plans for the redistribution of wealth were systematically postponed, diluted or abandoned. In part this reflected the Government's failure to introduce any significant measure of industrial democracy, as we shall see in the next chapter. It was also a result of the persistent postponement of the wealth tax. But it was mainly a consequence of the Government's failure to consolidate its own initial moves. It did tie pensions and other long-term benefits to the rise in earnings or prices, whichever was the higher, and short-term benefits to the rate of inflation; and accompanied this with a speedy increase in pensions and other benefits in its very first budget. Even its first pay norm was a flat-rate one, which served the low paid better than any percentage settlement was to do later. But the Labour Government then retreated from any further progressive taxation. Its pension reform was income-related, which only served to perpetuate the inequalities of the labour market into old age. It presided over a generalised fall in living standards between 1975 and 1977 which hit the poor particularly hard. It allowed the numbers of those in full time employment who earned less than the supplementary benefit poverty line to grow by 123 per cent.[65] It cut levels of planned social expenditure in spite of the growing need for spending on the poor, the old, the sick and the unemployed, and in 1977 it angered its supporters in the trade union movement by a particularly mean estimate of how great an increase in pensions was necessary under the 1975 Social Security Act. Most important of all, the Labour Government allowed, or failed to stop, unemployment rising at a dramatic rate, particularly amongst the young, the over fifty-fives, and women workers. The result was to leave over 6 million people in households with incomes at or below the official poverty line, and the inequalities of class as manifest as ever.[66]

In spite of this, the majority of trade union leaders were still prepared to act for very long periods as 'policemen' to the Labour Government's incomes policy, and as loyal allies of the Labour Government in its electoral struggle with the Conservatives. It is true that the degree of official trade union opposition to incomes control grew over time, as we have seen, and that the strikes against the Government's incomes policy in the winter of 1978–79 were official strikes, supported by the official trade union leadership. Yet that leadership always contained elements of ambiguity that reflected the leaders' identification with the Government, and their refusal to embarrass it by any policy of generalised confrontation. So in 1974 Len Murray repeatedly urged TUC guidelines (and especially the twelve-month rule) on individual unions, and at the 1976 Trades Union Congress, major trade union leaders bullied the National Union of Seamen into a settlement within Stage 2. As inflation touched 22 per cent the Leyland toolroom workers on strike in 1977 were urged back to work as fiercely by Hugh Scanlon as they were by Leyland management, the NEB and the relevant Government Ministers. Hugh Scanlon was even prepared, as were other AUEW officials later, to see the toolroom men sacked to 'save British Leyland', and it must have been hard for those toolroom men to see what distinguished their union leader from the management and Government with whom they were in dispute. Even in 1977 the TUC persistently forbade unions to defer settlements in order to escape the pay limits, or to bring more than one demand for wage increases in any twelve-month period. As rank-and-file opposition was blocking any official trade union support for the negotiation of a third round of pay restraint, the TUC still insisted that Stage 2 run without challenge to its very end: 'not merely in the national interest', Len Murray told the Health Service Employee's conference, 'but in terms of the self-respect of the union movement'.[67] Even a year later, when union opposition to wages control was less ambiguous, the TUC president could still call on trade unionists to 'work and vote for Labour',[68] and the unions in total could still aim at raising a million pounds to support the Labour Party's election campaign. It is this subordination of the bulk of the trade union leadership to a Labour Government that was less and less responsive to their general policy demands, and their loyalty to a Labour Government which was *not* the creature of excessive trade union power, which is the overriding feature of the unions' relationship with the Labour Government of 1974–79; and it is this which, in a later chapter, will have to be explained and assessed if the lessons of this Labour Government are to be drawn accurately and in full.

# CHAPTER THREE

# The industrial strategy of the Labour Government

## I

The Labour Party in opposition in 1972 let it be known that a future Labour Government would 'adopt a fresh approach to the relationship between government and industry'. The aims of that fresh approach were ambitious: to 'mould industry into a more humane and democratic form', to 'redress the balance of power between giant corporations and the community', to 'move forward the frontiers of public ownership' and 'to attack economic inequality in all its manifestations'. In declaring these to be their intentions, Labour leaders promised that they would achieve economic growth in a manner that was, in the words of the NEC document, compatible with the maintenance of 'full employment, a rising real level of public expenditure, a healthy balance of payments, decisive progress in eliminating regional disparities, stable prices and . . . rising personal incomes, particularly for those on average or below average earnings'.[1] Of course, such aspirations are the common stock-in-trade of manifestoes from any radical political party out of power, and can be found in a long line of Labour Party policy documents down the years. But the renaissance of the left wing of the Party within Labour's policy making process in the years after 1970 gave those aspirations a new significance. For by 1972 and 1973 it was clear that at least some sections of the Labour leadership felt that they were in a position to achieve economic growth and social justice at the same time, because of the radicalism of the industrial policies then being adopted by the Party's National Executive and Conference.

Not for the first time in the Party's history, its leaders in opposition reasserted their determination to gear industrial expansion 'to the real needs and priorities of the community as a whole, rather than to the short-term dictates of the market', and to do this by making 'a clear political commitment to industrial intervention and to economic planning, which must include an expansion of the public sector'.[2] In 1972 the Party's detailed proposals were still being formed, but even in that year the NEC document submitted to conference proposed the introduction of comprehensive price controls, extensive public ownership, the formation of a State holding company, greater public spending, tighter controls on multinational corporations, and the encouragement of industrial democracy. These policy initiatives were put forward as the key mechanisms by which a future Labour Government could achieve two broad planning objectives, which the Programme specified as

first, to ensure that our policies on consumption, inflation and the balance of payments are supported and supplemented by *uninterrupted industrial expansion* [and] second to reduce sharply the cruel disparities in living standards, job opportunities, economic power and wealth between different sections of the community.[3]

The 1972 Programme underlined the Labour Party's commitment to full employment. 'Given the right economic, regional and industrial policies,' the NEC told conference, 'and the necessary development of the public services, unemployment can be drastically reduced.' The answer to unemployment, according to *Labour's Programme for Britain*, was to 'increase the strength of public policy over private power'.[4]

Central to thinking on the left of the Party in this period was the recognition that industrial production was now dominated by a few large (and increasingly multinational) private companies, whose investment programmes, pricing policies and industrial relations practices must remain outside effective government control so long as public ownership did not penetrate into the manufacturing sector. This recognition inspired the proposal for a state holding company, or National Enterprise Board (NEB), which the 1972 Programme had mentioned, and which a Labour Party study group laid out in detail in a report published in April 1973. That group argued that previous Labour Governments had failed to achieve any fundamental change in the distribution of economic power, and had never effectively directed and planned economic activity in total, because they had left intact the private determination of investment policy in the productive and manufacturing sectors of the economy. The next Labour Government, the group argued, should go further than its predecessors, and should 'transfer economic wealth and power from a small economic oligarchy to the people' by extending public ownership into the centre of British manufacturing capital. The NEB was proposed as the main mechanism by which a future Labour Government should introduce public ownership 'into the strongholds of private industry' both by holding and overseeing existing government interests in joint public–private corporations and by rapidly increasing the number and importance of these joint public–private concerns. With ownership should go control, and the group looked to the NEB to use its dominant position to shape industrial activity in line with general Labour Government policy. In particular, the Board was to use its position in the 'commanding heights of the modern capitalist economy' to implement government policy on job creation, new investment, technological innovation, price restraint, export promotion, import substitution, and industrial democracy. At the same time, by creating publicly owned firms in the manufacturing sector, the NEB was to enable a future Labour Government to compete effectively against (and hence, it was claimed, to curb the power of) the big multinational concerns. The NEB, the group recommended, should aim to acquire (by compulsory purchase if necessary) a substantial base amongst the largest firms in the manufacturing sector, from which to exert a 'controlling interest over a large slice of the economy'. Indeed the study group went so far as to make known their opinion that, if it was to be effective, the NEB would have to take twenty to twenty-five of the largest hundred private manufacturing firms into public ownership[5].

This thinking found its way into the 1973 Labour Party Programme, which urged the next Labour Government to act 'directly at the level of the giant firm itself'[6], and to pursue there an industrial strategy with three main features. First, *public ownership* was to be extended, both through nationalisation of entire industries (the Programme mentioned North Sea oil, docks, aircraft production and shipbuilding, with the possibility of some public ownership amongst the financial institutions and the pharmaceutical industry) and through the activities of the NEB. This would give the next Labour Government a major presence in the manufacturing sector. In addition, the Government was to draw up a system of *planning agreements* with the remaining large private firms, to clarify their investment intentions and to facilitate the direction of State aid. Finally, a new *Industry Act* was to be brought into being, to give the appropriate Ministers extensive powers to obtain information from private companies, to invest in them, to purchase them outright if necessary, and to issue directives to them on a wide range of industrial matters, including prices, profits, investment programmes and industrial relations practices. In addition, the 1973 Programme urged that a future Labour Government should consolidate a system of price controls, extend industrial democracy, and tighten public supervision of multinational corporations. In all these ways the Labour Party planned to make economic power more accountable to the people, and to achieve a degree of economic growth which it felt a less interventionist set of policies could not guarantee. The 'regeneration of British industry' required nothing less, the Party claimed, than what it took to be a 'socialist industrial strategy'.

## II

It should not be forgotten that there were serious divisions within the Labour Party leadership on all this even before the Party returned to power. In opposition, these divisions were at their most visible over the proposal to specify the number of firms that a future Labour Government might take into public hands. At the 1973 Party Conference Harold Wilson managed to extricate the leadership from the commitment to nationalise the twenty-five largest private firms, as Party figures on the right and centre of Labour's ideological spectrum attempted to tone down the ambitious interventionism being advocated by men like Tony Benn and Eric Heffer. Roy Jenkins was not alone among former senior Cabinet Ministers in believing that the public takeover of 'a vast number of industries would not of itself remove the country's economic difficulties'.[7] Tony Crosland too was later reported as calling such proposals 'idiotic' and 'half-baked'.[8] But the strength of left-wing feeling within the Party was still sufficiently strong to ensure that the bulk of these proposals found their way into the manifesto on which the Party fought the February 1974 election, and to place Tony Benn (with Eric Heffer as his deputy) at the head of the Industry Department in the wake of Labour's election victory.

As a result the early public image that the Labour Government projected was that of a radical, interventionist administration. This was sustained in part by its price controls and pension increases. But throughout 1974 its radical centre seemed to lie in the Industry Department itself. As the national press waited for the Department's promised policy document on industrial strategy through the spring and early summer of 1974, journalists, Ministers and critics combined to produce a sense of impending radical change. We were repeatedly 'warned' of the system of planning agreements to come, and of the impact that the planned NEB would have on the boundary between the public sector and private enterprise. Apparently the Industry Department was contemplating the wholesale withdrawal of all public subsidies to the 180 largest private concerns, in order to renegotiate their return on a firm by firm basis. It was rumoured that only those companies prepared to sign five-year planning agreements, and to meet Government requirements on such things as employment, regional location, and export policies would then receive State financial aid. Moreover it was feared in many business circles that the NEB would take an unspecified (and large) number of private firms into public control, from which to dictate industrial strategy to those private firms that remained. This was certainly the role for the NEB that Eric Heffer publicly anticipated in June 1974. His future NEB would

influence major companies in every manufacturing sector through competitive stimuli by giving a lead on investment, would reorganise the industrial structure in each major sector in line with longer term public need rather than short term market considerations, reduce private monopoly power by inserting public enterprise competition, and create a more evenly balanced regional location of industry.[9]

This was in line with Tony Benn's claim in the Commons that the extension of public ownership from his Ministry would bring a fundamental and irreversible shift in the distribution of power and wealth in favour of working people and their families. In fact the new Secretary of State for Industry spoke less often than the volume of public denigration he attracted might lead one to suppose; but when he did, he too fuelled public expectations, and provoked public dissent from leading business figures, by talking in general and unspecific terms of the need for 'reform of a major kind',[10] and by publicly criticising the investment record of the major industrial companies to support his advocacy of the extension of public ownership. His speeches were full of the promise of the reallocation of economic power, and of the building of an industrial consensus through extensive consultation and open government, and his Department as a result consulted widely, with industrialists and unionists alike, as it tried to put together a strategy that would regenerate British industry and extend industrial democracy.

The Cabinet was visibly divided on the precise role of the public sector in this industrial regeneration, and these divisions were reflected in the moderate nature of the White Paper on *The Regeneration of British Industry* that eventually emerged from long Cabinet wrangling in July 1974. The White Paper contained *no* list of large firms earmarked for public ownership and avoided any commitment to such a pattern of nationalisation in the future. If the 'commanding heights' of British manufacturing were to be controlled, it was not to be by systematic and extensive public ownership. Instead the National Enterprise Board was recast in the mould of the Industrial Reorganisation Corporation of the previous Labour Government, closer in design and function to Harold Wilson's preference for a State holding company than to Tony Benn's more interventionist agency of direct and detailed public control. The list of industries to be taken wholly or partially into public ownership shrank: pharmaceuticals vanished from the list, and there was no mention of banks, insurance companies and building societies. Most striking of all perhaps, the tone of the White Paper differed significantly from the anti-private sector critique of the opposition years. There was no claim in the White Paper that the Government was seeking fundamental and irreversible shifts, nor that it was attacking the arbitrary exercise of economic power frustrating the national will. Instead the stress was on partnership and collaboration between industry, Government and the unions to create, amid economic growth, a vigorous, competitive and profitable private sector.

It is worth remembering at this point that it has been a characteristic of Labour Governments over the years to retreat from their radical pretensions in a gradual way, with more conservative policies accruing as the culmination of a series of incremental shifts in policy and statement, whose longer-term results are in each case obscured by terminology whose ambiguity serves to unite the various wings of a divided party. *The Regeneration of British Industry* is a classic example of this process of gradual retreat. It was presented to a Party in which all sections were agreed on the need for economic growth, and for a new kind of government intervention in industry to get it. But it was also presented to a Party whose left wing saw this intervention as one important route to the achievement of radical changes in industrial power and social justice. The White Paper promised new interventionist agencies, while remaining absolutely silent on the degree to which they would be used for radical industrial and social ends. That silence was already a defeat for the Left, and constituted the start of that retreat from the industrial objectives of the 1972 and 1973 Programmes which would accelerate and become more obvious later. But the very creation of vast new interventionist agencies served to obscure this at the time, and while men sympathetic to the left of the Party remained in charge of the Industry Department, neither the Labour Left nor its critics could be sure how ominous the White Paper's silences would prove to be.

In retrospect it is clear that the analysis of economic problems and their policy solutions offered in the White Paper precluded the radical shift in economic and social power to working people and their families that Tony Benn sought. The problem to which the White Paper addressed itself was a 'national one', of insufficient investment in manufacturing plant and equipment, of 'skill and ability' going unharnessed, or living standards put in jeopardy by the economy's vulnerability to international competition. The White Paper's 'solution' was also seen as a national one, of greater government intervention to galvanise a united and national economic effort. The language of the White Paper was the language of cooperation between classes in a common and shared striving for economic competitiveness. There was no sense in this White Paper of any incompatibility of interests between labour and capital, no sense of tension between Labour Party radicalism (or even the call for full employment) and the search for industrial regeneration, and no explanation of the pressures which capitalism must impose on its weaker competitive units, no matter how radical the pretensions of their politicians. Instead the Government committed itself to the creation of 'both efficient publicly owned industries and a vigorous, alert, responsible and profitable private sector working with the Government in a framework which brings together the interests of all concerned'. Further public ownership, planning agreements and the National Enterprise Board were to be the new mechanisms by which this was to be achieved, and the claims for the new strategy were still considerable. To quote the White Paper, the Government believed that its new initiatives would

contribute to the achievement of greater industrial efficiency, more and better investment, and a higher return on that investment. By thus entering into explicit partnership with industry the Government expect to raise the quality of management, develop industrial democracy, and to improve both the quantity and quality of manufacturing industry's contribution to the development and growth of the economy.[11]

The White Paper repeated the Government's intention to nationalise development land, the shipbuilding and aircraft industries, and the docks, to set up the British National Oil Corporation, and to extend public ownership into road haulage and construction. It also renewed its promise to create the National Enterprise Board, which (like the old Industrial Reorganisation Corporation) was to be given funds through which to provide investment for industry, in order to encourage efficient restructuring there. But (unlike the IRC) the NEB was in addition to take the proportion of shares, and therefore ownership, commensurate with the degree of investment funds provided, and in that way to carry public ownership into the profitable sections of British manufacturing industry. The Board was to be the channel through which the Labour Government would assist 'sound companies which are in short term financial or managerial difficulties', and by which future governments would 'operate directly to create employment in areas of high unemployment'. It was to be more than an ordinary merchant bank. True, it was to take over existing government funds in a number of private firms (notably Rolls Royce 1971 Ltd) and it was given the responsibility of 'securing the efficient management of the companies and assets vested in it'. Indeed its 'guiding financial objective' was explicitly stated to be 'to secure an adequate return on that part of the nation's capital for which it is responsible'. But the NEB's activities were to be hemmed about by tight criteria, some conventionally commercial, others less so. It was to give priority to projects creating jobs in assisted areas, to reducing monopolies, to strengthening the balance of payments by import substitution and export creation, and to extending industrial democracy. ('The NEB will play its part in ensuring that enterprises under its control provide for the full involvement of employees in decision-making at all levels.') It might also be called upon to depart from its guiding financial objective at the specific request of the Government, where Ministers believed that wider social criteria had to be given precedence; in particular (and ominously in the light of subsequent events) it might, according to the White Paper, 'on occasion be called upon to take over an ailing company which is in danger of collapse but needs to be maintained and restored to a sound economic basis'. The NEB was to be kept under tight government control, free to exercise its commercial judgement in carrying out its functions only within detailed financial guidelines laid down by the Government, and subject to written government approval before it could take a controlling interest in any company (or indeed take any minority interest involving more than £5 million of public money).

The White Paper was also full of details of the planning agreements to come. These three-year agreements were envisaged as a means of ensuring that the commercial intentions of the larger companies left in private hands were 'in harmony with national needs and objectives', and of guaranteeing that government aid was effectively deployed, by the systematic sharing of information. Half the White Paper was given over to this theme, although already the more radical elements of the opposition years had been shed. The Government did not intend, as had been suggested in 1973, to take statutory powers to compel a company to sign an agreement with it. Nor did the White Paper propose to deny public funds to companies refusing to enter the planning agreement system. Gone too was any intention to create a super planning Ministry, or to involve trade unionists as formal parties in the creation of planning agreements. Instead the Government hoped that the attraction of possible additional public aid would be enough to pull large companies into a voluntary discussion with Government (and separately with their own employees) on investment and pricing policy, productivity, employment, export creation and import substitution, product development and industrial relations. The length of the list of items was important, for the regular updating of these planning agreements (in a consultative process which would include trade unionists) was presented in the White Paper as an important part of the policy to extend industrial democracy; and to this end it was intended that the agenda of consultation within the planning agreement system would extend to all aspects of company policy other than those whose publication would seriously jeopardise either the company's commercial viability or the nation's military security.

## III

The Left of the Party saw in these proposals a way in which economic growth, social reform and a shift in class power could be achieved simultaneously. The Right and Centre expected less, but looked to State intervention to assist economic growth and employment by strengthening the economy's international competitive position. Time and events, however, were to make a mockery even of these more moderate aspirations. The severity and character of the economic crisis faced by the Labour Government as it entered office precluded any easy 'regeneration' of industrial performance, let alone any significant social reform. Indeed the very social and economic conditions which were necessary to re-establish the economy's competitive position involved the redistribution of power and wealth *away* from the very 'working people and their families' to which the Labour Party was supposedly committed. The Labour Government was to find that unemployment, cuts in public spending on social services, and a systematic reduction in working-class living standards were absolute prerequisites of renewed capital accumulation. Labour Ministers were to find too that the degree of social and economic retrenchment required to resuscitate British economic growth from so weak a base in 1974 was greater than even a Labour Government (with all its working-class political support) could deliver without bringing Ministers into growing conflict with sections at least of the organised working class on whom the Party's electoral success ultimately depended.

The character of the economic crisis faced by the Labour Government in 1974 is discussed in detail in the next chapter. What should be noted now is that the political agenda of the Labour Government was dominated by the most obvious manifestations of that crisis: by balance of payments deficits and a depreciating currency, by low rates of manufacturing investment, greater penetration of home and export markets by foreign competitors and an internationally low level of labour productivity, and by industrial stagnation, rising unemployment, high levels of government spending, a strong labour movement and a disproportionately high rate of price inflation. These 'surface' features of the 'British problem' preoccupied the Labour Government. They were the visible parameters within which policy was shaped, to which Ministers reacted, and against which success or failure was conventionally judged. But their intractability as problems reflected the extent to which they were actually manifestations of deeper processes at work in the world economy – processes to which the Labour Government had no real answer. These deeper processes, rooted in the laws of development of world capitalism, were less visible and less controllable than the surface phenomena to which they gave rise. But they were no less potent for that. On the contrary, the deepening crisis of world capitalism, with its particular impact on its British component, blocked the Labour Government at every turn. The necessarily combined but uneven development of world capitalism, the centralisation and concentration of capital on an international scale to which it gave rise, and the generalised tendency for the rate of profit to fall to which its productive units were inexorably subject, proved too powerful a set of processes for one tiny Labour Government to reverse.

So it was no accident that the Labour Government faced a massive balance of payments crisis and a depreciating currency in 1974. That growing balance of payments deficit was almost entirely the result of price movements, not of changes in the volume of trade. In 1973 imports rose 4 per cent by volume and exports 3 per cent. But the terms of trade fell 16.1 per cent, brought down by a depreciation in the pound and by a sharp rise in the cost of raw materials (especially oil). The movement of raw material prices reflected changes in world capitalism as a whole, and as such affected all the Western economies in some measure. But the diminution in the exchange rate of the pound was a particularly British problem, the consequence of the dwindling competitiveness of British capitalism alone. It was this competitive weakness in the nation's economic base that generated the harsh realities to which policy had to succumb. No matter how fine the rhetoric of Labour politicians, there was no way in which the economy's competitive position could be restored without a significant increase in the rate of exploitation of labour. Nor could the resulting balance of payments deficit be removed without a reduction in the level of domestic consumption, either public or private. Labour Ministers were to find that the industrial regeneration they sought required so great an increase in the productivity of labour that it could be achieved only by a large-scale restructuring of capital in which jobs would be lost and the labour process intensified. The balance of payments deficit (and later the fear of its return, via an excessive consumption of imports) precluded any rapid expansion of home demand that might soften the adverse effects of that restructuring on employment levels and living standards; and yet in a depressed world economy the alternative route to domestic economic growth (via an export led boom) was so difficult to achieve that it required a still greater increase in the productivity of labour. Even then, no industrial strategy could bring export strength while inflation rates in Britain were higher than in the economy's major competitors, and so in addition industrial regeneration required reductions in government social spending and hence in employment. In total, then, the pursuit of industrial regeneration in so difficult a context did not require a growth in living standards, job security and industrial power, as the Labour Left implied. It required just the reverse, and its pursuit led the Labour Government away from the rhetoric of left-wing radicalism towards state-initiated restructuring of British capitalism on a large scale. Public ownership, the National Enterprise Board and planning agreements did not bring a socialist New Jerusalem; but were used (or, in the case of planning agreements, abandoned) in the pursuit of a reorganisation of British capital, and a shedding of labour, that might leave what remained of the economy's manufacturing base better able to withstand strong foreign competition.

The process of retreat from the radical pretensions of the Labour Party in opposition was incremental rather than sudden and traumatic. This was partly because working-class militancy had itself to be dissipated and destroyed in a process of incorporation which was vital for British capitalism, and which the Labour Government achieved, as we have seen, only after July 1975. It was incremental too because it was in no sense planned. Labour politicians did not consciously decide to abandon their ambitions. Rather, in the normal way of Labour Governments, they tacked after events, responded to problems thrown up at them, and slid towards that role of servicing British capital at the expense of the working class which the ambiguities of their rhetoric had always foreshadowed, but which had never been their conscious intent. It is only in retrospect that the logic of the policy that they adopted is clear. But it is now clear, and it can be laid out as follows.


## IV

The opening stages in this retreat from radical purpose were marked by debates around the Industry Bill introduced in February 1975 to implement the proposals of *The Regeneration of British Industry*. In one crucial area the Bill proposed powers for the Government which even the July 1974 White Paper had not foreshadowed, in that it gave to the Secretary of State for Industry powers to compel companies to disclose information to trade union negotiators, powers presented by Tony Benn as a significant increase in industrial democracy. It also allocated £1000 million direct to the Industry Department, to provide financial assistance to particular firms and industries. In this it built on, and indeed retained the bulk of, the provisions of the Conservative Government's 1972 Industry Act which it was to replace. The Act also set up a legislative framework within which a voluntary system of planning agreements could be established; and it created the National Enterprise Board. The NEB was to have £700 million of public money in its initial budget, with an extra £300 million available upon parliamentary approval, with which to extend public ownership into the profitable sectors of manufacturing industry, and to reorganise production there as it accrued a profit on its investments. The Board was not given the power to purchase a company compulsorily (except where the Government wished to stop an undesirable foreign takeover), though it could buy shares on the open market, presumably even against the wishes of the existing directors. But there was no longer to be a limit of 50 per cent on the proportion of voting shares that could be taken by the State in return for public funds. Rather the NEB was given the power to invest up to £10 million in any one firm, or to take up to 30 per cent of its voting shares, without even seeking the specific approval of the Secretary of State. Thus the NEB was to function independently of the Department of Industry, subject only to the need for the approvals already mentioned and to the obligation of an annual report to Parliament. Where it acted as the channel for the Department in the provision of selective financial assistance (to 'lame duck' industries for example) it was to be given extra government funds.

The claims and counterclaims surrounding the Bill were enormous and predictable. On the one side, the Confederation of British Industry

(CBI) saw it as a major threat to the private sector of industry. On the other, Tony Benn declared its reforms 'the most fundamental since the war . . . designed to check and then to reverse the decline of our manufacturing industry'.[12] In fact, enormous as the powers of Government intervention were by previous standards, they were still modest, and so could hardly transform the whole investment record of British industry overnight.[13] Clearly the Government's hope was that the NEB would be a catalyst to generalised investment and effective management in the private sector, rather than the source of the bulk of that investment itself. The choice of the Board's first chairman, Sir Don (later Lord) Ryder was evidence enough of this. Ryder was a successful businessman of no known radical views, who shared Tony Benn's propensity for State intervention and industrial planning while lacking (publicly at least) his parallel concerns with industrial democracy and shifts in class power. Ryder made known very early on that his staff would be selected for their commercial and industrial skills, and would pursue conventional commercial criteria, and that the NEB's main function under his chairmanship would be 'the provision of equity funds for private companies which could not obtain enough funds from private sources'.[14] This was light years away from the Left's vision of the NEB's role when the institution was first proposed, and was not dissimilar in orientation to the old IRC which the Left had no wish to resurrect. So with Ryder's appointment, the NEB was placed firmly in moderate hands, and the worst fears of Tony Benn's critics were somewhat allayed. In any case, Benn was not at the Industry Department by the time the Bill became law. By then he had been moved to the Department of Energy, and his entire ministerial team had broken up, to leave industrial policy in quieter and less controversial hands.

From 1975 the Government settled into a straightforward tripartite industrial strategy of the kind governments have pursued in Britain ever since the war. True, this Government used greater amounts of public money, and the NEB remained an important interventionist agency, as we shall see. But the criteria by which it acted did not differ significantly from those dominant in private financial agencies. The scale and manner of its operation were insufficient to put the Government visibly 'in charge' of private investment, as the Labour Left appear to have hoped. And in any case the Government's own emphasis shifted under Eric Varley towards a cooperative planning exercise focused around the National Economic Development Council. The Labour Government continued to expand public ownership and to vaunt its 'industrial strategy', but that strategy came to amount to little more than an attempt at tripartite indicative planning and the creation of conditions for successful private capital accumulation – an attempt no different in purpose (or indeed in effectiveness) from that which had inspired its Conservative predecessor.

Such a development in industrial policy was not entirely unexpected. It had been clear to many in the right and centre of the Labour Cabinet from the very beginning that such an industrial strategy was unavoidable, that for all its rhetoric of reform a Labour Government would have to run a mixed capitalist economy in which a healthy (that is, competitive and profitable) private sector would be a vital part; and that if the Government were ever to achieve a sustained rate of economic growth, they would have to allay the fears of private capital and create the conditions for successful private profit-making. The radical rhetoric of Labour documents was recognised as a barrier to this; and many major Government figures found it necessary to reassure private capital regularly of Labour's moderate intentions. As early as May 1974 Denis Healey let it be known that 'the Government has no intention of destroying the private sector or encouraging its decay'. He told the CBI that, on the contrary, the Government wanted 'a private sector which is vigorous, alert, imaginative and profitable'.[15] That the private sector's own industrial leadership were less certain can be gauged from the number of occasions on which that reassurance had to be repeated. In July 1974 Harold Wilson promised that 'a clear frontier' would be defined between what is public and what is private industry so that private industry could have 'the necessary confidence to maintain and increase investment'.[16] James Callaghan repeatedly stressed, in his public speeches, that 'a company, whether publicly or privately owned, must be able to make an adequate return on the capital employed if workers in that industry were to get a decent wage and if the investment was to be replaced'. Indeed, as the falling value of the pound made the economy's export prices more competitive, he went so far as to argue that industrial needs should come *before* social policy, if we were to 'take advantage of an almost unprecedented position of competitiveness in the markets of the world'.[17]

Many aspects of Labour radicalism eventually proved to be casualties of that subordination of policy to industrial needs, and those casualties were not restricted to the social field. Policy on price controls, company taxation, public ownership and industrial democracy were all amended down the years to produce a less directive, more accommodating relationship between Government and private business than the Labour Party documents of the opposition years had implied. In its search for a cooperative relationship with private manufacturing capital, out of which economic growth and international competitiveness was to come, the Government retreated from its early intention to control and plan industry directly at the level of the large company. That is, it abandoned its intention to build a system of tight planning agreements with those sections of British industry that it chose to leave in private hands. The contrast between the aspirations of opposition and the actual development of policy could hardly have been starker. The original intention of the planning agreement system had been to give a future Labour Government control over the hundred large companies that dominate the manufacturing sector of the economy, and to give Labour Ministers a new means of achieving, not detailed day to day control over industrial tactics, but rather, as the 1973 Programme had it, of determining such companies' 'medium and longer term strategies . . . to achieve certain very broad objectives in terms of jobs, in certain regions for example, in investment or in exports'. A planning agreement would do this by providing the Government with up-to-date information on such matters as 'investment, prices, product development, marketing, exports and import requirements', with the company agreeing to assist the Government in achieving certain clearly defined objectives (on such things as employment in Development Areas) in return for the channelling of selective aid in its direction. The result, according to the 1973 Programme, would be that with publicity and the sharing of information would come greater government influence over industrial policy and greater accountability in this vital field.

This set of proposals for a planning agreement system reportedly originated from a paper submitted by Stuart Holland to a subcommittee of the Labour Party's NEC in 1972, in which the clear intention was to use planning agreements to control private industry *directly* at the highest level. It is worth noting that in the 1972 paper Stuart Holland apparently spoke of 'a strong case for making programme contracts [as planning agreements were initially known] compulsory, rather than voluntary [by] requiring leading firms by law to submit a true report of their medium term profits, prices, imports and exports'. He also proposed that government aid to industry should be used selectively, to enforce participation by large companies in the planning agreement system 'with the back up sanction of public ownership for notorious miscreants'.[18]

Measured against these initial intentions and aspirations, even the lengthy proposals for a planning agreement system outlined in Tony Benn's 1974 White Paper already represented a retreat in the face of opposition from private capital and within the Labour Party leadership. The White Paper, as we have seen, explicitly rejected any notion of compulsion, or the withholding of public funds from companies declining to participate in the planning agreement scheme. Yet in 1974 the Industry Department did intend to make such agreements the centrepiece of the Labour Government's relationship with private manufacturing capital. By 1975 that intention had largely gone, and Stuart Holland's proposals had not been amended so much as abandoned. Under Eric Varley the Industry Department prepared for planning agreements at an extremely leisurely pace in the face of industrial opposition and indifference.

The discussion document on planning agreements which eventually emerged in August 1975 marked the next stage in this retreat from the Party's initial intentions. It stressed that the relationship between the Government and a company should be 'wholly voluntary, based on consent', and should *not* involve direct trade union participation. Instead the Labour Government proposed that 'discussion leading up to a planning agreement [should] take the form of two dialogues – between company and trade unions, and between company and government . . . in parallel, or more probably in series'.[19] Yet in spite of this, the TUC remained a major advocate of the planning agreement system. In its *Economic Reviews*, and in its renegotiations of the social contract, the TUC urged the establishment of planning agreements at a company level, to supplement the planning at industry level to which the Government increasingly turned. While the TUC remained critical of the failure of companies to give adequate information to their trade unionists on strategic matters, such as investment plans and manpower intentions, it was even more critical of industry's refusal to sign planning agreements with the Labour Government, and by October 1977 union leaders were urging the Government to consider the use of sanctions.[20] For by then only seven companies had apparently even begun to negotiate planning agreements with the Labour Government, and only one, the Chrysler UK motor company, had actually completed and signed. (The Government also later (July 1978) signed a planning agreement with the National Coal Board, though it is not clear that this did more than formalise normal relationships between a sponsoring Department and a nationalised industry.) All seven of these private companies were heavily dependent on State orders and in Chrysler's case the planning agreement was a precondition for a massive government loan. Even with Chrysler, as we shall see, the planning agreement did little more than give government support to existing managerial policy before public money vanished into the hidden depths of the multinational company's internal costing system. Here, as elsewhere, the Labour Government by 1978 was as far from 'intervening directly at the level of the large firm' as it had ever been, and what industrial strategy it still possessed had left the Benn–Holland planning agreements far behind.

It is worth pausing for a moment to examine the creation of the planning agreement with the Chrysler motor company in greater detail, for there are important lessons to be drawn from it concerning both the radical potential of planning agreements in general and the innate conservatism of this Labour Government in particular. The 1973 Labour Party Programme had singled out multinational car companies for special mention, referring explicitly to Henry Ford's threat during a major strike to use United Kingdom profits to facilitate the transfer of production to Spain. The Programme argued that the power of such companies should be 'made more accountable within this country'[21] possibly through state-appointed directors, through NEB activity, through the extensive disclosure of information and through the application of anti-monopoly policies. Chrysler presented the Labour Government with a perfect test case for such controls. By 1976 it was no longer a strong and self-confident multinational. On the contrary, its car plants were in serious market difficulties (the UK company's share of the home market had fallen from 12 per cent in 1972 to only 5 per cent by October 1975) with losses in the multinational as a whole reaching $232 million in the first nine months of 1975 alone. The response of senior American management to the market difficulties of their United Kingdom subsidiary was fully in line with their multinational preoccupations: quite simply to remove a loss-making part of the company by closing entirely their UK operations from January 1976, so making 25,000 employees redundant and jeopardising as many as 70,000 other jobs in the related component industries.

In the face of this drastic suggestion the Labour Government was uncertain how to act. Ministers clearly disliked the social and electoral consequences of such large-scale redundancies, particularly since major Chrysler plants (as at Linwood in Scotland) were in areas of already high unemployment. But they were also aware that their new industrial strategy (discussed in a later section of this chapter) was opposed to funding weak industrial concerns, and that a revitalised Chrysler company could only intensify competitive pressures on the already nationalised and beleaguered British Leyland. In negotiations with senior Chrysler management, Ministers were free to choose from a wide range of policy options: from the total shut-down of Chrysler UK to the 'public ownership without compensation' that was in effect offered by the Chrysler management in their first talks with Labour Ministers in December 1975,* The Government's own 'think tank' report urged that Chrysler be closed completely, to ease competitive pressures on a British car industry that was, in their view, already 25 per cent too large, and a majority of the Cabinet opposed public ownership (in spite of their supposed generalised support of nationalisation) out of a recognition that a small national car company could not survive in the fierce competitive world of large multinational companies. Chrysler's complete closure was opposed by trade union leaders because of its effect on employment; and also, ironically, by the Iranian Government, who applied heavy diplomatic pressure to maintain Chrysler UK (and with it, the supply of kits to be assembled in Iran). This last pressure appears to have been decisive in persuading a deeply divided Cabinet to put together a £162 million rescue deal, within which the Government itself underwrote £72.5 million of Chrysler losses over a four-year period in return for a company undertaking (a public declaration of intent) to maintain its UK operations and to sign a planning agreement with the Labour Government. Ministers also backed management plans to sack 8000 men, and forced this on a reluctant work force by threatening to retract its financial guarantees unless the company was given full labour cooperation. A planning agreement followed in March 1977 in which Ministers gave public support to company plans to expand production and increase productivity.

Yet here, as elsewhere in the private sector, State involvement did not qualitatively alter the criteria governing investment decisions, nor did it significantly shift control of production away from management to either government or unions. The casualties of the Chrysler affair remain both the 8000 men who lost their jobs, and the 17,000 employees who, though 'saved' by Labour Government intervention, were subsequently subject to sustained pressure to increase productivity from Labour Ministers no less than from Chrysler management. Indeed the whole sorry story stands as a clear example of the problems endemic to the planning agreement strategy. The Government negotiated the planning agreement it required, and could claim (as it did) to have prevented large-scale immediate unemployment and the redirection of investment. But the *sharing* of information in the planning agreement made no difference to this outcome. As we have seen, Chrysler management were initially keen to give the Labour Government *complete control* over Chrysler UK, through public ownership, and had

* This was also proposed by Chrysler shop stewards in their submission to the Government in January 1976. The Chrysler management offered to *give* the Government its United Kingdom company, and to *add* £30 million towards the cost of redundancy payments!

to be persuaded by the Labour Government not to surrender their managerial responsibilities here in their entirety. Yet the Labour Cabinet did not decline public ownership because of political spinelessness alone. Ministers were also aware of the difficulties that would necessarily accrue to a small national car company obliged to compete with big multinational concerns; and they wanted no part of that. In that sense, their ultimate sanction over the multinational (a seizure of its national assets) was wholly without value. Moreover the position of Ministers was weakened still further by their dependence on Chrysler's own facts and figures in the negotiation of terms, and by their inability to control the costing processes *within* the multinational on which the subsequent supervision of public money depended. Chrysler's management simply milked the Labour Government, and used the promise of a planning agreement to do so, and they were able to succeed in this precisely because they were willing (indeed keen, as later events showed only too well) to withdraw their resources totally. This made perfect commercial sense from the multinational's point of view but it also meant, as Harold Wilson said, 'that the Labour Government [had] been presented with a pistol at its head',[22] and was thus less able to negotiate effectively with Chrysler's senior management because there was more at stake for the Labour Government than there was for the multinational itself.

In this case, the total vacuity of the Chrysler planning agreement was brutally demonstrated over the next two years, by the continuing weakness of the company's market position and by the events of July 1978, when the American management simply *sold* Chrysler UK to the Peuguot–Citroën motor company, without even telling the Government, let alone the unions, until the agreement was signed. Some planning agreement, this: the Labour Government did not even have advance notice of the sale, and had only just announced in the Commons the results of recent negotiations on Chrysler's future that it had completed with senior American management. The original planning agreement gave the Government a veto over such a sale, and this the Labour Government was technically free to exercise in 1978. But in reality it had little choice. It could go along with the sale, and hope that British jobs would be safe, or veto it and see Chrysler UK close completely. Its much-vaunted planning agreement, and its desire to share information between itself, management and employees, could not prevent this; and instead the Cabinet found itself obliged to start all over again seeking 'guarantees' from a new French management, only two years after 'saving' Chrysler from the abyss in return for American 'guarantees' that July 1978 proved to have been worthless.

All these defects seem endemic to planning agreements negotiated with international companies, whatever the degree of goodwill and cooperation involved, and must stand as serious problems for any future Labour Government that is tempted to resurrect such a strategy of 'industrial control'. In fact the defects of the planning agreement system run deeper still, as the Chrysler example again shows. For even the most perfect planning agreement conceivable could not give a Labour Government control over a company such as Chrysler, precisely because in public or private hands it is forced to compete with other multinationals and cannot shake itself free of the industrial policies which that competition necessitates. It is the existence of world competition, not of private ownership (of capital*ism*, not of capital*ists*, as I argue in the next chapter) which necessitates unemployment, an intensification of the work process, and a replacement of men by machines if costs are to be kept down and output potentials realised. It was Chrysler's size, not its American ownership, that left it vulnerable to competition as profits fell in the 1970s. As a result the planning agreement could not differ significantly from the kind of corporate plan that Chrysler management alone might have devised. The only major difference that State funding brought was to encourage Chrysler temporarily to keep production in the United Kingdom, rather than, say, concentrate it in France, and to that degree the planning agreement strategy helped to maintain employment among British workers, at least for a time, at the expense of other national working classes. But beyond that, the fact that company goals (and investment funds) were now underwritten by the Government in no way altered what those goals had to be. As it happened, in Chrysler's case there was no direct trade union involvement in the negotiation of the planning agreement, and this will probably provide more grist for those who would argue that a trade union presence would have altered the situation dramatically. But I doubt it. It would have been just as likely (as I will argue in Chapter 5) to have weakened working-class solidarity and undermined the unions' defensive strength by adding trade union voices to those of management and politicians who were already calling for greater productivity at the expense of Chrysler workers. If this is correct, the claims made for planning agreements by the left wing of the Labour Party must be countered by the recognition that the involvement of a Labour Government (or union officials) in a close planning relationship with senior management cannot qualitatively alter the industrial experience of the workers in private industry, nor affect significantly the criteria which govern policy on investment and labour relations in the private sector.

The failure of the Labour Government's planning agreements system reflected the degree to which senior management were prepared to resist policy initiatives which involved a full disclosure of information even to governments, let alone to the trade union movement; and indicated that the Labour Government was either unable or unwilling to force private companies to comply, for fear of alienating foreign investors, or of depressing profit margins still further by adding the costs of social responsibility to industries already under severe international competition. This degree of opposition, and of Labour Government retreat from initial intentions, will doubtless be enough to persuade the left wing of the Labour Party that planning agreements are a radical device, and that they do have something to do with socialism.* But the experience of Chrysler after 1975 would suggest that the Left is wrong, and that planning agreements are inherently flawed as a policy tool for democratic socialists. What Chrysler suggests is that a full planning agreement system would unite the State and private management in a common assault on working-class industrial power; and that as a result the close involvement of a Labour Government in the control of private industry through planning agreements cannot carry with it any easing of the burdens that fall on working people and their families in an internationally competitive world economy.

## V

If we are to understand the full complexity of the distribution of power between this Labour Government and the private sector, we must examine in addition two features of policy that indicate both the limits *and* the autonomy of the State in its orchestration of economic activity under capitalism: the blacklisting of firms and the retention of price controls. To take the blacklisting of companies briefly first, we find here a clear case of the limits which governments face when dealing with strong multinational companies, even when the government is pursuing policies which it believes to be in the interests of capital as a whole. The blacklist was a mechanism devised for Stage 3 of the Labour Government's incomes policy (when voluntary trade union 'policing' of the policy was no longer available to Ministers), as a way of ensuring

* It is significant that a major concession won by the Labour Left in the 1979 Labour Party election manifesto was a promise that a future Labour Government would 'conclude planning agreements with the major industrial companies, with the necessary back-up statutory powers to do so' (Election Manifesto, 1979, p. 10).

that employers in the private sector observed the stated pay norms. Employers signing collective agreements in breach of the pay norm were to find themselves blacklisted by public authorities, and as a result denied contracts with, and sales to, public bodies. This sanction was clearly a very real one, given the size of public sector purchasing of private sector commodities (both goods and services). We should note in passing that there was a heavy irony in the Labour Government's refusal to use sanctions against private employers who reduced employment or under-invested, when Ministers were willing to use sanctions against employers whose only 'crime' was that of being 'too generous', under union pressure, to their own workers. Yet we should also note that even when using sanctions in this limited way, the Labour Government could not in the end sustain its policy. For though it could (and did) discipline small nationally based firms for breaches of its pay code (by August 1978 seventy-four firms had been blacklisted, and fifty-five were still on the blacklist by October) the Government could not enforce a full set of sanctions against a big multinational without jeopardising future employment and investment by that company in the United Kingdom. In particular, when the Ford Motor Company signed a 17 per cent agreement with its militant work force in November 1978, the Government did not withdraw its financial support from the company, as the sanctions documents had implied that it would. It restricted its reaction to one of blocking public sector purchasing of Ford motor cars, while quietly confirming its £150 million loan to the Ford company to develop a new car plant in South Wales. In this case the risks to the company of defying the Government were less than those to the Government of a major row with the company, and in this way the impotence of the Government before the Ford Company matched that before Chrysler. Whether sanctions could have continued, and in what form, after November 1978 we cannot know, for the Government's parliamentary weakness led to the policy being defeated a month later, and this parliamentary defeat gave the Government a way of claiming that it was the Opposition parties who were responsible for its subsequent inability to maintain tight control over private sector pay. But the claim was disingenuous. The Government's parliamentary weakness only compounded dilemmas in its relationship with multinational capital that had become obvious as the Ford dispute progressed, and the blacklist must join planning agreements as an example of Labour Government policy blocked by the strength of international market forces and their institutional expression – the multinational corporation.

Price controls reveal different, and rather more subtle, things about the relationship between the Government and the private sector in the 1970s, and about the role of the State in advanced capitalism. They remind us that the Labour Government was subject to *contradictory* pressures in its dealings with private industry, and that this was often enough to create serious tensions between Ministers and the representatives of private capital even when the long-term interest of the two parties was actually in close accord. Price controls had to serve many audiences. They were foreshadowed in the Labour Party's 1973 documents as a mechanism for ending inflation (by controlling the retail prices of a number of key items in the average family budget) and as a barrier to excessive profits. The NEC anticipated that price rises might have to be sanctioned to provide a surplus for investment, but proposed in 1973 that where such a price rise loomed large in family budgets, the increase might still be blocked and any necessary investment provided from public funds with public control.[23] As a result price controls were presented in 1974 as part of the social contract, as a way of keeping inflation down and of creating the climate for voluntary wage restraint. But though the control of inflation and wage costs was vital to the long-run competitive position of British manufacturing capital in general, price controls ate away at short-term levels of profits and so undercut the accumulation of capital on which future economic growth depended.

The Labour Government found it politically impossible to abandon price controls in total, but had to amend them to ease their adverse impact on profits, investment levels and employment. Accordingly Labour Ministers altered them in stages, not consciously to subvert their initial purpose but rather more to move their emphasis away from social justice to the straightforward encouragement of investment. The trajectory of that change, as I argue in the next chapter, was established by the logic of capitalist market forces operating on a world scale; but the speed was fixed by the relative strength and militancy of the contending classes surrounding the British State. When working-class militancy was high, price controls were tight and subsidies on food were extensive. As militancy waned, subsidies were removed, tax loads on business were reduced, and the price code was systematically eased to facilitate, and indeed to encourage, private capital accumulation. As working-class militancy revived in 1979, the price code was tightened again, to remove the automatic profits safeguards it had hitherto contained, as a trade-off with the TUC which the Government was obliged to give in a vain search for voluntary wage restraint.

As we have seen the Labour Government initially focused its attention on retail prices, and Shirley Williams (the Prices Secretary) won a voluntary agreement from the retail consortium to hold down the prices of essential foods until the spring of 1975. At the same time she continued the price code inherited from the Conservatives, which restricted companies to profit levels typical of the period prior to control, obliged the larger among them to notify the Government of any proposed price rises, and allowed these only if the company had incurred certain unavoidable increases in industrial costs. These restrictions were eased in the November 1974 budget, to allow firms to pass on a greater percentage of their extra labour costs, to safeguard profits that had fallen below April 1973 levels, and to facilitate extra spending on plant and machinery; but these changes were insufficient to prevent a long CBI campaign against the Price Code as a barrier to investment and as a disincentive to industrial efficiency. Ministers were never willing to shed these controls in total. The political requirements of repeated incomes policy negotiations were enough to guarantee that. But they did regularly increase the reliefs within the Code which accrued to firms investing in new plant and equipment, and which allowed profit margins to rise. As the Labour Government's consultative document put it in February 1977, in proposing to continue the system of controls (and indeed to add to the investigating and price-freezing powers of the Price Commission), among the criteria that the Price Commission should follow must be the 'earning of a profit which gives a real rate of return on capital employed sufficient to meet the cost of finance, including compensation for the business risk, and to sustain investment in expansion, innovation and technical improvement'.[24] While a tight voluntary incomes policy remained, the Labour Government used its powers under the Price Code to penalise employers who gave wage settlements above the norm; and in addition (after August 1977) Ministers used the expanded Price Commission to investigate (and block) price rises caused by industrial inefficiency, including overmanning. Neither set of powers made the Price Commission popular with the CBI, who repeatedly urged that its activities be curtailed to allow firms to fix prices and plan investment without tight government surveillance; even the TUC was aware that too restrictive a set of price controls might erode the investment levels on which, in their view, future levels of employment depended. But the Labour Government could not and would not abandon its powers here totally. They were too important a pawn in the relationship with the unions that was vital to the economy's overall competitiveness, and they strengthened the Government's ability to encourage investment by giving differential price relief to that aspect of industrial costs. Of course price controls were no panacea for economic ills. The rate of price rises was very slow to ease, as we have seen, and industrial investment did not recover significantly in the face of world recession. But the Labour Government hung on to its price controls ever more firmly as the economic recession persisted, in order to give it some vestigial direct leverage on a vital aspect of industrial policy, as it sought to create the climate for generalised capital accumulation again.

So when examining the overall relationship between the Labour Government and private industrial companies after 1974, it must be said that Ministers inherited a set of extensive powers over firms in the private sector, which they then added to rather than abandoned. State aid was given and conditions were attached. Indeed the degree of State aid to private industry (in the form of loans and grants) reached new heights, and proved to be a vital part of investment funds for important sections of British manufacturing industry. Moreover price controls were retained, as we have seen, in spite of repeated business pressure to remove them. But it is significant that the degree of control that the Labour Government did exercise over the business élite did not bring with it the new (and more 'socialist') criteria of economic activity which the documents of the Labour Party in opposition had implied. At best, such controls enabled Ministers to delay the immediate impact (on employment in particular) that market forces imposed on private managements. But more normally the control or influence which Labour Ministers exercised over individual managements in private manufacturing industry was not used so much to delay as to *reinforce* imperatives established by the market forces of world capitalism: to increase productivity, reorganise production methods, intensify work routines, shed labour, sell frenetically and innovate perpetually. In other words, far from the Labour Government's entry into private industry altering the criteria that shaped the managerial function, as the documents of the years of opposition had implied, Labour Ministers were just as likely to tighten and to underline them.

# VI

In place of a direct planning arrangement with large private capital, the Labour Government turned in 1975 to the NEDC, as the vehicle through which to build a cooperative industrial strategy. Even with Tony Benn at the Industry Department the NEDC had been used for conventional tripartite discussions, with the main issue in 1974 being the search for agreement on a national strategy to boost investment and productivity. Apparently the NEDC had begun in 1974 to concentrate its discussions on in depth analyses of the problems of a particular industry or group of industries rather than restricting itself (as in the past) mainly to a discussion of economic targets at the level of the economy as a whole. It was this theme of industry by industry planning which was given major prominence by the Government when its revamped 'industrial strategy' was eventually announced in November 1975. The overall aim remained the strengthening of the competitive position of the British manufacturing sector, and in that strengthening State funds and extended public ownership remained important elements. But in addition the Government returned the emphasis of public debate to a preoccupation long associated with the NEDC, and with government indicative planning – namely the pursuit of increases in productivity across British industry as a whole, to be achieved on this occasion by tripartite cooperation on an industry by industry basis. As Denis Healey said in November 1975, the low productivity of British industry was so entrenched that it applied even within multinational companies, who were incapable of getting a yield per unit of capital in Britain that they could achieve elsewhere in Western Europe and Japan. 'If both sides of industry could combine at plant level to solve this problem,' he said, 'the effect would be dramatic not only on our output and our balance of payments, but on inflation too.'[25] If they could not, then by implication home markets would continue to be penetrated by foreign competitors, export markets would continue to shrink, the full advantages of each economic upturn would be dissipated by 'structural rigidities' in manpower and equipment, and 'all that socialism stands for in terms of social services and so on would be at risk because national performance in terms of industry has been poor'.[26]

So by November 1975 the keynote of the Government's economic policy was the search for greater industrial competitiveness through increased productivity and higher investment in a profitable private sector. Any alternative strategy of extensive public ownership, planning agreements and import protection had been rejected, and any search for enhanced productivity through industrial democracy had been postponed in the face of fierce CBI opposition. The preoccupations of Labour Governments in the 1960s had resurfaced: export competitiveness, cost effectiveness, high investment and an adequate return on industrial capital from whatever source. Indeed these problems had a new urgency now, as inflationary pressures eroded jobs and weakened the balance of payments – an inflationary process which only a significant rise in industrial productivity could bring down, if government spending was not itself to be drastically cut.

So the NEDC became the focus for much publicised tripartite examinations of economic problems, industrial sector by industrial sector, in order to locate those sectors which were most vital economically, those that were the strongest competitively, and those which were in need of assistance to protect output and jobs. The stress in all the early announcements on the new strategy from the Government side was that such an exercise was vital if public assistance was to be flexibly and effectively deployed, and if investment was to be planned and coordinated across industry as a whole.

Harold Wilson presented the new industrial strategy in terms reminiscent of the launching of *The National Plan* a decade previously: that national industrial performance could be improved by tripartite discussion, the agreeing of medium term economic targets, and the coordination of government assistance to industry on the basis of much fuller and more detailed information. What was new to the presentation of the industrial strategy was the Government's apparent intention of concentrating its aid on the sectors that were industrially strong and vital to the export drive, with the clear implication that less strong industrial sectors would be run down and their jobs lost. Although political pressure from the Liberals forced the Government in its April 1978 budget to add to their list of industrial priorities a new concern with the revival of small businesses, the main novelties of the industrial strategy after November 1975 remained this preoccupation with analysis and action on an industry by industry basis, and the Government's explicit concentration of extra resources on the industrially strong. To this degree at least, the Labour Government's industrial strategy differed from *The National Plan* of the 1960s. But the differences in presentation should not obscure the extent to which by 1975 policy had dropped back into a well-established pattern, one whose lack of success in the 1960s was to be repeated yet again.

Seen in this light, the new industrial strategy should be understood as an attempt to achieve the results of the planning agreement system by more conventional tripartite negotiations. The NEDC summits produced working papers, economic targets and specifications of sectoral needs, but they did not produce economic growth. Thirty-nine individual working parties reported in July 1976, recording for each industry in turn a familiar pattern of short-term bottlenecks, inadequate investment, insufficient penetration of export markets and deficiencies in manpower skills and training. They also listed the numerous ways in which the Government could help: both in its general economic and taxation policy, and through specific initiatives on export assistance, investment incentives and the provision of new working capital. The

Government responded in February 1977 with offers of assistance in export servicing, in industrial restructuring and in help for new product development, and to this degree the sector working parties did act as a new channel through which government policy to industry could be more effectively coordinated. As a result, by the end of 1977 a number of industries were receiving financial assistance under the Industry Act to help in restructuring (and these included textile machinery, printing machinery, machine tools and ferrous foundries); and five successful industries had been selected as a result of the working party reports to be recipients of detailed government assistance to increase their already strong world market position, through discussion on a company by company basis: industrial engines, construction equipment, office machinery, electronic components and domestic electrical appliance industries.

So after two years of the industrial strategy the Labour Government found itself with a new mechanism of communication with the private industrial sector, from which economic targets on an industry by industry basis were coming, and by which it could direct its own financial assistance. But what it did not find was either a marked improvement in industrial efficiency or sustained economic growth in the private sector. As late as February 1978 Denis Healey was stressing that 'the onus of the next stage of the strategy will be on industry and unions which must try to translate the analysis of the last two years into action'. In fact, February 1978 was, according to the Chancellor, 'blast off time for the industrial strategy' when its imperatives had to be communicated 'to the shop floor'.[27] The Government apparently apportioned an extra £250,000 to bring this about; and by then labour productivity had in any case begun to rise in twenty-one of the thirty-one industrial sectors for which detailed information was then available. In nineteen output was up. But so, in twenty-four of them, was the degree of penetration of the domestic market by foreign competitors.[28] Overall the picture was bleak. The index of industrial production did not rise significantly until well into 1978. As the Labour Government entered office in March 1974 it stood at 104.4 (January 1970 production levels equalling 100). By September 1975 it had *fallen* to 100; and by February 1978 it was still only 103.5. The economy did grow by 3 per cent in 1978, and private manufacturing investment returned to almost 1970 levels. But the signs were that even this modest rate of growth would slow in 1980, if not in 1979, and the Labour Government went to the country still waiting the 'industrial regeneration' that the Tony Benn White Paper had promised five years before.

## VII

The gap between promise and performance in the industrial strategy of this Labour Government was not restricted merely to its relationship with private capital. It was equally true of the new agencies and examples of public ownership whose creation constituted the other 'leg' of the Government's attempt to 'regenerate' British industry. As we have seen, the initial hopes for the NEB were very considerable, at least within the left wing of the Labour Party. In opposition, the Board had been seen as a mechanism by which a number of related aims could be achieved: the rapid increase of investment levels in manufacturing plant and equipment, the influencing by Government of the activities of the large manufacturing concerns through competitive nationalisation, the pursuit of criteria of economic activity other than those dictated by conventional market and commercial forces, and the redistribution of power *within* industry in favour of working people and their representatives. Though these intentions were modified as the proposals went through their White Paper and then their legislative stages, the NEB still emerged with the wide range of functions promised by the October 1974 manifesto:

> to administer publicly-owned shareholdings; to extend public ownership into profitable manufacturing industry by acquisitions, partly or wholly, of individual firms; to stimulate investment; to create employment in areas of high unemployment; to encourage industrial democracy; to promote industrial efficiency; to increase exports and reduce our dependence on imports; to combat private monopoly; and to prevent British industries from passing into unacceptable foreign control.[29]

When the powers of the NEB were initially proposed, the CBI organised a major campaign against them. The spokesmen of private capital were particularly concerned at the lack of parliamentary control over the NEB, with its apparent ability to acquire firms in the face of opposition from the boards of those firms, and by the possibility that NEB firms would enjoy an 'unfair' competitive advantage because of the Board's ability to cross-subsidise units within its portfolio. The Government, for its part, went to every length short of closing the NEB down, in an attempt to put these fears to rest. Both in terms of its personnel and its policies, the NEB was designed from the beginning to operate fully within the conventional managerial practices of a competitive capitalist economy. Senior NEB officials came from the right and centre of the trade union movement and from impeccably conventional industrial and financial circles. Lord Ryder's background has already been mentioned; his deputy, and later his successor, Sir

Leslie Murphy, came to the NEB from a career as a successful merchant banker, and both men took every opportunity publicly to reassure City and industrial interests of the Board's intention to operate on conventional commercial lines and to plan its programmes in close informal consultation with senior industrial personnel.[30] The much delayed guidelines which the Government eventually issued for the NEB in March 1976, after lengthy consultations with private industry, stand as clear evidence of these intentions. CBI fears of unfair competition were allayed by a set of guidelines which obliged the NEB to act in the manner of any major private company, subject to the City Code on Mergers and Takeovers, subject to government policy on price controls and fair trading legislation, and obliged to make its loans to companies on terms that carried at least the normal commercial rate of interest.[31] In this way the aspirations of the Labour Left that the NEB could be a vehicle for shifting class power, and a means of subordinating economic decisions to qualitatively new (and more socially responsible, even 'socialist') criteria that transcended market forces, simply did not materialise.

The obligation of the NEB to encourage industrial democracy was quietly dropped, in place of a vaguer obligation on the Board to make 'appropriate arrangements' with their subsidiaries to ensure that 'management is playing its part in furthering government policy in this field'. In addition the Board was under a clear obligation to obtain an adequate return on its capital, and this rate of return was set by the Government at a target of 15–20 per cent by 1981. This, plus the overriding preoccupation of the NEB with the strengthening of export competitiveness, forced the Board to be the advocate *par excellence* of conventional commercial criteria, and to insist that its newly acquired holdings must increase their industrial efficiency and reduce their costs. For workers in the firms that the NEB acquired, the arrival of the Government's new agency might avoid immediate redundancies, but it did not alter the long-term managerial pressure on them to restrict wage increases, intensify their work routines and tolerate redundancies. On the contrary, it was just as likely to add to these pressures. So the much publicised opposition by sections of senior management to the NEB's arrival (most notably the Rolls-Royce board's attempt to keep the NEB at bay, and the resistance to NEB moves in the tanning industry) should not be taken as evidence of the NEB's willingness to impose non-commercial criteria on private industry. When the NEB met resistance from the representatives of private capital, and it is significant that this opposition was rare, the resistance was motivated more by the desire of one group of senior managers to retain their

autonomy to pursue commercial criteria without NEB encouragement. The settlement between Rolls-Royce and the NEB in 1975
underlined the Board's determination to run the firm on conventional
lines,* even if that meant a diminution of industrial democracy and job
security for the workers involved. As the Board put it in its first annual
report to Parliament, it believed it to be 'no part of its job to prop up
non-profitable companies simply to maintain jobs. The only lasting
cure for the evils of unemployment,' Lord Ryder was reported as
saying, 'lay in helping industry to restructure, rebuild and redeploy
rather than spending scarce resources in supporting projects with no
future.'[32] It is not surprising then that by the end of its first thirteen
months, the NEB was able to report a profit of £51.3 million before tax,
as a result of investments of just under £500 million in thirteen
companies with assets of over £959 million, in a period in which
unemployment rose from 1,087,000 to 1,273,000.

Nor did the Board establish a significant public presence at the level
of the major hundred companies, as had originally been envisaged. It
was not provided with enough capital to enable it 'to control a
successful leading company operating in each of the key sectors in
industry and commerce', as the 1976 Labour Party Programme wished
it to do. Rather it was given just £1000 million to spend in its first four
years, and as a result concentrated its efforts on small and medium-size
businesses – on the very sector indeed which the Labour Party in
opposition had planned to leave alone in favour of planning agreements
and competitive public ownership at the level of the larger concerns.
What big firms the NEB ran it inherited from the Labour Government
as 'lame ducks', large employers of labour who had to be sustained and
restructured over a number of years under NEB supervision. British
Leyland is the most striking case of this; but Rolls-Royce 1971, Alfred
Herbert and Ferranti were others. At the very least, these large and
competitively vulnerable concerns absorbed a significant percentage of
NEB time and money. Rolls-Royce 1971 and British Leyland alone
reportedly took £450 million of the NEB's first £1000 million budget.

---

* The text of that settlement included the following: 'except as provided in this
memorandum, Rolls-Royce 1971 is expected to continue to operate on a normal
commercial basis like a company in the private sector' and 'the NEB's prime concern will
be to see that the Board of Rolls-Royce 1971 run the company efficiently and
successfully'. The exceptions mentioned committed the Rolls-Royce board, in preparing
its long term plans, to 'examine the case for locating any expansion or new undertakings
in an area of high unemployment' and 'take adequate steps to provide for the full
involvement of employees in decision making at all levels' (*The Times* 27 Feb. 1976,
p. 20). However, subsequent Rolls-Royce policy shows no sign of these exceptions
having affected policy to any significant degree.

At worst, their presence in the NEB portfolio involved the Board in the overseeing of long-term redundancy programmes in direct contrast to its official aims. The cumulative effect of their presence was to prevent the NEB from being the catalyst and controlling interest in a growing manufacturing sector, as had been intended. Instead the NEB simply reproduced at the level of the large firm that association between public ownership and industrial rundown and decline which the 1945–51 Labour Government had established at the level of industries as a whole.

The failure of the NEB to act as a successful catalyst of private investment and growth, and its subordination to normal commercial criteria and associated industrial practices (of labour intensification and forced redundancies) is clearest in its handling of British Leyland. When the Labour Government came to office in 1974 the car industries of all the industrial powers were already experiencing a sharp drop in demand for their products. This contrasted sharply with the expansion of car sales and production on a world scale in the 1960s, when each national car industry had invested heavily to exploit the growing demand. The European car industry was producing 15 per cent more cars in 1971 than it had a decade earlier, but by the early 1970s the rate of growth of demand was already beginning to falter. The sudden increase in oil prices in December 1973 accentuated that trend dramatically, and left the car industry over-capitalised (by as much as 25 per cent) on a world scale. The resulting increase in competition between car producers, and the generalised pressure on the industry's profits throughout the world, prompted car manufacturers everywhere to intensify the work pressure on an already alienated labour force and to reorganise production processes and employment totals in the pursuit of greater productivity. As a result 'mass redundancies, the reorganisation of jobs both within and between plants, reduced manning levels, faster track speeds, harsher discipline and tighter supervision'[33] began to affect General Motors, Chrysler and Ford in the United States, Fiat in Italy, Volkswagen, Ford and Opel in Germany, and Renault and Citroën in France. The British car industry in general, and the British Leyland Motor Company (BLMC) in particular, could not escape the imperatives set in motion by worldwide depression. Indeed the fall in world demand added to Leyland's already considerable problems, as each major car producer attempted to hold the level of its own output by penetrating further and further into the home market of its competitors. As the Labour Government began its relationship with British Leyland, that process was well under way, and British Leyland came to the Government for assistance precisely because it was too weak to withstand such growing competition unaided.

The causes of British Leyland's competitive weakness were not difficult to find. The company's levels of productivity in 1974 were low, and costs correspondingly high, by international standards. On one estimate, every man employed by British Leyland represented six cars a year to the company, compared to twelve in Europe generally and a staggering twenty-seven in Datsun plants in Japan.[34] This low productivity was in part a consequence of British Leyland's creation, 'the result of a series of defensive mergers and acquisitions under the pressure of market forces'[35] that an earlier Labour Government encouraged in 1968, which left the new company producing an overlapping and uncoordinated range of cars and parts in over sixty geographically scattered plants, with a labour force that was as high as 200,000 in 1972–73. Parts of the new combine were profitable and enjoyed strong market positions, particularly in commercial vehicles and specialist cars. But at the heart of the new combine was its 'volume' car producing component, the old Austin–Morris group of companies, who were already undercapitalised by international standards, with an outmoded product range and a chaotic marketing network. If that was not enough, the new management in 1968 inherited a complex network of different pay systems and work practices which had slowly evolved in British Leyland's component companies in the easier market conditions of the 1950s and 1960s, and which had come to embody considerable working–class strength. The 'rationalisation' of industrial relations thus became a vital part of the overall managerial attempt to cut production costs and raise productivity, and represented a serious challenge to the industrial power, job security and living standards of the work groups employed by British Leyland. Not surprisingly, that 'rationalisation' was achieved (to the degree that it has been) only at the price of considerable industrial unrest. British Leyland's strike record, by international standards, remained high through the 1970s. BLMC lost 11.5 million man hours in disputes in 1973 and 23.9 million in 1974. As Harrison and Sutcliffe remarked, these figures 'are much higher than the figures for other motor companies, though some of the losses in 1974 were probably provided by the management as an alternative to redundancies in the face of falling demand. Even so the losses must have significantly raised costs per unit of output.'[36] So too must the company's poor investment record. The combine in 1968 had less than half the capital per man employed of its major British rival (Ford), and was never able in the next ten years to generate the internal surpluses on which to make good that deficiency. The £400 million five-year investment plan adopted by British Leyland prior to nationalisation is a case in point. Large though the sums involved were, they compare unfavourably with the £1300 million that Volkswagen could be expected to invest in the same period, or with Fiat's £750 million, and were insignificant when set alongside the investment programmes of the major American concerns. Ford reportedly spent £580 million on research and development on the 'Fiesta' alone[37], and would invest (as would General Motors) 'as much in a year as BLMC [would] do over the next five'.[38]

It is not surprising then that, as international competition intensified, British Leyland should have begun to lose its share of the domestic car market at an alarming rate, and should have been driven to seek government assistance in the face of the banking sector's growing reluctance to provide from private sources the funds necessary for BLMC's new investment programme. The company had to invest on a large scale if its competitive weakness was ever to be alleviated. Yet its very weakness denied it the internal sources of investment funds that it required, and this combined with the general recession in world car demand to make private finance capital reluctant to intervene on an adequate scale, or at least reluctant to do so until British Leyland had first obtained government guarantees to protect its loan capital. By 1974 BLMC was close to a choice between government aid or voluntary liquidation, and as a result the prosperous Midlands were on the edge of an economic and social calamity of interwar proportions. For it should be remembered that, in turning to the Government for assistance, this was not just any old private company in competitive difficulties: in 1973 British Leyland was the seventh largest British company by turnover, and the largest by employment. It was the economy's largest single earner of foreign currency, contributing 40 per cent of British car exports and 4 per cent of total manufacturing exports. The company was simply too large and too vital a part of the export sector for the Labour Government to ignore. Indeed, as the only British owned car producer in the country's Big 4 (the other three were all American subsidiaries) BLMC was the only major car producer that a Labour Government could rely on to pursue its export strategy with singleminded determination; and the company's dwindling ability to do this effectively underlined the very weakness of British manufacturing capital which the Labour Government was committed to rectify.

As Labour took office it was presumably clear both to politicians and to senior management in the afflicted company that if Labour leadership was to achieve 'the regeneration of British industry', British

119

Leyland would have to be part of that regeneration. Yet the state of the world car market, and British Leyland's weak position within it, left the Labour Government with very few options. For all the fine rhetoric about industrial regeneration, and about the creation of a socially just society in which job security and a fundamental shift in class power would guarantee economic growth, Labour politicians quickly found that neither the most detailed planning agreement that they could design, nor the presence of the NEB, could alter the imperatives imposed on British Leyland management by the company's weak market position. The Government found, no less than BLMC before it, that the anarchic logic of a capitalist world economy imposed on its constituent units in an already overcapitalised industry the iron necessity, if those units were to survive at all, of yet greater investment programmes, further large-scale redundancies and tighter managerial control over the work practices of the labour force that remained. Every major car manufacturer experienced these necessities in the 1970s, but only the weaker ones were driven by them to seek State aid. Chrysler came and went, as we have seen, with its private autonomy intact. British Leyland did not follow Chrysler, precisely because its competitive position was weaker still, and because the degree of its integration into the structures of international capital was so much less developed. By the mid 1970s only the State was in a position to provide the scale of finance that British Leyland's revitalisation required. Accordingly the Labour Government found itself called upon to orchestrate the restructuring of this vital sector of British capital, by giving both material and *ideological* aid to the Company's management. For British Leyland needed more than money: it also needed the Labour Government's help to persuade its workforce to cooperate in the reorganisation of production and employment that the restructuring involved. The State's role here was if anything even more vital than in the mere supply and guarantee of capital sums, for the cost to be borne by BLMC's already hard-pressed labour force was to be considerable. The Labour Government's regeneration of British industry had necessarily to involve for them a *degeneration* in their degree of job security and job control, and it is this contradiction, hidden in the rhetoric of Tony Benn's White Paper, that subsequent events were to underline time and time again.

British Leyland came to the Labour Government for the first time in 1974, continuing a close dialogue with the Department of Industry that the company had begun under the outgoing Conservative administration. By 1974 the company was running at a loss that was obscured only by its low level of self-financed investment. Hit by the energy crisis and the three-day week, its Board was unable to generate internally the £100 million necessary for the next stage of its modest investment programme, and unable to raise that money in the banking sector without government guarantees. In December 1974 the Labour Government agreed to give those guarantees in return for 'a measure of public ownership' and for tight government supervision of company policy prior to nationalisation. The British Leyland Board from December 1974 was apparently required to obtain government consent before embarking on any capital expenditure in excess of £1 million, before undertaking new borrowing or before selling off any section of the company; and Tony Benn was to be consulted over any major wage negotiations, dividend payments or new service contracts to directors. Full public ownership came later, after the publication of the Ryder Report on British Leyland which the Government commissioned in December 1974, but it existed in practice from the time that the loans were guaranteed.

The Ryder report was a hastily drawn up, and in restrospect over-ambitious, survey of the company's problems and prospects. Its analysis of British Leyland's problems was accurate and conventional: that the company had 'too many men making too many different kinds of cars inefficiently with ancient equipment in badly laid out plants'.[39] The solution offered, though ambitious, was equally conventional. There was to be no system of workers' control. Nor were there to be any radical experiments in industrial democracy. The report merely proposed in this area the creation of extensive systems of consultation between workers and senior management, and a tight planning agreement relationship between management and the Government, while retaining the existing structure of managerial control under external NEB supervision. Nor did the report anticipate large-scale redundancies. On the contrary, it proposed that British Leyland should avoid redundancies by setting itself (and then attaining) ambitious sales targets, to increase its output of 'volume' cars by at least 50 per cent by 1982, in a market which even Lord Ryder did not anticipate would grow by more than 13 per cent, and to do this by adopting a truly massive investment programme of £2800 million between 1975 and 1982. Lord Ryder proposed, and the Government agreed, that public funds should provide up to half of that sum, with £200 million to be made available immediately, followed by sums up to a total of £900 million in stages through to 1978, with the remainder of the Government's £1400 million to be provided in the form of either loan capital or equity capital after 1978. These enormous sums of money were to enable the British Leyland Board to reorganise its production both geographically and through the standardisation of parts, to streamline factory layouts and to concentrate production of particular models in particular plants. The report contained no proposals for plant closures (though four plants were apparently earmarked for closure in paragraphs that were not published, but these employed at most 2000 workers). But it did stress the importance of achieving 'realistic manning levels' and the 'interchangeability of labour' if the targets of the investment programme were to be realised, and looked to full cooperation from the labour force through the new system of extensive consultation.

The Government agreed to follow Lord Ryder's advice to maintain BLMC as a producer of cars and trucks in both the volume and the specialist markets. Harold Wilson made clear in the House that the alternative, of allowing the Company to go into liquidation to shed its weaker units, was too stark, too costly in lost exports, and too likely to jeopardise upwards of one million jobs across British manufacturing industry as a whole. But significantly he refused to give an unlimited commitment: further money would be forthcoming only so long as productivity in the Company grew to justify it. As he said, the release of public funds 'will be determined in the light of the contributions being made to the improvements in the performance of British Leyland by *better industrial relations and higher productivity*. This is a condition to which the Government attaches great importance.'[40] In making that condition, the Government at long last revealed its true colours. Its concerns henceforth were to be with the restructuring of British capital within the existing constraints of world capitalist competition and its concomitant structures of managerial control. With such concerns, Ministers would soon be forced to demonstrate the emptiness of so much of their talk of industrial democracy and working class power. Their preoccupations with rising productivity led them instead to support managerial attempts to curb working-class resistance to the intensification of work routines and loss of jobs that such rising productivity so manifestly entailed. Shorn of their radical pretensions by the severity of British Leyland's problems, Labour Ministers began to show clearly the managerialism that lay beneath the fine words of the opposition years, a managerialism which had prompted an earlier Labour Government to urge the formation of British Leyland a decade before.

British Leyland's competitive weakness was not removed by public ownership. The company's share of the home market continued to fall. As the Ryder Report was published, British Leyland commanded 32.9 per cent of home sales, and the average for the year 1975 was 30.9 per cent. That share fell to 27.4 per cent in 1976, to 24.3 per cent in 1977, and reached as low as 20–22 per cent as the Edwardes's plan was published to replace Lord Ryder's report in January 1978. The better industrial relations on which the Government insisted also failed to materialise. In fact the very pursuit of greater productivity by the BLMC management fuelled a new series of unofficial strikes, as Leyland workers sporadically resisted attempts to speed the work process, and to achieve greater flexibility, mobility and interchangeability of labour within and between plants. Related managerial attempts to rationalise the pay structure, and to replace payment by results schemes by measured day work, were also a cause of industrial unrest, as management attempted to re-establish control over earnings (and hence costs) which they had effectively lost in the early days of British Leyland, when they negotiated with over fifty different groups of manual workers in agreements with different settlement dates in each plant. Such a rationalisation was bound to generate industrial unrest in the most favourable of circumstances, because both sides in British Leyland realised that what was at stake in management attempts to harmonise agreement dates, to reduce the number of bargaining units and to establish common rates for common jobs throughout the company was an attack on the freedom of work groups to negotiate locally to leapfrog on existing settlements, and to buttress their differentials. But these tensions were exacerbated to breaking point by the rigidities of the Government's incomes policy, which prevented Leyland's management from 'buying' industrial peace by settlements above the norm, made harmonisation difficult because of the twelve-month rule, and further eroded differentials though its initial £6 flate rate limit.

Instead of improved industrial relations, Leyland's management found themselves beset with unofficial stoppages: five in March 1976, a further eleven in the next six months, and of course the major eight-week unofficial strike of Coventry toolroom men in February–March 1977. By then rank and file opposition to pay policy, and the desire of skilled men for separate negotiating machinery through which to protect their differentials, was sufficiently strong to dominate Eric Varley's visit to Longbridge. As *The Times* reported of the industrial disputes then plaguing the company:

Superficially much of the trouble arises from the reorganisation of manning arrangements in a number of big plants, with the transfer of men to new jobs. But there is little doubt that shop floor discontent is also geared to the mounting groundswell against any further pay restrictions, and grievances over the steady erosion of skilled differentials.

Only through a return to free collective bargaining, stewards argued to Eric Varley, could industrial relations improve, and would 'it be possible to end many anomalies in wage rates and the erosion of skilled differentials, and provide the degree of flexibility in pay bargaining necessary to the success of the job transfer scheme'[41] at the heart of the restructuring programme. The Government went some way to meeting these demands in the special terms it allowed British Leyland under Stage 4 of its incomes policy; but this concession was not enough to prevent militancy against the Company's decision to close its Speke factory in 1978, or to stop a seven-week strike at the Bathgate plant over the terms on which new computerised machine-tools were to be used. Nor could it prevent a brief re-emergence in the spring of 1979 of the clash between toolroom men and the AUEW which had stopped production for eight weeks in 1977, nor a two-week strike in November 1978 which left 28,000 Austin–Morris workers idle.

These labour troubles were given vast publicity in the years of the Labour Government, to create a general impression that they were the cause of British Leyland's competitive problems. But they were not. They should be understood as reactions by hard-pressed working men to managerial policies which sought to re-establish BLMC's competitive position at the expense of the degree of job security, job control and standard of living that British Leyland workers had managed to win for themselves and their families in times of easier competition. The workers found themselves in the 1970s victims of the inadequate levels of investment pumped into British Leyland components in the past, called upon to suffer the cuts in incomes and jobs that the crazy logic of a competitive capitalist system imposed on its undercapitalised industrial units in times of recession. As Hugh Stevenson observed in October 1977,

The terrible fact is that even if by some magic wave of the wand all Leyland's industrial relations problems were solved, all manning levels came down to the right level over night and continuous production became the unbroken pattern, British Leyland would still not be able to produce cars which compared in price or value say, with those of several of its major competitors. The reason is that capital investment per employee has now fallen so far behind.[42]

The recognition of this eroded militancy no less than it shaped management. Trade unionists in British Leyland could see the necessity of restructuring. They understood 'as clearly as Mr Edwardes [the Managing Director] that productivity must be raised to the level of our international competitors in order to make British Leyland viable'.[43] But they had also to live with the adverse effects of that restructuring on their members. Resistance necessarily came, and had to be given expression, but in the end it was always dissipated precisely because Leyland workers alone could not end world competition in their industry, and as long as that competition remained, restructuring at their expense was the only way to strengthen the Company's market position. The costs to sections of the workforce were heavy, of that there can be no doubt, but time and again resistance petered out amid union and shop steward agreement to give 'full cooperation' to management policies of greater productivity and labour mobility.

Public ownership did not alter this. It simply brought the weight of the Government (and at times, of official trade unionism) down on the side of management in their call for greater productivity and the toleration of declining standards by British Leyland workers. The management's call for discipline and cooperation, and the threat of redundancies in its absence, had been unambiguous from the start. Derek Whittaker, the managing director of Leyland cars, repeatedly told Longbridge workers that only a 'total commitment' to improve productivity, accept labour mobility and end unofficial strikes could prevent the £120 million project for the new Mini from being abandoned and Longbridge itself being closed.[44] Ministers, on the other hand, were initially less honest. Harold Wilson in January 1975 chose his words carefully. Speaking of the company's industrial relations record, he said:

The rights and wrongs of these disputes (are) now a matter of history . . . what is not a matter for argument for the future is this. With public capital and an appropriate degree of public control involved, the Government could not justify to Parliament or to the taxpayer the subsidising of large factories involving thousands of jobs which could pay their way but which are failing to do so because of manifestly-avoidable stoppages of production.[45]

His underlying meaning was of course quite clear: the choice was between strikes and money, with the Government on the management's side. This was even clearer later when Eric Varley quite explicitly spelt out Labour's unwillingness to support Leyland workers in their opposition to the company's intensification of work processes. As the toolroom men struck in 1977, he was joined by leading trade unionists in condemning the action and blaming the strikers for jeopardising Leyland's future. Former left-wing union leaders Hugh Scanlon and Jack Jones, plus the entire executive of the Confederation of Shipbuilding and Engineering Unions, condemned the strike openly, in terms best expressed by Eric Varley in the House of Commons.

British Leyland has reported to the N.E.B. that since the major review of progress last summer there has been insufficient evidence of a reduction of industrial disputes or of improved productivity in Leyland cars and that the situation has deteriorated sharply in recent months. British Leyland has also stated that unless there is a substantial improvement in performance the generation of cash by Leyland cars, an essential component of the Ryder Report strategy, would be insufficient to support the Cars Plan. British Leyland would then be unable to recommend to the N.E.B. and the Government the injection of further funds for modernisation and expansion of Leyland cars. The N.E.B. has decided in those circumstances it would be unable to make further funds available for the Cars Plan, and I can tell the House that the Government accepts this position. . . . The simple fact is that if this company is to be successful, not only the £1000 million of government money is involved, but the profits which British Leyland cars make. . . . I want all those at Leyland, including those on unofficial strike today, to be clear that their future employment and the future of their company is in their hands. They can kill it or they can save it.[46]

It is hardly surprising that, in the face of such total opposition, and threatened with such awful consequences, the toolroom men eventually returned to work with their main demands unachieved. Yet the Government did not, in the end, live up to its threat to cut off the supply of public funds. £30 million was released to British Leyland in March 1977, an extra £50 million came from the NEB in November 1977, and yet another £150 million in April 1978. But it did retreat from the ambitious targets of the Ryder report, and supported a new management's plan to reduce employment in the car division. For by the middle of the toolroom workers' strike BLMC's trading losses were running at about £10–15 million a *week*. Fear that the Mini project would be cancelled eroded militancy in the summer of 1977, as did the NEB's much publicised consideration (in May 1977) of whether to close four plants and lay off 60,000 men in its pursuit of profitability. So, though the bus and truck division had a two-week strike over pay in September 1977, the toolroom men who had held out for eight weeks in the spring did not in the end implement their threatened resumption of militancy in the autumn, and shop stewards at Longbridge were unable to persuade their members to stage a one-day token stoppage called in August 1977. More significant still, the initially fierce opposition of shop stewards in the TGWU to the company's scheme to complete the 'rationalisation' of the wage structure petered out amid inter-union rivalry and a ballot of all Leyland workers. By a two to one majority on an 87 per cent turnout Leyland employees agreed to cooperate in a scheme to establish a common implementation date for collective agreements in all thirty-four car plants, and to see pay parity phased in across the plants by November 1979, only (ironically) for the scheme to run into trouble with the TUC because of its breach of the twelve-month rule. This erosion of local TGWU strength was followed by initial union and shop steward support for the Edwardes plan which split British Leyland into four subsidiary companies, and proposed the destruction of 12,500 jobs. Resistance to that unemployment did develop later, with a campaign by the unofficial shop stewards combine committee to keep production of the TR7 at Speke, but in the end even this failed to prevent Speke's closure.

British Leyland's troubled development was central to the reality of the Labour Government's industrial strategy. The Party entered office claiming that public ownership and State control could create a new climate of social justice, higher living standards and enhanced working-class power. These claims were echoed in the demand for full public ownership put to the Ryder Committee by Leyland shop stewards early in 1975. The shop stewards got the public ownership they sought, and in the newly nationalised concern enjoyed as full and developed a system of industrial consultation (a three-tier system of joint management councils) as could be found anywhere in British manufacturing industry. But participation did not bring power. It did not even improve industrial relations. Instead, militancy became unofficial, often pursued (as in the case of the toolroom workers) in the face of official trade union condemnation, and aimed at the establishment of new and separate negotiating structures which might be more responsive than the old to the grievances generated in the restructuring of Leyland's production processes. The new participatory machinery, far from shifting class power within British Leyland, in fact marked another stage in the incorporation of trade union officials and shop stewards into the managerial function within British capitalism. Neither the entry of shop stewards into joint management councils, nor the superintendence of British Leyland by a Labour Government through the NEB, altered in any significant way the criteria by which British Leyland's management operated, nor did it lessen in any way the competitive constraints which beset the Company on all sides. The whole thinking of the Labour Left, that participation with management would bring power over the managerial function, was based on the assumption that management controlled its universe in the first place, and that as a result 'control' was there to be shared in a democratic fashion. But this was to misunderstand the nature of capitalism itself. As the Counter-Information Service (CIS) report put it, 'the irony is that the speed of this hand-over-fist competitive race is beyond the control of any of those taking part in it. It hurtles on with a motion of its own, and sucks in massive resources, beyond society's real needs for the goods its produces; simply because of the need of the participant companies for the profits to survive'.[47]

The Labour Government entered car production at a time when, through the world car industry as a whole, the big multinational companies were rationalising their production on an unprecedented scale, because of the competition between them, in order 'to centralise, co-ordinate and integrate the whole production process on a global basis'.[48] In the true manner of anarchic capitalism, each car producer was forced to react to an already overcapitalised industry by investing further, only to find the pressure on profits reappearing at a still higher level of investment, requiring a still higher level of sales to maintain company viability. In such a situation public ownership could not make the difference its advocates had claimed. Tight market-generated imperatives remained to dominate BLMC's management, and these demanded the reorganisation of production, the destruction of jobs, and the intensification of the work process.* The intervention of the Labour Government permitted those processes to be carried on without the immediate and massive redundancies that British Leyland in private hands would have been forced to create. But the presence of public money did not remove the force of competitive pressures, nor free British Leyland from the necessity of following the developments set in motion by its major competitors. Rather it drew the Labour Government into adding its voice to that of management in the company's concerted attack on the degree of job control, job security and living standards attained by Leyland workers. Far from achieving 'a fundamental and irreversible shift in the balance of power and wealth in favour of working people and their families', public ownership in the car industry completed the alliance of management and the State *against* any such shift, and demonstrated more visibly than any other aspect of Labour Government policy the limits that exist on reformism within a capitalist State.

VIII

Nor was British Leyland an isolated example within the public sector. Its experience was typical of government policy in the manufacturing

---

* This was made very clear by British Leyland's chairman in his report for 1978. 'There is a popular misconception', he was reported as saying, 'that B.L. is subject to different rules than those which apply in other commercial undertakings and that endemic overmanning will be accepted by the B.L. board and paid for by the public. The facts are different. The B.L. board's terms of reference are to run the company on strict business lines.' (*Financial Times*, 24 April 1979, p. 28.)

section of the public sector as a whole. The streamlining of production methods under competitive pressures, the forced redundancy of large groups of workers, and the erosion of work practices that embodied working-class industrial power were no monopoly of British Leyland. The story in the British Steel Corporation is all too similar, with the same pattern of initially radical promises being lost in financial crises that forced Ministers to give public support to the destruction of jobs and to the closure of plants. In the case of steel, the Labour Party in opposition were well aware of management plans to cut employment by 30,000 by 1982, and to rationalise production methods and plant locations, in the pursuit of competitiveness in world markets. In opposition at least, Labour politicans found that these plans involved 'redundancies of an unacceptable scale . . . without any coherent plan for providing new employment for those affected'; and they promised 'a new deal for steel by the next Labour Government' which would involve the immediate freezing and reconsideration of all the plans for closures and redundancies, the guarantee of long-term expansion to the British Steel Corporation, and full consultation with management and unions 'to ensure that wherever possible unavoidable redundancies are phased to link with newly available employment'.[49] It should be stressed that policy in 1974 and 1975 remained remarkably loyal to that aim. In February 1975 Ministers postponed British Steel Corporation plans to make 13,500 men redundant, by slowing down the closure of uncompetitive plants in areas of already high unemployment, at a cost to the Corporation of £100 million a year. The Corporation's chairman and Tony Benn clashed openly in May 1975, as the Labour Government blocked further proposals for the destruction of up to 20,000 jobs by 1976. That immediate confrontation was resolved in the Government's favour, with the unions agreeing to a six-point plan to cut the total wage bill and increase productivity without compulsory redundancy; but such settlements only exacerbated competitive difficulties for the British steel industry which the world recession had already created. The British Steel Corporation was already subject to fierce international competition (its share of even the United Kingdom steel market had dropped to 53 per cent by the middle of 1978). The Corporation had a history of government-inspired price restraint policies which had eroded internal sources of investment funds. It had too much of its capital tied up in plants which were technologically obsolescent. It had a labour force of over 200,000, which was at least 30 per cent greater than its share of world demand could sustain. And for all these reasons, it moved steadily into financial crisis by 1977. By then, productivity in the British steel industry was anywhere between 25 per cent and 184 per cent below that of its major competitors, which left it particularly prone to falling demand as output levels in the world economy continued to stagnate.[50] The Corporation lost £225 million in 1975–76, £95 million in 1976–77, and £443 million in 1977–78. By then the plants 'saved' in 1975 were again in jeopardy, and the rate of voluntary redundancy under the January 1976 agreement was so low (only 2200 men left the industry in nearly two years) that the spectre of forced unemployment could be avoided no longer.

For all the Labour Government's fine words about a 'new deal', the logic of competitive pressures from the world market eventually shaped policy here, as elsewhere in the public sector. In February 1978, in the face of union opposition, Labour Ministers refused to pay steel workers even the going rate of 10 per cent until they agreed to a programme of plant closures and job losses, softened only by unprecedentedly high levels of severance payments to those made redundant. Five thousand men left the industry in the first quarter of 1978, and 12,000 more were to follow as the plants 'saved' in 1975 were closed in 1978. The Government also deferred plans to open new steel-making plants in areas of high unemployment, and made clear their determination to restore financial viability by closing other high-cost plants and by 'further rationalisations'.[51] By then, closures were not prevented by the absence of alternative sources of unemployment in the areas affected, as the Labour Programme in 1973 had intended, nor was the Government prepared, as it had been initially, to withstand the market pressure to concentrate production in a smaller number of modernised steel plants.

In steel, as in cars, public ownership did not enable the Labour Government to replace or control market forces. At best, it permitted market-dictated processes of unemployment and intensified work routines to be introduced more slowly than might have been the case in private hands. In the end, jobs were still lost and the government-inspired delays, by compounding the industries' competitive difficulties, made the long-term job loss even more severe. Labour Ministers found that, to a degree, they could 'socialise' the losses of these industries through the provision of public funds, though even this was restricted by their own propensities to run down the rate of subsidisation of the public sector (as in the November 1974 budget) and to set commercial targets for returns on public sector investment as part of their general attempt to curb the growth rate of public sector spending in total. But even Labour Ministers, though reluctant to create unemployment and social deprivation, could not continue for long to pour large quantities of public money into industries that had fallen behind in the world competitive stakes without coming under very heavy pressure from the Opposition to streamline production and employment levels, and without finding themselves short of public funds for other cherished policy objectives. Such political pressures soon obliged Ministers to add their own voices to those of management, in the call to subordinate industrial policy to the dictates of the world market, and transformed even radical Ministers into the most adamant proponents of international competitiveness. The Party's social conscience remained, but was rapidly and necessarily subordinated to economic imperatives.

In the public sector as in the private, the Labour Government's initially radical aspiration to control and shape economic activity in a manner compatible with social justice and a growth in working–class power ended in state-supervised restructuring of production and an explicit subordination of policy to the goals of international competitiveness and commercial financial viability. The consequence of public ownership for the workers in the steel industry and in British Leyland was not greater control over their own work situation, but rather the threat and reality of unemployment, and an intensification of work routines which brought increased productivity at the cost of tighter supervision and a generalised replacement of men by machines. Where trade union rights had grown through new structures of consultation, these had served to lessen worker resistance to this deterioration in their working conditions and job control; with the paradoxical impact of actually marking a *decline* in real working-class power and a growing division between workers and their representatives. In the public sector, as elsewhere in the Labour Government's industrial policy, in the confrontation between radicalism and the market forces of world capitalism, it was radicalism that had succumbed.


# IX

One area of the Labour Government's industrial policy remains to be examined in detail: that of industrial democracy. As we have already noted on several occasions, this Labour Government began its period of office with an ambitious programme of industrial regeneration and social reform, committed, on paper at least, to the shifting of class power *within* industry by an extension of industrial democracy. The Party's understanding of such a term, it must be said, has never been a particularly extreme one. It has never taken industrial democracy to involve the total subordination of the managerial function in industry to workers' control, still less the establishment of institutions capable of enforcing socialist criteria on economic activity. The Labour Party has always left that responsibility to the Parliamentary Party, in spite of the inability of Labour Governments in practice to avoid succumbing to market forces beyond their control. Instead, even on the left of the Party, industrial democracy was understood as involving two processes: the strengthening of the defensive rights of workers (both individual rights and the collective rights of workers as trade unionists) *against* the exercise of managerial prerogatives, through trade union legislation, employment protection, and health and safety measures; and in addition, the *sharing* of the managerial function, through the disclosure of information to strengthen and widen collective bargaining, and the placing of workers on boards of directors, in the context of an unaltered world competitive economy. Yet even on this more moderate understanding of what an extension of industrial democracy involves the performance of the Labour Government after 1974 did not match earlier aspirations, though here the retreat has been made more complex by divisions within the unions themselves. This story too requires to be told if the full record of this Labour Government is to be understood.

The discussion on industrial democracy, dormant in the labour movement since the 1930s,[52] was revived within the Labour Party by the report, in June 1967, of a working party chaired by Jack Jones. That working party urged the Government to increase worker participation in workplace and industrial affairs through a very considerable extension of existing trade union rights and powers within industry. It called for new legislation to guarantee union recognition, to win improved facilities for workplace representatives, and for training shop stewards, to protect trade union activists against unfair dismissal, to give general rights of notice, appeal and compensation for all workers subject to redundancy, and to increase the quantity of information available to union negotiators (on questions of manpower and remuneration, industrial ownership, costs, prices and profits, and development, production and investment decisions). But significantly in the light of what was to follow, it did not press for worker representation on the boards of companies in the private sector. Indeed it rejected this 'as a suitable starting point for the extension of industrial democracy', preferring instead to see collective bargaining extended and statutory protection of trade unionists strengthened before any consideration was given to the advantages and functions of worker directors. Only for public sector industries did the working party call for boardroom representation. Otherwise the report resisted any idea of creating new channels of worker representation in favour of developing existing structures; in its words, industrial democracy understood as 'a *single channel* of worker representation based on trade union organisation and involving a further development of the scope of collective bargaining'.[53]

This report, and the subsequent statement by the NEC to the Labour Party conference in 1968, proved a crucial source of ideas for subsequent policy in this field. The main elements of the Employment Protection Act can be traced back to it; so too can the preoccupation with restricting industrial democracy to existing trade union structures, which was to be such a matter of contention after the publication of the Bullock Report a decade later. But on that later report's main concern (worker representation on the boards of private companies) the 1967 report's caution was matched by the TUC's own evidence to the Donovan Commission in the same year. The TUC then suggested legislation to allow firms to appoint worker directors if they wished, but the majority Donovan Report[54] felt unable to recommend even this, because of the clash of interests and functions it seemed likely to cause for the worker directors themselves. Clearly no one in a leadership position in the labour movement in the late 1960s was prepared to call for legislation compelling firms to create worker directors, and the whole issue was overshadowed until the early 1970s by Labour's electoral defeat and the furore over the 1971 Industrial Relations Act.

The issue was raised again by Jack Jones early in 1972, when he called for 'a major involvement of trade union representatives on management boards', with those representatives to be elected through, and to report back to, the shop steward system within the company concerned. The first Liaison Committee statement in July 1972 was less specific on details, but it too called for 'work on a programme to promote the widespread development of industrial democracy',[55] and by January 1973 the TUC was demanding that a two-tier system of supervisory and executive boards be created, with shareholders and worker representatives having equal representation on the supervisory board. The driving force in all this was reportedly Jack Jones himself, and other Labour leaders picked up the cue. Tony Benn was particularly enthusiastic. 'We reject as a party and a movement,' he told the 1973 Labour Party conference,

the idea that one worker on the board is industrial democracy. We reject co-ownership; we reject the phoney works councils not rooted in the strength and structure and tradition of the trade union movement. All these are window dressing. . . . We will not accept the existing pattern of nationalisation as the form for the future. We have had enough experience . . . to know that nationalisation plus Lord Robens does not add up to socialism.[56]

Even Harold Wilson joined in, with a major speech on industrial democracy in Edinburgh, in which he picked out areas in which the Labour Government after 1974 did take action: in the reform of the procedure surrounding redundancies and dismissal, in the field of industrial health and safety, on facilities and training for workshop representatives, and on the extension of collective bargaining to include 'work routine, factory layout, work–load arrangements, assembly–line speeds and techniques as well as general production methods'.[57] He too mentioned worker directors, promising experiments in the public sector whilst avoiding any specific commitment on private sector boards. This ambiguity found its way into Labour's 1973 Programme, where worker representatives on boards were mentioned as one possibility currently under review, in a section which stressed the importance of extending and strengthening the procedural rights of workers and trade unionists, the importance of collective bargaining and the need for companies to disclose information to workers and trade unionists 'on a much wider basis'.[58] All this lay behind the Labour Party's election promise in February 1974 to 'repeal the Industrial Relations Act as a matter of urgency and then bring in an Employment Protection Act and an Industrial Democracy Act, as agreed in our discussions with the TUC, to increase the control of industry by the people',[59] repeated in October 1974 as a promise to 'introduce new legislation to help forward our plans for a radical extension of industrial democracy in both the private and public sectors'.[60]

In the event, progress on industrial democracy went more slowly than the manifestoes implied, although initially this was not clear. The Trade Union and Labour Relations Act was passed, amid a fierce parliamentary row over its provisions for the closed shop; and later an Employment Protection Act and an Industry Act reached the statute book, both of which contained procedures by which the Government could compel firms to disclose information to worker representatives. The Industry Department under Tony Benn gave much publicised support to a number of small worker cooperatives, and a committee on the extension of industrial democracy in the public sector began work in February 1976. But there was no Industrial Democracy Act to complete the process. Instead a fierce internal wrangle within the Labour Cabinet produced a delay, in the form of a Committee of

Inquiry into the extension of industrial democracy in the private sector. All the TUC managed to salvage were tight terms of reference for that committee, and the presence among its membership of the men who had engineered the revival of TUC interest in the whole field, Jack Jones and David Lea.

There can be no doubt that the Trade Union and Labour Relations Act, and the Employment Protection Act, marked an important advance in the procedural rights of workers and trade unionists in industry. Moreover the latter Act, in company with the Industry Act, did lay down procedures by which the Government could compel firms to disclose information. Those powers were sufficiently potent to generate a CBI campaign against them. Indeed it is significant that the degree of opposition from private capital intensified to near hysteria at precisely that point at which the Labour Government moved from strengthening worker rights against management to the area of power-sharing between workers and management. The CBI treated the proposals on the disclosure of information as the thin end of a wedge that would erode managerial autonomy in sacrosanct areas of industrial power, and reacted accordingly. But in fact neither the design nor the implementation of the Government's proposals lived up to the aspirations in opposition that there would be a significant increase in the information available to trade unionists. The failure of the Government to negotiate a wide set of planning agreements (and their willingness to exclude direct trade union representation in the negotiation of the few that were signed) compounded this.

The obligations on an employer under the Employment Protection Act were restricted to issues involved in collective bargaining; and though collective bargaining was widely defined by the 1974 Trade Union and Labour Relations Act it did not extend coverage to such matters as product costs, marketing and pricing policy or detailed investment plans. Nor was the employer, even when engaged in collective bargaining, obliged to verify the information he supplied, or to do more than to appear before ACAS if he failed to disclose information as specified by the Act. Disclosures under the Industry Act were potentially wider in scope, situated as they were in the context of the planning agreements system, but the procedure of disclosure was indirect and complex, with the Minister receiving the information and then serving notice on the company to transmit relevant sections to the appropriate union representatives. The appeals procedure, when companies resisted such ministerial orders, was even more elaborate and time-consuming. Indeed, the Industry Act was weaker than the Employment Protection Act in two important respects. Its coverage of firms was narrower, applying only to firms in manufacturing industry, and it gave trade unionists no statutory right to information, but left the initiation of the disclosure procedure to the discretion of the Industry Secretary. Given the resistance of private industry to these disclosure provisions, and the growing reluctance of Ministers to alienate private management, it is not surprising that the unions have found neither of these Acts adequate to their requirements for full and detailed information on a wide range of industrial matters in their pursuit of industrial democracy.

The Government's direct initiatives in industrial democracy also proved ineffectual. At the beginning, Tony Benn's Ministry did give assistance to three worker cooperatives: to Triumph motor cycle workers at Meriden, to workers formerly employed by the Scottish Daily Express, and to Fisher–Bendix workers at Kirkby. The sums involved were small, around £10 million in total; but they were enough to keep all but the newspaper cooperative viable until 1977, when Fisher–Bendix and Meriden both received extra government funds, the latter receiving theirs in a package between themselves, the Government and the General Electric Company (GEC). But Government enthusiasm for worker cooperatives waned (though they retained powers to give small loans to worker cooperatives under the Industrial Common Ownership Act where such proposals had 'a reasonable chance of success'[61]) and the Kirkby cooperative was allowed to collapse early in 1979.

Subsequent ministerial attempts to strengthen industrial democracy by their own direct actions focused more on the public sector boards. When the Government took Harland and Wolff, the Belfast shipbuilders, into public ownership in July 1974, it made support conditional on the introduction of moves 'towards genuine worker participation in all the decision-making processes of the company'. That culminated, three years later, in five worker directors joining five executive and five government nominees on the company's board. The initial draft of the Aircraft and Shipbuilding Industries Bill obliged the management in those industries 'to promote industrial democracy'; but lack of enthusiasm for the idea of worker directors among union activists in the industries apparently persuaded the Government to amend this to an obligation merely 'to bring in a form of industrial democracy acceptable to the unions in the industry'. They failed to find a way of resolving the dilemmas that an extension of industrial democracy generated in the fields of national health and local government, where the 'employers' were themselves democratically elected and accountable; but they did oversee (as we have already observed) the introduction of complex schemes in British Leyland and the British Steel Corporation, whose unions and shop stewards found themselves participating in extensive systems of consultation with management at all levels through new joint management councils. And the Government did at least pass legislation by which the Post Office could begin a two-year experiment in industrial democracy in January 1978, in which six trade union worker directors joined six management nominees and four independents on a new Post Office Board, the trade union worker directors being free to report back to their constituents in the unions involved. The Government hoped that such schemes would also be established in other nationalised industries but only the British Steel Corporation had followed suit by the time that the Government went to the polls in 1979.

However the real fight against the extension of industrial democracy into the area of power sharing came from private sector management, in the wake of the Bullock Report. This resistance had been foreshadowed in the evidence to Bullock, and in the division of opinion within the Committee of Inquiry itself. In its evidence the TUC proposed its fifty–fifty worker director scheme, and discouraged individual unions from submitting counter-proposals. The CBI, and a number of major employers' federations and large companies, countered this with opposition to any legislation which would impose worker directors on private industry, preferring voluntary schemes of employee participation settled on a company to company basis. These divisions were reflected in the two reports which eventually emerged. The majority report stayed close to the spirit of the TUC proposals. It recommended that companies (including subsidiaries of foreign companies) which employed more than 2000 people should set up one board, made up by the '$2X + Y$' formula of equal groups of worker directors and shareholder nominees plus a smaller group of independent directors. Such a structure should not however be compulsory, but should be established only after a vote of all employees had indicated both that a majority of employees voting desired such a change, and that at least one-third of the workforce were favourably disposed towards it. The resulting worker directors should be union nominees, selected or elected from a joint representation committee of all interested unions in a particular company. These worker directors would not be formally mandated by their particular union, but would be expected to report back to their constituents. The minority report, on the other hand, aimed 'to design a system of worker directors that would give the least possible power over management decision-making to employees in general and to trade union representatives in particular, whilst encouraging participation below board level'.[62] It proposed only that all companies be obliged to set up participatory machinery within four years, with employees free to vote on whether to create worker directors three years later. Even then, financial institutions and the subsidiaries of foreign companies were to be excluded, the trade unions were not to enjoy any monopoly of worker director places, and any resulting worker directors were to make up only one-third of the seats in the supervisory board of a two-tier board structure in the holding company alone. The resistance of sections of private capital to power-sharing was thus visibly underlined.

The publication of the Bullock Report prompted a major offensive against the majority proposals by the CBI and by leading individuals in senior management and finance. This campaign seems to have been motivated in part by genuine concern among senior industrialists that a full disclosure of information to worker directors might jeopardise commercial secrets, and that such a shift in class power might discourage foreign investment, slow necessary changes in manning levels and labour practices and so erode still further the competitive strength of the British manufacturing sector. To this degree, the CBI was unconvinced by those (including Lord Bullock himself) who argued the reverse: that greater worker involvement would spark industrial efficiency and greater competitiveness. But it is clear too that a considerable degree of the opposition to Bullock (as also to planning agreements) was promoted by the 'caste' mentality of senior management, and their horror at having to abandon managerial prerogatives to even this slight degree. To this extent, the counter-arguments they used against Bullock were reflections of deeper class interests that would tolerate no intrusion of working-class institutions into the managerial sphere. This lay behind CBI proposals that the only major legislative requirements on large companies should be to negotiate participation agreements with their employees, free of any obligation to create a system of worker directors of the Bullock type.

CBI anger was greatest at the proposal to restrict the choice of worker directors to members of trade unions, a fight on behalf of the 'disenfranchised' non-trade unionist which the CBI had also maintained for members of occupational pension schemes and for health and safety officers appointed under other pieces of government legislation. The CBI countered the Bullock proposals by stressing the importance of 'quality' rather than 'representativeness' as the key to successful industrial leadership, and by arguing that capital would be more difficult to raise where companies had workers on their boards. The CBI anticipated that the implementation of Bullock would slow down managerial decision-making, and make it less efficient; and CBI leaders supplemented their own threat of withdrawal from NEDC working parties on the industrial strategy with public warnings of the difficulties of implementation when managerial resistance was so marked. 'Flexibility', 'voluntarism' and 'gradual progress' became the watchwords of the CBI campaign to resist legally imposed, union-nominated worker directors, to block any proposal to give parity to employee-elected and shareholder-elected directors, and to prevent the trade unions enjoying a monopoly of nomination in any worker director scheme that the CBI failed to stop. As Lord Watkinson told the NEDC in February 1977,

> if, in spite of this, the Government decides to press ahead with legislation based on the Bullock majority report, it will not only be introducing highly divisive legislation; it will also be showing complete disregard for the efficient management of our major companies on which the economic future of the country depends . . . the industrial growth that we all wish to see will not happen and the objectives we have set ourselves will not be achieved.[63]

In their opposition, CBI spokesmen were joined by voices within the trade union movement. The TUC was more divided on worker directors than its evidence to the Bullock Committee implied. Left-wing union leaders were opposed to a nominal involvement that could bring no change in power; right-wing union leaders rejected any attempt to involve trade unionism in the managerial function; and even union leaders keen on an extension of industrial democracy (David Basnett for example) remained unconvinced that a rigid system of worker directors was the best way to achieve it. Jack Jones's TGWU remained committed to worker directors under his leadership, but the string of unions opposed was considerable, and included the NUM, the EETPU, the NUGMW, UCATT and the AUEW.* Yet the TUC continued to press for the implementation of the Bullock report, especially after its 1977 Congress had passed a compromise resolution urging legislative backing for unions and workers wanting parity of representation on company boards, while generally strengthening the procedures of collective bargaining. As the CBI campaign built up in the summer of 1977, the TUC continued to insist that unions alone

---

* National Union of Mineworkers; Electrical, Electronic and Telecommunication and Plumbing Union; National Union of General and Municipal Workers; Union of Construction, Allied Trades and Technicians; Amalgamated Union of Engineering Workers.

should monopolise the nomination of worker directors in the private sector, and that the Government should press ahead with the generalised introduction of worker directors in the nationalised industries. The 'single channel of representation' had been the central issue of the Labour Party working party report of a decade before, and the TUC hung on to it, as CBI opposition grew and as the Labour Government's parliamentary dependence on the Liberals pushed ministerial thinking away from the 'single channel' position.

The Labour Government was trapped between contradictory pressures. It was busy seeking wide agreement in industry and the City for its general economic strategy. It needed specific trade union support for future wage restraint and it depended on Liberal votes in the Commons. As a result, Ministers promised legislation on industrial democracy, but regularly failed to produce it. Immediately after the Bullock Report was published, a White Paper was promised for the summer of 1977. Later this was postponed to the autumn, and in fact did not appear until April 1978. The Cabinet itself was divided. Edmund Dell, as the Minister responsible for drafting any Bill, preferred to build a wide agreement that could take in many CBI objections to the majority report. Albert Booth, at the Department of Employment, apparently took a more pro-Bullock line. But the positions of the TUC and the CBI were not simply different: they were incompatible. The CBI wanted voluntary participatory machinery built slowly from the bottom up: the TUC wanted worker directors at the top immediately. The CBI rejected any proposal to give the trade unions a monopoly of the nomination of worker directors: the TUC would settle for nothing less. The CBI opposed equal representation of employee representatives and shareholder directors: again the TUC wanted at least this. And as Edmund Dell's proposals moved towards those of the CBI, in the face of business opposition and under the Liberal Party's pressure to depart from single-channel representation, the situation was complicated by divisions between the unions, and by regular opinion polls that reported a general lack of interest in worker directors among rank and file trade unionists.

In the end, the Government's White Paper retreated from the Bullock proposals. The Government stressed the desirability of a *voluntary* move to industrial democracy, buttressed by fall back statutory powers for employees and unions where no voluntary agreement was forthcoming. The statutory route to industrial democracy was to take two stages. Initially, the proposed legislation would oblige all companies employing more than 500 people to consult regularly on all important company matters (including investments, mergers, takeovers and closures) with a joint representation committee (JRC) of elected shop stewards. The White Paper gave the trade unions the right to set up these JRCs, but added rights of participation and appeal for non-unionists. Later (and certainly not before 1984) JRCs in the bigger companies (employing 2000 people or more in the United Kingdom) would have the right to initiate a ballot of all employees on whether worker directors should be appointed. If the ballot supported the idea, the committees would decide how these worker directors were to be selected and the individuals chosen would normally join the supervisory board of a two-tier board system (unless the company chose to retain its unitary structure). Worker directors would not initially have parity of representation. They would only constitute one-third of the board, with a view to attaining parity later; they would have the same responsibilities as other directors, and would not be mandatable by the unions who selected them. Not even these watered down proposals became law before the general election. Instead, in the Queen's Speech in November 1978 the Government announced its willingness to discuss its White Paper once more with management and union representatives before bringing its much delayed Industrial Democracy Bill to Parliament. Yet neither its own lack of a parliamentary majority nor the continuing chorus of opposition from the CBI and other spokesmen for industrial and financial capital (not to mention the occasional trade union leader) suggested that that Bill would have a quick or an easy passage.

For the fate of the Bullock Report is in line with the rest of the Government's plans for the reform of British industry. The push to industrial democracy petered out in the face of sustained opposition. The Labour Government's determination to strengthen the procedural rights of individual workers and trade unionists against arbitrary managerial practices was sustained, and this legal change constituted the TUC's major gain from the social contract. But when the Government went further, to consider a strengthening of trade unionism that involved a sharing of power with private management, through the disclosure of information, planning agreements and worker directors, it met solid resistance from the political spokesmen of private capital. Only in the manufacturing sections of the public sector were new systems of consultation developed under this Labour Government, and even here participation brought no significant change of industrial policy or class power. In the private sector, the Government bent before fierce opposition, as its political will for reform waned in the face of persistent industrial stagnation. As a result, through large sections of British manufacturing industry the right of management to make its crucial industrial decisions in private and in secrecy remained as intact when the Labour Government went to the country as it had been when the Party first took power in 1974, and yet another aspect of Labour radicalism in the years of opposition had come to nothing.


X

The industrial policy of the Labour Government after 1974 was marked by two overriding characteristics: the ambitions of its initial aspirations and the limited nature of its actual effects. The language of 1973 and 1974 was radical and optimistic, implying that a Labour Government, precisely because it was prepared to extend public ownership, control private capital and experiment with industrial democracy, would succeed, slowly but surely, in its pursuit of economic growth, social justice and a shift in class power 'in favour of working people and their families'. In the event, the Labour Government did *not* achieve sustained economic growth or full employment. It abandoned its attempt to control the private sector through planning agreements, and proved to be quite as capable as earlier governments of providing large amounts of public funds (as to Chrysler) without adequate public control. Where it did extend public ownership, through the NEB or in the nationalisation of whole industries, the change in ownership did not alter the basic criteria directing economic activity. Instead Labour Ministers became ever more 'managerial' in the tone and content of their policy statements, bringing the material and ideological resources of the State to the aid of managements who were already intensifying work processes and shedding labour throughout the manufacturing sector. The much publicised pursuit of industrial democracy was a major casualty of that State–employer alliance, either degenerating into a joint consultative system (as at Leyland) which only added the voice of official unionism to those already articulating managerial policy against trade union members, or being blocked entirely (as in the case of the Bullock Report) by union divisions and employer opposition. Behind the language of social justice and socialist advance the Labour Government maintained the very goals, perspectives, and fundamentally antagonistic relationship to working-class industrial power, which the Party in opposition had denounced, and brought the State machine into an ever closer relationship with centres of private capital in an increasingly singleminded pursuit of economic growth.

In part, these developments reflect the defeat within the Labour Government of the left-wing Ministers whose voices had been so dominant in the years of opposition. The shared concerns of all Labour Ministers with economic growth and state intervention could not hide for long the fundamental divisions within the Party, between those who thought that greater democratic control (through a radical Labour Government) and working-class participation in management (through industrial democracy) could allow qualitatively new criteria to dominate investment and inspire efficiency, and those who recognised that such transformations in the distribution of power within British industry could only intensify competitive weaknesses and erode still further the already depressed levels of profits and output. The full significance of that division is discussed in Chapter 6; all that should be noted here is the way in which the development of the Government's industrial policy threw into relief defects in the Labour Left's analysis of their situation which guaranteed their ultimate defeat.

The Labour Government began its period of office under left-wing influence, claiming that it could build a coalition of interests between all sections of the community behind the goal of economic growth. In doing so its leading members did not recognise initially that in a fiercely competitive and stagnant world economy, growth could come only at the price of changes in industrial practices and levels of employment that would *add* to the work burdens and social deprivations of large sections of the Party's own working-class electorate. Labour politicians in 1974 seemed to believe that the problems besetting British industry were those of ownership and control on the one side, and bad communications, inadequate information and poor planning on the other. They seemed to feel that with men in control of industry who were sympathetic to Labour (via public ownership), with greater trade union involvement, and with extensive consultation at senior management level, the problems of industrial inefficiency and low output could be overcome. In fact private ownership and élite control, inadequate communications and poor planning were not the root cause of industrial stagnation and falling employment, as Labour politicians were to learn; and the changing shape and muted impact of the Government's industrial policy should be taken as an index of that learning process. Instead they were important surface manifestations of deeper processes at work in the world economy, which Labour politicians had no means even of recognising, let alone of bringing under their control. It was these processes which literally drowned the industrial strategy and reformist hopes of the Labour Government after 1974.

These processes in the world economy lay far beyond the control of any élite group, even when that group professed loyalty to Labour's own radicalism. As we have seen, the world economy in the 1970s was in a recession of a severity last seen in the 1930s, and was dogged by inflation. That recession was accelerating the restructuring of capital on a world scale and shifting investment, production and employment *away* from the United Kingdom. As a result, the Labour Government found that, far from regenerating British industry into high and sustained economic growth, its industrial policies came to constitute a rearguard action against the 'deindustrialisation' of the British economy which these world processes were setting in motion; and that even so ineffective a rearguard action as Labour Ministers were able to mount had to be paid for at the heavy price of abandoned social reforms, rising unemployment and (for long periods) falling living standards. Powerful competitive forces in the world economy imposed tight imperatives on British manufacturing capital, if production in the UK economy was to remain profitable; and the Labour Government came to discover in consequence that it had to encourage an intensification of inequality, and a growth in the rate of exploitation of labour, if economic growth was ever to be attained. Not for the first time in the history of the Party, a Labour Government found its social reform programme and its industrial strategy in contradiction, and had to curtail its reforms in the search for the sustained economic growth that continued to elude it. It is this, rather than any weakness of political will within the Labour Government, or any capitalist conspiracy outside the Party, that gave Government policy its trajectory after the heady reformism of 1974.

In conclusion it is worth noting that, contrary to the claims of the Conservative and Liberal parties, public ownership under this Labour Government did not lead to 'creeping socialism', if by socialism is understood either a shift in class power towards working people, or even the ability of a popularly elected radical government to impose non-market criteria on economic activity. What happened instead was that, under a veneer of radicalism, the Labour Government came to play an important role in the restructuring of British industry to facilitate its return to profitability, and in the process came to intensify working-class job insecurity, and lack of job control. The 'socialism' of the British Labour Party generated, as it ever will, only an ever more 'managed capitalism' in which the State plays an enhanced role, but in which class power remains firmly and unevenly entrenched.

This is not to say that the Labour Government became simply a tool of big business, as the analyses of many on the left might be taken to imply. The relationship between private capital and the State under a Labour Government is more complex than such a 'sell out' thesis would suggest. Of course, much of the development of the Government's industrial strategy does provide evidence for those who would argue that business and finance are the dominant forces in British political life. There are many examples of policy initiatives abandoned because of business opposition, and these included those sections of Labour policy that had been given the greatest radical veneer in opposition. The fate of the planning agreements system and the demise of industrial democracy must be the starkest examples of this in the 1970s, to set against the earlier defeat of the Industrial Relations Act and the development of the social contract as examples of trade union power. It is also clear that large multinational companies proved far more difficult to control than Labour politicians appear to have anticipated in opposition, as the vacuity of the planning agreement with Chrysler again suggests. Moreover, the very pursuit of economic growth as a basis for social reform committed the Labour Government to seek the conditions by which the accumulation of capital could go on apace; and to the degree (as I argue later) that such an accumulation process remained locked in a world capitalist economy, so to that degree also was the Labour Government pulled into the servicing of capital and forced to bolster a weak British capitalism at the expense of its own working-class base.

All that seems to me to be undeniable. Even so it should not leave us with a view of this Labour Government as simply and directly subordinated to any section of (or indeed, the mere puppet of the spokesmen for) British capital. Such a view would make a mockery of the complexities of power this narrative so far has sought to illustrate. It should not be forgotten that the Labour Government entered office with wider aspirations and with constituencies other than private capital to serve, and that these too had their impact on policy initiatives and their subsequent development. The Labour Government's own interventionist propensities combined with the weakness of British manufacturing capital to propel Ministers directly into the accumulation process, both directly supervising it in the expanded public sector and indirectly orchestrating it (through price controls and State aid) in the private sector. The Labour Government also found that the restructuring of British capital required more than material aid. It also required extensive working-class cooperation, which the State alone was in a position to call into being. That cooperation was won in part by simple, old-fashioned ideological pressure, by the beating of the drum of crisis and sacrifice in time of national disaster, and by appeals to working-class loyalty to 'their' Government. But it was also won by the granting of material concessions to the working class in line with the Labour Government's own professed radicalism. Here the motives of Labour politicians and the long-term requirements of capital accumulation were at one. Price controls and welfare provision stand as two examples of this – policies which were anathema to sections of the industrial establishment but whose role in guaranteeing working-class moderation made them vital components of the long-term needs of British capital. So if the Labour Government turned out to be a capitalist one, engaged in the restructuring of British capital at the expense of the working class – and I argue in the next chapter that it must be seen as such if its whole development is to be understood – then it was a capitalist government prepared to act *against* the policy demands of sections of (and at times, all of) British capital in its determination to guarantee a long-term prosperity to the economy's industrial base and to meet its political obligations to its predominantly working-class electorate.

Of course, as working-class militancy was defused by such radicalism in and after 1974, and as the economic constraints tightened, such 'concessions' to popular demands could be, and were, eroded; and the gap between business demands and Government policy narrowed. But to the end of this Labour Government, the coincidence of policy between, say, the CBI and the Cabinet could never be, and never was, total; and that gap reflected the balance of class forces which the Labour Government had to coordinate in its pursuit of capital accumulation. What the industrial policy of the Labour Government demonstrates is not the simple and unambiguous political power of big business in Britain in the 1970s, so much as the intractibility of British capital's competitive weakness. It is the intractibility of *capital*, and the fragmented political universe it generates, rather than any monolithic power of *business*, which has to be grasped as the key to the development of policy under this Labour Government, and to the consideration of which we must now turn.

# PART TWO

# The explanation of the record

# CHAPTER FOUR
# *The determinants of Labour politics*

When the record of this Labour Government is set against the aspirations of the programmes prepared in opposition, it is clear that Labour Ministers in the 1970s met problems in the implementation of their intentions that were of such a scale as to effectively nullify the radicalism of the opposition years. The heady optimism of 1973 and 1974 that the Labour Party in power could use its close relationship with the trade union movement and its declared propensity for state intervention in industry to create a more equal and just society in which jobs were secure and economic growth sustained – all this had long gone by 1979. Moreover, solutions to the main economic problems with which Labour Ministers were faced in 1974 continued to elude them. Economic growth was slow and sluggish, unemployment high, and inflation rates only slightly lower than when the Labour Government entered office. The NEB was a pale shadow of the institution designed in opposition. Planning agreements had simply not materialised. A significant degree of industrial democracy had not been achieved. And the degree of poverty and social inequality remaining in 1979 stood in stark contrast to the Labour Party's claim in opposition that it could achieve a 'fundamental and irreversible shift in the balance of power and wealth in favour of working people and their families'. Of course, not all the Party's aspirations had been lost. In particular, the legal and procedural powers of trade unionism had been consolidated, and this was an important advance for the labour movement. Moreover, if public spending had not grown as Labour Ministers had planned, at least the Cabinet had struggled hard to resist the kind of dismantling of the social services that their Conservative opponents, and many influential private individuals, had urged on them. But not for the first time in the Party's history, a Labour Government entering office ambitious and confident left office more defensive and conservative, with its more radical promises unfulfilled; and it is this pattern of limited success and frustrated radicalism which we must now attempt to explain.

# I

The starting point of such an explanation must be the immediate political universe within which the Labour Government had to operate, and to which the character and aspirations of its own leading members made a significant contribution. It should not be forgotten that the development of policy so often reflected the accidents of personality and the impact of political commitments within the Cabinet. This Labour Government's political composition was not quite that of its predecessor of 1964–70. The left wing of the Party was stronger within it, partly as a result of the inclusion of men like Michael Foot and (briefly) Eric Heffer, excluded from office hitherto, and partly because of the conversion of established Labour Ministers (most prominently Tony Benn) to more radical positions. Their presence acted throughout the Government's period of office as a barrier to the full sway of conservative pressures to which Labour Ministers were regularly subject in their dealings with civil servants, industrialists and financiers. There seems in addition to have been a collective determination among Ministers to avoid any repetition of the traumatic events of 1969, and this kept the Cabinet unusually close to leading trade union officials, and true to the procedural points of the social contract. The Government was determined to strengthen *official* trade unionism, and it did. Its concern with unemployment levels was undoubtedly genuine, and the overt 'managerialism' (and even antipathy towards trade unionism) which became so much a feature of the tone and content of Labour policy between 1966 and 1970 was much more muted this time. But it was there nonetheless. For the radicalism of the Labour leaders did not survive the years of office, and the presence within the Cabinet of a majority of men on the right and centre of the Party prevented any left-wing domination of the kind suggested by the adoption of the 1973 Programme.

The development of policy was thus first shaped by the nature of the Labour Party coalition, as this was reflected in the personalities, ambitions and political commitments that were represented inside the Labour Cabinet. That pattern of coalition was complex:[1] not least because of the persistence until the sad and untimely death of Anthony Crosland of a Gaitskellite revisionism as well. So to this degree there was some justification for the propensity of the political press to reduce policy disagreements within the Cabinet to the simple question of a struggle between individuals, to a 'battle between Healey and Benn', with the Chancellor increasingly in the ascendancy. Of course such descriptions did not explain why the choice over which the fight occurred was as it was, nor did a simple polarity of left and right exhaust the nuances of coalition within the Labour Party. But there can be no doubt that the presence of certain individuals within the Cabinet, each armed with a particular view of what was happening, of what was important and of what could be achieved, and each intensely ambitious in his or her own right, is an essential first element in any full explanation of why this Labour Government did not lose its close relationship with official trade unionism as it struggled for economic growth, and yet why this struggle for economic growth took it away from its initial programme.

The development of policy also reflected the weak *parliamentary* position of the Government. Its shaky hold on power encouraged Ministers to tolerate features of policy to which they were opposed in order to guarantee the passage 'before it was too late' of other pieces of legislation to which they were heavily committed. Michael Foot's defence of the Government's record at the Tribune meeting at the 1975 Labour Party conference relied heavily on this argument, and stressed the danger to the labour movement of any returned Conservative Government. From March to October 1974 the minority position of the Labour Government left it particularly vulnerable: subject to periodic threats of defeat on votes of confidence by a grand coalition of the fragmented Opposition parties; humiliated by irritating defeats on the detail of legislation in the Commons, and by opposition in the House of Lords to certain sections of its Trade Union Bill; and reminded repeatedly of its own precarious hold on power by the defection or death of MPs from its own ranks. From March to October 1974, with opinion polls reporting Labour and Conservative support in the country to be evenly matched, the political life of the new Labour Government was dominated by its own minority position, and by the inevitability of a new election.

That situation was only changed slightly by the Labour Party's acquisition of the tiniest of parliamentary majorities in October 1974. A majority of three for a party in which two of its members were under police investigation was not the strongest base from which to launch a busy legislative programme, and even that slender majority did not survive long. Technically, the majority was lost in February 1976, with the defection of two left-wing Labour MPs into a new Scottish Labour Party. In fact, divisions within the Labour ranks, and the inevitable incidence of sickness and unavoidable absence from the House by Labour backbenchers, was often to threaten policy before then. The Labour Government was unable to avoid periodic defeats on minor matters of detail: in the committee stage of the Police Bill in February 1976, for example, and on the second reading of the Bill on redundancy rebates a year later. Eric Varley had his salary as Secretary of State for Industry cut briefly in February 1976, when party managers failed to prevent a temporary Conservative majority on a vote of censure. Bigger defeats also came as a result of the Government's minority position and internal divisions. Two left-wing MPs forced the Chancellor to raise tax thresholds in June 1977; two right-wing Labour MPs had only to abstain in November 1976 to defeat their own Government's Dock Labour Bill, and that in a week in which the House of Lords had forced the Government to postpone the nationalisation of aircraft, shipbuilding and associated industries for at least twelve months, and had sent back four other Bills in a much amended form. All that occurred in the last week of one parliamentary session; and the Government fared no better in the next. By June 1977 it had been forced to abandon that session's major piece of legislation (on devolution for Scotland and Wales) when forty-one of its own backbenchers and eleven Liberals refused to cooperate with the Government's parliamentary timetable. In addition the Cabinet had repeatedly to delay publication of its Bill on direct elections to the European Assembly as four senior Ministers resisted its major clauses. As late as December 1978 the Government was unable to avoid the parliamentary defeat of its policy of sanctions against companies making settlements in excess of its income policy norms; and it was forced to go to the country in 1979 by its defeat on a motion of confidence – the first time this had occurred in British politics since 1924.

That the Labour Government should have been so vulnerable to defeat at any time in its last three years of office was a result of a series of appalling by-election results that reflected only too accurately its diminishing hold on popular support. Those by-election defeats were themselves foreshadowed in disastrous local government election results in 1976 and 1977. In May 1976 Labour lost control of many of its traditional strongholds in Wales, and Conservative gains were considerable throughout the English local government system. A year later, Labour lost control of the Greater London Council (GLC), and four of its six English metropolitan county councils, and saw the

Scottish National Party (SNP) capture 107 seats in the Scottish district elections. The Scottish results were particularly significant, implying a possible loss of seventeen out of forty-five vital Labour seats in Scotland in the next Parliament in any early general election. This pattern was repeated in the systematic swing to the Conservatives in English by-election after English by-election: in ten by-elections between June 1976 and April 1977 the swing to the Conservatives was never less than 7 per cent (at Grimsby in April 1977) and was at one time as high as 22 per cent (at Walsall the previous November). By April 1977 a Labour majority in the October 1974 general election of 23,000 at Ashfield was insufficient to prevent a Conservative taking the seat; and Labour had to govern as a minority party through the first half of 1977, knowing that any immediate general election would probably leave it defeated on the scale of 1931.

The most immediate political consequence of all this was the pact agreed between the Labour Cabinet and the Liberal Party in March 1977. Precipitated by a vote of confidence initiated by a reluctantly militant Conservative Opposition, the pact left the Labour Government formally dependent on Liberal support for its continuance in office. The initial pact between the two parties guaranteed Liberal support to the Government only to the end of the current parliamentary session, and this in return for the regular consultation of Liberal opinion by Labour Ministers, and in effect, for Labour Government openness to Liberal policy on indirect taxation, industrial democracy, direct elections to the European Assembly and the cessation of further public ownership. The Liberals made much of their new role, publicly parading their team of Shadow Ministers and stressing their determination to stop 'the further expansion of socialism'.[2] But in practice the Labour Government seemed only slightly and intermittently embarrassed by them. Certainly the Cabinet's decision to include a form of proportional representation (the regional list system) in its Bill on elections to the European Assembly, in the face of opposition from within the Parliamentary Labour Party, reflected Liberal pressure. So did the Chancellor's temporarily embarrassing inability to add a 5½p tax to petrol as part of his 1977 budget strategy. Harold Lever's new-found interest in the problems of small companies in 1978, the passage of the Conservative amendment to the 1978 budget reducing income tax by 1p, and the Government's inability to reply by increasing employers' National Insurance contributions by 2.5 per cent (they settled for the Liberals' 1.5 per cent instead) are further examples of the Liberal presence. The eventual Government proposals on industrial democracy also reflected Liberal views, as did the revamped proposals on devolution for Scotland and Wales which were presented to the 1977–78 session of Parliament. But over time it was the Liberals who were most embarrassed by their new role as maintainers in office of a government whose main lines of policy were already set. On purely constitutional issues, the Liberals could exert considerable leverage. But as policy touched the economy, they could only hope to shape the details and this is indicative of the kind of constraints which governments now face, to which the rest of this chapter is addressed. It was only with the greatest difficulty (and amid much public dissent within the Liberal parliamentary ranks) that David Steel was able to renew the pact with the Government into the next parliamentary session. In 1977–78 the Labour Government remained in power aware that the Liberals expected concessions in ten specified areas of policy, including legislation for direct elections to the European Assembly, devolution and industrial democracy, and especially the persistence of a Stage III incomes policy based on the maintenance of a 10 per cent limit on pay settlements in the public sector. All these were Government aspirations in any case, but the Liberal pact existed to toughen the resolve of Ministers subject to counter-pressures, and to win significant differences of detail in the legislation proposed.

It should not be thought however that the pact with the Liberals was the *cause* of the Labour Party's inability to pursue the more radical elements in its policy. Once established, the Liberal pact was one important *extra* factor for Labour Ministers to bear in mind. But as Neil Kinnock said in a radio interview immediately after the first pact was signed, it was nonsense for David Steel to claim that the significance of the pact lay in its prevention of any 'further extension of socialism'. That expansion had already been abandoned by a Labour Government under pressures that were rarely parliamentary in origin, and which only occasionally even found expression in parliamentary terms. The Liberal–Labour pact either restricted itself to purely constitutional questions (proportional representation, devolution and the like) or, on wider policy, merely reinforced patterns of Government activity already established. The main attraction of the pact, to both parties, was its ability to delay the electoral annihilation to which both seemed liable in the first half of 1977, and which, in the Labour Party's case at least, reflected popular reaction to the Government's failure to overcome problems (of inflation, unemployment and stagnation) which had nothing to do with constitutional niceties and which did not originate within the parliamentary arena. The two-year Liberal pact, that is, saw the Labour Government through from a period in which they were 16.5 per cent behind the Conservatives in the Gallup Poll to one in which they were only 2 per cent behind, and to a period in which by-election results (both in Scotland and in England) gave only an average 5 per cent swing against them.

## II

Simply because the Labour Government was politically weak, it would be quite wrong to assume that political factors alone explain the development of its policy and the drift away from radical pretensions. The key to that drift, as is presumably obvious to even the most casual observer, lies outside Parliament, in the relationships that existed between the Labour Government and the power groups it faced, and in the origins of the problems with which those relationships had to cope. In an earlier study of the Labour Party[3] I argued that whenever the Labour Party is in power it faces a complex set of interlocking centres of private power, whose general effect has been to erode the early radicalism of successive Labour Ministries. Each Labour Government since 1924 has tended to enter office with too inflated a sense of the power which it will be free to exercise, and too optimistic about the ease of reform and regeneration of a total society by a single parliamentary party. I argued then (1975) that the Labour Party is, of course, a coalition, and that many of its centre and right-wing MPs are only too aware of the difficulties and constraints they must face, and only too keen to shed the radical policies imposed on them at Labour Party conferences in opposition. I argued, too, that on the left of the Party generally, among those who agreed with Tony Benn that 'we are here to change society',[4] the conviction exists that, in spite of these constraints, a Labour Party with a parliamentary majority can achieve a programme of radical reforms if the political will to do so exists in the parliamentary leadership as a whole. But a detailed examination of the history of Labour Governments would suggest that in power Labour Ministers increasingly succumb to more moderate aspirations and more conservative policies as they experience the constraints which can be exercised against a reforming government by the centres of private power: by civil servants, by industrial firms and spokesmen for organised business, and by financiers, international financial agencies and foreign governments. In the face of this entrenched body of powerful private interests, each Labour Government to date has found that its one point of potential social power outside Parliament – the trade union movement – has been insufficient to act as a complete counterweight to the powerful orthodoxies of economic opinion to which Labour Ministers have been subject, and that as a result the main legacy of periods of Labour office has not been so much important social reforms as a growing tension between the Party and its disappointed supporters.

It is neither necessary nor desirable to repeat the detail of the argument here. The thesis that ran through *The Labour Party and the Struggle for Socialism* can still be read as a guide to the experience of the Labour Government that was just entering office as the study was published. Indeed what is striking about the years since 1974 is how the development of policy by this Labour Government has generated examples of precisely this set of constraints on Labour radicalism. A full explanation of what has happened to the Labour Government since 1974 requires much more than a specification of the way in which private élites blocked radical policies; but such an explanation requires that blocking to be established first, by a listing of what evidence is available on the interconnections between Labour Ministers and significantly placed groups of private power holders.

The most immediate group of people with whom Ministers have to deal are their own civil servants, and it is clear that this relationship continued to be a potential source of conservatism for a reforming Government. The full story of the way in which policy was formulated inside the ministries after 1974 has yet to be made public, but such evidence as has emerged continues to justify the view that day-to-day dealings with civil servants had a powerful impact on the development of Labour policy. Lord Crowther Hunt's survey of civil service power[5] stressed its growth, and the difficulty of ministerial control; and as the years of office lengthened after 1974 this power became an increasing theme in the Labour Left's explanation of what was going wrong. Hence Tribune's repeated condemnation of 'the Treasury mind', which received some indirect support from civil service opposition to the publication of the Crossman diaries on an earlier Labour Government. In these, Crossman gave his account of how difficult it can be for a Minister to overcome opposition to his policy from within his own department. Of course the diaries have to be handled with care. They are only one man's account, and there can be no guarantee either that his experience is typical or that his recollections are entirely reliable. But he repeatedly recorded the way in which his relationship with senior civil servants became a major problem for him, as an MP who at least at the beginning of his parliamentary career stood on the left of the Party.

This theme in the Crossman diaries received even greater emphasis in Joe Haines's strident condemnation of the way in which Treasury officials apparently pressed for a statutory incomes policy in July 1975, as reported in his controversial account of his years as Harold Wilson's press secretary, *The Politics of Power*. If this account is to be believed, there can be no doubt that Treasury conservatism stood as a major barrier to Labour Party radicalism, that civil service opposition to trade union power was marked, and that Labour Ministers could find their own bureaucrats so zealous at cutting public spending programmes that, as in August 1977, public sector expenditure would fall more rapidly than the Cabinet had intended.[6] It is clear, too, from Joe Haines's memoirs, as it was from a reading of the press in the opening year and a half of this Labour Government, that a reforming government must expect to come under pressure both from within the government machine and from business spokesmen outside, if only to shed its more radical personnel. According to Joe Haines, Labour Governments are perennially subject to 'the battle between the elected and the appointed';[7] and Harold Wilson, he reported, was under heavy pressure to sack Tony Benn (and Eric Heffer) through the first fifteen months of the Labour Government's period of office.

This example of extra-parliamentary pressure against the retention of office by radical ministers also serves to underline the fact that the Labour Government experienced many constraints from outside its own machinery. Its membership of the EEC provided a whole set of limits on its freedom of manoeuvre, through the standardisation of legislation and the necessity of implementing agreed EEC policy (not least on the thorny issue of 'unfair' subsidisation of nationalised industries) that gave the Labour Left repeated evidence for its defence of British sovereignty against the Brussels bureaucracy. At least one Minister – the Attorney-General – found the judiciary to be an obstacle, as they overturned his initial decision not to ban a trade union boycott of mail to South Africa. And, as we have already seen, a very large amount of the time of key Labour Ministers, particularly at the significant moments of policy adjustment, were taken up in direct negotiations with senior managerial personnel in private industry, and with the representatives of international financial agencies and financially powerful governments.

Historians of the CBI will correctly characterise this Labour Government as less responsive to CBI pressure than its 1964–70 predecessor; and at the level of the peak organisations of capital and labour there can be no doubt that throughout this Labour Government Ministers were more sympathetic to TUC personnel and pressure than to its CBI equivalent.[8] This is indeed so important an aspect of this Government's record that it requires separate and detailed assessment, which will come in Chapter 5. For the moment it must be stressed that the influence of organised business was not absent between 1974 and 1979. The CBI won from the Labour Government a steady erosion of its initially severe price controls, and was the main vehicle by which the Bullock Committee recommendations on industrial democracy were effectively blocked. And if the peak organisations of the business sector found Ministers less responsive than usual, individual firms found no such barrier between themselves and the government machine. This Government faced a higher degree of industrial concentration than any previous Labour Government. In common with other Western governments, the Labour Cabinet faced a world economy in which the largest 650 companies, operating on a multinational scale, were responsible for a combined turnover of 773 billion dollars a year in 1973, greater than the GNP of any country outside the USA and the USSR.[9] By 1970 one-half of the manufacturing output of the British economy came from just 140 firms, and financial institutions (particularly insurance companies) accounted for 55 per cent of all shares quoted in the Stock Market.[10] In this way, the growth of industrial concentration and capital ownership had gone hand-in-hand, with major consequences for the distribution of political power and for the autonomy of Labour Governments.

As we have seen, some features of Labour policy were direct casualties of that private concentration. The Government did not manage to impose an effective system of planning agreements on the top 100 companies, as it had intended. Nor was the NEB able to act as the catalyst for large-scale industrial reinvestment and growth as private industry's reluctance and inability to expand its scale of investment in the face of persistent inflation (and at times high rates of interest) persisted, and as larger and larger amounts of NEB funds were absorbed into the 'baling out' of British Leyland. The whole story of the Labour Government's involvement in the car industry after 1974 is relevant here. The ability of a multinational company to negotiate with a British Government on the basis of equality, with its worldwide preoccupations standing as a major barrier to any easy subordination of its policy to that of any one national government, was made explicit in the dealings of Labour Ministers with the senior managerial personnel at Chrysler. For all the brave talk in opposition of industrial regeneration through greater state control, the Labour Government went to a general election after more than five years in office with the British manufacturing sector still internationally weak, and with the big multinational corporations as autonomous of direct state control as ever.

The most visible set of external constraints, however, did not come from the manufacturing sector but from the world of finance, and from the direct negotiations on credit, trade liberalisation and world economic growth which the Labour Government held periodically with the finance ministers, central bankers and heads of state of the strong industrial powers: with the United States, with West Germany and with Japan. In many public speeches Labour Ministers stressed the dependence of their policies of economic growth and full employment on the willingness of these strong economies to reflate their levels of domestic demand and (in the case of Japan) to adjust the balance of their trade with the United Kingdom. In neither of these endeavours were Labour Ministers successful. Instead they were driven back, at critical junctures for the development of policy, to seek sources of foreign credit: from Arab governments with massive petrodollar surpluses, from central banks, and from the IMF. In seeking such credit, policy at home had to be tailored to meet foreign demands, initially indirectly, in that the Government felt itself obliged to follow internal policies which would persuade foreign creditors that an extension of credit was worth while, and eventually directly, as the Labour Government found the IMF willing to lend an extra credit-tranche in December 1976 only in return for a written undertaking that domestic economic policy would follow the lines agreed in negotiations between Treasury officials and IMF investigators in the autumn of 1976. Before that the Labour Government found that the power of big multinational companies and other foreign sterling holders to devalue the pound by speculative selling could force them to design policies that would reassure extremely nervous foreign exchange markets. That Ministers periodically failed, with resulting runs against the pound, only made it even more imperative as time passed that policy should be geared to stabilising the foreign exchange rate of the currency, and hence to reassuring foreign holders of sterling balances. This preoccupation alone cost the Government its radical policies, as cuts in public spending emasculated the aspirations of the opposition years. Then, after December 1976, when the pound stabilised against the background of by now orthodox government policies of retrenchment and wages control, the Labour Government still experienced periodic visits from IMF inspectors, keeping a watching brief on the continuing implementation of the economic policies which had been agreed in the sterling crisis.

So to understand the experience of Labour in office it is necessary to grasp the power – the power to initiate, the power to resist, the power to block and the power to circumvent – which is enjoyed in a society like ours by significantly placed groups of private individuals. Senior civil servants, senior managers in private industry, senior bankers and financiers, and major figures in foreign government had an impact on the policy of this Labour Government which was far in excess of their numbers; and it is for this reason that the character of the élites which the Government faces must constitute the first stage of any analysis of the development of Labour policy. But such an élite analysis is only a first stage, and the argument must now be carried further. The character of private élites in British society, important as it is as a constraint on Labour Governments, is not the main problem which faces the Left in Britain today. Rather, a full explanation of the development of Labour Government policy requires the recognition of the interconnections between the character and power of private élites and the nature of the economic and social processes which generated them, and to which they (no less than the Government) are now subject. It is not the class structure alone which constrains Labour radicalism, but the impact through that class structure of the *capitalist* economy on which it is built.[11]

This becomes particularly clear when we examine those features of the Labour Party's experience in office which the character of the élites it faced does *not* explain: when we examine, that is, those features of Labour Government experience in the 1970s which stand in sharp contrast to the experience of the first Wilson Governments of 1964–70. A full analysis of what happened to this most recent Labour Government has to explain, for example, how it was that Labour Ministers kept such a distance between themselves and the CBI, and why (and with what consequences) they established, in contrast, so intimate a set of relationships with the senior members of the trade union movement. The character of the élites themselves is little help in examining this. Nor can an explanation of Labour Government policy development which focuses on the character of the élite structure faced by Ministers adequately explain why the issues with which that structure, and that Government, were concerned, changed over time, when the élite structure itself, and even the personnel of successive Labour Governments, remained largely unaltered between 1964 and 1979.

To know that Labour Governments face conservative civil servants, businessmen and bankers remains essential to any explanation of how Labour Ministers in the 1970s perceived and reacted to the problems of inflation and unemployment with which they struggled. But it will not of itself explain why inflation and unemployment have come to be the main issues preoccupying Ministers and élites alike. Nor does it explain why inflation and unemployment have proved so difficult a set of issues for Labour Governments to resolve. And finally, no élite-based analysis can of itself explain the degree of autonomy and independence which even Labour Governments enjoy *against* the élites they face, nor specify the changing character of the role which the State clearly plays in accommodating the interests of some sections of the élite structure at the expense of others. To handle these questions it is necessary to go beyond the character of the élites to examine the economic, social and political processes to which both government and private élites are subject.

To do this it is essential to note first that in the 1970s neither private élites nor public figures either understood or were in complete control of the main processes which shaped the world economy over which they presided. This was the Labour Government's basic dilemma, that it did not control the origins or determinants of the processes it sought to handle and which it had to handle if its policy promises were to be realised. This lack of control went along with a lack of understanding within the Labour leadership (and indeed within the government machine generally) of the basic causes and character of the world it tried to govern. Of course it is true that each section of the economic power structure – the public bureaucracy, private business, international banking and finance – had a particular and often very complex view of the way prices and jobs, profits and growth were related. Each enjoyed a limited degree of autonomy and leeway in the handling of their affairs, such that how they reacted to developments in the world economy (and in its British section) helped to determine the route which those developments would then take. It would be ludicrous to claim that the managing director of a big multinational corporation, or a senior banker, were passive tools of unseen economic forces; and it is precisely for this reason that the character, aspirations and self-definitions of the private élites faced by Labour Governments must constitute a vital part of any analysis of the processes shaping government policy.

But the freedom of action of these élites was itself constrained, and the nature of those constraints has to be grasped as *the* key to the ultimate determinants of Labour Government policy, and as *the* problem to be faced by those attempting to devise a strategy for the Left in Britain in the 1980s. Simply because the reaction of significantly placed élites to their common experience of inflation and stagnation conditioned the development of those overriding features of economic and political life in the 1970s, it should not be thought that any one élite, or any group of élites, was actually responsible for the deliberate and conscious initiation of these overriding social evils. No group, and certainly no individual, no matter now well placed they were, controlled the entire economy. No one group invented inflation, nor was responsible, as a conscious act of private policy, for the rapid increase in world prices after 1970, not even the oil ministers of OPEC. No one individual or group fixed the rate of economic growth. No particular institution determined the relationship between levels of unemployment, levels of capital accumulation and the rate of increase in the price of consumer goods. Rather the élite structure acted as a framework within which governments had to react to problems and relationships of this kind, problems that were common to (and given and fixed for) the élites no less than the governments. Only to a limited degree did private élites specify independently the problems which the Labour Government faced, and the limits within which it had to operate. To a far greater degree these powerful institutions and personnel surrounding the Labour Government acted as mediators, channels, definers of problems and processes that were rooted elsewhere, beyond their control. This is the overriding feature of the power structure faced by the Labour Government in the 1970s.

What gave the business and financial élite their power (and their specific interests) was not simply the position they occupied in an international and interconnected industrial economy. What gave them their power and their interests, and what defeated the Labour Government, was the fact that that world economy was a *capitalist* one, subject to its own laws of development, its own contradictions and points of internal tension. It was the nature of international capitalism over many decades that had generated the structure of institutions and élites (including the trade union leadership) the Government had to face; and it was the particular character of the postwar development of world capitalism that gave the Labour Government of 1974 its agenda of problems: inflation, unemployment, stagnation, international competition, working-class militancy and social inequality. To understand the dilemmas facing the Labour Party in office in the 1970s it is essential to explore the significance of this fact in all its complexity, and to trace out the degree to which the response of Ministers to the élites and problems they met was conditioned by the fact that they did *not* recognise the capitalist nature of the universe in which they had to operate. To understand the events of the 1970s, to assess the true impact of élite constraints, to place the power of British trade unionism, and to discuss the future of the Left in Britain, the question of capitalism had to be faced, and its impact on British politics fully understood.

## III

There is a very distinct sense in which the unease surrounding the public use of a term like 'capitalism' reflects almost perfectly the central ambiguity that is faced by those who would defend capitalist institutions. Particularly when challenged, they clearly require a term with which to encapsulate the defining features of a social and political system to which they are so heavily committed that the prospect of any preferable alternative seems literally inconceivable, yet the very use of the term seems to allow for the possibility of just such alternative systems of production and exchange, whose absence must then be explained and whose inferiority must continually be demonstrated, or at least asserted or implied. It is no accident that fashions in terminology seem to follow variations in economic performance. In periods of social stability and economic growth the limits of the possible under capitalism are rarely evident or tested, and few people need to use the term. To talk unproblematically of 'industrial society' or 'the economy' becomes enough for all but the most intransigent communist. But in periods of severe recession, the *character* of this economy necessarily becomes an issue again. Defenders and critics alike must then widen the boundaries of debate, and with it the vocabulary of political discourse. When 'capitalism' is the regular subject of public debate in countries in which the Left is dominated by non-communist social democratic labour parties, this is a fair indication that economic and social difficulties are deepening.

Ever since Edward Heath reportedly denounced certain aspects of the Lonhro affair as 'the unacceptable face of capitalism' the term has been used with greater frequency than hitherto in public debate in Britain. For the first time since the 1940s it is now fairly conventional for at least left-wing Labour MPs periodically to specify that which is 'wrong with Britain' as its *capitalism*, and the solution which they have to offer as some form of 'socialism' – though there is a very distinct tendency (which is significant politically, as I argue later) for neither term to be very clearly or precisely specified. This is to be regretted, since such precision is vital if a full understanding of our situation is to be grasped. I discuss in Chapter 6 my sense of unease with the Labour Left's characterisation and its alternatives. But this is less important a task than that of providing a coherent alternative explanation of why the difficulties facing the Labour Government have to be understood in the context of the imperatives running through a system that is capitalist at its core. It is the argument of this book that the building of that explanation requires a return, not the speeches of Tony Benn, but to the writings of Karl Marx. The Labour Government's failure to achieve its policy objectives flows from its failure to recognise (and to adjust its whole political practice to the recognition) that the world it faces is still capitalist in the sense that Marx used the term; and therefore in order to understand the world in which we now live it is essential to begin by drawing heavily on Marx's characterisation of nineteenth-century capitalism. Of course this is a minority view, though one that is somewhat fashionable among left intellectuals these days; and the reader will do well to remember both that the interpretation and reinterpretation of Marx's analysis is full of controversies and pitfalls, and that the whole area is a minefield of sectarian dispute and political apologetics. But in spite of these difficulties, the task of relating Marx's writings to our times must be undertaken, and this is now being done by a growing number of young writers on the British Left. For them, and correctly in my view, it is significant for the lack of impact of Labour Governments over the years that Marx's writings are not widely known or studied in the British labour movement, and that even the vocabulary of a Marxist analysis of capitalism will sound strange to the ear of many a British socialist. This only makes it more essential than ever that in an analysis such as this, nothing should be taken for granted, and no prior familiarity with Marx's writings should be assumed, but that the analysis should rather be built logically, step by step and slowly, to indicate precisely the illumination of our present difficulties which such a Marxist strategy of analysis can bring. So for the moment (and with apologies to those already well versed in Marxist scholarship) I wish to leave the immediate problems of British politics in the 1970s on one side, to examine Marx's characterisation of nineteenth-century capitalism in some detail, as a base from which to return later, better equipped to isolate what seems to me to be the true nature of our current situation.

Marx's method in *Capital*, as is perhaps well known, was to proceed by abstraction and successive approximations to lay bare what he called 'the natural laws of capitalist production . . . the tendencies which work out with an iron necessity towards an inevitable goal'.[12] To locate these, it was necessary, Marx argued, to go beneath the appearance or surface of market relationships to move ever closer to the isolation of the essential processes that gave surface phenomena their shape: to move from the study of prices and exchange relationships to the study of values and the relationships of production. Marx's analysis was rooted in his wider 'materialist conception of history' by which he argued that what distinguished men and women from other animal species was, ultimately, that they and they alone worked systematically on their natural environment to produce the food, and clothing, the dwellings and the other artifacts by which to sustain themselves. And that this *process of labour,* in all but the most rudimentary forms of social existence, involved men and women in the establishment of regular and cooperative relations with others. The form that those social relationships took bore an intimate connection to the methods of production available to those generations of people, so that the whole historical process could be understood, Marx wrote, as 'nothing but the succession of the separate generations, each of which exploits the materials, the capital funds, the productive forces handed down to it by all preceding generations, and thus on the one hand continues the traditional activity in completely changed circumstances and, on the other, modifies the old circumstances with a completely changed activity'.[13] This view of history was central to Marx's analysis of capitalism: that, at any point in time,

There is found a material result; a sum of productive forces, an historically created relation of individuals to nature and to one another, which is handed down to each generation from its predecessor; a mass of productive forces, capital funds and conditions which, on the one hand, is indeed modified by the new generation, but also on the other prescribes for it its conditions of life and give it a definite development, a specific character . . . circumstances make men just as much as men make circumstances.[14]

This is not to say that, for Marx, men and women were to be understood solely as generations of producers. Clearly they also develop intimate and many-sided personal relationships, complex political structures and cultural systems, which then condition the nature of human activity. But a close examination of historical experience suggested to Marx that political, social and economic epochs could best be distinguished from each other by the forms of production and the associated set of social relationships which predominated within them; and that moreover, when all the complexities of social structure had been allowed for, it remained remarkably true that those predominant social relationships had always tended to take an antagonistic and a class form. In epoch after epoch, the population would be split internally, divided into a large class of producers generating artifacts by their labour, yet dominated by a smaller ruling class who were not engaged directly in production themselves, but who survived by expropriating in various ways the surplus part of the subordinate class's production for their own private use. Thus Antiquity – the city states of Greece and Rome – rested in their essence on a slave form of production, in which a slave-owning ruling class lived off the agrarian surplus of a slave-based economy;[15] just as in the pure form of European feudalism a military and religious ruling class expropriated the surplus produced by the mass of the population who were tied to the land as serfs. Each system of production, slave or feudal, Marx said, had its internal motor of development, and its own internal set of contradictions, such that in the end each went into internally generated decay. But what is crucial for an understanding of our present situation is not the detail of Marx's economic history: it is rather that, for Marx at least, capitalism is to be understood as yet another system of production and associated set of social relationships, the most recent the Western world has known, with its own historical origins in feudalism, and its own particular set of social contradictions. The world has not always been capitalist, Marx argued, nor need it always continue to be. But while capitalism prevailed, certain inexorable tendencies, certain natural laws, would be evident within it, which would condition the freedom of manoeuvre of governments, employers and workers alike.

What then were these natural laws? To isolate them it is necessary first to make clear how capitalism differs from the feudalism which preceded it. Production in feudal Europe was overwhelmingly agricultural in kind, and subsistence in purpose; capable only of sustaining a tiny (often urban) concentration of artisan producers working on agricultural materials (leather, corn, hops, and the like) and on simple metals. It was a society in which trade and exchange was relatively restricted, and in which the ruling class's expropriation of the serf's surplus product was open and direct. By a mixture of political and religious domination the ruling class successfully obliged the bulk of serf labour in feudal Europe either to work their lord's land directly for part of the working week, or later to commute that labour duty into a tax payment in cash or in kind. The capitalism that emerged from that feudal society was not a system geared to subsistence farming, nor one that expropriated its surplus in so open and so political a way. Under capitalism, and really for the first time in human history, production came to be geared exclusively to exchange. What was to be produced were goods and services to be sold as *commodities*, things that were not consumed by the immediate producer. Money and trade stood, and still stand, at the heart of capitalism, as do the two great social classes whose creation over many centuries brought feudalism down.

The rise of capitalism required the creation and growth of a class of men who lived by exchange, whose purpose was to enhance their own surplus by the making and exchanging of goods. Merchants, landowners, industrialists and eventually financiers, formed the new capitalist class, owning the raw materials and tools – the capital – with

165

which other men and women would make commodities from whose sale the capitalist class would prosper. The emergence of such a class, with such a set of preoccupations, involved a complex process of legal and political changes whose overwhelming impact was to consolidate the rights of private property, and which served to quicken that other unparalleled social transformation of an unprecedented scale which capitalism required: namely the creation of a proletariat. For capitalism was not, and is not, simply a system of commodity production. Even slave economies could be that. What is new to capitalism is that labour-power itself has become a commodity. Capitalism, for Marx, is a system of commodity production based on free wage labour, and its creation required the transformation of a European peasantry tied to the land in various forms of serfdom into a proletariat divorced from any rights over the land and obliged as a result to sell their labour in return for money wages. This creation of a proletariat happened slowly in England, more rapidly in later capitalist nations; and in England it involved initially the sale of labour to an emerging merchant class, then to a commercialising agricultural land-owning strata, and only finally to the industrial capitalists of the post 1760 period. But everywhere the process was in essence the same, and involved the creation for the first time in human history of a mass of labourers who, because they were denied ownership (or any other rights) over either the materials and tools with which they worked or the commodities which their labour produced, were as a result obliged repeatedly to sell their labour to a capitalist ruling class, to agree that is, to produce commodities in return for money wages.

It was Marx's view that, in this process, the true nature of social relationships became obscured behind the fetishism of commodities, and that nowhere is this inversion of reality more evident than in the analysis of the new social order offered by bourgeois economists. In their writings, the new forms of social relationships created by capitalism were taken as natural, inevitable and unproblematic, and the task of economics restricted to the analysis of the market process by which commodities, once produced, circulated and were consumed. Yet beneath this sphere of circulation, Marx argued, lay the production process, and at its heart, the crucial relationship between wage labour and capital that held the key to the overall development of capitalist society. For Marx this relationship between wage labour and capital was necessarily exploitative and antagonistic. Capital, whether expressed in the form of money, stocks, machinery or unsold finished goods, existed and could grow, Marx wrote, only by the expropriation of the surplus value of labour power. The capitalist started out with his stock of wealth which he wished to enhance by initiating a process of production and exchange. This circuit of production (from his original money $M$ into commodities $C$ and back into money $M'$) required the value of $M'$ to exceed that of $M$, and somewhere in the circuit that increment of value had to accrue. Since Marx worked with the assumption in Volume 1 of *Capital* that commodities, once produced, exchange at their value, and even in Volume 3 that 'the law of value dominates the movement of prices',[16] he was able to argue that a fully developed capitalism does not need to rely on processes of buying cheap and selling dear in order to generate profits, even though such 'swindling in exchange' remains a feature of imperialism, and was the prime source of merchants' capital in the early stages of capitalist development. In a fully developed capitalist system, Marx argued, the acquisition of a surplus occurs in the prior process of production, in the exploitation of labour power by capital. Under capitalism labour is itself a commodity, bought and sold like any other. And as such it has a value in the exchange process, one determined (as was the exchange value of all commodities for Marx) by the amount of socially necessary labour power that had gone into its production.* The exchange value of labour time was thus fixed by the socially necessary amount of other people's labour that had gone into the production of the commodities which the labourer and his family would consume to sustain themselves. Yet labour was no ordinary commodity, according to Marx. It alone had the unique feature of being value-creating. The application of labour power to other commodities (raw materials and semi-finished goods) enhanced their value in the subsequent process of exchange. It was from this gap between the value which labour created and the wage price it received that the capitalist found his surplus value and his subsequent accumulation of capital; and it was the ratio between the surplus value produced and the mass of values consumed by labour ($S/V$ in Marx's notation) that established the rate of exploitation of labour.

It should be noted that not all labour, for Marx, generated extra value. Only labour that was directly exchanged with capital for the purpose of augmenting capital added to the total stock of values available to the

---

* As Marx explained in volume 1 of *Capital*, the amount of time required to produce a given commodity (and hence to fix its value in the exchange process) would be determined by the state of technology prevailing and the customary speed of work. To work more slowly, or to use outdated machinery, would not give extra exchange value to the commodities produced, but would simply (via competition) drive the sluggish out of production altogether, leaving prevailing modes of technology and work paces as 'socially necessary'. Crucially, of course, technical change could *reduce* the socially necessary amount of labour time required to produce a commodity, and this pattern of technical change is, for Marx, a significant feature of capitalism.

167

capitalist class as a whole: and this meant that the existence of a large body of unproductive workers engaged in government and industrial supervision could only reduce the amount of surplus available for reinvestment as capital. But for 'productive' labour the situation was clear: capital would employ labour only so long as the capitalist, in exchanging the goods produced by his labour force, could realise in that exchange more values than were consumed in the wages of the labourers he employed. The wage bargain would help to mask that exploitation, with wages apparently fixed as a full payment for the entire stock of values produced by the labourer in the wage period. But in reality wages would tend to reflect only that part of the working day equivalent to the time involved in the production of the commodities which the labourer himself would consume. The remaining hours of the labourer's day would provide surplus value, which when realised by the capitalist through the sale of the day's entire production, would constitute the profit on which future capital accumulation depended.

According to Marx, the capitalist was a new actor on the human stage. By his position in the predominant system of social relations under capitalism he was driven necessarily to seek constantly to enhance the stock of values that was his capital, and he could do that only by repeatedly reimmersing it in the processes of production and exchange. In societies where production was geared to the satisfaction of the producers' immediate needs, the production process could be expected to end whenever those needs had been met. But under capitalism, where production was, and remains, geared to the repeated expansion of the stock of values that is capital, then the process became endless. The only way in which capital could be expanded was by the further expropriation of surplus value from the labour time of the proletariat, and that involved the repeated organisation by the capitalist class of production and exchange.[17]

For this reason, according to Marx, capitalism became the first social system in which the perpetual striving to expand production came to predominate, such that capitalism's propensity for what now would be called 'economic growth' served to distinguish production in our epoch from the more static and set production patterns and levels of its feudal predecessor. Capitalism, as Marx and Engels made clear in *The Communist Manifesto*, institutionalised change, and in the process became the first system of production which necessarily operated on a world scale. Yet with this propensity for growth capitalism also brought instability, anarchy, and the deprivation of the working class. Sections of the *Manifesto* made that clear, too. Thus on the one hand the *Manifesto* is a hymn to the success and productive potential of the new social order.

The bourgeoisie, during its rule of scarce one hundred years [Marx and Engels wrote in 1848], has created more massive and more colossal productive forces than have all preceding generations together. Subjection of Nature's forces to man, machinery, application of chemistry to industry, and agriculture . . . what earlier century had even a presentiment that such productive forces slumbered in the lap of social labour.

But with this growth has come anarchy too.

The bourgeoisie cannot exist without constantly revolutionising the instruments of production, and thereby the relations of production, and with them the whole relations of society. Conservation of the old modes of production in unaltered form was, on the contrary, the first condition of existence of all earlier industrial classes. Constant revolutionising of production, uninterrupted disturbance of all social conditions, everlasting uncertainty and agitation distinguish the bourgeois epoch from all earlier ones. . . . Modern bourgeois society, with its relations of production, of exchange and of property, a society that has conjured up such gigantic means of production and exchange, is like the sorcerer, who is no longer able to control the powers of the nether world whom he has called up by his spells.[18]

This contradiction between the immense productive potential that capitalism releases and its anarchic social effects grows out of the tension between wage labour and capital that lies at the heart of the system. For according to Marx, if the capitalist class can survive only by enhancing the stock of values that it expropriates from the labour it employs, only two general strategies are open to it as a class: either to lengthen the working day of the labour force in absolute terms (to increase, that is, the proportion of labour time spent in the production of surplus value) or to reduce that part of the working day necessary to sustain labour (either by intensifying the labour process, or by increasing labour's productivity, both of which would act to reduce the amount of socially necessary labour time absorbed into the production of the commodities which labour itself consumes). In fact there are real limits to the extent to which the working day can be lengthened: both the physiological limits set by the human body, and the social limits set by working-class resistance. And similar limits are bound in the end to block any persistent intensification of the labour process, though pressure to make labour 'work harder' remains a regular feature of capitalist production. So for these reasons and over time, the main consequence of capital's need to grow manifests itself as a tendency to increase the productivity of labour by the application of machinery to production. Persistent and unavoidable technical change, and the perpetual addition to the volume of the means of production, are the main initial consequences of the search for the accumulation and reaccumulation of capital.

But of course the systematic application of machinery to production alters the balance between machinery and men in the production process – alters what Marx refers to as the *technical composition of capital*. In doing so it acts to reduce the proportion of new values being added to the production process. As the scale of production increases, as the size of the means of production grows, the amount of new value being added, as a proportion of the total stock of values (capital) involved in production, falls because this new value can only be provided by the diminishing proportion of labour input into the whole production process. That is, for Marx, there is an inexorable tendency under capitalism for the changing technical composition of capital (machines : men) to be mirrored by a changing *organic composition of capital* (the ratio of constant capital to variable capital in his terminology, or 'the amount of labour time set in motion by a given capital'[19]). The greater productivity of labour which the application of machinery produces guarantees that the organic composition of capital will not change as rapidly as its technical composition; but as the stock of capital grows down the generations, it becomes harder and harder for the capitalist class to achieve a growth rate in productivity which will more than offset the effect on the organic composition of capital that results from a diminished dependence on labour power in production, such that in the end this will be reflected (other counter-tendencies aside), according to Marx, in the propensity of the rate of profit to fall.

This gives capitalism its central contradiction. Capital can grow only from the expropriation of the surplus value of labour power, and is therefore dependent on the application of labour to production. But to increase that surplus capitalists must apply ever more and more machinery to production, so reducing the proportion of their total outlay which can yield a surplus. The only solution available to capital is the perpetual expansion of its scale of production, thereby increasing the total volume of surplus value while allowing the rate of surplus to fall. For labour this means that capitalism pursues contradictory tendencies: creating an ever wider proletariat as a basis for capital accumulation, while at the same time shifting the pattern of production away from labour power to machinery, from living to dead labour, in Marx's terminology. This *law of value* – or as he had it, this 'general absolute law of capital accumulation' – has the effect of creating unemployment (Marx's 'industrial reserve army') and of bringing down the rate of profit unless counter-tendencies operate.* Such counter-tendencies act either to alter the organic composition of capital or to increase the rate of exploitation of labour, and *their potency will ultimately be determined*, Marx argued, *by the relative strengths of capitalism's two great social classes, by the degree of working-class resistance and struggle*.

The general propensity for the rate of profit to fall can be ameliorated, as we have seen, by the associated growth in labour productivity, which so cheapens the mass of products that more and more of the working day is left as a source of surplus value. It can be ameliorated by any lengthening of the working day or intensification of the labour process that the capitalist class can achieve, by their ability to hold wages below their value, by cheapening the elements of constant capital, or by foreign trade. However, Marx argued, none of these counter-tendencies were inexhaustible. The degree of working-class resistance would block any persistent capacity to increase the exploitation of labour directly; in addition, the physical limits that exist to the total amount of surplus value that any one worker can produce (namely the maximum length of the working day) and the fact that increases in productivity of a sufficient scale will be progressively more difficult to achieve, means that eventually the changing organic composition of capital will result in a declining rate of profit. The underlying contradiction between wage labour and capital will then leave, on the surface of economic relationships, a cruel paradox for the employing class: that the mass of profits can grow, and the exploitation of labour intensify, but still the rate of profit will have a tendency to fall.

This propensity of the rate of profit to fall was, for Marx, only the most important manifestation of the underlying character of capital itself: namely its contradictory relationship with wage labour. That contradictory relationship meant that the productive system under capitalism 'was necessarily driven to seeking a higher and higher productivity of labour in order to produce sufficient surplus value for the continuous reproduction and expansion of the growing capital'. But

---

\* There is currently a dispute on the status of these counter-tendencies: whether they too must be seen as a tendency of equal or greater force than that of the tendency of the rate of profit to fall. The question is critical, for if the counter-tendencies are of such force then the motor of change and crisis under capitalism comes to be the degree of working-class struggle – that is, the focus of crisis moves from the sphere of production to that of distribution (or at least the focus of analysis must shift from the inner logic of capital to the determinants of working-class reality and political radicalism considered *sui generis*). For various positions in this debate, see G. Hodgson 'The theory of the falling rate of profit', *New Left Review*, 84 (1974, pp. 54–84), I. Steedman, 'Value, price and profit', *New Left Review*, 90 (1975, pp. 71–80) and B. Fine and L. Harris 'Recent controversies in Marxist economic theory', in R. Miliband and J. Saville, eds, *The Socialist Register* (Merlin Press, 1976).

this did not produce unending and smooth economic growth. On the contrary, Marx argued that the process of expansion under capitalism was necessarily contradictory in character. The rate of surplus value could not in the end rise as rapidly as the mass of surplus value. Inevitably, at some point, the system would generate 'an underproduction of surplus value in relation to the growing mass of total capital'.[20] At that point, given the degree of labour exploitation prevailing, any further capital invested would not yield sufficient profits, and the process of expansion would be blocked. Capital would be momentarily overproduced in relation to existing levels of exploitation, and capital and labour would both experience a typical capitalist crisis. This is the kernel of Marx's argument, that the inner logic of capital, the contradictory relationship it experiences with labour, gives a perpetual instability to a capitalist economy, gives it a propensity to crisis; and although any particular economic crisis has to be explained 'out of the real movements of capital production, credit and competition, it is the general tendency of the accumulation process itself, and the long-run tendency of the rate of profit to fall, that constitutes the basis of that explanation'.[21] Or as Marx put it in Volume 3 of *Capital*, 'the real barrier to capitalist production is capital itself'.

It is worth examining Marx's view of capitalist crisis in a little detail, not least because of the controversy which still surrounds its interpretation.[22] Within the Marxist camp two schools of crisis theory have tended to emerge: one stressing the way in which crisis is caused by the necessary underconsumption of the mass of the working class (that is, by the overproduction of consumer goods), the other emphasising the problems of the producer goods sector, and the impossibility of sustaining a sufficient rate of profit to finance further expansion there. Marx himself stressed the role of both processes in the creation of crises. The possibility of such a crisis, of a breakdown in the regular pattern of economic activity, was made possible by the very separation of the act of production from that of consumption, which occurs on a major scale for the first time under capitalism. As Marx made clear in Volume 1 of *Capital* there is always some chance that the two would fall out of line, that the amount of commodities available for sale would no longer coincide with the volume of commodities that the market would absorb. Indeed, he stressed that capitalism ultimately could not avoid this contradiction, between its need for high levels of demand through which to realise profits and its parallel need for low wages to facilitate accumulation; and in this sense the restricted purchasing power of the mass of the working class remained for Marx the ultimate form in which capitalism's propensity for crisis manifested itself. But he recognised, too, that the anarchy of capitalism's market relationships made crises of 'disproportionality' unavoidable also. Whenever the production of investment goods fell out of line with the needs of the consumer goods sector, crisis could ensue in the form of a chain reaction of company failures, factory closures, unemployment and falling wages. The fact that money was used to lubricate the process of production and exchange under capitalism also generated the possibility of crises resulting from a breakdown in the flow of money – crises of confidence and credit. Indeed, Marx pointed out that any specific disturbance in the circulation of money could generate crises, not simply in market relationships, but crises that went back into the production process itself, shutting factories, laying off workers and leaving machinery idle. It required only political instability, a crop failure, bad banking practice or corruption in vital financial insitutions to set such a crisis in train.

The fact that such an incident could generate a crisis was not of itself an explanation of why that crisis should happen, nor of the form that such a crisis would take; and economists who attempted to argue that such explanations sufficed were heavily criticised in *Capital*. For Marx, a major defect of the bourgeois economics with which he was familiar was that, precisely by restricting its analysis to the sphere of circulation (to an examination of the market process, to seeing how goods already produced were exchanged) it could not hope to understand that the roots of market instability lay outside the market, in the prior process of production in which commodities gathered the values by which they would later be exchanged. For Marx, the key to capitalist instability lay in the social relationships surrounding the production process, such that, although the instability of capitalist production always manifested itself at the level of circulation, as a crisis of underconsumption, it did not originate there. The origins, and ultimate source of resolution of capitalist crisis, for Marx, lay in the contradictions between wage labour and capital in the process of production itself.

For as the rate of profit falls, Marx argued, competition between individual capitals can be expected to intensify. Precisely because 'capital exists and can only exist as many capitals',[23] competition between different capitals provides the mechanism through which the inherent tendencies of capital are realised, and as such incessant competition becomes capitalism's most evident feature, 'the essential locomotive of bourgeois economy' as Marx called it.[24] It is through competitive struggle that the total level of surplus generated is divided between various capitals (both between national capitalisms, between sectors within any one national capitalism, and between individual firms within any productive sector); and as the tendency of the rate of profit to fall operates, the competitive mechanism becomes crucial as the means whereby capital can be restructured to generate the basis for a fresh period of accumulation. The struggle for profits throughout the production process will inspire the development of new inventions, new markets, new sources of raw materials, whose temporary generation of a price advantage for the successful innovator will soon be eradicated by their general adoption through the system, and later by yet more innovation by competitors. In this way the rise and fall of firms and industries, and the perpetual readjustment of work processes and skills, are unavoidable under capitalism; and this instability and flux is never more evident than in the periodic depressions which hit the world economy as a whole.

Marx's theory of capitalist crisis cannot be divorced from his general analysis of the total process of capital accumulation. For Marx, that process was necessarily crisis ridden, a perpetual race between the rising organic composition of capital (which erodes the rate of profit) and the rising rate of labour exploitation (which acts as a counter-tendency to sustain it). In periods of economic upswing, when such counter-tendencies are in the ascendancy, the rate of capital accumulation, and the growth rate of total profits, will be more than sufficient to offset the tendency of the rate of profit to fall; and in this period employment will rise and real wages can increase whilst profit margins are still sustained. As Paul Mattick puts it: 'If the accumulation is large enough, the greater mass of capital at a higher organic composition will yield the same or a greater profit than that brought forth by a smaller total capital of lower organic composition.'[25] When this ends, as necessarily it must as the counter-tendencies to the propensity of the rate of profit to fall begin to weaken, the full force of capitalist crisis develops again.

In these periods of crisis in capitalism, when capital is temporarily overproduced in relation to existing levels of surplus value, the competitive nature of market relationships acts as the main mechanism by which the total stock of capital is reduced to a level commensurate with a new period of accumulation. War, and the physical destruction of capital stocks, will achieve the same result; but more normally it will be attained by the abandonment of obsolete capital units, by the swallowing, that is, of weaker and smaller capital units by larger and stronger ones in which higher levels of labour exploitation already exist. The resulting unemployment of labour in such a crisis also permits real wages to be depressed, and reduces the ability of labour to resist processes of 'rationalisation' (the intensification of existing work patterns and the extensive mechanisation of production) which together allow for a revival in the rate of expropriation of surplus value by the larger capital units which survive. The instability of capitalism thus manifests itself, for Marx, in the periodic abandoning of old capital stocks, *the increasing centralisation and concentration of capital*, and the greater exploitation of labour, which together allow profitability to be restored and a new cycle of capitalist production and competition to begin. In this way the crisis, 'whilst representing an end to the accumulation process, is nevertheless the precondition for its continuation on a higher level'[26]. Such crises in capitalism are thus not simply the most dramatic manifestation of the tension between wage labour and capital; they are also the mechanism by which that tension is temporaily abated, and a new period of economic growth initiated.

It is clear, too, from Marx's writings that this propensity to crisis would never of itself generate the *final* breakdown of capitalism, though many later Marxists introduced such a determinism into the analysis. For Marx, crises were only a manifestation of the deeper contradiction between wage labour and capital, a contradiction which would always be resolvable so long as labour itself was prepared to bear the instability and deprivation that this would involve. In this very important sense, *capitalism's capacity to transcend its crises always depended on the combativity of its working class*; and the relative strengths of the various national capitalisms were bound to be intimately affected by the degree of supineness of their respective proletariats. For Marx, the degree of class struggle, though not itself the cause of the tendency of the rate of profit to fall, certainly conditioned its speed, and critically affected the distribution of that diminishing surplus between the competing parts of the capitalist world economy. Marx himself felt that such forebearance by the emerging working class would only be shortlived, and that ultimately the crisis of capitalism would manifest itself *politically*, in the rise of a revolutionary socialist proletariat. He argued that work under capitalism would be a profoundly *alienating* experience, as men and women came to find that the activity which was most defining of their humanity – productive labour – was reduced to the level of a commodity, a thing to be bought and sold, and the needs of its suppliers subordinated to the prior demands of capital expansion and commodity production. Marx argued, too, that the constant competitive struggle that was endemic to capitalism would be experienced by the proletariat as a process of perpetual instability, job insecurity and work pressure; and that this would erode working-class toleration of, and support for, the new social order. He was well aware that in periods of economic upswing real levels of wages might rise, and that this might help to consolidate working-class toleration of the capitalist system. But it was his view that over the long period, the working class would experience a widening gap between their living standards and those of the bourgeoisie, that unemployment would come to be an ever greater threat to them, and that the incidence and severity of economic crises would deepen, with all that that entailed for general impoverishment, and for working-class oppression.

For all these reasons Marx anticipated that the necessary response of labour to this would be a collective one: first defensive in trade unions, and later assertively political; and that the working class would go forward from a rejection of capitalism's impact on their lives to the creation of a totally new social order. It was not his view that capitalism would manage to find new and prolonged methods of legitimation that would prevent the rise of revolutionary movements against it. For him, the indication of capitalism's contradiction lay in the growing tension between society's productive potential and its actual social deprivation (between the *social* development of the productive forces and the *private* nature of capitalist appropriation), but its resolution could only be a political act, by a revolutionary socialist working class; and that revolution, he believed, would not be long in coming.


# IV

What is the relevance of all this to the situation faced by Labour Governments in Britain? Of course there is no way in which *Capital* can be taken as a total and unambiguous guide to the detail of social and political life a century after its publication. The very claim that it can be must be dismissed as ludicrous, and indeed profoundly non-Marxist in its specification of the relationship between theory and practice. Whatever *Capital*'s status is, it is not that of Holy Scripture, and the Left has suffered too long from the reduction of scholarship to the studying of holy writ, and from the use of quotations from the founding fathers of Russian Bolshevism as a substitute for much-needed fresh analysis. After all, Marx's writings contain a number of very serious errors; not least, his underestimation of the degree of political stability which capitalism in Western Europe and the United States would experience through the incorporation of the working class into the ruling political structures. That, after all, is the critical legacy with which present Marxists have to come to terms, a legacy which Marx certainly did not expect and to whose prevention his whole life work was dedicated. Nor did he anticipate that a revolution would be made in his name in the most backward of the major capitalist nations in 1917, and that in its isolation, that revolution would degenerate into a political dictatorship which would use his writings to justify the consolidation of the very system of wage labour to whose transcendence he was so dedicated. In any case, those writings remained incomplete at his death, and their characterisation of capitalism remained highly abstract and approximate, and it would be dishonest to pretend that their central categories and assertions are without their problems and their critics. To this day, both within and beyond the Marxist tradition, unresolved debates continue on the status and adequacy of the labour theory of value, on the problem of translating Marx's analysis of value formation under capitalism into an adequate theory of price determination, on the propensity of the rate of profit to fall, and on the epistemological status of Marx's categories and their susceptibility to empirical refutation.[27]

The thesis that underpins this analysis of the Labour Government is that this 'celebrated "failure" of Marxism is a failure not of economic theory but rather of the social and political expectations based on it'.[28] Yet in the 1950s few would have argued that so much could be usefully salvaged from the wreckage of working-class revolutionary failure and Stalinist degeneration. Until recently in Western Europe it was conventional among the vast majority of practising economists (outside the Communist parties) to dismiss Marx's economic writings as anachronistic, rendered redundant at the level of micro-economics by the rise of marginalism, and at the level of the national economy by the writings of John Maynard Keynes. And these developments in the field of economic theory seemed to be matched by the very dynamism of capitalism to which Marx attached such importance, such that the economies of Western Europe in the postwar period seemed for many commentators to be far removed from the capitalism that he described. Political and economic stability in the West since 1945, high levels of personal consumption on a mass scale, the new and enlarged role of the State, the rise of trade unionism, the emergence of new managerial strata, the sophistication in technology, the degree of capital concentration and the sheer volume of production – all were singled out by a generation of writers and political analysts in the 1950s to demonstrate the irrelevance of Marx's theoretical legacy. Anthony Crosland's writings within the Labour Party, and those of John Strachey, remain major examples of the explicit rejection of Marxism by the postwar generation of social democratic intellectuals.[29] But the optimism of that generation has come to grief on the re-emergence of unemployment and inflation in the Western economies, and on the difficulties of handling the re-emergence of these phenomena in

177

conventional Keynesian terms. The truth of Paul Mattick's remark that 'the Keynesian solution to the economic problems that beset the capitalist world can be of only temporary avail, and that the conditions under which it can be effective are in the process of dissolution'[30] is now more obvious. To understand the Labour Party's predicament in office in the 1970s requires more than the categories of Keynes and the optimism of Crosland. The writings of Marx have their relevance again.

If the problems facing Labour Governments in the 1970s and 1980s are to be correctly specified, they must be approached through an analysis of the world which the Labour Party seeks to govern. Such an analysis must be able to say why particular institutions and processes pose such a set of problems for individual Labour Governments, why particular issues come to preoccupy political debate in one period only to dwindle in importance in the next, why particular patterns of political and social cleavage prove so tenacious, and why the institutions created and sustained by the labour movement (both trade unions and the Labour Party itself) have only a limited impact on (while making a quite consistent set of responses to) these dominant institutions, cleavages and issues. Indeed the acid test by which to distinguish the relative merits of the various theories offered in explanation of our current political condition lies here: in their relative ability to make intelligible the full complexity of postwar experience in the fields of economics, industrial relations and government policies – to make clear, that is, the totality of the main processes to which the Labour Party has had to respond and which even now provide its agenda of action, its targets for control, and its ultimate constraints. Such a total analysis will obviously be many-sided, and will require much more than an explanation of the logic of economic activity in the West. It will involve, among other things, a detailed assessment of the nature of political parties, the character of cultural systems, and the dynamics of social stratification. But the overwhelming impact of economic issues on political life necessitates that, at its core, such an analysis must be able both to explain this primacy of the economic and to specify the defining features of economic life in our epoch. It must be able to explain in a detailed, consistent and integrated fashion a whole range of contemporary economic phenomena, including the pattern of economic activity in the West since 1945, the sequence of booms and slumps, employment levels and inflation, the differing strengths of the national economies, the rise and significance of multinational corporations, the role of international financial agencies, the origins and character of tensions and disputes in industrial relations, the nature and determinants of working-class political loyalties, and the changing role of governments in economic and social life. Clearly such an undertaking is a formidable one, necessarily tentative and exploratory in kind. But the task, though vast, is not impossible. There *is* a coherence and an underlying logic in the sequence of institutions, cleavages and issues that Labour Governments have faced – the logic of capitalism itself. So what must hold the analysis together is the recognition that the world is still *capitalist* in the sense that Marx used the term. The law of value still operates throughout its major economic and social processes; and this means that if we are to grasp the nature of the choice before the Labour Party we have first to specify the character of postwar capitalism and its consequences for the British labour movement and the British State. It is for this reason that the preceding outline of Marx's analysis remains relevant, for it provides the means by which the true nature of the Labour Government's dilemmas can be isolated and understood.

How then are we to understand the postwar boom and its culmination in stagnation and inflation? We must begin by recognising that the postwar boom would have been inconceivable without the interwar depression of world capitalism, and in particular that it required for its occurrence both the destruction of militant labour movements in the fascist period and six years of worldwide war. These traumatic events, appalling as they were, at least prepared the conditions for a fresh period of capital accumulation. The resulting period of sustained economic growth had at its base the massive destruction of capital between 1939 and 1945 and the associated political, military and economic supremacy of the United States. America, alone of the capitalist powers, emerged from the war with its economy intact, able to impose a new economic and political order on the entire world economy outside the Soviet bloc. Its postwar dominance established the dollar as the basis of world currency, and opened non-communist markets to American capital. A significant feature of the postwar period was the supply of American capital to the Western European governments, to restore Western European private capitalism and to open European markets to American goods. After 1952 the United States government ran regular balance of payments deficits, as American capital came abroad and as United States defence spending which helped to protect that capital continued to grow; and this supply of American currency (supported by sterling) lubricated world trade as the gold standard had done in the heyday of British industrial supremacy. The destruction of European economies during the war, the availability of large supplies of cheap labour, and the

179

cooperation of labour movements (both social democratic and communist) in postwar reconstruction, guaranteed that capital an adequate return, and the 1950s was characterised by a high level of profitability and rapid capital accumulation. This partly reflected the persistence of unequal exchange between the re-emerging Western economies and their Third World suppliers of raw material, primary produce and cheap labour – a legacy of colonial domination and the relatively low levels of demand from Western economies still recovering from the destruction of war. High profitability also reflected, in the ex-fascist countries, the low wage levels which private capitalism could impose on working classes whose defensive institutions had to be rebuilt after the fascist holocaust, and whose bargaining power was in any case eroded by the plentiful supply of cheap labour available in the immediate postwar period.[31] High profitability in the 1950s also reflected the pattern of technological change, as the social productivity of labour in the capitalist economies as a whole rose dramatically through the establishment of new capital-intensive industries developed in the United States before and during the war, particularly vehicle manufacture, electrical goods and chemical products. Through the 1950s and 1960s the productivity of labour doubled every ten years in Japan, every fifteen years or so in the major continental economies, and every thirty years or so in the United States and the United Kingdom.[32] This rising social productivity, representing as it did a much higher level of labour exploitation than capitalism had achieved in the interwar years, was the base on which the unprecedented levels of personal consumption were established in each of the capitalist economies by the mid 1960s.

This long period of sustained growth contained its own slowly emerging contradictions, as the counter-tendencies to the propensity of the rate of profit to fall which the 1945 settlement had released slowly lost their power.[33] The consolidation of United States' domination over postwar capitalism, and the defeat or incorporation of various labour movements, had removed the immediate danger of renewed depression in 1945, but could not eradicate the basic propensies of the capitalist world economy. Indeed in the end it would intensify them. In the early postwar years there was no discernible generalised trade cycle in the western economies. United States' recessions in 1948–49 and 1957–58 were not reflected in parallel drops in output and employment throughout the OECD area. Economic management by individual nation states gave each economy its own rhythm of growth and recession; and in the fastest growing economies (Germany and Japan) growth in the 1950s and early 1960s was uninterrupted. The rate of growth in these economies might slacken at times, but output in total would not fall. However, by 1966 the generalised trade cycle was visible again, and in the last decade the behaviour of the world economy has become 'more erratic, sharp booms alternating with steadily longer periods of stagnation. . . . The boom of 1973 saw the fastest rate of growth ever recorded by the OECD area. Even the United Kingdom grew at a rate of 5 per cent. It was followed in 1974 by the start of the most serious recession the OECD has faced since 1945.'[34] The severity of the crisis is indicated by the scale of unemployment and inflation in the major OECD economies after 1974. Inflation rates throughout the OECD were three and a half times higher in 1974 than the average for the entire decade 1961–71, as the mini-boom which had generated this price rise gave way to rising levels of unemployment and to falls in GDP which began in 1974 and which persisted well into 1977.

Such a pattern of generalised inflation, unemployment and recession would have been inconceivable a decade before, when the contradictions and crises of a world capitalist economy appeared to have been transcended by the Keynesian policies of each national state. What was not obvious in the mid 1960s, but is now unavoidably clear, is that the postwar settlement contained its own emerging set of contradictions of a fairly conventional kind. The very dominance of the United States dollar and the worldwide mobility of American capital helped eventually to consolidate strong capitalist competitor economies in Germany, Japan and (to less a degree) France, where the social productivity of labour gradually overtook that prevalent in the United States. German and Japanese capitalism stockpiled US dollars with increasing reluctance, as the United States' deficit on foreign trade turned from a basis for their own capital accumulation into a fetter on their capacity to realise profits from commodity exchange. The dominance of the dollar was further weakened by the American military involvement in Vietnam, whose effect on the American balance of payments was so severe that in August 1971 dollar convertibility into gold was stopped, and in December 1971 the dollar was devalued, and with it the stable monetary basis for the sustained growth in World trade destroyed.[35] The re-emergence of strong competitor economies also intensified the demand for precious raw materials, and eventually eroded (in the upswing of the trade cycle at least) the favourable terms of trade on which high rates of economic growth and relatively stable prices in the West had been built. The rise in oil prices was, in this sense, simply the most dramatic and important shift in a whole series of primary product prices, which acted to accentuate, rather than to cause, international monetary instability and rates of domestic inflation which the consolidation of strong national capitalisms in Western Europe and Japan, and American indebtedness, had already begun to create.[36]

A further major consequence of the re-emergence of strong national capitalisms was the intensification of international competition. At the level of each national economy, the re-emergence of problems of private capital accumulation in the late 1960s acted as a powerful incentive to this process, as governments looked to export-led booms to generate profits, employment and price stability, and experimented to varying degrees with competitive devaluations, trade blocs, protectionism, and national drives to increase productivity. Nowhere was this intensification of international competition more obvious and more serious than in the heavily capitalised growth industries of the boom years: in vehicle manufacture, electrical goods, pharmaceuticals and chemical goods. It was in these industries that the profits crisis of the late 1960s was particularly severe, and among whom in consequence the 'merger boom' of the same period was most heavily concentrated.[37] Indeed, these mergers drew attention to those features of the postwar capitalist economies which do most to explain the recurrence of a world-scale trade cycle by the late 1960s, namely the increasing internationalisation of both industrial and financial capital. Of course it is true that one feature of the postwar settlement from the 1940s was the international domination of the dollar, and the associated establishment of international financial agencies, like the IMF and the World Bank, which effectively consolidated the hegemony of American capital by 'policing' the operations of weaker national capitalisms. Indeed the autonomy and visibility of these institutions has perhaps grown since the 1960s, as the hegemony of American capital has given way to a more complex struggle between two or three 'super' capitalist powers, whose collective interests gain some degree of orchestration through institutions such as the IMF. What the re-emergence of strong national economies from the 1950s, and the associated intensification of international competition, has done is to further that process of internationalisation, by leaving industrial production in the growth sectors of the Western economies in the hands of large multinational corporations, serviced by the parallel consolidation of increasingly complex interlocking international banking arrangements. The very accumulation of 'unwanted' American dollars in the central banks of Western Europe in the 1960s gave this mushrooming of international banking institutions an extra twist, by providing a base for the emergence of a large Eurodollar and Eurobond market, whose provision of credit lay outside the effective control of any one national government, and to which the. manufacturing sectors of international capital turned for the supplies of credit on which their continued existence increasingly depended.

It was in these manufacturing sectors of international capital that the very longevity of the postwar boom produced its ultimate contradiction, in the consolidation of strong labour movements whose memberships' postwar experience of full employment and rising wages generated expectations that were ever more difficult to fulfil. In the very industries in which the boom had been built, British governments by the mid 1960s faced well-organised work groups prepared to fight to maintain jobs and living standards; and this situation was repeated, to differing degrees, across the OECD economies as a whole. The existence of a large 'industrial reserve army' of peasants, artisans, small traders, women and foreign workers had been a crucial prerequisite of the sustained accumulation of capital between 1948 and 1960; and the increasing exhaustion of these sources of cheap labour after 1960 shifted the balance of economic and social power against capital, and left the working class as the ultimate barrier to any easy increase in the rate of exploitation of labour. Yet it was only by increasing the exploitation of labour as investment occurred that sufficient profits could be produced to compensate for the tendency of the rate of profit to fall. It was the re-emergence of this tendency which explains the intensification of international competition between the big multinational corporations from the mid 1960s onwards, and which holds the key to the growing instability of even the once 'affluent' car industries of Western Europe, and to the growth of unemployment among their once secure and relatively well-paid labour force.[38]

So by 1973–74 all the major indicators of a growing capitalist crisis were to hand: the reappearance of a generalised trade cycle, monetary instability, a significantly higher rate of concentration and centralisation of capital, a growth in the intensity of international competition, the exhaustion of the industrial reserve army, a falling rate of profit, calls for the intensification of labour, and working–class militancy. By the early 1970s, the spectre of the 1930s was being recalled in the speeches of politicans and in the headlines of newspapers, as capital was once more overproduced in relation to existing levels of labour exploitation. But this time the crisis had a new feature. It was accompanied by high rates of price inflation; and that this was so reflected a particular characteristic of the postwar boom which we have yet to discuss fully, and which has enormous significance for the freedom of action of Labour Governments, namely the role of the State in the accumulation of capital and in the realisation of profits.

High levels of government spending have come to be a significant feature of all the major capitalist economies in the postwar period. The share of government expenditure in Gross Domestic Product was between 25 and 35 per cent in all the major OECD countries except Japan in the 1950s, and with the exception of Japan again, rose in the 1960s to between 32 per cent (USA) and 40 per cent (in Britain and Italy). That scale of spending has reflected the various tasks which have fallen to governments in the postwar period: tasks which have had, as their essence, the prevention of capitalist crisis, and which have included the maintenance of high levels of employment and demand, the provision of defence and other services that are 'unproductive' of surplus value, the restructuring of capital and the maintenance of the existing social and political order. What has to be grasped, if the true nature of the Labour Party's situation is to be understood, is the character of this relationship between government functions and the existing economic and social order. Postwar governments of whatever political persuasion have had to operate within, take their agenda of problems from, and ultimately service, the laws of motion of the international capitalist economy that has surrounded them. Policy has had to be shaped within parameters established by the inexorable tendency of capital to centralise and concentrate, to develop in a combined but uneven manner, and to show a propensity for its rate of profit to fall.

This is not to argue for a simple economic determinism. Governments have continued to enjoy significant degrees of autonomy within those parameters, and how they have reacted to their national economies has reflected factors other than the purely economic. Their own political aspirations and, critically, the pattern of class forces which they have faced, have been among the factors which have conditioned governmental responses in ways that have often been vital in determining the development of the international economic system. There has been no one-to-one relationship between economic imperative and political response. There is always an element of the accidental in government policy: the personality of a Minister, the foibles of an economic adviser, the substance of ruling orthodoxies, faulty government statistics – all play their part, but a part that is within limits. Even the scope of the accidental is constrained. All governments have experienced very real and definite limits on their freedom of action, regardless of their political persuasion. As Fine and Harris put it, 'political class struggle and ideological tensions affect the extent to which the State can permit crises to develop at any given time. . . . the State can postpone crises, moderate their depth and precipitate crises, but it can never abolish them. For it is ultimately bound by the laws of capitalist accumulation.'[39]

In other words, the activities of governments have continued to depend on the generation of surplus value, and their ability to realise their own policy objectives has continued to depend on the 'health' of their national capitalism in the overall competitive struggle. To guarantee that health, governments have found themselves playing new roles that reflect the developing character of monopoly capitalism and the way in which its contradictions could not be postponed without State assistance. In the name of a multiplicity of ideologies and political positions, governments across the western world in the postwar period have found themselves playing a greater and greater role in assisting the realisation of profits, in attempting to facilitate private capital accumulation, and in stabilising potentially disruptive class relationships. This greater role for the State has helped to sustain the long postwar boom and to guarantee its ultimate culmination in stagnation and inflation.

The pattern of government involvement in industrial and social life has varied between different national capitalisms, and these differences have reflected the different pattern of class forces, political traditions and electoral expectations that the uneven development of capitalism since the nineteenth century helped to initiate, and which the different pattern of postwar development has helped to sustain. What is striking, when a comparison of governments in the OECD area is undertaken, both between countries, and between governments in any one country, is how similar their roles and actual performance have been.[40] Though governments have been unable to abolish the tendency to crisis in the capitalist economy, they have, through demand management and various distributional policies, so altered the conditions for profit realisation as to postpone the development of crises and to moderate their effects. They have also encouraged the restructuring of capital by financial assistance, public ownership and general industrial supervision. In the immediate postwar period, the conditions for private capital accumulation became so favourable that the role of the State was restricted to that of general lubricant, sustaining demand, employment and class peace by welfare spending and armament programmes. Even in Britain the interventionism of the Attlee Government was replaced by the revival of private capitalism in the boom years of the 1950s. But as the contradictions of the postwar settlement began to emerge in the late 1960s, the scale of government activity across the OECD area began to increase, government employment became even more important as a way of offsetting the job loss resulting from private sector restructuring, and the efficacy of government demand management began to wane. This tendency to greater government activity was common to all the capitalist powers as the great boom ended, but the degree of government activity varied between national capitalisms. Throughout the OECD area the differing scale of government involvement in economic activity (and the share of GDP absorbed by the public sector) grew with the relative weakness of each national capitalism.

In general therefore, governments in the postwar period have found themselves taking unprofitable sections of private industry into public hands, there to perform (more or less quickly, with greater or less degrees of enthusiasm, depending on their political ideology and the balance of class forces that they faced) the shedding of obsolete capital and the reduction in the labour force which had proved impossible under private ownership. Indeed, only the increasing scale of public sector employment in the postwar period has prevented the re-emergence of large scale unemployment, as the shift back to labour-saving investment in private industry has intensified. Governments have found, too, that they have been called upon to provide an extensive infrastructure of social capital – roads, medical and education services – as a context in which private capital accumulation could flourish. And politicians have found it essential to contain trade union demands and working-class militancy by the extensive provision of social services and by policies designed to maximise employment and protect living standards. Moreover, politicians of many shades of political opinion have found in office that the ability of the remaining capitalist sector to maintain its level of profits (and hence its rate of capital accumulation, economic growth and employment levels) has depended on a sustained and a high level of government spending: both to purchase directly a sizeable percentage of the commodities produced in the private sector and, through the financing of the subsequent budget deficits, to sustain the institutions and levels of private credit which had already begun to play so important a role in profit realisation and capital accumulation in the private sector in the interwar years. By spending so much, governments in the postwar years have helped to maintain the high levels of employment and personal and social consumption which have guaranteed the stability of the political and social order within which private capitalism could flourish; and in this way they have created expectations in their electorates, and strong pressure groups in their political universe, which now stand as blockages to any easy and politically painless breach of this process as the contradictory nature of the State's role has again become evident.

For vital though this State spending has been for postwar private capital accumulation and resulting economic growth, it has contained its own contradictions. From the point of view of private capital accumulation, the crucial feature of much State spending outside the manufacturing sections of the nationalised industries (or more precisely, of the employment that it sustains) is that it is not directly productive of further surplus value. Vital as it has been to the realisation of profits by the maintenance of high levels of domestic demand, and no matter how indirectly vital it has proved in providing the general social preconditions for private capital accumulation, government spending (and the employees it directly sustains in the public sector bureaucracies) has to be supported out of surplus value produced in the capitalist sector and transferred to these employees by taxation. This is not to say that all employees in the public sector are in this sense a burden on capital, nor to imply that all private sector employees are productive of surplus value. The matter is more complex than that.[41] But it is to say that, as the State's role has grown, the number of workers who have to be supported out of the surplus value created in the capitalist sector has increased.

This contradiction manifests itself most obviously at the level of taxation. State expenditure has to be funded, either by taxation (directly on wages, or indirectly on products purchased by wages) or funded by budget deficits and public borrowing. In either case this constitutes a problem for private capital. To the degree that higher taxation inspires higher wages, so the pressure on profit margins becomes greater and the more likely it is that governments will urge social contracts that keep the burden of taxation on the working class by preventing compensatory wage demands. Yet public borrowing is if anything more problematic for capital. For governments to borrow while attempting to maintain a fixed money supply tends to price out all but the most profitable private borrowing. Yet to borrow while allowing the money supply to rise merely fuels an inflationary process which reduces effective demand, increases costs, undermines international competitiveness and erodes profitability. These pressures are handlable for private capital only so long as the social productivity of labour continues to grow. For in essence what a high level of public spending (and employment of labour which is unproductive for capital) requires is a higher rate of exploitation of labour, a higher rate of expropriation of surplus value, than would otherwise be the case. Here then is the central contradiction of the role of State spending in monopoly capitalism: that sustained government spending has proved vital to the maintenance of high levels of capital accumulation, which is itself required to increase the social productivity of labour which alone can sustain large numbers of 'unproductive workers'. But the very scale of capital accumulation which this generates in the end alters the organic composition of capital and erodes the rate of return on investment; so that the propensity of the capitalist system to generate a reserve army of the unemployed and to restructure itself though crisis is not negated by State action. It is only delayed, and obliged to reappear later, on a greater and more dramatic scale.

Where then does inflation fit into this picture? Here, as elsewhere in capitalism, first appearances can be deceptive. There is no denying that the rise in oil prices, the tripling of commodity prices between 1971 and 1974, and the steady depreciation of the pound, played a large part in the determination of the high rate of inflation experienced by the British economy under the Labour Government; and many commentators have been tempted to leave the explanation there. But such 'accidental' factors are not a total explanation, nor indeed are they accidental. They are themselves rooted in the changing character of monopoly capitalism and its differential impact on particular nation states. We have seen already how the very consolidation of strong national capitalisms in the end destroyed the stable international monetary system that had kept price inflation low, and shifted the terms of trade in certain key commodities against the industrial West. Both these aspects of intensified international competition had marked inflationary consequences in the late 1960s and early 1970s. Yet their prominence of late should not be allowed to draw attention away from the fact that inflation is, in any case, endemic to this stage of capitalist development, and would have occurred (and indeed has occurred) in economies in which the exchange rate of the currency is strong and in which the dependence on foreign imports of oil is less. Factors which help to explain the differential impact of inflation should not be taken as explanations of the existence of inflation in total.

In fact it is clear that inflation is no new feature of capitalism. Indeed the very tendency of the rate of profit to fall as the organic composition of capital alters and as working-class militancy intensifies builds into the world system a propensity for individual monopoly producers to hold, or if possible to raise, their prices. The 1930s made clear that, left to their own devices, monopoly capitalists could not sustain a level of demand, and hence their prices, at a rate sufficient to compensate for their own declining profitability; and that institutions of demand generation were vital to their continued realisation of profits and further capital accumulation. In this way the development of private (and State-controlled) credit from the 1930s – as a vital mechanism to permit the realisation of profits and avoid recession by maintaining high levels of demand – proved essential to allow capital accumulation to continue at these higher prices. The development of credit gave capitalism in the postwar period its stability at the price of built-in inflation, as the supply of money grew at a rate faster than the rising social productivity of labour could generate extra commodities for purchase. It should be said in passing that this development of private credit institutions also generated high employment of private 'unproductive' workers, with the same relationship to private capital accumulation as the State bureaucrats discussed above. State spending made its contribution here as an extra inflationary force: partly by its borrowing adding to the general availability of credit (and hence to the money supply); and partly by the purchasing power of its employees not being matched by any concomitant increase in the supply of commodities. Such a contradiction was manageable so long as the level of capital accumulation was sufficient to sustain a high rate of increase in the social productivity of labour; and in the boom years high government spending and a growing money supply did not generate inflation rates of more than 3 or 4 per cent on average. The contradiction only became obvious, and inflation acute, when that pattern of capital accumulation faltered.

Inflation is, of course, a monetary phenomenon, but its causes lie in the production process, in the contradiction between those forces generating excessive money supply and those eroding the social productivity of labour and hence the supply of goods. What erodes the rising social productivity of labour under capitalism is the falling rate of profit, which results from the changing composition of capital that generated rising productivity in the first place, but which comes to produce a rate of return incompatible with further private capital accumulation. What delays that incompatibility is the high level of government spending. 'Without it the organic composition of capital would long ago have risen so much and the rate of profit fallen so low that accumulation of capital would have ceased.'[42] But government spending itself generates further inflationary pressures, and in the end intensifies the problems of capital accumulation that hitherto it had acted to facilitate. This paradox will emerge most starkly and earliest in national capitalisms in which the social productivity of labour is relatively low, not least because the defensive strength of their working classes is well established. It will be most evident there because the State had a greater role to play in order to compensate for deficient private capital accumulation and to meet working-class demands for social reform; and because the resulting growth in the money supply will face a lower than average social productivity of labour, and hence have earlier and greater inflationary consequences. That economy will then find itself doubly bound: inflation-ridden because of relatively low capital accumulation in the past, and with low capital accumulation in the present and future because its higher-than-average rate of inflation acts as a barrier to successful competition, sales and profit realisation, and (through the weakening of its currency) erodes still further its internal levels of cost competitiveness. Britain in the 1970s found herself in just such a situation.

Although the paradox is thus starker in some national economies than in others, ultimately it is felt throughout the world system. Falling profitability necessitates higher and higher prices which can only be sustained by ever greater private credit and public loans. Each extension of credit facilitates the increased exploitation of labour only by altering the organic composition of capital and intensifying the propensity of the rate of profit to fall. This in its turn can be compensated only by still further rises in prices and yet greater State spending, as the rising cost of private credit and the uncertain conditions discourage private capital accumulation still further. But this expenditure only intensifies the rate of inflation and, through its impact on rates of interest, squeezes even more private capital accumulation out of the system. As inflation soars governments cut back their spending, restructure capital and allow unemployment to rise, in an attempt to generate private capital accumulation again. Governments, that is, swing backwards and forwards between tolerating high levels of unemployment and high rates of inflation. But the preoccupation with inflation in the end always predominates, because any differentially high rate weakens so severely the competitive position of the national capitalism on which the Government depends to sustain even existing levels of employment and social services. The cost of unemployment is restricted to the unemployed alone, so long as political radicalism does not result. The cost of inflation hits society in total, and undermines the ability of private capital to accumulate surplus value. Nor does the problem ease with time. On the contrary, the struggle of governments against inflation and unemployment must prove increasingly unsuccessful as the contradictions intensify. Not even internationally coordinated government action can do more than reduce unemployment slightly (by a collective reflation), for even that would be bought at the price of a leap in the rate of inflation of such a scale that the fear of it has so far proved sufficient to block such collective action. Indeed the pattern of government policy internationally has so often been the reverse, with the recent slowdown in the rate of inflation achieved only at the cost of a large rise in unemployment and a significant fall in industrial production between 1974 and 1977. As David Yaffe has put it, the contradictions endemic to the postwar settlement are now becoming all too evident. The booms are becoming 'shorter and shorter, accompanied by higher and higher rates of inflation, and the slumps longer and more severe. [This] shows the crisis of overproduction of capital cannot be postponed any longer. The return of a world wide depression becomes increasingly near.'[43] A Labour Government has to struggle in office, that is, surrounded by a world economy in which profitability can only be restored by an extensive attack on working-class living standards, job security and work routines on a world scale. It is that context of action that has made a mockery of the claims made in opposition that in power a Labour Government could build a new Jerusalem.

## V

Nowhere have the growing contradictions of postwar monopoly capitalism been more evident than in Britain in the last decade; and this holds the key to the experience of the Labour Government. Once the first and mightiest of the capitalist powers, by the 1970s British capitalism was amongst the weakest of the major industrial economies, the legatee of the perennial competitive struggle and the necessarily uneven pattern of development that characterise world capitalism as a system. Capital had long found it more profitable to settle outside the United Kingdom, and the international importance of the City had facilitated that movement. Even before 1914 capital exports had reached 7 per cent of national income, and Glyn and Sutcliffe estimate that 'the value of British owned capital abroad in 1913 was probably greater than the total American capital abroad today'.[44] In the 1960s 'the outward movement of British capital was massive. Between 1962 and 1969 there was an increase of £3425 million in direct investment abroad, £2500 million in portfolio investment and £12,275 million in financial claims. . . . Although foreign investment in the UK was also substantial, British interests invested abroad were nearly 70 per cent more than foreign interests invested here.'[45] One consequence of this was to give a lower than average rate of investment in manufacturing plant and equipment. Investment as a percentage of GNP between 1960 and 1972 was only 16–18 per cent in Great Britain, lower than any of its major capitalist competitors. As a result the growth in labour productivity in this economy was significantly lower than that in its Italian, West German, French and Japanese equivalents. As Mandel notes, this, together with the relative strength of the British labour movement, meant that

> Britain became the only imperialist power which proved unable to increase the rate of exploitation of its working class significantly during or after the Second World War: the rate in the UK was now stabilised at the lower pre-war levels in the new epoch. From a capitalist point of view the result was evident: an erosion of the rate of profit, and a much slower rate of economic growth and accumulation than in the other imperialist countries.[46]

In consequence each successive Labour Government in the postwar period found itself faced with an economy whose international competitiveness was persistently dwindling. In the immediate postwar period this was not so obvious, as the wartime destruction of major competitor economies gave British capitalism and its export sector a temporary advantage which did not survive the re-emergence of German, French and ultimately Japanese competitiveness from the mid-1950s. From 1955 onwards British capitalism faced rapidly growing national competitors: the average annual rate of growth of the British economy between 1955 and 1968 was only 2.8 per cent, that of Japan was 9.7 per cent, of France 5.5 per cent, Germany 5 per cent, and the United States 2.9 per cent.[47] The full consequences of this persistent pattern of under-investment, limited labour exploitation and slow economic growth were obscured through the 1950s by the rapid expansion of world trade. Full employment, rising living standards and an entrenched labour movement were consolidated in that period as British capitalism maintained the volume of its production while perpetually losing more and more of its share of the growing total trade in commodities and services through the world economy as a whole. Between 1948 and 1972 British exports (f.o.b.) fell from 12.2 to 6.6 per cent of the total exports of the OECD economies, and the international indebtedness of the economy grew.[48] This was enough to dog British governments from 1957 onwards with balance of payments crises, stop–go policies and an eventual (1967) devaluation of the pound; and to familiarise both politicians and their electorate with the requirements of the international sources of credit to which governments repeatedly turned. United States governments, international banking consortia, the IMF and Arab sheikhs all served as sources of short-term funds as the international indebtedness of the economy persisted. This indebtedness was also enough to draw each successive government from the mid-1950s into playing a greater and greater role within the economy: attempting to maintain demand and employment levels by their own spending programmes and by the expansion of private credit, while aiding industrial profits by repeated experiments with incomes policies, industrial restructuring, investment grants and direct aid to individual industries and companies.[49]

Even this was not enough to prevent a major crisis of profits in British manufacturing industry in the late 1960s, or to prevent the largest wave of industrial mergers (the centralisation and concentration of capital) since the 1920s. Glyn and Sutcliffe estimated that the share of profits in companies' net output almost halved between 1964 and 1970, so that 'by 1970 profits had totally evaporated in metal manufacture, ships, planes and cars. . . . In most other manufacturing industries the stated profit rate had fallen by at least a third between 1964 and 1970, and outside manufacturing profitability fell a lot in wholesale distribution and transport.'[50] This problem of profitability persisted in the 1970s. After-tax profits remaining to industrial companies in 1973 in real terms were worth less than half the profits of 1972, and less than one-fifth of the profit levels of 1963.[51] As the Labour Government came into office the manufacturing sector of British capitalism was experiencing a major crisis of liquidity, with the rising money level of its profits unable to cope with the increased cost of stocks, taxation and interest repayments without recourse to sizeable borrowing from the banking sector. This declining profitability went hand in hand with a merger boom of gigantic proportions. By the time the Labour Governments of the 1960s left office the largest hundred manufacturing companies in the United Kingdom were responsible for between 40 and 50 per cent of total manufacturing output. When the Attlee Government left office twenty years before that figure had only been 20 per cent. This figure of 40 per cent gave British manufacturing capital a greater degree of market domination even than their equivalents had achieved in the United States.[52] By 1970 the number of firms responsible for producing half the economy's manufacturing output had fallen to 140; and that figure is likely to be even lower by now.[53]

Many of the problems (and responses) which were to characterise the Labour Government after 1974 were thus foreshadowed in the Labour Governments between 1964 and 1970. Those Governments created new agencies (the Ministry of Technology and the Industrial Reorganisation Corporation), through which to aid industrial

---

* 'Over the years State subsidy of the private sector has assumed massive dimensions. It has been estimated . . . that, by the late 1960s, it came to nearly 7% of the national product, and was equivalent to nearly half of all private sector fixed capital formation, excluding housing . . . amounting (by 1972–73) to between £2,100 million and £2,300 million, or £8 million per working day' (S. Holland, *The Socialist Challenge*, Quartet Books, 1975, pp. 65–7).

restructuring, and large quantities of public money were used to facilitate the concentration and centralisation of capital.* Those Governments also attempted to increase the rate of labour exploitation by initiating productivity agreements throughout British industry, and by restricting (for a period at least) increases in incomes to a government-vetted productivity scheme. They also – and this is a lesson which the Labour Left ought to take to heart – used their ownership of basic industries to replace labour by capital within the industrial parts of the public sector. The total impact of these policies on employment levels was dramatic. Between 1964 and 1974 350,000 employees left the coal industry, and 325,000 left the railways; and the latest steel programmes, as we have seen, suggest that that process is not yet over. Productivity agreements, stagnant profits and industrial restructuring repeated this shift away from labour in the private sector as well. Employment in coal and petroleum products fell by a reported 8.5 per cent between 1964 and 1973, in other metals and engineering by 11.9 per cent, in bricks, pottery and glass by 14.2 per cent, in construction by 16.8 per cent and in food, drink and tobacco by 9.4 per cent. Overall, total employment in British manufacturing industry fell from 8,033,100 to 7,504,000 between 1970 and 1975, and this fall was particularly concentrated on 'direct' productive workers. Their numbers in British manufacturing industry fell by 571,000 in the five-year period, as the number of indirect employees there rose by 5700.[54]

The total effect of this was to add almost half a million people to the register of the unemployed between 1959 and 1972, and to drive at least 300,000 other people out of the labour force altogether. Nor is this of itself a total reflection of the loss of labour from manufacturing industry. Part of the surplus was absorbed into the expanding sectors of employment that were non-productive of surplus value, into the white-collar public bureaucracies and into private sector employment in banking, insurance and finance. These sectors have been the fastest growing sectors of employment in Britain since the war,[55] reflecting the degree to which only the systematic expansion of private credit and finance, and public spending, have prevented generalised unemployment. Yet the legacy of this trend, to governments in the 1970s, has been twofold. It has left levels of inflation that have eroded still further the already precarious international competitiveness of British capitalism; and it has involved a level of personal taxation that has actually reduced net take-home pay as a percentage of personal income.[56] So by the time the Labour Party returned to office in 1974 it found itself trapped between a level of inflation that was undermining an already shrinking manufacturing sector, and a level of taxation which prevented any easy financing of further government spending essential to maintain demand and to prevent large scale unemployment – spending which had been foreshadowed in the election manifesto on which the Party had defeated its Conservative opposition, and on which its political agreement with the trade union movement had been based.

It was only so long as there was no generalised intensification of contradictions within world capitalism as a whole that the inflationary consequences of this pattern of government policy could be contained and the rate of job loss restricted; as the growth in world trade faltered, and the rate of job loss restricted. As the growth in world trade faltered, competition intensified, so the relative weakness of British capitalism produced acute problems of inflation and stagnation for both Conservative and Labour governments in the 1970s. The inheritance of the Labour Government in 1974 was particularly depressing: a weak capitalism in the midst of world recession. The Labour Party came into office at a time when, through the international system as a whole, the contradictions of the 1974 settlement were becoming obvious, as the counter-tendencies to the underlying propensity for profit rates to fall were everywhere weakening. The unbroken postwar boom had already given way to the reappearance of a generalised trade cycle, in downturn by 1975; and the logic of greater government involvement in economic management as *the* postwar way of avoiding world crises of the 1930s type, was culminating in all the major economies in inflation and unemployment, as rates of profit fell and as international competition intensified. Even if the British economy had been amongst the strongest of the national capitalisms, the Labour Government would have found it difficult to implement its policy aspirations in so hostile an environment, especially given the centrality to Labour Party thinking of the very extension of State spending by which inflation was being fuelled. Labour's commitment as a party to greater social spending and to full employment ran counter to the general re-emergence of capitalist instability, with its propensity to shed labour and to require the curtailment of any public sector employment that was 'unproductive' of surplus value.

What made the situation worse for the Labour Government was that Britain was among the weakest rather than the strongest of the capitalist powers, experiencing in full measure the propensity of capitalism in crisis to generate unemployment and abandon obsolete investments. Indeed, the weakness of British capitalism left it vulnerable in a world recession to a series of self-sustaining disabilities which further curtailed the possibilities of Labour Party reformism. The uneven development of world capitalism and its associated movement of capital out of Britain over the years, and the strongly entrenched position of the postwar British working class, meant that the Labour Government inherited an economy in which the social productivity of labour was relatively low, whose international competitiveness was in consequence being systematically eroded, and which had already generated as a result high levels of international debt. The strength of the working class and the lack of international competitiveness, with its resulting low rates of return on capital, not only acted as a disincentive to further capital investment and hence as a barrier to any easy reversal of the historic tendency of British capital to be exported; it also necessitated high levels of government spending to maintain demand and employment, thus giving the economy a disproportionately high rate of price inflation. This high rate of inflation was reinforced by the heavy dependence of British capitalism on imported raw materials, and hence by its particular vulnerability to the impact on the terms of trade with the Third World of the reappearance of the generalised trade cycle after 1967, and of the political instability of the Middle East after 1971. The total effect of this was to leave the pound vulnerable and capable in its fall of generating yet further inflationary pressures.

The very weakness of British capitalism which kept the pound weak also left the Labour Government with a particular problem with its own trade union base. For the regeneration of British industry to which the Labour Government looked required the very policies to whose avoidance the union–Party alliance in opposition had committed itself. Previous Labour, and more recently Conservative Government attempts to regenerate British industry through direct attacks on working-class industrial power (through industrial relations Acts) and on working-class market strength (through statutory wages policies) had already stimulated widespread industrial unrest. The number of days lost in strikes in 1972, for example, was higher than for any year since the General Strike. Yet the logic of the Labour Government's search for export-led economic growth required large-scale unemployment and a reduction in government spending in non-productive areas, to restore profitability and a higher rate of labour exploitation. The electoral survival of the Labour Government, on the other hand, depended on the support of a trade union movement that was strongly entrenched in the interstices of British capitalism, many of whose members worked in that 'non-productive' public sector, and all of whose members had an expectation of rising living standards inherited from the years of the postwar boom. To follow the logic of capitalist regeneration threatened this electoral support, and threw into question the whole *raison d'être* of the Labour Government. But to temporise with the trade union movement amid so weak a capitalism was only to add to inflation and stagnation. The Labour Government of 1974–79 could not fail to lose.

Such a 'Catch 22' situation has happened to Labour Governments before.[57] Not for the first time in the history of the Party, the policy objectives of this Labour Government were grounded in inadequate theory, and its aspirations proved incompatible with a capitalist world in growing difficulties. The Government looked to the regeneration of British industry to guarantee employment, and to high public spending on social services to guarantee trade union support. But as it entered office its leading figures had not come publicly to recognise or admit that industrial regeneration in a capitalist system required major unemployment, and had as its prerequisite a lower rate of inflation that itself required lower government spending in the social area. Nor were they prepared to face publicly the tension between the need of British industry for a higher rate of labour exploitation (and a consolidation of its profit margins) and the trade union movement's opposition to wage control and their demand for price restraint. Far from being able to afford the greater social services which Labour Ministers promised, British capitalism could hardly sustain the degree of state spending to which it was already subject. As Yaffe has argued, to cope with the expense of the non-productive sector the rate of exploitation of labour in the productive areas of British capitalism had steadily to be raised. This required a higher organic composition of capital and a fall in the size of the employed labour force relative to this growing capital. The maintenance of full employment by the Labour Government over a long period therefore required the very growth in employment in the non-productive sector whose reduction was essential if the burden on private capital accumulation was to be eased.[58] The problems with which the Labour Government struggled – the way in which low investment in the past seemed to preclude high investment and economic growth in the future, the way in which the weakness of the pound generated further speculation against sterling, and the slow disintegration of its social contract with the trade union movement – all these were manifestations of contradictions deep in capitalism itself, consequences of the propensity of capital inexorably to move to the point of maximum return in the face of a declining rate of profit, and of the manner in which the contradictory nature of the relationship between capital and labour becomes increasingly manifest as that decline intensifies.

## The explanation of the record

The Labour Government had no way out of this series of impasses which could avoid rising unemployment. To increase government spending would fuel inflation, erode capital accumulation and threaten long-term employment. To cut back government expenditure would destroy its own electoral programme, make profit realisation by private industry difficult, and reduce employment in the public sector. Of course the Labour Party in opposition had claimed that its special relationship with the trade union movement held the key to economic recovery; and so in a way it did, though hardly in the manner which Labour politicians initially had in mind. For only the Labour Party was able to hold trade union support as it slowly and with reluctance succumbed to the capitalist pressures around it. Only it could (and only then with increasing difficulty) retain working-class cooperation while the growing 'managerial' tone of its policy drowned any vestiges of early radicalism. This shift in tone and policy has been described in many ways within and beyond the Party: as the victory of Healey over Benn, of the Treasury over Transport House, or realism over radicalism. But however described, its occurrence left the Labour Government able only to salvage some remnants of its early aspirations as the pressure of problems swept over it. Indeed, given the severity of the economic conditions it faced, the Labour Government's loyalty to official trade unionism throughout its period of office remained striking. But inexorably it was pulled, as a Government, away from the heady optimism and naïve euphoria of March 1974 into a fuller appreciation of the imperatives operating on it. Unemployment was allowed to rise in an attempt to reduce inflation; grandiose schemes for public sector expenditure were abandoned in the same process. The social contract was redefined as a policy of wage control, by which the real living standards of the Labour Party's electorate could be systematically cut over a number of years. The restructuring of British capitalism was financed by the State, both within the extended public sector and by direct negotiations with major private firms[59]. In neither case did the presence of a *Labour* Government alter fundamentally the criteria of action by which those industries were to function. On the contrary, efficiency and productivity remained the key preoccupations of Ministers and senior management alike, the shedding of labour a main consequence of the Government's industrial policy, and the reaffirmation of the importance of profits a frequent occurrence. Nor could the Labour Government easily do otherwise. It was trapped between powerful international agencies and institutions over which it had no direct control (multinational corporations, international financial agencies and foreign governments) which acted as the mechanism by which the imperatives of capitalist crisis were transformed into policy. The nature of that crisis gave the Labour Government its agenda of problems: inflation, stagnation, dwindling profits, and intensified international competition. The force of the crisis gave the Labour Government little leverage over multinational corporations and international financial agencies. Indeed the vulnerability of even large multinational corporations to drastic falls in profits meant that they were often in no position to tolerate Labour Party radicalism at their expense. And the intractability of inflationary pressures and their intimate connection with high levels of government spending meant that the Labour Government could not generate fresh capital accumulation without the adoption of policies which were antipathetical to the Labour Party's aspirations in opposition for more social spending, greater social equality, and more working-class industrial control.

Only the trade union movement stood as a counterweight to all these pressures; and as I argue later, it had neither the theory, the will nor the international leverage to reverse the pressures entirely. Trade union resistance, ambiguous and halfhearted as it was, to the retreat of this Labour Government from its promises in opposition, only reinforced the electoral pressure on the Government to postpone yet higher unemployment by tolerating higher inflation. But this could not avoid the electoral consequences for a trapped Government, caught as it was within 'the fundamental contradiction between the economic need to increase the rate of exploitation and the political need to reduce it'. There is a general lesson here for social democratic labour politics:

The credibility of social democracy depends on its ability to grant reforms to the working class without endangering the reproduction of capital. If it cannot improve workers' living standards it will, eventually, lose its political base as its actions continually give the lie to its rhetoric. If its reforms eat into accumulation too much, on the other hand, the resulting economic crisis will both damage workers' living standards and necessitate a redistribution of capital to promote accumulation.

It is sometimes possible to walk quite a long way along this tightrope without toppling off. In a sustained boom, when the economy is growing steadily, workers' living standards can grow absolutely, and can even be improved relatively by cutting capitalists' consumption or running down the rate of accumulation a little, without damaging profitability too much. This is one reason why reformism is such a powerful ideology – it works sometimes.

A period of crisis is not one of those times though. The central requirement then, if capitalism is to survive, is an increase in the rate of exploitation, to provide the resources and incentive for further accumulation. Any attempt to implement major reforms will deepen the crisis. Failure to grant them, on the other hand, will lose the party its political base. This is the essential contradiction facing a reformist party in a capitalist crisis.[60]

## The explanation of the record

One final set of comments ought perhaps to be made in this chapter, on the relationship between the Labour Government's actual situation and the way in which Labour politicians, journalists and other political leaders have presented it. The particular severity of inflation and stagnation in Britain has helped to sustain those who have wished to lay the blame for present ills firmly on British shoulders. Indeed the Labour Left and the *Daily Telegraph* do at least agree on this – that what is wrong is here at home: in the faults of British financial and Treasury institutions, or British management or British trade unions. Yet it should be clear by now that the Labour Government actually faced a crisis rooted in international capitalism as a world system. Even its differential impact on various national economies, including the British, should be understood as a consequence of the necessarily uneven development of that world system and of the differential degree of working-class organisation and resistance to which it necessarily gives rise. In a competitive struggle, someone has always to be at the bottom. Particular national features may explain why one economy is there rather than another; but no amount of national tinkering can remove the systemic necessity for some economy's subordination. Inflation, stagnation, cuts in public spending, large-scale unemployment, are features common to all capitalist countries in the 1970s, unanticipated consequences of the tendency of the rate of profit to fall, and of the way in which that tendency has been held at bay since 1945 by the extension of private credit and by large-scale public spending. Inflation and unemployment hit the weaker economies more severely, but they affect even the stronger economies in some form. The Labour Government found that a weak economy under capitalism tends to stay weak: that nothing short of the total emasculation of the labour movement and immense human misery can reverse the propensity of capital to flow from areas of low labour productivity to those of high, with self-fulfilling consequences. The Labour Government found, too, that though the logic of its position pulled it towards international cooperation in favour of expanded production, that cooperation never went beyond the signing of paper manifestoes because the inflationary consequences of such a move would be too great. Needing greater world trade to ease its own inflationary problem, the Labour Government found it could not eradicate inflationary pressures (and the fear of them) from this stage of monopoly capitalism without either destroying monopoly capitalism or, through massive unemployment, destroying its own electoral base. Lacking any notion of how to replace monopoly capitalism and having no wish to generate mass unemployment the Labour Government was left helpless, a spectator of its own uncertain electoral fortunes as economic growth remained limited and unemployment remained high. Thirty years after the start of the postwar boom, Labour politicians found themselves at an impasse which little in their political perspectives and experience equipped them to handle, an impasse whose intractability reflected the fact that 'the barriers to further expansion are rooted deep in the political and economic features of the mixed economy',[61] which the Labour Party had spent the postwar years creating and sustaining.

Yet few commentators on British politics have been prepared to concede so much. Instead, the conventional method of explaining the nature of Britain's economic ills has been to lay the blame squarely on the shoulders of the very social groups or political forces who in fact are the least responsible for the economic decline they are supposed to have generated: the trade unions and the Labour Left. A full understanding of the political choices facing the labour movement in the 1980s must therefore go beyond an analysis of the Labour Government's problems to include an explanation of why the forces that attempt to bolster Labour radicalism should always prove to be so weak. It is to the gap between the public image and the private reality of union power and Tribunite influence that we must now turn to complete our explanation of the Labour Government's record in office since 1974.

# CHAPTER FIVE

# The political power of trade unionism

## I

It has become a commonplace of conventional political analysis to draw attention to the growing political power of British trade unionism. There is nothing new in such an observation, but the public image of excessive trade union power has been greatly reinforced in recent years by the presence of leading trade union figures in the committees surrounding government, by the willingness of the TUC to announce its own Economic Reviews and associated budgetary policy, by the way in which politicians of both parties publicly negotiate for trade union support, and by the way (as with the miners in 1973–74) in which that support is sometimes not forthcoming. When the Government had reached the point, as it had in the summer of 1977, of publicly leaving the design of the next stage of incomes policy to the TUC, only to find the TUC unwilling and unable to cooperate in this way, it is hardly surprising that people like Professor S. E. Finer could begin 'to wonder whether free collective bargaining [was] still compatible with the traditional practices of parliamentary democracy . . . and to wonder what, if this (was) the case, parliamentary democracy (could) do about it'.[1]

The argument on excessive trade union power has been couched in many ways, and with differing degrees of moderation. Professor Finer is content to stress the 'socio-economic leverage' enjoyed by sections of the labour movement because of their 'indispensability'. 'Without the function they, or rather some of them carry out,' Finer wrote, 'the society would collapse. It is the power to withhold a function, that constitutes their strength: not their power to coerce.'[2] Such functionality allows them, according to Frances Cairncross's similar formulation of the problem, 'to put tremendous political pressure on the government', to 'raise the trade-off point between stable prices and

stable employment' and to exploit the politically sensitive nature of
public sector services, whose disruption 'because of industrial action by
a public sector union . . .' would quickly bring the government 'under
public pressure to restore the service by making an award'.[3] The result,
if Paul Johnson's extreme presentation of the case is to be believed, is
that 'British trade unionism has become a formula of national misery',
fuelling inflation, hitting the poor, sustaining capitalist values of a 'free
for all', and slowing down the rate of economic growth. Dogged by
poor quality leadership, in Johnson's view, the trade unions have
refused to allow 'the emphasis [to] shift progressively from the
outmoded sectionalist methods of unionism to the universalist methods
of political socialism'. Instead,

they have flatly declined to allow the smallest diminution of their power to
press the sectional interests they represent. Indeed they have steadily, ruthlessly
and indiscriminately sought to increase that power. And in recent years, and in
particular in the last five years, they have exhausted or beaten down any
opposition and have finally succeeded in making themselves the arbiters of the
British economy.[4]

Yet this picture of 'the new barons', dictating policy to governments
and 'holding the country to ransom' in the pursuit of 'sectional' goals, is
profoundly misleading. As we have seen, the general drift of
government policy after 1974 was *not* to the liking of many trade union
leaders. Nor did the Government implement the full range of policy
aspirations developed within the Labour Party in the years of
opposition. What trade union leaders enjoyed under the Labour
Government was not so much the power to determine the *substantive*
drift of policy as the ability to participate in a new set of *procedural* rights
which created the very impression of influence that the resulting drift of
policy so often belied. Trade union leaders were consulted on a scale,
and with a degree of publicity, never before seen in peacetime. From
their consultations emerged, among other things, legislation bringing
enhanced rights to individual workers, particularly rights in the event
of redundancy and dismissal. And at critical periods in the Labour
Government's history, those consultations took the form of public
negotiations with leading TUC members, to win their support for
government initiatives. All this served to sustain the popular
mythology of trade union power. But publicity is never the most
reliable index of influence. At best it is an indicator of importance, not
of leverage. Trade union leaders were important to this Labour
Government because their support was essential to the successful
implementation of policy in key areas. To this degree, the trade union

leadership enjoyed power: the power to be consulted, to be listened to, even to resist; and this resistance was at its most visible after August 1978, when union resistance to a Stage 4 incomes policy came into the open. But even then, the resistance was not initiated by the trade union leadership. They acted only as spokesmen for memberships they felt they could no longer restrain, and a major reason for their growing lack of ability to restrain rank-and-file wage pressure was their previous failure to enjoy positive influence over the development of government policy.

What the trade unions enjoyed under this Labour Government was the power to block the smooth implementation of policy in politically sensitive areas, and it was this that made their support vital to Labour Ministers. The Government settled, as we have seen, into a strategy of curbing inflation and rekindling levels of domestic investment by a process of wage restraint and restricted government spending. Trade union militancy was bound to threaten that strategy and force the government into the toleration of even higher levels of unemployment or greater domestic inflation than the Chancellor required. Pay restraint was therefore a vital ingredient in the Government's overall scheme of things, and it was this which the TUC was called upon to deliver, and for which the Labour Government was prepared to pay a price. But the price had limits. The Government was not prepared to buy that restraint at the price of its general economic strategy; and as a result it resisted TUC calls for more rapid economic expansion and lower levels of unemployment. It met those calls as far as it could, within constraints imposed by the political power of organised capital and by the intractability of the inflationary process in a weak capitalist economy. But so tight were those constraints, and so intractable those processes, that basic trade union aims (on economic growth, job security and living standards) were simply not 'delivered' by this Government for large periods of its time in office. The TUC's alternative economic strategy of reflation and selective import controls was repeatedly rejected by a Labour Cabinet subject to stronger pressures and more deeply rooted economic imperatives that any that Congress House could mobilise.

The publicity surrounding TUC–Labour Government relationships signified not TUC power, but rather the new role into which leading trade union officials were being pulled by the logic of that relationship. Trade union leaders were public and visible under this Labour Government because they acted as invaluable assistants in the pursuit of policies which Labour Ministers could not implement without voluntary trade union support. In the beginning trade union leaders won in return significant legislative changes and elements of social reform, but by the end all that was available to sustain them, as income restraint grew unpopular with their memberships, and as cuts in public spending and persistent unemployment eroded the earlier promise of fundamental social change, was the strength of loyalty to the Labour Party within the ranks of trade union officialdom, and a general fear that a divided labour movement would herald the return of the Conservatives to power. Amid the publicity of regular Government–TUC consultations, trade union leaders superintended cuts in the living standards of their members, and were helpless to prevent rising unemployment. What the majority of union leaders could and did prevent, until late in 1978 at least, was any attempt to resist these cuts and job losses by a return to the industrial militancy of the 1970–73 period. It is this that has to be explained – not so much the power of the trade union leadership over this Labour Government, but rather their subordination and loyalty to that government and their willingness to play a role which inevitably brought them into conflict with the aspirations of at least a significant section of their own rank and file.


## II

The conventional explanation of this, in left-wing literature on trade unions under capitalism, runs as follows: that the subordination of trade union demands to government policy, and the moderation of rank-and-file militancy by trade union leaders, reflects their 'incorporation' into the ruling economic and political orthodoxies of the day, and their resulting propensity to act as 'managers of discontent',[5] extensions of the State in its attempts to discipline the working class as it protects the rate of return on capital. On this argument, the most militant trade union leader finds himself 'in a situation riddled with contradictions that, as a trade union leader, he [is] quite incapable of resolving. . . . Trade unionism express[es] the contradiction between Labour and Capital, but [is] not the means of resolving it;'[6] and as a result the full-time union official becomes subject to pressures which he is ill placed to resist. Precisely what those pressures are, and exactly why and how they operate to shape and moderate trade unionism, varies with the author. In the cruder explanations of what Tony Cliff called 'the dead weight of the trade union bureaucracy'[7] left-wing critics have accused trade union leaders of 'selling out' the interests of their members, by a mixture of ambivalent leadership and downright deception motivated in each case by their preference for industrial peace and their own individual social advancement. More subtle analyses have pointed to the *necessary* gap which exists between the full-time national official and the membership he is supposed to represent, and to the sense of personal and social isolation this generates for the trade union official himself, a gap and a degree of isolation which arises from the inevitable change in job content, lifestyle, and social position experienced by men as they rise through the trade union hierarchy. And so the analysis is carried forward, to stress the way in which trade union leaders, while often opposing the detail of government policy, repeatedly accept the terms of reference and the specification of 'problems' and 'policy options' laid down for them by Ministers, senior civil servants, businessmen and the Press. In this way they become vulnerable, so the argument runs, to the full force of bourgeois hegemony, subordinating themselves and their members to economic orthodoxies which do not accurately reflect the true (and antagonistic) nature of the relationship between labour and capital, but which serve instead to lubricate the effective running of a capitalist economy whose continuation requires at best the retention, and at worst the intensification, of the very patterns of social inequality and economic instability to which trade unionism has ever been a collective working-class response. It is therefore not surprising that trade union leaders, for all their fine rhetoric, become 'masters of the shabby compromise',[8] 'parasites on a class struggle that they can articulate but never resolve',[9] obliged to go along with policies (indeed often to canvass the very policies) that result in a diminished degree of job security, job control and real wages for their members. It is in this way that they constitute, it is claimed, one important element in the 'State Ideological Apparatus', by which capitalism reproduces itself, and by which working-class subordination 'to the rules of the established order'[10] is perennially maintained.

To understand fully the role which the trade union leadership has played in the development of policy since 1974, it is necessary to realise the strand of truth that runs through the 'incorporation thesis'. There is an inevitable distance between the full-time national official and his members, which affects left-wing and right-wing union leaders alike. That distance, and its impact on the industrial aspirations and political radicalism of trade union leaders, is partly a result of personal factors. Most national trade union officials are men in their fifties and sixties; and the very fact that they are older than the majority of their members is itself significant. There can be very few trade union leaders who lack the desire to leave their mark on national policy, on the labour movement, or on the pages of official histories; and the fact that they have at most ten or fifteen years of active trade unionism left must encourage the short-term view, the acceptance of compromise now in order to win some gain, however partial. Even if this is overdrawn, officials in their fifties or sixties are likely to have been officials for twenty or thirty years. Their direct experience of work on the shop floor, or in the office or classroom, ended a long time ago. As officials they live away from their members, have different pay and conditions, and are removed from the solidarities and loyalties sustained by daily contact with fellow-workers in an industrial setting. So that even where trade union leaders do retain a close affection for, and identification with, their social origins, those identifications have to be a conscious artifact, a determination to stay close to members who must be seen at a distance as 'the lads' or 'cases', rather than as individuals known personally and in the round. For the daily routine of a trade union official is different from that of the bulk of his membership. It involves a steady succession of paper work, committee meetings, preparing and giving speeches, consultation and confrontation with men of influence and status (senior civil servants, managers and politicians), even the occasional visit to a television studio or space in the national press. These differences do not guarantee that trade union leaders will be more moderate than their members, but they do set them apart, and deny to the trade union leader an intimate network of personal contacts with ordinary trade unionists from which to view, even to resist, the other pressures that operate on him.

What then are those pressures and why should they pull the trade union leader towards moderation? Some are organisational, rooted in his responsiblity for his union as an organisation, and in his own need to protect and defend his position and powers within it. The very fact that union funds and organisational viability can be put at risk by major industrial action is often sufficient to give a trade union leader a distinctly less enthusiastic and militant attitude to a particular wage demand or strike call than might otherwise have been the case. The leader's need to maintain his status in the eyes of governments and employers by being able to 'deliver' agreements which he has signed, and the knowledge that excessive militancy by strongly placed groups of members may create difficulties for the union among workers who are equally ambitious but less industrially strong, can encourage him to look askance at unofficial strike action and unconstitutional forms of industrial behaviour, no matter how legitimate the specific grievances happen to be. And the very involvement of trade union officials in regular negotiations acts as an additional force moderating radicalism, by encouraging tendencies to 'incrementalism' in the official's aspirations and perspectives, and by encouraging him to 'reduce' problems to a scale that is 'soluble' within the parameters established by 'the other side'. Such pressures are hard to avoid. As Richard Hyman has noted,

> A union representative who questioned the very institution of wage labour, the subordination of employees to employer, would have to operate in his routine activities as if capitalism were permanent, would have to fight the battles for improvements and reform according to the nature of the terrain, which is that of realistic calculation in a capitalist economy and a capitalist state.[11]

In all these ways the perspectives of the majority of trade union leaders must be shaped by the *defensive* and *reactive* character of trade unionism as an activity under capitalism. Since 'contemporary trade union action involves coming to terms with the power of capital rather than attempting to overthrow that power, collective bargaining is a process of defensive accommodation to the existing power structure, and involves the relief or suppression of immediate grievances rather than any attempt to tackle the underlying causes of workers' problems'. With this as their daily function, trade union leaders learn to accommodate and to compromise, and to restrict their aspirations to that of providing 'merely a protective function within the constraints of capitalist domination of the employment contract'.[12]

Then, in addition, trade union leaders are regularly exposed to pressure for 'moderation' and 'responsibility' from politicians, employers and the Press. The very language of public debate and news reporting, and the ability of Ministers, bankers and leading industrialists publicly to specify the trade unions' range of 'legitimate' action, puts trade union leaders on the defensive, and helps to erode any vestigial militancy. Trade union leaders face an 'asymmetrical culture',[13] reflective of the uneven distribution of social power and privilege in a capitalist society. By 'asymmetry' I mean three things. First that 'the language and concepts employed by trade unionists in the social construction of their world are closely intertwined with evaluations, legitimations and belief systems that owe their shape to the distribution of social power and its historical development'.[14] Trade unions and their leaders operate, that is, in a cultural system whose very categories reflect the expectation that trade unions should occupy a subordinate role, and that their members should enjoy only limited amounts of social power and influence. From this it follows that trade unionists find themselves liable to condemnation by significantly placed politicians and public commentators if they widen the range of their policy demands, to take in the specification of how the representatives of capital (in industry and finance) should act. At best, to do this is to be 'left-wing', 'sectional' or 'political', according to the major press and television commentators, and as such in need of explanation and justification; at worst, it is to exceed the 'legitimate' scope of trade union activity, and as such to be condemned. Yet the same commentators find no parallel qualms in reporting the much more regular and influential policy demands of bankers, industrialists, foreign governments and overseas holders of sterling. Their demands are not castigated as 'illegitimate', 'political', or outside the scope of proper pressure group activity, but are treated as 'facts of life', reflective of national rather than of sectional interests, for whose articulation governments should be grateful and to which trade unionists should subordinate their own narrower, more 'selfish' and 'shortsighted' aspirations. This is clearest of all in the asymmetrical world of assumptions, language and news reporting that trade unionists face whenever a trade union is sufficiently resilient to such pressures as to threaten a national stoppage.[15] Then, as V. L. Allen has described so well, the pressure to 'moderation' and 'responsibility' is particularly heavy.

Strikes take place within a hostile environment, even though they are a common every day phenomenon. They are conventionally described as industrially subversive, irresponsible, unfair, against the interests of the community, contrary to the workers' own best interests, wasteful of resources, crudely aggressive, inconsistent with democracy, and, in any event, unnecessary. The morality which assesses strikes in these terms acts on employees so that they approach strike action with severe inhibitions. Union officials are particularly prone to the anti-strike environmental influences because they are frequently made out to be responsible for the behaviour of their members. Once they are committed to a strike call, union officials tend to become defensive, apologetic and concerned about taking strike action. When they are actually engaged in a strike they are frequently motivated by a desire to end it quickly, irrespective of the merits of the issue.[16]

What this means in practice is that trade union leaders have to operate under a gale of pronouncements which single out trade union restraint (and working-class sacrifice, though this is more euphemistically specified normally in the language of 'restraint' and 'moderation') as the key to economic growth. The partial nature of the analysis that underpins such announcements is not made clear. The language used serves to obscure the manner in which priority is being accorded to the interests of other groups, whose aspirations are being taken as unalterable, inevitable, even just. The 'facts of life' to which trade unionists are repeatedly subject, even by Labour politicians, are thus heavily slanted to produce the working-class 'restraint' which their articulation is designed to achieve. Unemployment, the Prime Minister (James Callaghan) told the 1976 Labour Party conference, 'quite simply and unequivocally . . . is caused by paying ourselves more than the value of what we produce. . . . it is an absolute fact of life which no government, be it left or right, can alter.'[17] There is little doubt that the Prime Minister spoke sincerely, and his sincerity doubtless helped to persuade his audience of the validity of his assertion. Yet the assertion was no more than a tautology, an empty definitional truth which left unexplored the structural causes of unemployment and inflation, beyond its clear implication that trade union wage demands were their primary cause. The superficiality and slant of the assertions underlying such economic analyses helped then to perpetuate a degree of trade union restraint and powerlessness which the analysis itself reflected. It is true that private capital accumulation required a cut in working-class living standards in the 1970s, and that there was nothing a Labour Government could do to avoid that need so long as private capital accumulation remained the motor of economic activity. The Labour Government's powerlessness in the face of such imperatives doubtless educated Mr Callaghan in the 'absolute facts of life' to which he referred, and encouraged him in his turn to exploit the one element in his power structure (the trade unions) whose activity could be shaped by rhetoric alone. But that cannot alter the fact that his presentation of the choices before the labour movement was a highly partial and misleading one.

I discuss later the full significance for trade union power of these underlying imperatives of capital accumulation. What has to be grasped for the moment is the remarkable degree of self-confidence which trade union leaders have to possess if they are successfully to withstand this kind of perpetual ideological pressure. It is not surprising that, on issues other than those concerning the immediate organisational integrity of trade unionism itself, they seem only too happy to operate within the same categories of analysis, and with similar specifications of problems and possible solutions, as the civil servants, employers and politicians with whom they have to deal. As Richard Hyman has noted,

On rare occasions the point may be explicitly stated that 'the argument from the national interest is but one of a rich repertoire employed by those whose interests are different from those of trade unionists' (TUC. *Trade Unionism* 1966, p. 62). Yet far more commonly, trade union spokesmen endorse the ideological vocabulary of capitalism: 'this Movement is as conscious of the national interest as the government is and much more so than most of our critics'. Feather's comments at the time of the debate over Labour's 'penal clauses' are typical: the assumption that it is meaningful to use such concepts as 'national interest' or 'the country's problems' is uncriticised, and the fundamental ideological argument is thus lost by default.[18]

This subordination of trade union leaders to the full force of cultural orthodoxy in a society such as ours remains a major factor moderating their influence even on a Labour Government, and helps to explain why in the 1970s trade union leaders continue to play the role that Trotsky found their predecessors playing forty years before, 'lieutenants of capital in the intensified exploitation of the workers'.[19]

## III

Powerful and important though the argument on 'incorporation' is, it cannot be taken as a total explanation of the gap between the image and the reality of trade union power since 1974. Certainly a major implication of its less sophisticated variants – that the conservatism of trade union leaders was matched by, and served to frustrate, industrial and political militancy in the union rank and file – is clearly false. What is significant about industrial relations since 1974 is the abrupt drop in industrial militancy, and the remarkable degree of self-discipline and moderation shown by the entire work force through more than three years of wage restraint, falling living standards and heavy unemployment. That restraint was not an artifact of conservative trade union leadership, except to the degree that a coherent, alternative and convincing alternative to wage restraint was not forthcoming from the majority of trade union leaders. A tiny group of 'left' trade unionists kept a degree of opposition alive; but between 1975 and 1978 they met no major sustained rank and file response. There was simply no large-scale pressure for any breach with the Labour Government's policy. Rather, both the vast majority of union leaders *and* members operated within a similar universe of discourse, one in which there was a qualified acceptance, however reluctant, of the force of the Government's arguments for pay restraint. This was far less a matter of leadership incorporation than of an entire class's cultural subordination, a passive if reluctant integration into capitalism's ruling ideology of necessity. As Len Murray put it, 'the policy has only stuck over the last couple of years because of the generality of feeling that this was the right thing, the sensible thing to do – and because everyone else was doing it'.[20]

The full significance of such a total class subordination to the ruling orthodoxies of the day is discussed in the last chapter. It is enough to note here that when that period of pay restraint did not produce significant reductions in inflation rates and unemployment, as it had not by the summer of 1977, rank-and-file pressure was strong enough to block the cooperation of trade union leaders in any third round of pay restraint. This pressure, when it came, was still insufficiently strong to prevent most settlements in the third year of the policy being around the 10 per cent target set by the Government. Moreover it was sectional and sporadic, preoccupied often with the maintenance of differentials *within* the working class and a return to a reliance on the supremely capitalist forces of supply and demand in the labour market. It had no wider social and political ambitions than a return to 'free collective bargaining'. But it at least demonstrated that the degree of incorporation to which trade union leaders can be subject has its limits, in the degree of rank-and-file resistance to which capitalism necessarily gives rise and which trade unions must articulate, in however muted a form, if their leaders are to be in a position to act as 'the managers of discontent' that even Labour Governments now require.

Moreover it is always a mistake to treat the national trade union leadership as a homogeneous and undifferentiated bloc. Such men are not all cut in the same mould. On the contrary, their actions and public statements reflect more than external pressures, and are shaped by their own personalities, aspirations, political perspectives and past experiences. Trade union leaders have invariably served a long and tough apprenticeship on their route to national office; they are almost always strong personalities, used to articulating and imposing their will; and they hold different views from one another on the desirability of industrial militancy and political radicalism. There is, in each generation of the union hierarchy, a group of more radical men, able to resist to a degree the calls for moderation. They are sustained in part by a socialist political philosophy; in addition and quite often their roots in and sympathies with the Communist Party provide an alternative ideological and political base which, however moderate by revolutionary standards, constitutes one bulwark against total subordination to conventional orthodoxies. And their militancy can be sustained by the particular character of the memberships they serve: either by its industrial strength (as with radicals in the NUM) or by its craft exclusiveness (as in ASLEF). When we talk of the TUC's subordination to government policy in the 1970s, the existence of these men should not be forgotten. They kept alive a minority strand of opposition within the official leadership of British trade unionism when incomes policy was in its heyday in 1975 and 1976, and remained there to capitalise on the failure of incomes control to generate economic growth and long-term price stability.

Yet under this Labour Government their impact was limited, and even their opposition to Labour policies was muted and ambiguous. That this was so reflected another feature of British trade unionism which the thesis on 'incorporation' tends to obscure, namely the degree to which the majority of trade union leaders make their *own* contribution to their subordinate relationship with governments, as a result of the Labourist perspectives which they bring to bear on their definition of legitimate political power in a modern industrial society. The vast majority of trade union leaders have always stood full square with their parliamentary colleagues on this: 'have always rejected any kind of political action (such as industrial action for political purposes) which fell, or which appeared to them to fall, outside the framework and conventions of the parliamentary system'.[21] This Labourist faith, with its denial of the necessary incompatibility of labour and capital, and its equation of politics with parliamentary action, has always left trade union leaders vulnerable to appeals for 'moderation' in the 'national interest', even from Conservative Governments. This is as true now as it was in 1926 when J. H. Thomas explained his pathetic leadership of the General Strike by claiming that 'in a challenge [by the unions] to the constitution, God help us unless the Government won'.[22] Len Murray, less flamboyantly, echoed those sentiments in 1977 when he told Brian Connell: 'We recognise the supremacy of Parliament, we value Parliament . . . at the end of the road we know – this is really coming to the heart of it, that where the thing really happens is in Parliament.'[23] Of course, when J. H. Thomas spoke, the direct involvement of governments in wage settlements and industrial relations was relatively restricted. But it is clear that his attitudes have persisted unaltered into a new era, when governments directly employ probably 40 per cent of all trade unionists and make policy on incomes, inflation and unemployment, that intimately affect the rest. As a result it is no longer the case that the attitudes of trade union leaders to Parliament have little regular impact on industrial militancy. Just the reverse: Labourism as a political perspective erodes trade union militancy against government policy by underestimating the class constraints that operate on the State and by sustaining instead a belief throughout the senior levels of the trade union movement that strike action against governments is in some way less legitimate than strike action against the private employer.

At least with a Conservative Government there remains in the minds and speeches of trade union leaders some sense of a class division between government and unions, which helps to soften the impact of the Conservative claim to speak 'above class' and for the nation as a whole. These defences are not there with the Labour Party in power, and were especially low after 1974 when the recent experience of confrontation with the Conservatives had reinforced the trade union leaders' traditional belief in the necessity of Labour's return to office. The positive commitments of trade union leaders to the Labour Party, and the close links they enjoy with Labour politicians, thus always leave them particularly prone to subordinate union demands to the general drift of Labour Government policy. This subordination was only too evident after 1974, for the union leaders' unusually close involvement in policy formation within the Labour Party between 1970 and 1974, and their regular and close consultation thereafter, did more than begin 'a process of gradual enlightenment about the real constraints of government',[24] it also drew trade union leaders into a partial responsibility for, a sense of identification with and a commitment to the general drift of government policy. Far from acting as barriers to policy that added to unemployment and falling living standards, many trade union leaders were drawn into a recognition of how and why such a development was occurring, and came to play the role of spokesmen for policies that were in some important sense 'theirs'. Disagreements persisted of course, on the timing and necessity of reflation and import controls, but this did not remove the general sense of identification with the Government and its policies in the minds of the bulk of the trade union leadership.

That sense of identification was reinforced by the historical connections that bound Labour Party politicians and trade union officialdom. As we have seen, the dominant position of the trade unions within the Labour Party's formal decision-making processes did not mean that union leaders were prepared or able to 'hi-jack' the Party to their point of view. On the contrary, 'with the party . . . union leaders have always shown considerable political restraint, and the degree of this restraint has been far more remarkable than the degree of power they have exercised'. This degree of trade union restraint within the Party reflected in part the TUC's reluctance to undermine its ability to negotiate with any Government regardless of party (and in the process possibly to split a united and growing membership) by being too closely identified with the Labour Party. But it also reflected, as Lewis Minkin has noted, the trade union leaders' 'high degree of loyalty to the Labour Party, a Labour Government and to "the Movement"'. 'That there was an instrumental quality to that loyalty is obvious. But the emotional element is not to be under-estimated.' This is true even of the new left-wing union leaders who came to positions of influence in the AUEW, TGWU, NUM and USDAW after 1967. In their dealings with Ministers *within* the institutions of the Labour Party, and when dealing directly with the Cabinet as conventional pressure groups, their concern for 'the party's electoral viability, for its organisational cohesion and preservation during times of crisis, and for the success and continuation of a Labour Government in office'[25] continued to act as very powerful forces moderating trade union demands and shaping trade union reactions to government policy. So too did fear of the Conservative alternative. Indeed the weaker the Labour Government became politically the more the loyalty of trade union leaders to it reduced the pressure they could bring to bear.

In this sense the trade union leaders' loyalty to the Labour Party had paradoxical results. That loyalty encouraged trade union leaders to sustain the Labour Government at virtually any price. The Labour Government's failure to control unemployment and inflation generated tensions among the rank and file of the trade union movement which, had the Government been Conservative, the trade union leadership would have articulated more fully. They could not do so with a Labour Government, and especially with one dependent on Liberal votes, without running the risk of seeing the feared Conservatives return to office, and so they spent the last years of the Labour Government visibly trapped: seeking to avoid any political embarrassment for a Government whose impotence in economic affairs was eroding its already weak electoral base, yet under growing pressure to articulate industrial dissatisfaction to which an unreformed economy was giving rise.

The true 'feel' of the trade unions' actual impact on the Labour Government can be found in Len Murray's 1977 interview with *The Times*. There he made very clear that trade union power had its limits, that Labour Governments no less than Conservative ones have been known to reject trade union demands, and that this of itself need not weaken the relationship between the unions and the Labour Party as many had anticipated.[26] The relationship between the unions and the Government remained strong, he argued, because *both* sides saw the necessity for the general drift of policy, however unpalatable this was to sections of the trade union movement and however many points of detail remained in dispute. When asked where he stood in the current debate on the excessive power of particular pressure groups, this was his answer:

I might almost wish it were true, with my purely T.U.C. hat on. Anyone who knows how we've battered till our knuckles have bled on the doors of government to try to get expenditure in certain areas and been met with a blank refusal must realise that this is so. After all the cuts in public spending we didn't throw our hats in the air. The Government said this is what we are going to do. It is we who went along with it, the T.U.C., by and large. Some of our unions are very much opposed to it because it affected them individually as unions. It would lead, they argued, to deterioration in the quality of services which they thought ought to be maintained – housing, health and so on. It was the Government which decided that major political issue and we grumbled, but we went along with it. We nagged about certain things like food subsidies and nursery schools. . . . We were presented there with a very definite decision by the Government, with parliamentary approval, that this was going to be the pattern of public spending. We went along with it, amongst other reasons, because we saw the need to shift resources from the public sector, the public services sector, into the private manufacturing sector. Oh yes, we've urged, we've argued, we've proposed: but to suggest that we've determined is nonsense . . . is totally in conflict with the facts.[27]

Len Murray's assertion that the TUC, no less than the Labour Government, 'saw the need to shift resources from . . . the public services sector into the private manufacturing sector' can be taken as yet further evidence of the TUC's incorporation, its lack of a coherent alternative specification of the causes (and cures) of the economy's poor performance. And so it is. But the 'need' was no artifact of Establishment economists. As we have seen, the size of the 'non-productive' sections of the public sector did exacerbate problems of private capital accumulation in Britain in the 1970s. And this serves to remind us that what gave such economic orthodoxies their force, and what blocked trade union power, was not merely the social and political strength of the élite structure that the labour movement faced, nor the coherence of that élite structure's economic views. It was also the relationship between such economic orthodoxies and the real structural constraints faced by trade unions and Labour Governments in advanced capitalism.

In other words, it is not enough to restrict our analysis of the power of trade union leaders under a Labour Government to an examination of their subordination to prevailing economic opinion and to an understanding of their political commitment to the Labour Party. Such cultural factors, though vital, have themselves to be explained. Trade union power was restricted not just by a hegemonic power structure, but by a power structure subject to *capitalist* imperatives and processes with which strong and militant trade unionism was bound to come into conflict. So the persistent hesitation of trade union policy, and its ultimate failure to determine government policy, must not be seen simply as a response to the dominance of prevailing beliefs. It must also be seen as a consequence of the material reality that those beliefs reflected, and of which they were a part. For there are *real* limits to trade union power under capitalism, which have to be recognised by the Left if the genuine choices of strategy and tactics currently available are to be located. Analysis has got to move beyond the assertion of 'leadership failure' to the recognition of the systemically induced constraints that operate on trade unionism as a working-class institution under capitalism.

## IV

It should be said that trade union leaders themselves seem only too aware of these constraints. They experience daily the truth of the assertion that, as trade unionists, they can only react to, but cannot control, the basic *institutions* of international capitalism, nor prevent capitalist *processes* eroding Labour Government attempts at major social reform. They know only too well that excessive trade union militancy, and refusals to accept incomes policy norms, can inspire reactions from significantly placed groups of businessmen, financiers and governments, reactions which may seem capricious and irrational but whose consequences are, for all that, no less real and damaging to the living standards and job security of their members. They know that union intransigence can affect the exchange rate of sterling, make foreign loans difficult to raise, or dissuade investment by multinational corporations, and that such responses can lower the rate of economic growth and thus in the long term undermine levels of real wages and security of employment for rank-and-file trade unionists.

The contradictory pressures that trade union leaders face are in this sense real; they are always subject, even in periods of rapid economic growth, to the danger that trade union success in the immediate period will be bought at the price of more difficult negotiating conditions later. That contradiction is even starker when economic growth is missing, when – as for the British trade union movement in the 1970s – bargaining had to occur against the background of a competitively weak economy, in which rates of investment were already low, exchange rates already unstable, and foreign competition already sufficiently intense to prevent the maintenance of full employment at existing levels of real pay. What could trade union leaders do, trapped as they were in the midst of a weak capitalism? The overriding immediate pressure on them from their own rank and file was to maintain existing levels of pay and employment. Yet, as any survey of economic debates at the TUC makes clear, trade union leaders recognised the impossibility of sustaining even the *status quo* without a major restructuring of British capitalism that must, in the short period at least, threaten jobs and living standards even more. TUC hesitation and powerlessness came not just from subordination to prevailing economic orthodoxies; it also reflected the recognition by trade union leaders of the real dilemmas faced by the Labour Government and the resulting danger that trade union resistance to falling living standards in the immediate period might block the restoration of British capitalism's competitive edge on which future living standards depended.

These real constraints on British trade unionism in the 1970s have been referred to by certain non-Marxist commentators as 'the pay paradox'. Peter Jay for example, in his column in *The Times*, repeatedly pointed out that trade union pressure for higher real wages has a propensity to be counter-productive. In part, he argued, this occurs because successful wage bargaining across the labour movement as a whole will (with a fixed or only slowly changing exchange rate) tend to reduce the competitiveness of the export sector, with a resulting deficit on the balance of payments, deflation to correct that, and unemployment in the export sector. However, so long as the balance of payments deficit continued to grow, trade union pressure can be said to have raised the real level of national income as a whole. What the Labour Government found in the 1970s was that it is exceptionally difficult to run a balance of payments deficit permanently without a falling exchange rate generating internal inflation, and without external financial demands to lower the social wage. Yet more seriously, according to Peter Jay, such pay pressures 'either force the government to expand monetary demand to accommodate the new higher level of domestic costs, so underwriting an acceleration in inflation, or cause an unavoidable rise in unemployment while pay and costs are forced down again',[28] for rises in real wages require either that real national output should grow, or that the income of non-workers should be cut. The latter can be achieved only by squeezing profits or taxing the rich, or by cutting the level of government spending on the unemployed and the already poor; and rises in real output are likely to be threatened by the pressure of rising wages (and any associated inflation) on profit margins and interest rates. So, Peter Jay would argue, the cumulative effects of trade union pressure for rising wages are likely to be higher levels of unemployment or inflation, with no significant shift in the distribution of income, or social power, between capital and labour.

It is possible to go a certain way with the school of bourgeois economists who argue that trade unions can have no direct influence on the level of real wages of the working class as a whole, and with their claim that trade union pressure can threaten long-term living standards if it erodes already hard-pressed profit margins, slows the growth of productivity or discourages investment. But where the monetarists' position is profoundly misleading is when it carries with it the clear implication that, without such trade union pressure, problems of profitability, productivity and capital accumulation would be self-correcting. They are not. I have argued earlier that the relationship between capital and labour in a capitalist system is a contradictory one: capital needs labour as its own source of growth and yet constantly retreats from its use in order to stem the tendency of the rate of profit to fall. So trade unions in their turn find themselves in a contradictory relationship with capital: requiring capital accumulation on a large scale to maintain employment and wages, and yet experiencing a long-term tendency for capital accumulation to intensify the rate of exploitation of labour and to generate ever higher levels of 'normal' unemployment. With the rate of profit vital to renewed capital accumulation under capitalism, trade unions have to negotiate in a system in which that rate has its own tendency to fall. Only an altered organic composition of capital and an intensification of the rate of labour exploitation can stem that tendency, yet each of these processes will affect trade union members adversely, and demand a union response. Only very rapid capital accumulation can create a world in which, temporarily at least, profits and wages can grow together, and this is the world which trade union leaders repeatedly seek. But the degree of restructuring of British capitalism that this would require, with the resulting dislocation of trade union power and working-class living standards, repeatedly oblige trade union leaders to stand as a block to the very processes they wish to see. This is not to say, as critics of trade unionism have it, that wage rises are a cause of inflation, or trade unionism the cause of low productivity; inflation is structural to capitalism at this stage of its development, and low productivity endemic to a labour force alienated by their treatment as commodities. But it is to recognise that a period of further capital accumulation requires a significant rise in the rate of exploitation of labour, to ameliorate problems of profit realisation and investment caused by inflationary pressures rooted outside the trade union movement. The rate of growth of profits is in this sense determined by the inexorable tendencies of capitalist development, and not by trade union militancy alone: but it is tempered by the severity of the class struggle to which those tendencies give rise; and trade unions, looking for a 'healthy' economy in which to bargain, are faced with the paradox that their strength as unions can impede the health they wish to foster.

Trade union leaders and rank-and-file union members do not oppose technological change, press for greater wages and resist managerial policy to the degree that they do, out of a misguided bloody-mindedness and collective stupidity. Indeed, precisely because the necessity for greater output if living standards are to rise is generally recognised throughout the union movement, trade union resistance to change under capitalism is invariably halfhearted. Resistance is inspired by the *costs* which technological change under capitalism brings to the workers subject to it, and by the irrationality and instability of patterns of capital accumulation dictated by the law of value. It is precisely because the process of capital accumulation under capitalism is so flawed, and so destructive of working-class living standards and job security, that trade unionism is vital. The paradoxical consequences of trade union defensive action are not rooted in unionism, but in the contradictory nature of capital itself. This has to be realised if the real limits on trade union power are to be grasped. Trade union leaders cannot prevent problems of public policy and realities of economic life being presented in the way they are, for these are the exigencies of capitalism to which they, like everyone else, are subject. Nor can they prevent the contradictory relationship between capital and labour generating the contradictory pressures which they face as trade union leaders, and which as trade unionists they cannot resolve. The long-term tendency of capitalism to accumulate through crises gives a perennial instability to working-class life, and to trade union power. In a weak capitalism, already beset by inflation and unemployment, the need for fundamental restructuring adds to that instability, and erodes trade union leverage. Successful trade unionism aspires to bring a shift in power and wealth towards labour, and yet requires sustained capital accumulation. But successful capital accumulation in Britain in the 1970s requires a shift of power and wealth *away* from labour, and a diminution of trade union effectiveness that is at variance with the long-term aims of collective working-class action. Trade unionism in a weak capitalism is thus in a particularly intractable dilemma, a dilemma from which there can be no escape so long as the transcendence of capitalism is kept from the agenda of trade union politics.

V

In such a situation the range of choices available to the trade union movement is very restricted. An individual union leadership under heavy rank-and-file pressure will always have the option of pushing for a wage settlement that is higher than the average, even though the general consequences of that are likely, because of its impact on price levels and eventually on the general level of demand for labour in the economy as a whole, to be a redistribution of incomes and job security within the labour movement, from the ill-organised and the unemployed to the well organised and the relatively powerful. But as far as the trade union movement collectively is concerned, the range of choice is different, and fourfold. One available option is the conventional strategy of the right wing of the union leadership, explicitly to subordinate labour's demands to those of capital, to go for a restoration of profits by tolerating an intensification in the rate of exploitation of labour, through productivity deals, wage freezes and reductions in manning levels. Invariably and eventually the price to be paid for that strategy is rank-and-file unrest. But right-wing union leaders have been prepared to tolerate that, so long as any resulting unofficial militancy has remained sporadic and unconnected, on the gamble that the restoration of high growth rates in the economy as a whole would make their unpopularity temporary. The other three strategies would see themselves as avoiding that dilemma. The Labour Left strategy for the trade unions in the 1970s was to sign a broad agreement with a Labour Government, trading income restraint for government policies which used State action both to speed investment and to create greater social equality. Left critics of that strategy within the trade union movement have two strategies from which to choose: to demand an end to state control of wages and a return to industrial militancy under the slogan of 'free collective bargaining', or to seek to politicise industrial militancy as part of a revolutionary working-class strategy behind an international socialist programme.

This latter is as nebulous as it is vital, and will be discussed again in the last chapter. What makes it so pressing, however, are the contradictions associated with each of its alternatives. The right-wing strategy is flawed in its belief that the subordination of labour to capital need only be short-term, that there is a once and for all solution to British capitalism's competitive weakness which can be found by 'restraint' now if that restraint goes deep enough. As we have seen, the contradiction between capital and labour is perennial to capitalism; and at this late stage in capitalism's development the maintenance of adequate levels of profit will repeatedly require higher levels of unemployment in each slump (by means of a changing organic composition of capital), and higher rates of labour exploitation as a base for each industrial recovery. So the subordination of labour to capital in this period will not prevent a similar requirement in the next, and it is for this reason that a strategy calling for government action to break the stalemate of private capital accumulation has been so attractive of late to left-wing trade union leaders. But their strategy has been that pursued between 1974 and 1979 and has achieved neither sustained economic growth nor rising living standards, subject as it is to all the limitations imposed on a reforming Labour Government by capitalist recession.

Indeed it is the failure of that 'social contract' route which has given renewed strength to the call for a return to free collective bargaining. Yet this desire to be rid of state controls on wages, important as it is, attacks the symptoms but not the causes of the trade unions' present impotence, and shows a faith in the desirability of market mechanisms and Keynesian policies that is hard to square either with the present state of international capitalism or with any socialist condemnation of market capitalism. Free collective bargaining is clearly attractive to those trade union leaders under heavy rank and file pressure, with strong bargaining positions, but for the trade union movement as a whole, a return to free collective bargaining on its own will not, except in the very short run, avoid the falling living standards associated with wage restraint. It will merely alter the processes by which living standards fall, as price rises and unemployment have the effect that frozen money wages had previously. If the barrier to rapid capital accumulation is an overproduction of capital in relation to existing levels of surplus value, an increase in surplus value will be necessary for capital accumulation, come what may; and if real wages cannot be cut by the incorporation of trade union leaders and the 'voluntary restraint' of the entire working class, then unemployment and inflation will do the same job in a different way. And when free collective bargaining is linked to a demand for extensive import controls, it will inevitably curtail further the already sluggish levels of world trade, with serious consequences for unemployment (if not here, then abroad). The free play of market forces in the domestic labour process, plus the export of unemployment, is hardly an adequate socialist answer to an international crisis of capitalism.

It seems inevitable that trade union leaders advocating either the social contract strategy or a return to free collective bargaining will run into increasing problems of credibility with their members. The lack of return (in the form of investment, growth and rising living standards) will make it increasingly difficult to sustain wage restraint within a social contract, and the impact on prices and employment of any return to free collective bargaining will call into question the claims made for it by those specifying wage control itself as *the* problem to be overcome. Indeed, as David Yaffe has argued, effective working-class resistance to government policies of retrenchment must make the crisis worse, and by pretending that this is not so those left-wingers in the trade union movement who campaign for free collective bargaining as a total solution to working-class ills leave themselves particularly vulnerable to rapid loss of support when any implementation of their demands makes this obvious. In this sense a period of free collective bargaining could be a precursor to another period of voluntary wage restraint just as it was in 1974–75. As Yaffe and his colleagues have insisted,

Unless it is argued that the defence of the living standards of the working class will deepen the crisis, unless it is understood that there can be no resolution of the crisis within capitalism that is not wholly at the expense of the working class, then it will not be possible to train a revolutionary vanguard and build a revolutionary movement in this country.[29]

Neither Arthur Scargill nor Jack Jones can provide a successful way forward for British trade unionism. The experience of 1974–78 reinforces the importance of the recognition that the limits of effective trade unionism are established by the law of value under capitalism, and that challenging those limits can never be a purely economic or a narrowly British affair. Trade union resistance has to be widened into a revolutionary socialist struggle or succumb to its own contradictions. The argument, after all, is not new, that left to itself collective bargaining is bound to succumb to the dictates of capital, as rank-and-file trade unionists, no less than their leaders, see the 'necessity' for restraint as the lesser of two evils. Ben Fine has recently put it like this.

Struggle within the wage system cannot by itself bring down capitalism. For if it is pursued beyond the point where accumulation has collapsed workers cannot help but be aware of the consequences of their action, and wage demands will pale into insignificance against more fundamental threats to the capitalist relations of production. Workers are faced with the choice: either moderate wage claims or investment slackens with falling employment. This is the conventional wisdom, and the consciousness necessary to reject this wisdom requires the wisdom to reject capitalism. In other words the wage system poses strict historical limits on the level of wages. Challenging those limits can never be a purely economic struggle.[30]

Trade union leaders, historically as now, have shown neither the will nor the inclination to take on so awesome a task as the overthrow of capitalism, and have rarely been pushed towards such an aspiration by any large-scale politicised rank-and-file pressure. But this cannot alter the fact that until the truth of Ben Fine's remarks is widely realised within the trade union movement the gap between the appearance of power and its reality will persist, and trade union leaders will continue to share with their parliamentary colleagues in the Labour Party a persistent inability to prevent the aspiration for social justice and general prosperity from disintegrating before the imperatives of a process of capital accumulation to which they can respond but over which they can exercise no ultimate control. It was for this reason that the disappointments of office between 1974 and 1979 were not experienced within the labour movement as a process setting parliamentarians against trade unionists. For those disappointments were experienced as a *shared* sense of impotence, in the face of a crisis whose intractability defeated Ministers and trade union leaders alike.

Such limits on the power of trade union leaders should come as no surprise to those readers long steeped in the left-wing literature on the role and character of trade unions under capitalism. In a classic article on the limits and possibilities of trade union action, Perry Anderson put in general terms the contradictions operating in the 1970s: that trade unions are, at one and the same time, 'an opposition to capitalism and a component of it',[31] expressing tensions in the class struggle under capitalism, but incapable themselves of challenging or transforming a class society as such. Trade unions, as Anderson noted, follow the 'contours' of capitalism. They take their organisational structure and their demands from the capital-dominated environment of the factory. They enjoy as their ultimate sanction only a *negative* withdrawal of labour, and wield only a sectoral power potential against the universal force of capital, such that in consequence trade unions are capable of sustaining only a sectoral or 'corporate' sense of class in their working-class base. But such a recognition of the limits of trade union power should not blind us to the importance of strong trade unionism. It would be a mistake to slide from an analysis of the subordination of trade union leaders before the State to a specification of trade unions as simple extensions of the State – part of the 'ideological State apparatus which serves to reproduce the capitalist social formation', to use the conventional terminology of the followers of Poulantzas and Althusser.[32] Their specification is attractive because it draws attention to a critical function of modern trade union leaders, as guarantors of industrial peace and working-class restraint. But it misleads when it fails to locate the limits on that process of leadership incorporation. What has to be recognised is the *contradictory* role of union leaders in modern capitalism, the cross pressures operating on them, and the degree of autonomy which these necessarily generate for the trade union function. The degree of incorporation to which trade union leaders succumb is limited by the strength of rank-and-file pressure, pressure which can never be entirely absent under capitalism because of the adverse impact of the law of value on the lives of trade unionists and their families. The intensity of the class struggle clearly varies, and in the determination of that intensity the degree of trade union incorporation plays a vital part. Hence the preoccupation of politicians with the winning of union leaders' support. But the class struggle has roots outside the trade unions, and stands as a force restricting the total subordination of trade union policy to government dictates; and in this sense the defensive role of trade unionism remains strong, as a way of offering vestigial resistance to unemployment and the intensification of work routines, and as a base upon which working-class self-confidence and political assertiveness can grow.

Industrial militancy is a vital ingredient in the move to a socialist society, and a rejection of wage restraint is critical to the education of a new generation of workers in the true nature of State power under capitalism. But trade unionism of itself cannot resolve the dilemmas to which it is a response, and unpoliticised industrial militancy will ever run into the paradoxes which surround working-class resistance under capitalism. The system's compensatory mechanisms that act to nullify the effect of industrial militancy are strong precisely because they operate automatically, through a set of market mechanisms that require no central orchestration by a ruling class. Unemployment or inflation, low investment or high labour exploitation, are choices dictated to the labour movement by the inexorable logic of a fully developed capitalist economy. Trade union action can affect the balance between unemployment and inflation, investment and labour exploitation, but it cannot remove the choice itself; nor can it prevent trade union resistance to one side of each choice having adverse consequences on the other. The visibility of this last process will leave trade unions blamed for inflation or for low investment when in reality the fault is not theirs. The structuring of the choices to which trade unionism is a response lies deep in capitalism; and the recognition of this is the first stage on the journey from industrial militancy within capitalism to political action against it.

The full discussion of this must wait until the last chapter. What is clear now is the true nature of the relationship between the trade union leadership and the Labour Government between 1974 and 1979. The close involvement of trade union leaders in consultations with Labour Ministers was a major *procedural* gain which helped to cement the already strong ties of personality and ideology between the two wings of the labour movement. But the substantive issues on the agenda of that consultative process were not fixed by trade union pressure. At best, trade union leaders enjoyed the power to choose the lesser of two evils in situations in which the alternatives were not of their making or choice; and in that way the potential of their newfound procedural powers was drained of its substance by the severity of the crisis which surrounded unions and Government alike. That crisis did not divide them. On the contrary, with the exception of left-wing preoccupations with free collective bargaining, both groups operated within roughly similar definitions of the causes and consequences, the necessities and policy options that the crisis generated. The range of options was sufficiently wide to permit serious disagreement on individual issues, and on these, particularly when questions of general economic strategy were involved, the trade unions as often as not found themselves as one pressure group among many, rarely enjoying the immediate leverage of other more significantly placed groups of financiers and foreign governments. The initial rush of reforms in 1974 could not be repeated; and Labour Government–trade union relations thereafter became a matter of salvaging what the trade unions could from a package whose total viability was eroded by the persistence of stagnation and unemployment. All that the trade unions could do was to hang on to the Labour Party out of fear of a Conservative Government which might repeal the procedural gains and intensify unemployment, in the hope that time would bring a relaxation of the constraints under which the Labour Government had to operate. The Labour Government for its part clung to the trade union leadership with equal desperation, as a way of maintaining an increasingly unpopular policy of wage restraint while waiting for the same revival of trade and prosperity. The much vaunted alliance between the two wings of the labour movement persisted, but its significance for policy waned as both Ministers and trade union leaders stood immobile and impotent before a world whose major social and economic processes remained outside their comprehension and control.

# CHAPTER SIX
# *The weakness of the Labour Left*

Trade union leaders were not the only section of the British labour movement to be regularly denounced in the British press in the 1970s. As their political leverage over the Labour Government visibly waned, and so long as trade union moderation became too obvious to ignore, the attention of newspaper editors and television journalists switched to the supposed threat posed to stable democratic government by Tribunite MPs and their left-wing supporters among the Party's constituency activists. Reg Prentice played an important role in orchestrating this view of the Labour Government's vulnerability to left-wing domination, justifying his own resignation, first from the Cabinet and then from the Party, in terms of a revulsion from a 'growing emphasis on class war and Marxist dogma' within the Labour Party.[1] This was at its worst, he claimed, in the NEC's 1976 Programme, on which the next manifesto would be based. The content of that programme, including as it did proposals for extensive public ownership, the abolition of the House of Lords, and the insistence that MPs be subject to a re-selection conference in their constituency party before each general election, committed the Labour Party, in Prentice's view, 'to the most extreme socialist policies to which any major political party in Britain had ever been committed'. 'It was no exaggeration,' he told the House of Commons, 'to say that this is a Marxist concept designed by Marxists which would take us a long way along the road to a Marxist society.'[2]

Of course such charges were not new. They are the stock in trade of every right-wing newspaper editor short of copy. But Reg Prentice's status (and his much publicised troubles with his own constituency party) seemed to give them a new credibility, and were certainly much cited by those claiming that the Labour Party was in the grip of extremists, 'drifting to the left', subject to 'creeping Marxism', or even, at its most melodramatic, 'infiltrated to a terrifying degree by crypto-communists and fifth columnists', with ten of its MPs 'little less than the equivalent of undercover political agents for alien political creeds'.[3] The defection of other Establishment figures within the Labour Party – Woodrow Wyatt,[4] Paul Johnson, even Lord George-Brown – seemed to offer yet further proof that the significant determination of policy lay with the Left of the Party, and that the Left's influence was growing. Since nothing could be further from the truth, the policy and impact of the Labour Left must be examined again before a final verdict can be given on the character, determinants and potential of Labour Government policy in the 1970s.[5]


I

Certain features of Labour Party politics after 1970 helped to sustain this image of left-wing power. There can be no doubt that the Left within the parliamentary party, the constitutencies and the unions made much of the running in the years of opposition.[6] The drift to the left in the trade unions after 1967 left the Party in opposition with a new constellation of political forces, as Tribunite MPs allied with trade union figures to formulate and carry through the Party's annual conference a set of policy proposals more radical than any that had inspired the Labour Governments of the 1960s. Left-wing policy proposals after 1970, as we have seen, stressed the need to subordinate market forces in the economy to democratic socialist ones through public ownership, planning agreements, strengthened trade unionism and industrial democracy, and emphasised the need for public expenditure and for changes in taxation and social welfare payments to create a more socially just society, one free from poverty and less scarred by class inequalities. As we have also seen, the original social contract between the Labour Party leadership and the TUC did contain a number of the policies that had been traditionally canvassed by the left of the Party: the extension of public ownership, the creation of machinery to control private industry, and commitments to trade union legal reforms, to industrial democracy, and to heavy public spending on education, health and social welfare. Party leaders agreed to renegotiate the terms of EEC membership in line with left-wing demands to break with a capitalist Europe; and the Party formally united behind a commitment to shift class wealth and power 'in favour of working people and their families' in a way which would have been inconceivable only a decade before.

Nor did a return to office in March 1974 immediately dispel left-wing hopes that radical policies would follow. The Tribunite group of MPs was at least eighty strong in the new Parliament, and leading figures of the parliamentary Left were given important government posts. Michael Foot, a leading Tribunite of the 1960s and the biographer of Aneurin Bevan, went to the Department of Employment; and the newly radicalised Tony Benn became Secretary of State for Industry, with two left-wing MPs as his Ministers of State. These men were subject to an almost unceasing tirade of press criticism and Conservative condemnation that sustained the Party's radical image through the first fifteen months of the Government's term of office, as they produced White Papers which were remarkably true to the spirit and the letter of the 1973 Labour Party programme in which the campaigning of the opposition years had culminated. In this, Michael Foot and Tony Benn were given the full and public support of the Party machine outside Parliament. The Party's General Secretary regularly acted as spokesman for *Party* policy, as did the NEC, on which left-wing influence had grown in the wake of the drift to the left in the trade unions after 1967.[7] Indeed, as Government policy after July 1975 moved away from the aspirations of the 1973 Programme, the NEC kept alive the hopes of the Left (and the image of a divided and potentially radical party) by regularly producing policy proposals and planning documents that were in line with Tribunite criticisms of the Labour Government's economic strategy.

Many features of the Labour Party's internal politics acted to sustain this image of left-wing influence after 1974: not least the NEC's decision to appoint a self-professed Trotskyist as the Party's Youth Officer, the appointment of a Tribunite MP to the Party Treasurership vacated by James Callaghan, the periodic public condemnation of Trotskyist infiltration into constituency parties by Labour Prime Ministers, the presence of the Trotskyist 'Militant' group among the Party's Young Socialists, the left-wing campaign to remove the Parliamentary Party's right to select the Party leader, and the intermittent evidence of left-wing campaigns in several constituency parties to unseat right-of-centre Labour MPs. It is a measure of the Left's presence under this Labour Government that the right and centre of the Parliamentary Party should have felt the necessity to agitate so vitriolically against Tribunite policies and Trotskyist influences,[8] and to create their own factional organisation. Yet in doing this, they only reinforced the very image of a radical and divided party which they strove so hard to dispel, and helped to sustain the popular vision of a Cabinet under left-wing domination that was so at variance with the actual development of policy.


## II

The first important defeat for the Left during this Labour Government came on the question of EEC membership. The Conservative's decision to enter the EEC in January 1973 had bitterly divided the Labour Party, with the majority (though not the entirety) of anti-EEC pressure coming from the Party's Left and trade union base. The decision to renegotiate the terms of entry in the event of a Labour Government being returned to office, and the later decision to put these renegotiated terms to the British people in a referendum, were attempts by the Party leadership to paper over the deep divisions of principle that made the EEC so sensitive an issue at every level within the Labour Party. Leading figures on the right and centre of the Party felt sufficiently strongly to vote with the Conservatives in favour of EEC entry, and to resign the deputy leadership (as Roy Jenkins did in 1972) or (in Shirley Williams's case) to announce their intention of withdrawing from public life if the referendum was lost. Feelings on the left of the Party were equally strong, inspired primarily by the fear that membership of the EEC would drastically restrict the ability of a Labour Government to introduce socialist policies. As Michael Barratt Brown put it, 'all the economic institutions, rules and regulations of the EEC are designed to achieve just one economic end: that the allocation of resources . . . is determined in the market by the return in profit to private capital', and 'on the other hand, the system of political organisation in the EEC has just one political end, to prevent any one of the member states from breaking away from the capitalist embrace'.

Whether we look at it from the point of view of our trade deficit (the deficit with the original six countries of the EEC is now running at £200 million a month), our loss of control over capital movements, exchange rates, agricultural policy, sources of food imports; of the switch of our tax system to VAT; of the threat to our regional development policies and economic planning strategy from regulation by bureaucrats in Brussels, not only is the freedom of manoeuvre of a reforming Labour Government effectively narrowed down but the prospects for an advance to socialism are seriously set back.[9]

It was this fear that EEC membership would add yet another layer of obstacles to Labour Party radicalism that inspired the motion carried (against NEC opposition) by the Party's 1974 conference, demanding safeguards to guarantee a Labour Government's right to control industry, to restrict movements of capital and labour, and to settle its own policy on taxation, food subsidies, imports and defence. It was this fear that turned the Labour anti-marketeers into eloquent defenders of parliamentary sovereignty, and encouraged the Labour Left to present the referendum as an opportunity to defend, in Tony Benn's words, the five basic democratic rights threatened by the EEC. As he put it in a letter to his constituents:

The power of the electors of Britain, through their direct representatives in Parliament, to make laws, levy taxes, change laws which the courts must uphold, and control the conduct of public affairs, has been substantially ceded to the European Community whose Council of Ministers and Commission are neither collectively elected, nor collectively dismissed by the British people, nor even by the people of all the Community countries put together.[10]

The Labour Party manifestoes in February and October 1974 had specified seven particular areas of EEC membership for renegotiation. The Party required major changes in the Common Agricultural Policy, to maintain access to British markets by low-cost producers outside Europe. It required the next Labour Government to negotiate new and fairer ways of financing the Community's budget, to establish the freedom of British governments to pursue effective regional, industrial and fiscal policies, and to achieve an agreement on capital movements which would protect employment and the balance of payments in Britain. The Labour negotiators were, in addition, to safeguard the interests of producers in the Commonwealth and the underdeveloped world, to resist any tax harmonisation that involved extra taxation on necessities, and to 'reject any kind of international agreement which compelled us to accept increased unemployment for the sake of maintaining a fixed parity'. The Left of the Party felt that the terms negotiated by James Callaghan in Dublin early in 1975 fell 'very far short of the negotiation objectives which have been party policy for more than ten years';[11] and in this they had the backing of more than half the entire Parliamentary Labour Party. The renegotiated terms were carried through the Commons only with Conservative support, as the anti-Marketeers gained the votes of 7 of the 23-strong cabinet, 31 of the 62 junior ministers and 107 of the 199 backbench Labour MPs. The terms were also rejected by a two to one majority at a special Labour Party conference in May 1975, and by 8,436,094 people in the referendum in June. But the Labour Left lost this last and vital vote, and did so decisively. Though some leading anti-Marketeers had stooped to the wildest jingoism in their campaign, and though others had repeatedly stressed that EEC membership facilitated the export of capital, threatened British jobs and made regional and industrial aid more difficult to provide,[12] EEC membership was still supported by over 17 million people in the June 5th referendum. The Left's campaign, on an issue selected and pushed by left wing agitation, ended in a 67.3 to 32.7 per cent landslide victory for the Right and Centre leadership of the Party; and no section of the British political élite had been given electoral backing on that scale since Ramsay MacDonald's National Government victory *against* the Labour Party in 1931.

Left-wing members of the Parliamentary Labour Party did not abandon the EEC fight entirely after June 1975, but they were seriously weakened by the referendum result. Left-wing control of the Industry Department was abruptly ended after the referendum result was known; and on Harold Wilson's sudden resignation in March 1976, the Parliamentary Labour Party rejected left-wing candidates for the Party leadership in favour of the man who had renegotiated the entry terms, and who personified the conservatism of the Party centre. Though the national press was struck by the size of parliamentary support for Michael Foot in that leadership election (he led on the first ballot), the Party's new deputy leader had by then long made his own somewhat uneasy peace with the industrial and economic strategy to which the Labour Left maintained so spirited an opposition. For with Tony Benn's departure from the Industry Department, the Government's industrial strategy systematically shed the very innovations on which the Left had depended. In particular, as we have seen, no system of planning agreements was forthcoming, no rapid moves to industrial democracy were achieved, no more worker cooperatives were supported, and no attempt was made by the NEB to 'seize the commanding heights' of private manufacturing capital, as had initially been envisaged. As a result the left wing of the Party could still feel that *their* industrial strategy had not been tried, and that this Labour Government, like Labour Governments before it, had missed a golden opportunity to pursue a democratic socialist industrial strategy. The EEC vote did not cause that failure, but the scale of the pro-Market majority no doubt speeded its arrival. For with the limits of the Left's electoral support so visibly exposed, the Tribunites' opponents within the Labour Cabinet were in a much stronger position to shape the subsequent development of general economic policy, and to ignore the calls within the Cabinet for the forthright pursuit of a left wing economic strategy.

From June 1975 the backbench Tribunite group moved into

increasing opposition to the general drift of government economic policy, as they saw – in Stuart Holland's words – 'the rethink in theory and policy which followed the 1970 election defeat transformed under the present Government into a half-hearted State capitalism, rather than a major challenge to capitalism itself'.[13] Left-wing satisfaction with the Chancellor's second budget in July 1974 proved to be shortlived. Praised in the columns of *Tribune* in July 1974 for breaking with 'the Treasury orthodoxy which has had such a disastrous effect on the course of British economic revival since the war',[14] Denis Healey came under heavy criticism in November 1974, when his recasting of Government economic strategy involved a deliberate decision to let unemployment rise and price controls to ease. In part, left-wing anxiety at so early a stage in the Government's life reflected the fear of Tribunite MPs that, as was indeed to be the case, the Government would give tax concessions and financial aid to private industry without channelling that aid through the National Enterprise Board, and so miss an opportunity to establish government control over large sections of private sector investment. But it also reflected their recognition of the growing pressure for short-term deflationary measures, and the toleration of long-term unemployment, to which the Chancellor was subject, and to which Labour's programme in 1973 was supposed to be an alternative. As Brian Sedgemore put it in December 1974:

The experience of the last three decades and the performance of private industry makes it clear that investment-led growth cannot be achieved by conventional Keynesian demand management and fiscal concession policies. Investment-led growth will only come about through direct investment in industry through the operation of planning agreements and the National Enterprise Board. Without these tools . . . however competitive exports are made and however much 'slack' is created through unemployment, it will be home demand that will take up surplus labour, and not necessarily in productive areas; without these tools there will be phony sprints for growth; and without them balance of payments difficulties will reoccur and unemployment will be brought back as a cure.[15]

As Government policy failed to respond to such left-wing arguments, Tribunite criticisms of each successive stage of the Government's retreat became ever more strident. Anthony Crosland's decision to end the freeze on commercial rents from February 1975 was condemned in *Tribune* as a surrender to the property speculators and banking sector; and the July 1975 decision to pursue a counter-inflationary policy by imposing wage restraint was criticised as a 'panic measure', a 'fatal error', a 'disaster', and a surrender to Treasury and banking pressure. The July 1975 crisis saw the first major clash on general economic policy between this Labour Government and its own left wing, with Tribunite MPs rejecting the view that high levels of public spending and trade union wage demands were the main causes of inflation, and offering instead an alternative strategy of selective import controls, restrictions on the export of capital, price controls, compulsory planning agreements and the extension of public ownership into the finance houses, and through the NEB. They were well aware that, in spite of ministerial claims to the contrary, the July 1975 pay policy would 'prove to be a preliminary to pay laws and spending cuts rather than an alternative to them';[16] but they could not prevent that policy from being implemented, nor block the cuts in public spending which inevitably followed. Left-wing anger with the February 1976 cuts in planned public expenditure was sufficient to persuade thirty-seven Labour MPs to vote against the Government, and so defeat it in the House; but the Left rallied to the Government's defence in the vote of confidence that followed, so that the Government survived and the cuts continued unabated. By then, relations between the Tribunite group and the bulk of the Labour Cabinet were badly strained. Left-wing control of the Home Policy Committee of the NEC gave left-wing views on extra platform; and it was from here that the watered-down Industry Bill was criticised in March 1975, and a call for early reflation, selective import controls and the protection of social expenditure urged in November 1975. But the Left was insufficiently strong, even on the NEC, to win the special Party conference it demanded after the February 1976 White Paper on planned government expenditure; and neither the resignation of Joan Lestor from the Government nor Eric Heffer's call to the labour movement to fight the cuts 'as we did over *In Place of Strife*'[17] could shift the Government from its resolve. On the contrary, as unemployment rose through 1976, the Government cut public sector spending twice more: first in July, and then in December after the lengthy and much publicised negotiations with the IMF. By then the Chancellor had long rejected the Left's alternative economic strategy as 'totally unrealistic', and the left Labour MPs as 'out of their Chinese minds'.[18] Certainly he was able to defeat the Left's case when Tony Benn presented it to the Cabinet in the midst of the IMF negotiations,[19] in spite of the thirteen to six NEC vote against further public sector non-military spending cuts, later supported by as many as 105 backbench Labour MPs. Even as the Healey budgets became less deflationary in 1977 and 1978, left-wing criticism did not abate. Unemployment remained too high, pay policy too rigid, and the economy insufficiently protected by import controls or guided by state intervention to satisfy a parliamentary Left who feared not simply the electoral consequences for the Labour Government, but also the social costs of what they took to be the Cabinet's failure to pursue a socialist industrial and economic strategy which, in their view, was the only basis for long-term economic growth and financial solvency.

The starting point of the Tribunite critique of the Healey strategy was the recognition that 'the heart of Britain's weakness lies in its comparatively poor record of investment, especially in manufacturing industry', and that the responsibility for that lay, not with the unions or the Government, but with private industry and the financial institutions of the City. The case for public ownership was made in part on the simple grounds that 'the investment expansion Britain desperately needs is too important to be left to businessmen and financiers alone', particularly when the growth of monopolies in the financial world had already given 'the handful of major banks and insurance companies . . . a massive amount of . . . power'.[20] But it rested too on the belief that, in any case, the investment record of British industry was so poor precisely because business and financial élites were too prone to put their own class interests before those of the nation as a whole. They were too prone to speculate in property, land and works of art, to the detriment of the supply of funds to manufacturing industry. They were too prone to export abroad, and to invest in manufacturing competitors there, instead of directing investment to an already undercapitalised British industrial base;[21] and they were too preoccupied with their own short-term profit requirements to be the proper guardians of the long-term needs of British industrial regeneration. In all this, Tribunites argued, they were serviced by a powerful but profoundly conservative Treasury and Bank of England, whose leading officials subscribed to outdated economic orthodoxies, were regularly apt to give misleading and inaccurate forecasts and advice, and were, it was suspected, more concerned with blunting Labour radicalism and trade union industrial strength than with achieving an adequate rate of economic growth and full employment.[22] In the Left's view, the Treasury's caste mentality and the selfish class motives of the senior businessmen and financiers with whom the Treasury identified had combined to deny to British industry the buoyant home markets and the working and investment capital 'that industry so desperately needs'.[23]

The Left's major criticism of the 'Treasury mind' was that it regularly opposed the adoption of Tribune's alternative economic strategy. That strategy developed slowly, and came to have a number of components. In an early and rather tentative document in January 1975, the

Government was urged by left-wing MPs to provide the NEB with at least £1,000 million a year with which to buy its way into profitable firms (not just into firms in difficulties) in order to act as a catalyst for manufacturing investment generally. This early document talked of the way in which economic control 'would be greatly facilitated by the public ownership of the banks and insurance companies', and by the introduction of selective import controls (on finished goods not imported from Third World countries) in order to 'encourage the growth of firms concerned with import substitution, to ensure that key industries have the raw materials and components they need, to see that the whole plan is not frustrated by excessive import bills and to maintain full employment'.[24] In addition, the Government was urged to press planning agreements on the biggest hundred companies as a way of encouraging import substitution, the idea of petrol rationing was floated, and unemployment was to be tackled by selective aid to particular hard pressed industries, most noticeably the construction industry.

By the end of 1975 the alternative strategy was clearer, and the tone more strident and critical. Though individual MPs and trade union leaders each had their own list of individual demands, and although there were significant differences of opinion within the Parliamentary Left on the desirability of import controls or the necessity for incomes policy, even so Brian Sedgemore's nine-point alternative strategy can be taken as generally representative.

Import controls
An end to sterling's role as a reserve currency
Price controls and an incomes policy
Planning agreements
Muscle to the National Enterprise Board
Industrial democracy
Public ownership of the financial institutions
The maintenance of Labour's social programmes and defence cuts.[25]

Certainly the Left generally rejected Denis Healey's deflationary strategy, his tinkering with monetarist targets, and his toleration of a depreciating currency and rising unemployment. In general the Tribune group demanded, as did the TUC, a reflated and planned economy protected by some degree of import controls and stimulated to economic growth and full employment by high levels of government spending and extensive public ownership. The alternative industrial strategy of the Left called for the NEB to be given enormous extra sums to buy its way unrestricted into profitable private industry. It called for a systematic and compulsory negotiation of planning agreements with large multinational companies to reduce the degree of unnecessary imports within such companies, and to reduce the incidence of transfer pricing there. It called too for an extension of industrial democracy, and the selection of men sympathetic to public ownership to head publicly owned concerns. The Left demanded the public ownership of the major banking and insurance companies, by emergency legislation if necessary, to give a reforming Labour Government direct control over the supply of important funds to industry. It advocated tight exchange controls to restrict the export of capital. It urged a termination of sterling's role as a reserve currency, with all the volatility that that had brought to the movements of money in and out of the City. The Left also urged the Cabinet to introduce selective import controls, in order to protect jobs, to give weak industries a breathing space in which to strengthen themselves against fierce international competition, and to prevent a reflationary economic policy from being undermined by a sharp deterioration in the balance of payments. And the Left was adamant that cuts in non-defence public spending accentuated, rather than eased, the depressed state of private investment, and that the resulting loss of employment was not simply socially appalling and electorally disastrous for the Labour Party, but was also an indefensible waste of real resources and a cause of heavier government borrowing. Its answer to inflation was renewed investment through the NEB, coupled with tight price controls and a degree of wage restraint that could only be guaranteed by the systematic pursuit of social justice, by the insistence on (rather than any retreat from) a freeze on high incomes, the introduction of a wealth tax, and the protection of the social wage. In Tony Benn's words, it was the view of the parliamentary Left that 'the spiral of inflation and industrial collapse must be broken by a return to full employment, massive investment and systematic support for firms in trouble'[26] and not by the IMF dictated deflationary strategy and retreat from the 1973 *Programme* on which the Labour Government actually settled after November 1974.

It was this alternative economic strategy which the Labour Party conference voted to accept in 1976, and which the Labour Party's NEC presented as the Party's mid-term manifesto in June 1977: it was also the strategy which the Cabinet decisively rejected only eight weeks after the 1976 Party conference, in its agreement with the IMF. Indeed it must stand as one index of the failure of the Labour Left between 1974 and 1979 that they were still fighting, in the build up to the 1979 general election, for the party leadership to include in the election manifesto the very policy proposals to which the Party had apparently been committed in 1973 and which had then constituted the centre of the Party's 'radical' image, namely abolition of the House of Lords, compulsory planning agreements, further public ownership, stronger price controls, an expanded NEB, state control of at least part of the funds of the major private financial institutions, genuine industrial democracy, a wealth tax, improved social benefits, and policies to create a million and a half new jobs.

Most of these issues did in fact resurface in the 1979 Labour Party manifesto, as did the Left's opposition to the Common Market and their promise to 'bring about a fundamental shift in the balance of wealth and power in favour of working people and their families'. But the overall tone and image of the 1979 document was significantly less radical than its 1974 predecessors, and the record of five years of Labour government could not but give the manifesto's more radical promises a distinctly hollow ring. In fact it is probably accurate to say that their inclusion in the party manifesto told Labour's electorate more about the Left's vestigial strength in the party machinery outside parliament in the build up to a general election than it did about the likely impact of the Parliamentary Left on any future Callaghan government. Certainly by 1979 there was little electoral enthusiasm for either the Labour Government or its left wing, and there was no way in which the Labour Left could prevent Tribunite MPs from suffering as heavily as any other section of the Party in the defeat which took the Labour Government back into opposition.

## III

The failure of this generation of the Labour Left to control the drift of government policy is fully in the tradition of the Labour Party. Under each Labour Government to date, initial left-wing optimism has quickly turned into frustration and opposition as policy has drifted away from their prescriptions. As I discussed at length in *The Labour Party and the Struggle for Socialism,* each generation of left-wing parliamentarians within the Labour Party has faced a cruel choice of strategies in the pursuit of influence. Left-wing MPs could act as an 'open conspiracy' within the Labour Party, organising themselves as a faction to agitate for a left-wing programme. Or they could wait, compromise with the existing drift of policy, in the hope that its bankruptcy would eventually become obvious, and give the Party leadership no choice but to accept a left-wing alternative. As I argued there,[27] each strategy was fraught with difficulties. To organise separately was vital if pressure was to be maintained on Labour Cabinets subject to heavy conservative influences; and yet to organise separately always exposed leading left-wing figures to the possibility of censure and to the imposition of disciplinary sanctions. To organise separately was also to risk alienating, by open agitation, the very Party leadership that the Left wished to persuade; and certainly, by the impression of Party disunity that it necessarily created, separate organisation served to weaken the electoral appeal of the Labour Party in the build up to a general election. And yet not to agitate, particularly in the build up to a general election, was to miss an opportunity to educate both the labour movement and the Labour Cabinet in a left-wing alternative, and to fail to dissociate, in the electorate's mind, Labour's Left from the Party's right and centre as public dissatisfaction with a right-wing Labour Government inevitably developed. As a result, the strategy of waiting for a 'ripe time' and compromising now constantly postponed the 'ripening process', and gave the Labour Left no hope of creating any groundswell of electoral support for its programme. On the contrary, it seemed doomed to consolidate the position of right-wing and centre parliamentarians, whose refusal to implement left-wing programmes had necessitated the choice of left-wing strategy in the first place.

Historically, the left wing of the Labour Party has handled this dilemma by waxing first hot and then cold in its campaign for an alternative programme. Invariably, and especially early in a new parliament, left-wingers have been prepared to vote occasionally against their own Cabinet, and to publicly criticise the drift of policy; only to fall back into line whenever votes of confidence were mentioned and when elections loomed. Left-wing MPs have invariably looked outside parliament, to the extra-parliamentary institutions of the Labour Party, for support, and have urged greater Labour Party democracy and conference control; only to find either that the right wing of the Party was stronger in the trade union movement with its bloc votes, or (on those rare occasions when this was not the case) that extra-parliamentary control was not acceptable to a Labour Cabinet struggling with economic difficulties. Instead, the Labour Left has found itself subject to repeated calls for unity, and for the end of factionalism; and its leaders in particular have had to tread a very narrow tightrope, unable to speak openly without the danger of dismissal from the Cabinet, and all too prone as a result to make their peace with orthodox economic policies as the price of office. Indeed the dilemma of left-wing Ministers has always been a particularly acute

239

one. Office was attractive to aspiring left-wing politicians for obvious
and quite legitimate personal reasons, and also because it was the key to
the implementation of the policies to which they were committed. But
as a minority voice in a Labour Cabinet, influence was hard to win, and
the question of resignation or dismissal on some matter of principle
could never be avoided for long. Yet resignation could only bring a
total lack of influence in the short term; while the retention of office
(though giving some influence and permitting some treasured
commitments to be implemented) also involved an acceptance of
collective responsibility and hence an obligation to defend (if only by
carefully chosen silences) the very drift of policy to which the left-wing
Ministers were privately so opposed.

All these dilemmas and developments have been evident again since
1974. There were occasions, particularly in March 1976, when
left-wing back benchers were prepared to defeat their own
Government, and when the left-wing dominated NEC was willing to
issue a mid-term manifesto critical of Labour Government policy. But
those same MPs were quick to support the vote of confidence that
followed, and the NEC was reluctantly willing to tone down its
mid-term manifesto to merely 'a basis for the Party's campaign work'[28]
for the sake of Party unity. The Left, particularly in the Cabinet, was
subject to repeated calls for discipline, unity and an end of factionalism.
Harold Wilson made a particularly clear call for this over the issue of
joint British–South African naval manoeuvres in November 1974.
Robert Mellish, Wilson's Chief Whip, made another in March 1976
telling the Left 'to stop parading their consciences' or face a general
election. James Callaghan repeated the call when first elected leader, and
later when Tony Benn abstained in an NEC vote critical of government
expenditure cuts.[29] In spite of Callaghan's appeal for an end to
factionalism, the Tribune group itself was not prepared to disband; but
nor was it prepared to carry its campaign openly and systematically into
the constituencies when this was suggested in December 1975. As its
chairman Arthur Latham said, to do so would be to create 'the
impression of a party within a party',[30] and this he was not prepared to
do.

The Left's leading figures in the Cabinet experienced the usual set of
acute personal dilemmas. When Harold Wilson made his November
1974 call to three left-wing cabinet Ministers to resign or to give full
public backing to government policy, apparently all three came 'to the
brink of resignation late one night before giving way'.[31] Thereafter they
pursued somewhat different strategies. Each kept alive in the public
mind his or her own dissatisfaction with the drift of policy, by carefully

chosen public announcements on isolated issues. Otherwise, different personal strategies predominated. Some resigned, to speak freely; others accepted office, to seek influence; others remained silent, to keep office. Eric Heffer and Joan Lestor, each in their own time and place, in effect resigned and went to the back benches, to gain the freedom to criticise policy developments which, as junior Ministers, they had been unable to prevent. At the same time, and moving in the opposite direction, Margaret Jackson and (temporarily) Bob Cryer accepted junior office, in spite of left-wing criticisms, ostensibly in the pursuit of that influence over government policy which Joan Lestor and Eric Heffer had failed to enjoy.[32] Within the Cabinet, Judith Hart was sacked against her will by Harold Wilson, only to return to office under James Callaghan; and outside the Cabinet Brian Sedgemore came and went as Tony Benn's PPS, sacked by prime-ministerial order. Tony Benn, for his part, chose to wait his time. Beyond a regular speech to the Labour Party conference on the evils of capitalism, and periodic minor acts of rebellion within the NEC, he accepted effective demotion after June 1975, tolerated repeated prime-ministerial warnings to observe collective responsibility, and kept silent in public in order to be free in private to put the left wing case to the Cabinet. If James Callaghan is to be believed, Tony Benn's position, though patient, was also painful. 'I've got him on the end of a rope,' the Prime Minister told reporters, 'and occasionally I give a sharp jerk on the noose.'[33]

Only Michael Foot seems to have gone further, and initially to have tolerated, and then fully to have accepted, the case for wage controls that he had hitherto opposed. There is a personal irony here, in the biographer of Aneurin Bevan following the route of accommodation with the Party's right and centre that Bevan took after 1957. But the political trajectory of Michael Foot after 1974 is not quite that of a Bevanite accommodation with Gaitskellite revisionism. As Michael Foot could and did argue before left-wing audiences, this Labour Government had implemented important labour legislation under his guidance which had to be consolidated by the retention of Labour in office; and loyalty was at a premium after 1975 because of the Government's minority position and because of its dependence on Liberal votes which left-wing agitation could only jeopardise. The Left's dilemma in the face of the Liberals was particularly acute; for the Left needed to keep a Labour Government in office if there was to be any hope of radical measures, and yet this particular Labour Government stayed in power in 1977 and 1978 only because of a pact with the Liberals which explicitly excluded the implementation of Tribunite policies. Faced with this dilemma, the Labour Left could neither force policy nor risk a general election; and their weakness was compounded by the switch of loyalty of leading trade union figures after July 1975. When Jack Jones publicly clashed with Ian Mikardo at the 1975 Labour Party conference he was only underlining the extent of the Left's defeat: deserted by major trade union allies, compromised by the Liberal pact, outvoted in Cabinet, and subject to a degree of right-wing factionalism within the Party that was reaching new and vitriolic heights.

## IV

Nevertheless it would be a mistake to treat the Labour Left's failure to control the drift of Labour Government policy simply in terms of the Left's weak position inside the Party. For this Labour Left, unlike the Bevanites of the 1950s or even the Socialist League of the 1930s, lost the struggle for influence from an opening position of considerable strength. The Labour Party Programme of 1973 contained the bulk of the Left's demands, and was buttressed by strong trade union support. As the Government began, the Left enjoyed an unparalleled strength on the NEC and in the Labour Cabinet, and was able to maintain those positions throughout. Most important of all, there were crucial moments when the Labour leadership generally were actively looking for policies other than those dictated by IMF economists, and were open to persuasion from the Left to a degree unparalleled since the 1930s. If Stephen Fay and Hugo Young are to be believed, James Callaghan set aside a day in the midst of the IMF negotiations for the Cabinet to consider the Tribunite view.[34] That the Tribunite view did not win majority Cabinet support cannot, then, be explained simply in terms of the hostility of Party leaders to it. Tony Benn's failure to persuade his Cabinet colleagues on that crucial occasion may, in part, have to be explained by deficiencies in his powers of argument, and be taken as one indication of the strength of anti-Tribunite factionalism within the Parliamentary Labour Party. But his failure to carry the day also reflected serious deficiences in the Left's own analysis and alternative programme which even Cabinet Ministers sympathetic to the Left could not ignore. If the failure of the Labour Left to win this Government to its views is to be understood, it is to the nature of the Left's analysis that ultimately we must look.

The Labour Left's programme in the 1970s was underpinned by what was, by previous Labour Party standards at least, a well developed and serious body of economic and political analysis. Stuart Holland in particular attempted to provide a fully integrated and exhaustive account of developments within modern capitalism, from which to generate a 'socialist challenge',[35] a strategy for socialism capable of inspiring the entire British labour movement. Central to his thesis was the recognition of industrial concentration, the rise of what he called a 'meso-economic sector', whose economic and political leverage had blunted the conventional weapons of economic policy on which Labour Governments had relied for too long, and whose control and subordination to socialist purposes now required new policies and new interventionist institutions. In particular, Holland's writings stressed the failure of previous Labour Governments to remove the class inequalities that still scar British society, and their inability even to control or to stimulate the private economic sector which that class system sustains. In his view, such a failure was in part a product of defective strategies: an over-dependence on Keynesian techniques of economic management that were no longer sufficiently powerful to cope with the new concentrations of private economic power. Moreover, previous Labour Government failures were also seen as products of over-dependence on a body of social democratic revisionist theory, associated especially with the writings of Anthony Crosland, which made Keynesianism a central feature of Labour Party thinking, and which failed to turn the 'transcendence of capitalism' into the overriding preoccupation of Labour Government policy. To restrict the activity of Labour Governments to Keynesian methods of *demand* management was, on this argument, to retreat from an earlier socialist emphasis on the need to control the processes of *supply* in a capitalist economy; and Holland's 'strategy for socialism' required a return to that preoccupation in the face of the growing power of the private monopolies.

On Holland's own figures, the rise of monopoly power was too obvious to ignore. 'In fifteen of the twenty-two main industrial and service sectors in the economy', he wrote, 'four firms or less control more than half of the total industry's assets. In twenty of the twenty-two main industries and service sectors, fewer than six firms control half of the assets.' Moreover it was his estimate that the top 100 manufacturing firms in Britain would control two-thirds of manufacturing output by 1980; and that that degree of concentration represented a marked shift from their market position in 1950, when they controlled only 20 per cent of total output: 'the top 100 firms have now created a new domination over the mode of production, distribution and exchange in the heartland of the British economy'.[36]

Their presence there was said to alter qualitatively both the workings of a capitalist economy and the problems faced by Labour Governments attempting to exert effective control over the nation's economic activity. The large firms, operating on a multinational scale, *set* prices rather than responded to them, and pushed those prices up even in a depression, as a result both of the complex and privileged arrangements they enjoy with the big international banking institutions, and of their own speculative activity in world commodity markets. It is the presence of these large firms, Holland argued, that has created the persistence of inflation in depression with which Keynesian analysis has so much difficulty; and it is their size which gives government price control policies a tendency to be counter-productive, by freeing them from the resulting pressure on profits which destroys so many of their smaller competitors. The failure of price control policies to stem inflation is just one example of the general situation in which governments find themselves, in which their conventional techniques of demand management prove to be particularly ineffective in the face of the large multinational corporations. Even changes in interest rates, reductions in company taxation, general investment and depreciation allowances, and government control of industrial development certificates do not seem to give governments any significant leverage on the investment policies of the top 100 companies.[37]

This government impotence is a result, Holland has argued, firstly of the fact that 'the big league firms which already dominate the domestic British economy, are themselves multinationals, and can use their power to locate investment and jobs outside Britain to bargain terms which suit them more than the government for their operation in Britain'. But it is also a consequence of the fact that the new multinational companies 'can suspend the normal constraints and incentives of the price mechanism in transactions between their subsidiaries in different countries. In such transactions these companies are their own main market. By trading between subsidiaries they side-step the market mechanism underlying Keynesian international trade models'. In other words, as international trade has increasingly shifted from trade between *different* companies in different countries to trade between the *same* companies in different countries, so the 'economic sovereignty of the home country or a high-tax welfare state economy' has been eroded in several ways: by the system of transfer pricing already mentioned,* by the multinational companies' ability to

---

* It is always open to a multinational company in the United Kingdom to buy an import from another section of the company abroad at an artificially inflated price, which effectively transfers profits out of the United Kingdom, reduces the level of taxation which its profits here attract, and adds an extra element to the economy's total import bill.

reduce the effectiveness of a competitive devaluation, by their access to privileged sources of credit abroad, and by their own speculation in foreign currency movements. In Stuart Holland's view, the multinational companies' strong position is then further enhanced by the existence of a public sector infrastructure whose pricing policy indirectly subsidises their industrial costs, and by the extensive list of direct subsidies which successive British governments have provided to private firms as an incentive to investment and job creation. In total,

In both domestic and international policy the modern capitalist state is plunged increasingly into the dark by the simultaneous trend to monopoly domination at home and multinationalism abroad. Keynesian policies are increasingly eroded both by the increased market power and self-financing of the big league at home, and by their capacity to thwart government taxation, monetary and exchange rate policies. Prices in Britain and the other mature capitalist economies are increasingly decided by that level which leading companies determine as sufficient to maintain smaller and less efficient companies in being, whilst disguising the abnormal profits secured through their own increasing gains from size and multinational spread.[38]

The solutions that Stuart Holland offered grew directly from his analysis. If transfer pricing is to be avoided, and trade union bargaining power not undermined by the artificial restriction of declared levels of profit within the United Kingdom, a statutory obligation on multinational companies to reveal information on exports and imports becomes vital. To guarantee effective democratic control of economic activity, the Labour Government must go further, and extend public ownership directly into the large company sector; and not just to restrict nationalisation there to 'lame duck' firms like British Leyland, but also to ensure that 'the new public enterprise [is] represented in companies whose internal efficiency and scale is sufficient to match that of the remaining private sector leaders'. Only in this way can publicly owned firms act as leaders in levels of investment, patterns of innovation and rates of productivity, and so both *push* investment levels up and *pull* the rest of the private sector after them. The existence of such publicly owned firms would leave the Labour Government, for the first time, in a position to coordinate its macro-economic policy with a meso-economic (large firm) sector whose investment policies could be made to directly respond to nationally specified requirements. The presence of publicly owned large companies, according to Holland, would give a Labour Government countervailing power over the private companies that remain – power to compete directly and so erode abnormal levels of profits, power to undertake directly tasks that incentives to private industry had not stimulated, power to implement directly regional location and import-saving policies to which private multinational concerns had proved so resistant, and power that could be further enlarged by the systematic negotiation of planning agreements throughout the meso-economic sector, and by the extension of industrial democracy there. In Stuart Holland's view, the purpose of the planning agreement should be to bring investment back to the United Kingdom, to force 'the leading private sector firms . . . to reach deep into the kinds of funds which they had been syphoning abroad through transfer pricing in meeting their future investment needs'. To enforce this, a Labour Government should not hesitate to use its sanctions against the recalcitrant: to withdraw its assistance from, and to publish details of planning agreements negotiated with, multinational companies refusing to coordinate their investment policies with those of the State. In Stuart Holland's words:

What the country notoriously lacks is the high growth which is technically feasible if enough leading companies simultaneously expand investment and orders from other companies. The planning of such linkages between leading firms in a co-ordinated expansion, focussed on price restraint and an improved trade position lies in our grasp if sufficient public enterprise ranging through manufacturing industry can be directly harnessed to the broad wave of investment we need. However, we can only escape the vicious circle of the go-stop syndrome and enjoy the benefits of 'virtuous circle' expansion if public enterprise in big league firms ranges through manufacturing industry as a whole. Otherwise some industry cylinders will fire, others will not, and the economy will continue to stagger from go to stop or lose momentum over the long run.[39]

Stuart Holland's analysis is attractive, but superficial. His strategy for socialism, for example, never faces adequately the *political* problems associated with its implementation. Throughout he exaggerates the openness of the Parliamentary Labour Party to radical views and gives insufficient weight to the potency of the constraints that can be imposed on a reforming Labour Government by the concentrations of private capitalist power against which those reforms are aimed. As I have argued elsewhere, the Parliamentary Labour Party is unlikely to make the major shift of programme and aspiration which the Left requires,[40] not least because of the external constraints to which a left-wing Labour Government would be subject. In this respect it is significant that when Tony Benn presented the alternative economic strategy to the Labour Cabinet in November 1976, it was apparently this fear of external retaliation that dissuaded many of his Cabinet colleagues from following his lead. The Left was aware of this danger (that, for example, import controls here might inspire import controls elsewhere), but discounted it.[41] The right and centre of the Party, on the other hand, have always tended to stress its near certainty. But the Parliamentary Left were in no position to deny that the possibility of retaliation existed, and that British capitalism was particularly vulnerable to any retaliation that might come.

Indeed, given the growth of defensive protectionism in the world economy as a whole, it is hard to see how some form of retaliation from other important national capitalisms could be avoided. Yet even if it was, import controls are not the only form of potential external reaction, and it is clear that the Labour Left's alternative strategy would be likely to meet fierce opposition from holders of capital abroad. It is difficult to see how its introduction could avoid being accompanied by a serious flight from sterling which would add to the very inflationary pressures and international indebtedness to which the alternative strategy was supposed to be an answer. Moreover it is hard to see how tight exchange controls, and rigorous planning agreements to prevent transfer pricing, could do other than encourage multinational companies to redirect their investment away from the United Kingdom, at the cost of the employment, and enhanced competitiveness, which the alternative strategy was supposed to guarantee. And, if 1974–75 is any guide, the Left could also expect both an hysterical press campaign against 'Bennery' to erode its internal support, and fairly consistent Treasury and US Government opposition.

Stuart Holland at least has faced this question of the reaction of multinational companies to the introduction of tight planning agreements and competitive public ownership by a left-wing Labour Government; and has acknowledged that such a government might face 'blackmail, either in individual cases on location, or more generally in the form of the threat to close down in this country or locate all further expansion abroad'. But it is a danger he discounts, and one he implies can be overcome by firm government action. 'If they then threaten to locate abroad', he wrote, ' . . . a socialist government should not hesitate to bring them into public ownership.'[42] Elsewhere, in apparent inconsistency with this suggestion of punitive nationalisation, he suggests both that a Labour Government could reduce the problem by avoiding confrontation with foreign-based multinationals initially, sticking instead to home-based companies, and that it should organise international working-class action (both trade union action and Left Social Democratic and Euro-Communist political action) against the foreign subsidiaries of multinationals that resist Labour radicalism. Yet the first of these suggestions is less a solution than a postponement of the issue; and the second is probably precluded by the overall *nationalism* of his programme and by the *parliamentarianism* of his strategy. Why should a section of a foreign working class strike to protect an English nationalist Left? And how is such a Left to orchestrate the simultaneous election of Left Social Democratic and Euro-Communist governments in Italy, France and Britain, not to mention West Germany, the United States, Japan and Taiwan?

Such opposition by international capital would no doubt reflect the narrow class interests of a profoundly self-confident and arrogant ruling caste. But it would also reflect the fact, as social democratic critics of Holland were not slow to point out, that a left-wing programme which, in the short period at least, would 'let wage increases rip . . . add substantially to the public sector deficit, and . . . squeeze profits'[43] could only weaken still further the international competitive position of an economy already subject to a disproportionately high rate of inflation and low rates of private manufacturing investment. So though the Labour Left could no doubt legitimately condemn all these countermoves as either selfish or shortsighted, they could not avoid the real economic consequences that such a tension between a Labour Government and the spokesmen of international capital would have on the ability of that government to 'regenerate' British industry while maintaining the real value of working-class living standards and the social wage.

Indeed, the political weakness of the Labour Left in its conflict with more moderate forces within and beyond the Labour Party ultimately turned on this very point: on the inability of any government, of whatever political persuasion, to do what the Left claimed was possible, namely to strengthen the competitive position of British capitalism without at the same time having to intensify the rate of exploitation of labour. The Labour Left were ultimately politically weak because their economic analysis was defective. As should now be clear, the crisis of international capitalism to which the Left's programme in the 1970s was a response, was itself an amalgam of three related but distinct elements. At its base, the stagnation of the world economy in the 1970s, the intensification of international competition, and the concentration and centralisation of capital, were consequences of the working out of the law of value, and in particular of the dwindling impact of those forces which had for thirty years held at bay the tendency of the rate of profit to fall under capitalism. The British manifestation of this reappearing crisis was particularly acute because of the historic weakness of British capitalism in the face of American, German and latterly Japanese competition, and because of the particular constellation of class forces within the United Kingdom to which that weakness had given rise, and by which it was compounded. Finally, the particular form of the crisis, as a coincidence of inflation and stagnation, seems to have been a consequence of the role which State spending come to play at this particular stage of monopoly capitalism. A socialist analysis of the crisis, on which an adequate left-wing strategy could be built, had to treat all three features of the present conjuncture with equal seriousness. What is characteristic of Stuart Holland's analysis is his almost total preoccupation with the second of these three interrelated features, that is, his concentration on the British aspects of the crisis alone.

A number of things followed directly from this. The systematic failure of the Tribunite Left and their associated intellectuals to recognise the role which State spending plays in fuelling inflation in the present crisis allowed them repeatedly to offer increased social expenditure as an alternative to inflation, when in fact it was a major cause of it. Their associated inability to recognise the underlying force of the law of value under capitalism allowed them to ignore the full political significance of the existence of *market processes,* and hence to concentrate their attention instead on the predominant institutional form of monopoly capitalism – the multinational corporation. It allowed them to imply that the imperatives directing the activities of these companies were a product of the structure of their ownership and command, and not a consequence of the existence of capital as such. The Labour Left were thus able to move from a valid recognition that concentrations of private power in multinational companies, the City and the Treasury allowed certain individuals to shape policy in a conservative and selfish way, to the falsely drawn implication that in some way these people were therefore responsible for the agenda of problems – of inflation, stagnation and unemployment – that they attempted to turn to their advantage. What the Left's argument (on the necessity of public ownership of the banks, for example) did was to claim too much for public ownership. It might well remove the worst excesses of private speculation, and be welcome for that; but private financiers did not invent, and certainly did not control, the market imperatives to which they responded, and their replacement by public servants (or, in the Treasury's case, by economists sympathetic to left-wing causes) could not take those imperatives away. So when the Labour Left criticised the private banking system for failing to lend sufficient amounts of medium and long-term investment to the British manufacturing sector, the banks could not deny the truth of the assertion. But they could point, quite validly, to facts other than their private ownership for the explanation: not least to the Labour Left's own recognition that 'over the past three years interest rates have been relatively high and the rate of return on investment has been falling'.[44] The Labour Left conceded that these market processes played a role, but failed to appreciate the full significance of the concession.

In other words, the Labour Left was, and remains, too keen to offer public ownership as *the* way of qualitatively altering the workings of an international capitalist economy, when neither a full analysis, nor the actual practice of the public sector, can avoid the conclusion that a publicly owned, or even a worker–controlled, British manufacturing industry would still have to succumb to the systemically induced necessity to intensify the rate of exploitation of labour in order to survive in an internationally competitive capitalist world order. This is not to say that public ownership would make no difference. The precise mechanism by which that imperative would be experienced would differ after public ownership, in that the direct pressure of private profit would be replaced by a slower-acting, more obviously political pressure to stop 'wasting' public money by subsidising uncompetitive state industries. But the effect would ultimately be the same. For the 'regeneration' of British industry's competitive position requires a dramatic increase in the social productivity of labour, and this cannot be created by a change in the structure of ownership alone, but only by an increase in the rate of exploitation of labour through an alteration in the organic composition of capital, no matter who or what owns that capital stock. That necessarily involves a shift in class power *away* from the working class, not towards it. By restricting their analysis to these *surface* phenomena of ownership and control the Labour Left denied themselves a theory that was capable of isolating the essential processes of capital accumulation at work beneath the surface. As a result, they also cut themselves off from any form of political practice that was capable of preventing the consequent inevitable succumbing of their state ownership structures to the same underlying imperatives. That the Parliamentary Left has been 'betrayed' so often is not a measure of their opponents so much as an index of the inadequacy of their theory.

The Labour Left's analysis was accurate when it pointed to the propensity of private capitalists to put class before nation, and their own immediate profit requirements before the long-term interests of the manufacturing sector of the British economy as a whole. The Labour Left was correct too to argue that a publicly owned banking sector might be less likely to encourage property speculation and investment in similar non-productive commodities. But the Labour Left could not adequately explain why private capital is such a barrier to British economic growth when, until recently at least, it presented no such

problems for economic growth in West Germany and Japan; and the
Labour Left's analysis was defective when it went on to imply that there
was a way of 'regenerating' the competitive position of British
capitalism which did not involve British workers and their families
having to pay the price of that regeneration. There is not. High
investment in the manufacturing sector is no longer a sufficient
guarantee of full employment. Just the reverse: 'Capital stock in
manufacturing industry including plant and machinery nearly doubled
in the period 1963–76 while employment was cut by 15 per cent . . . the
simple fact is that new investment in productive industries, including
transport and distribution, and in finance and commerce too, now
reduces rather than increases employment opportunities.'[45] Moreover,
the factors which dissuade multinational corporations from investing in
Britain are precisely those which the Labour Left seek to strengthen,
namely the British labour movement and its industrial defensive
power. Cheap labour, weak unions and the absence of working-class
political power have pulled investment away from the United
Kingdom, and the Left cannot pull it back whilst strengthening the
British labour movement still further. Here is the ultimate paradox for
Left social democrats, and one of growing importance as capital
becomes ever more internationally mobile: that a strong labour
movement, insisting on industrial and political rights for workers and
their families, is the main barrier to the very industrial regeneration that
the social democratic leaders of such a labour movement wish to create.
The interests of capital and labour under capitalism are not simply
different. They are mutually antagonistic and incompatible; and
because the Labour Left's theory is insufficiently developed to
recognise that, their resulting political practice must in the end fall foul
of incompatibilities whose centrality they have failed to recognise.

As a result the Labour Left could establish a significant degree of
public ownership in 'the commanding heights' of British manufacturing capital, could move its own personnel into senior managerial
positions there, and could negotiate the tightest set of planning
agreements with the private firms remaining, *and still find* that the
resulting managerial policies were unable to differ in any significant
way from those which untrammelled private management would have
pursued. British Leyland is a clear case of this, British Steel is another,
Chrysler UK a third. Chrysler is particularly significant for the Labour
Left, for there was a multinational company actually asking for the
Labour Government to use its ultimate sanction (public ownership
without compensation), only to find the Labour Government
unwilling to do this because of the way in which the separate public

ownership of Chrysler UK would have added to, rather than eased, the company's competitive difficulties. Public ownership had no obvious answer here to a British problem created by world market forces. Yet British Leyland and British Steel did involve extensive public ownership. Moreover they and Chrysler UK had a close planning agreement type of relationship with the Labour Government; and all three developed extensive systems of worker involvement and information sharing at senior managerial level. Yet, contrary to the claims of the Labour Left, this sharing of information made no qualitative difference either to managerial policies or to the working-class experience of labour within these concerns. The problem for the men and women employed by British Leyland was not that information was not shared, but that the information to be shared was depressing. Each of the three industrial concerns was forced by the logic of the competitive world system in which it operated to intensify the rate of exploitation of labour, and to make a significant percentage of its workforce unemployed. Public ownership did not alter the necessity of this, for retrenchment was dictated not by the structure of ownership but by the firm or industry's position in a competitive world system that was itself in difficulties. What public ownership did was not to enhance the control that working-class men and women exercised over their own environment, but rather to add the voices of Ministers and senior trade union officials to those of a senior management team who were already attempting to intensify the work process and to reduce working-class industrial control in the search for an adequate return on capital. In spite of the Left's institutional changes (public ownership, planning agreements and industrial democracy) the men and women who actually produced the cars and the steel still paid the price for the 'regeneration' of the competitive position of the industries in which they worked, either by losing their jobs altogether or by seeing their work processes intensify. The institutional changes demanded by the Labour Left could delay the start and the initial severity of this process, but could not remove its necessity. For that, as we have seen, was imposed on a competitively weak capitalism by a world depression to which the Labour Left, for all its talk of a siege economy, had no effective answer.

## V

In that sense it is significant that the issue on which the Labour Left was prepared to fight so hard as to threaten the internal unity of the Labour Government was not unemployment, but the question of entry into Europe. The crux of the Labour Left's position was that, no matter how much mention in passing was made of international capitalism and its crisis, what the British working class actually faced was a British crisis, with a British solution. EEC entry was opposed precisely because it eroded the capacity to make that autonomous national response. But once more the Labour Left deluded themselves, and failed their potential audience, by letting their response take the shape dictated by the *appearance* of international capitalism, and by avoiding the harder job of penetrating beneath that appearance to the essential processes that created it. A national response is an intelligible one to a recession of world capitalism, but it is also superficial and ultimately self-defeating. International competition is experienced in national terms, precisely because it is mediated through national political units, and because in consequence the rise of competitor economies can and does create a national experience of relative decline, as in Britain in the 1970s. But the forms in which capitalist crises occur are not the cause (nor are they the means of resolution) of that crisis; and *to respond in national terms is to move not against capitalism, but with it,* both by directly facilitating the increased expropriation of surplus value behind a rhetoric of socialist national regeneration and by reinforcing non-class, jingoistic responses that divide the world's proletariat. Of course the Labour Left claimed that its aim was to strengthen the capacity of a democratic socialist British economy to fuel world economic growth, from which all would benefit, and to use import controls only to slow down a still growing British consumption of foreign produce that would not cost the jobs of workers abroad.[46] But this was all nonsense in the midst of a world recession. In such a situation any effective system of import controls could only ship unemployment abroad, and force another working class to pay the price that world recession would otherwise extract from British workers and their families.

What seems a simple solution to increase employment and competitiveness in one country – import controls and export led growth – becomes reactionary when viewed as a whole. Jobs saved in one country become lost in another in a period of growing capitalist crisis. Unemployment is thrown on to workers elsewhere. International trade, already falling, will fall further still. As one country takes protectionist measures, another will retaliate in order to survive. The laws of capitalism cannot be overcome in this 'commonsensical way'.[47]

Moreover, the Labour Left did themselves and their supporters no service when they created the impression that the alternative to EEC control of capitalist development was Labour Government control from Westminster. As Heath and Wood have argued:

> The left reformers fail to understand the basic realities of modern capitalist production – the existence of an international division of labour and a world market. They have no answers to pro-Marketeers . . . who [have] argued that 'in or out of the EEC our economy will be influenced by judgements made beyond these shores'. And yet thousands of car workers presently on short time already have some knowledge at least of the effects of international capital.[48]

The Labour Left were correct to see in the EEC a further barrier to Labour Party radicalism, but quite unjustified in restricting their specification of that blockage to the tiny Brussels bureaucracy. The basic blockage to Labour Party radicalism was the strength of Western European (and Japanese and American) capital, and its penetration into the British national economy; and that would not go away even if Brussels control could somehow be circumvented. Moreover, by couching their argument in the language of 'national sovereignty', the Labour Left disguised the real issue of the *international* exploitation of the working class of which the EEC was but one more manifestation.* They made the problem one of 'democracy' and not of 'capitalism'. By setting the problem up as a national question with a national solution, the Labour Left strengthened by their opposition to EEC entry the underlying thesis of the very ruling class against which they struggled: that British workers and their rulers have interests in common against foreign capitalists and foreign workers alike. The logical result of that class collaborationist chauvinism is not socialism, but a corporate state.

The Labour Left's failure to specify adequately the processes at work in the world economy, and their traditional and misplaced faith in the 'capturability' of the capitalist state for socialist ends, turn their alternative strategy into a *threat* to those working-class living standards, job security and political power that it purported to defend. The State, according to the Labour Left, could use public ownership and State planning to curb capitalist excess and introduce socialism. In fact, public ownership and State planning invariably prove to be the mechanisms by which the State rationalises those sectors of capitalism which private enterprise lacks the resources to do on its own. The State, according to the Labour Left, could galvanise economic growth as an alternative to unemployment, whereas in practice, of course, the State invariably facilitates and orchestrates processes of capitalist restructuring in which

---

* Not all the anti-Marketeers were guilty of this. Edward Thompson's eloquent defence of the anti-Market position was a notable exception (see *Tribune*, 2 May 1975, p. 5).

systematic unemployment now plays a major part. And the Labour Left talked the language of 'national' regeneration, of 'our' industries and 'our' manufacturing plants, which only helped a capitalist state to incorporate a whole working class into a voluntary acceptance of its own subordination. Even if the Labour Left's alternative strategy could have been implemented after 1974, the result would not have been socialism, not even when that term is understood, as by the Labour Left, as involving merely 'a fundamental and irreversible shift in the balance of power and wealth in favour of working people and their families'. At best it could have produced a high growth capitalism with intensified work routines and a higher 'normal' level of unemployment. More likely, given the intractability of British capitalism's competitive weakness, it would only have resulted in a lower social wage, high unemployment, and a corporatist planning structure whose very existence would have been evidence enough of the drift of power and wealth away from working people and their families.

Precisely because that is the drift of the Labour Left's analysis, it is not simply inadequate for socialists. It is dangerous. For in spite of the fears that international capitalism had of 'Bennery', the programme of the Labour Left, once stripped of its radical pretensions, marches with the grain of capitalism, with certain of its long-term structural requirements. This, after all, is what the Labour Left has done before. The 'socialism' of the 1930s proved the bedrock a decade later of a revitalised welfare capitalism. Consistently equating socialism with the relative stability of a high growth competitive national economy, Labour Left theoreticians repeatedly come to specify as *socialist* those forms of State activity that are vital to *capitalist* regeneration. The Labour Left has long had a dangerous tendency to equate socialism with the defence of *national* capital against other, foreign-based international capitals, and it is here that the Left's chauvinism on the EEC fits in to its general economic analysis. It is because the Labour Left wishes to strengthen capital based on, and oriented to, the United Kingdom economy, employing British workers to produce commodities in competition with commodities produced by foreign nationals, that its strategy of import controls and parliamentary sovereignty go hand-in-hand. It is for this reason too that Left Labourites find themselves occasionally in unholy alliance with the most reactionary elements of the Conservative Opposition. Yet such a strategy is surely open to the critique of those on the right and centre of the Party who argue that, whether we like it or not, British jobs, living standards and welfare provision are best guaranteed through a reliance on international capital and a rapprochement with multinational corporations. In fact, in simple capitalist terms, it is hard to see how an attempt to isolate, protect and regenerate a nationally based capitalism can succeed when the degree of internationalisation of capital ownership (and increasingly of production) is already so advanced. Nor, in socialist terms, can a reliance on either national or international capital give British workers the degree of control over their lives that the Labour Left requires. For that, on the contrary, as I argue in the next chapter, will come only through an alliance with foreign workers against *both* multinational and nationally oriented capital which the chauvinism of the Labour Left so often impedes.

The Labour Left's failure to understand the underlying laws of motion of the world capitalist economy permits them in their programmes to combine a pre-eminently capitalist focus on competitive efficiency with an aspiration for enhanced working-class industrial, social and political power. Since the two are in practice incompatible, it is not surprising that in power Labour Governments' pursuit of one is at the expense of the other. Nor, given the power of market forces under world capitalism, and the Labour Left's own dependence on high rates of economic growth to sustain its social programmes, is it surprising that it is the radical veneer of working-class emancipation that is the inevitable and speedy casualty of the implementation of left-wing programmes by Labour Governments.

This has consistently been the case since 1945, and is particularly likely under Labour Governments to come. For in a world in which the international restructuring of capital is moving investment to those areas where high rates of surplus value can easily be expropriated from weak labour movements under repressive political regimes, the resulting 'deindustrialisation' of Britain is particularly ill-suited to a yet further enhancement of working class industrial and political power. If the Labour Left genuinely want to create a fundamentally just social and economic system, they will have to do more than try to plan British capitalism back into a position of world competitive strength. They will have to learn the lessons of this Labour Government, see the impotence of a national strategy in an international recession, and design their political programme accordingly.

# PART THREE

# The consequences of the explanation

# CHAPTER SEVEN
## *The lessons of Labour in power*

### I

What lessons can we learn from this period of Labour in power? The first is that we should regard with scepticism the more ambitious claims conventionally made by Labour politicians in their years of opposition. This Labour Government, like those before it, came to its next general election with the usual mixed and dismal record, having failed either to implement or to achieve precisely those targets or policies to which its left wing had pointed as evidence of the Party's commitment to radical change of a democratic and socialist kind. The retreat from radical purpose is particularly striking in this Labour Government, since it began its life with a far greater degree of self-confidence than had its predecessor in 1964, with a newfound veneer of radical aspirations that had few parallels in Labour Party history, and with the usual desire to demonstrate that a Labour Government, unlike a Conservative one, could engineer sustained economic growth and social justice for all. In fact, as we have seen, the Government's radical initiatives on the industrial front were either blunted (as was the NEB) or repeatedly postponed (as were planning agreements and the promise of industrial democracy). A wealth tax has yet to materialise, and the Labour Left's alternative economic strategy has remained just that: an alternative rejected in favour of more conventional policies of wage controls, cuts in social expenditure, and the use of incentives to draw economic growth out of an unreformed private sector. Of course the Government's record is not one of total failure. The initial strength of the Left, and the continuing defensive political leverage of the trade unions, encouraged the Government to extend public ownership, and to consolidate a new body of labour law that extended the procedural powers of unions and workers when facing management and government. Moreover, the Labour Cabinet came to the general

258

election with inflation close to 10 per cent, with the pound stable, and with the private disposable incomes of those in employment enjoying a temporary boom. All this stood in stark contrast to the bleak years of 1975-77, and gave Labour politicians the material on which to defend their record. But these meagre successes were won at the very heavy price of unemployment, cuts in social spending, industrial stagnation and a failure to achieve that fundamental and irreversible shift in the balance of power and wealth in favour of working people and their families which the 1973 Programme had given as Labour's first priority. Edward Thompson had defended British autonomy against the EEC on precisely that priority: that in the next five years with this Labour Government outside the Common Market[1] one can glimpse, as an outside chance, the possibility that we could effect here a peaceful transition – for the first time in the world – to democratic socialist society'.[1] Yet as always it was just this transition which the Labour Party in power did *not* achieve, a failure of radical purpose which must stand as the first lesson to be drawn from events since 1974.

This is not to say that the Labour leadership, or the majority of commentators on the right and centre of British politics, need necessarily see this Government as a failure. On the contrary: Ministers might well argue that they salvaged all that could be salvaged from a world economy in deep recession, and that they successfully resisted the drastic dismantling of the social services that seemed imminent in the financial crisis of 1976. Moreover the success of governments is normally measured by yardsticks other than those of radicalism, and the Labour Party's claim to office in 1973 rested on more than a promise of social transformation and economic growth. Labour politicians also promised to heal the bitterness of a divided society and to end the politics of confrontation between trade unions and the State. This they managed to do for four years at least. For all the failure of its radical ambitions, the Government did engineer and then sustain a remarkable degree of working–class industrial and political moderation, of a kind which few commentators thought possible as Labour entered office. The 'explosion' of industrial militancy that occurred under the Conservative Government between 1970 and 1973 was abruptly ended. Though unemployment grew, work processes intensified, and real living standards fell for large periods of this Labour Government's years in office, Ministers still managed for over four years to all but remove official strikes (the firemen apart), to avoid all but the most sporadic and ineffective unofficial militancy, and to preside over four rounds of wage restraint. In the end, the degree of working-class resistance to incomes policy developed into protracted industrial disputes of the 1970–73 kind, to demonstrate the limits of even a Labour Government in this critical field; but the industrial struggles of 1978–79, and the subsequent election defeat, should not distract our attention from the remarkable degree of working-class industrial restraint that Ministers managed to orchestrate prior to the Ford workers's' strike in the autumn of 1978.

This was a major political achievement (Denis Healey once quite rightly called it 'something of a miracle'[2]) and a vital one for an already weak British capitalism. The initial docility of trade unionists in the face of the Labour Government's incomes policy must stand as a salutary reminder to the socialist Left of the strength of labourism among the British working class, and of the general role that is always played in periods of capitalist crisis by social democratic political parties. The events of 1975–78 in particular emphasise the accuracy and importance of Leo Panitch's argument that 'the function of the Labour Party in the British political system consists not only of representing working-class interests but of acting as one of the chief mechanisms for inculcating the organised working class with national values and symbols and of restraining and reinterpreting working-class demands in this light.'[3] As James Callaghan put it in the House of Commons,

It is . . . because I believe strongly that only a Labour Government can at present carry the country through the economic circumstances, in which we have to have a difficult combination of asking trade unions for sacrifices from their members at the same time as we are restraining public expenditure and getting the unique proposal and agreement from the CBI that they will encourage manufacturing industry. The Labour Government are the government which can carry this through, and it is in that sense that I wish them to stay in office.[4]

Of course, all governments attempt to do this, but what makes Labour Governments so useful to the ruling groups in British capitalism now is precisely the way in which their roots in the labour movement give them a unique capacity to act as effective 'managers of discontent', able to subordinate working-class aspirations to 'national' needs that are taken as being coterminous with the stability and prosperity of capital, and in that way to 'legitimate existing society and militate against the development of a revolutionary political consciousness' amongst its working-class supporters. What is striking about this Labour Government is how successfully it managed that task, how easily (and for what length of time) it managed to hold at bay the tensions within the labour movement to which that task necessarily gave rise, and how convinced its leaders remained that only by 'pursuing national concerns could working-class interests be satisfied'.[5]

All of which brings us to a second lesson to be drawn from events since 1974. It would be misleading to create the impression that the Labour Party is a 'class party', in the sense of one seeing itself as fighting *for* the working class *against* a hostile bourgeoisie, and asking to be judged in that light. Labour Party aspirations and world visions have never been so unambiguous and clearcut. It is true that the defence of working-class, and particularly trade union, interests has always been an important plank in Labour Party thinking (the Gaitskellite years apart). It is also true that the need to advance the power and wealth of 'working people and their families' was a familiar theme in Party debate after 1970, and that this theme was given a distinctly working-class tone and interpretation whenever it was used. Listening to debates in the Labour Party conference in 1973 you could be forgiven for thinking that only manual workers worked. But even so, the sense of class has always been muted in Labour Party thinking, and has always been given second place to interests and needs deemed to be vital to 'the nation' as a whole. When in government, this has given Labour politicians a perennial preoccupation with finding a basis of compromise between working-class and ruling-class interests that in practice has involved the subordination of working-class interests to the imperatives of capital accumulation. The Labour Party's belief that 'its national concerns embrace the needs of the working class as well'[6] has consistently fortified Labour Ministers in their resolve to block immediate working-class aspirations in the pursuit of a national renaissance that is always just around the corner, one which repeatedly fails to materialise even though its proximity seems to invite yet another year of working-class restraint. The very sensitivity of Labour politicians to working-class deprivations to which the process of capital accumulation gives rise makes them all the keener to get that process successfully completed and behind them; and their mistaken conviction that it is *inadequate* capital accumulation, rather than capital accumulation itself, which brings unemployment and social inequality consistently obliges them to urge restraint in the short period in return for easier times to come. For three years this Labour Government was extradordinarily successful in sustaining working-class restraint, in spite of the persistent absence of easier times; and in doing so gave British capitalism as industrially quiet a labour force as any in Western Europe. It was the Government's *success* in disciplining the working class which constituted the reverse side of the failure of its radicalism, and which must be recognised as the second lesson to be drawn from these years of Labour in power.

When we come to ask why this pattern of success and failure came to predominate, a third set of lessons comes into view. Anyone who wishes to use the experience of this Labour Government as a base from which to assess the range of potentially viable political strategies in the 1980s must begin from the recognition that the radicalism of the Labour Government failed ultimately because the problems to which that radicalism was supposed to be an answer proved to be more intractable than even left-wing Labour analysts supposed. And they proved to be so intractable because they were bedded in (were indeed manifestations of) the character of the international economy which surrounded the British State. The lesson to be drawn from this experience of Labour in power is that the international economy is capitalist, long established in its monopoly phase, subject to the laws of motion that Marx first laid out, and already subject to a deep and growing crisis. Moreover, any analyst of British politics has to recognise that the British section of international capitalism is already weak, and that the concentration and centralisation of capital on a world scale to which the system necessarily gives rise is now producing an international division of labour at odds with the Labour Party's determination to maintain the number of manufacturing jobs in the British economy. British governments, that is, now have to fight against the grain of international capitalism.

In addition, the Left has to recognise (as indeed the Labour Left has already attempted to do) that the multinational corporations, which are the main institutional form of the international division of labour, will not respond to conventional methods of economic management; and that moreover, as the Labour Left does not yet seem to have grasped, a tiny parliamentary élite, however well intentioned, cannot by itself effectively shape the policies of corporations that operate on a global scale and which are themselves subject to fierce international competition and dwindling profits.[7] The Labour Left in particular has yet to face the full political significance of the fact that capitalism's propensity to accumulate through crises makes any serious attempt to stabilise and control a capitalist economy at best problematic; that the current conjuncture of inflation and stagnation blocks any easy route to national economic competitiveness through greater government spending; that the very strengthening of the labour movement to which the Labour Left looks as a basis for economic recovery can only accentuate an already hostile international division of labour by encouraging beleaguered multinational corporations to move their resources away to 'safer' political climates; and, given the contradictory relationship between labour and capital which lies at the heart of capitalism, that a period of sustained capital accumulation can only be bought at the price of the very unemployment and greater rate of labour exploitation which the parliamentary Left seem to think that sustained economic growth can avoid.

In other words, if there is a central contradiction in a capitalist universe between the Labour Party's two goals – full employment and economic growth at one end, and a shift of power and wealth to working people and their families at the other – any political strategy seeking both must find a way of transcending the capitalist structure which sets the two apart. The problem will not go away. On the contrary, there is enough evidence that every future Labour Government is likely to face even tighter economic constraints. Short-term factors, such as North Sea oil, may create breathing spaces; but the long-term tendency of international capitalism is to tighten the integration of State structures and private capital, and to perpetuate that weakness of the British economy which has already given postwar British politics their perennial themes. Moreover, the conditions which underpinned the long postwar economic boom have now given way to a long period of relative stagnation, low profits and high unemployment. This means that if Labour politics continue to tailor themselves to the immediately possible, Labour politicians will find their freedom of manoeuvre ever more severely restricted, and their electoral base accordingly ever more vulnerable.*[8] This surely is the major lesson of the electoral defeat of May 1979.

There is also enough evidence to suggest that although the constraints of international capitalism will be tight on all British governments, they will be tightest of all on a Labour Government. For the instabilities of capitalism will also create grievances and deprivations in the rank-and-file of the trade union movement which will find some echo, however muted, in Labour Party radicalism; and Labour Governments will thus continue to enter office armed with policies which, among other things, reflect mass resentment at capitalist instability but whose implementation will threaten the structures of privilege on which capitalism depends. Labour Governments, that is, will not only face problems common to all British governments. They will also face opposition, and to the degree that their left-wing grows in strength, they will find the going tough.

Indeed there are general lessons to be drawn from the Labour Government's experience about the character of capitalist power in

---

* The vote for the Labour Party fell to 36.9 per cent in 1979, it lowest since 1931. Indeed the trend of dwindling Labour Party electoral support is virtually unbroken since 1951: at 48.8 per cent (1951), 46.4 per cent (1955), 43.8 per cent (1959), 44.1 per cent (1964), 47.9 per cent (1966), 43.0 per cent (1970), 37.1 per cent (February 1974) and 39.3 per cent (October 1974). The 36.9 per cent of the vote captured by the Labour Party in May 1979 represented only 28 per cent of the total electorate.

## The consequences of the explanation

Britain in the 1980s. The labour movement has got to grasp that the strength of capitalism lies not simply in its *institutions* but also in its *processes*; and that the 'capture' of key institutions (by public ownership, planning agreements, worker directors or whatever) cannot of itself change the imperatives to which the new Labour men of power would be subject. The situation of a Labour Government is very like that of a stone dropped into a pool – surrounded by an ever widening set of ripples. If the innermost set of constraints (ripples) are parliamentary, and the next the civil service, followed by the institutions of private capital, then the ultimate ripple-circle of constraints is set by the competitive processes of the world market through which capital is accumulated and realised. Labour radicalism has to reach that outer ripple if its control of all the rest is in the end to bring a new set of criteria to play in the determination of economic activity and in its dependent social priorities. Westergaard and Resler have described this ultimate level of constraints clearly in a passage which is worth quoting at length, and which the British labour movement might usefully take to heart.

In any society, the pattern of people's lives and their living conditions take the form which they do, not so much because somebody somewhere makes a series of decisions to that effect: but in large part because certain social mechanisms, principles, assumptions – call them what one will – are taken for granted. . . . In a capitalist society the social mechanisms and assumptions which are generally taken for granted in this way are those, in the first instance, of private property and the market. It is they which largely determine the living conditions of the people and the use of resources. And they clearly favour the interests of capital: they confer power on capital in a very real and tangible sense. But the proof of that power is not to be found only, or even chiefly, in the fact that capitalists and managers make decisions. It is to be found in the fact that the decisions which both they and others – including government – make, and the sheer routine conduct of affairs without definite decision-making, in the main have a common denominator: an everyday acceptance of private property and market mechanisms. It is taken for granted, 'in the way things work', that profit should be the normal yardstick of investment in most areas of activity: that the living standards of the propertyless majority should be set primarily by the terms on which they sell or once sold their labour: and so on. . . . power is to be found more in uneventful routine than in conscious and active exercise of will.[9]

Nor is the State machine which the Labour Party inherits free from subordination to that same 'uneventful routine'. On the contrary, it is clear again, as it has been under each Labour Government to date, that Labour politicians in opposition consistently overestimate the capacity of the State machine to subordinate itself to their control for radical ends. This Labour Government found the civil service staffed by men and women unsympathetic to Labour radicalism. They found the

264

State's controls over the key agencies of economic growth, the multinational corporations, both inadequate and difficult to strengthen. They found the State to be already a major employer of labour in its own right; and they found, in both their dealings with the private sector and in their relationships with the nationalised industries, that the achievement of their own growth and financial targets, and the pressures of significantly placed élites, combined to pull Labour Ministers into policies of capital restructuring that brought unemployment and intensified work routines in their wake. That is, the Labour Party found itself at the head, not of a neutral State, but of a capitalist one, and one that was ever more intimately integrated into the interstices of private capital and preoccupied with the problems of capital accumulation. The State has a vital role to play at this stage in monopoly capitalism, in the restructuring of capital, in the maintenance of demand and profits, and in the maintenance of social order and working-class control. The modern State is now *the* institution *par excellence* for the specification of the collective interests of capital; and though this role gives it a degree of political autonomy which Labour radicals hope to exploit, that autonomy is limited by the distribution of class forces in the wider society.[10] State power is a function of class power, and not an alternative to it; and the hope of Labour radicals to use Parliament as an alternative to the social and industrial power of the working class could not be more misplaced. If Labour radicals wish to use their hold on the democratic State to curb capitalist power they have to find an answer to the integration of the State with the institutions and personnel of international capitalism. The Labour Government of 1974–79 had no such answer, and its subordination to the imperatives of capital was all too clear.


## II

That the Left must find such an answer becomes obvious once we examine the social structure which more than seventy years of Labour Party politics has left intact. Social democrats and Tribunites may disagree about many things, but that socialism has something to do with equality remains a belief that is common to them both. Yet British society is still profoundly unequal, divided by the inequalities of class. Class differentiation is as visible here as anywhere in Western Europe, since divisions of sex, age, race, religion and region play a vital but relatively subordinate role in the British structure of social inequality, at least if Northern Ireland is left out of the account. Class differentiation is most evident at the place of work, where in general those who are paid less than the average are the very ones who, paradoxically, also experience less than the average degree of job security and control, who work in more than averagely severe conditions, and toil for longer, at more socially disruptive times. The evidence is plentiful that it is manual workers who work the greatest amount of overtime, who are most subject to shift work, who experience the worst working conditions, who are most likely to be subject to tight supervision, who are most prone to industrial accidents and illnesses, who have the least access to occupational pensions, and whose earnings are the least secure (most obviously because of the threat of unemployment and short-time working, but also because of the absence of increments and the disproportionate dependence on bonuses, overtime and piece rates).[11] Even the affluent car workers' experience is in this sense typical of the way in which 'a catalogue of broad class differences in conditions of employment soon becomes tedious, because the patterns repeat themselves with only small variations'.[12] For the permanence of the car workers' affluence is now threatened by the structural decline of their industry in the face of fierce international competition, like many more traditional workers before them; and even when this was not evident, in the 1960s, they still had to work long hours, including shifts and weekend working, in bad conditions and subject to the inexorable pressure of the assembly line, in order to receive a wage comparable to, or at least near that common among senior management and professional workers. Car workers were at least fortunate. They had the industrial power to make that bargain. Most manual workers do not, and yet they experience very similar and adverse employment conditions.[13]

Nor can manual workers expect their earnings to rise steadily over the years, and to culminate in an adequate level of pensions. On the contrary, the inequalities and instabilities experienced by manual workers in British industry give them a vulnerability to poverty in economic depression, in personal sickness, and in old age that the middle class lack. Most manual workers, even if they can avoid the short-time working and redundancy to which they are increasingly vulnerable, will experience a diminishing earning power in their forties and fifties, and face the certainty of near-poverty in old age. Their experience here is neither random nor accidental. It reflects the lack of property, and the consequent dependence on the sale of their labour power, which characterises the social position of the manual (and increasingly the routine white-collar) worker in an unstable competitive capitalism. But it means that it is the manual working class who generally 'get the least of what there is to get' and have to work hardest for it. It is from their ranks that 'are, so to speak, recruited the unemployed, the aged poor, the chronically destitute, and the sub-proletariat of capitalist society'.[14]

The Labour Party faces a society in which access to the consumption of the goods and services which we all collectively work to produce is unevenly divided, again on class lines. The concentration of private wealth continues to be significant, and continues to be a function of privilege, not of effort, a consequence of the inheritance of already accumulated stocks of capital. Though the ownership of houses and consumer durables has widened, 'the share of the personal wealth of the top 20 per cent of the population has shown a remarkable stability, 89.8 per cent in 1960 and 85.7 per cent in 1974, despite the supposed onslaught of equalitarian government policies and aggressive union pay claims'.[15] The richest 1 per cent still 'have as large a slice of income after tax as the poorest 30 per cent of the population',[16] at a time when 4,500,000 people are drawing supplementary benefits and when an additional 100,000 families (containing 300,000 children) have members working full-time but earning insufficient to bring their incomes above the official poverty line.[17] With such a pattern of inequality in the distribution of income and wealth, it is not surprising that class differences are starkly evident in the occupation of types of housing, in the quality and length of educational provision, in the ownership of consumer durables (from televisions to cars) and in the use of the welfare services. Even the incidence of illness and the timing of death follow class lines.[18]

The persistence of these inequalities is enough to sustain and justify the presence of a *radical* party in British politics in the 1980s. Their source is enough to explain why that radical party ought to be a *socialist* one. For the roots of inequality in British society are not accidental. They reflect neither the distribution of aptitudes between people, nor any inevitable consequence of industrialisation as such. When all the complications and nuances of explanation have been allowed, it must be recognised that the source of class divisions in Britain is capitalism itself. As Westergaard and Resler correctly argue,

The continuing inequalities of wealth, income and welfare that divide the population are among the most crucial consequences – the most visible manifestations – of the division of power in a society such as Britain. Those inequalities reflect, while they also demonstrate, the continuing power of capital – the power, not just of capitalists and managers, but of the anonymous forces of property and the market.[19]

## The consequences of the explanation

It is the process of capital accumulation through the expropriation of surplus value that necessitates the inequalities of power and reward at the place of work, and generates there both the alienation endemic to industrial production and the work pressure, the tight supervision and the long hours characteristic of manual labour. It is capitalism's inherent anarchy, its propensity to replace men by machines, and its subordination of human value to a preoccupation with competitiveness and profit, that brings unemployment, job insecurity, industrial decline, the destruction of old skills, and inadequate investment to burden workers and their families. And it is the past accumulation of capital, and the hierarchies of command that its protection and furtherance has necessitated, that provides the base on which the uneven distribution of rewards has come to be based.

Some men and women face one set of life chances (and other men and women face other and more limited sets) because of their different positions in the class structure of a capitalist society. It is because some people successfully lay claim to the ownership of the means and the product of the collective act of labour, and because these same people occupy positions of command within the private (industrial, financial and administrative) hierarchies that constitute the central owning institutions of contemporary capitalism, that they can monopolise the greater part of the social product, and can transmit the advantage of their class position more or less easily to their offspring. Conversely it is because the majority of men and women in the society do not own either the means or the products of their collective labour, and because they occupy subordinate positions in the private hierarchies of command, that they experience a different and more limited set of life chances. It is because the manual working class (and increasingly the routine white-collar worker) occupy the bottom position in these hierarchies, and are totally denied property rights over the means and products of their collective labour, that their experience of the instabilities and inequalities of such a social order are so extreme. And it is because capitalism and inequality are inseparable in this way that the removal of the latter cannot be divorced from the question of socialism itself.[20]

It should be said that capitalism does give some hope to those who would replace it, by the inequalities of experience that it generates, by the solidarities of class that it necessitates, and by the struggle between social groups to which those inequalities and solidarities give rise. As I have said, the accumulation of capital through the expropriation of surplus value creates and requires a necessary set of inequalities at the place of work – inequalities in work experience, in rewards and in power which alone constitute the social relationships within which capital can be accumulated. The fact that these inequalities are collectively experienced generates collective loyalties. The fact that the superiority of one group is the product of the subordination of another pulls these loyalties into an antagonistic relationship. The fact that, in essence, the antagonisms are between the producers of wealth and its expropriators pulls those antagonisms towards a simple polarity of class. Of course, differences of work experience and rewards generate patterns of group solidarity which cut across simple class divisions, and these sustain institutions with a vested interest in their retention. Divisions *within* the working class over the question of differentials is a clear and topical example of this. The character of white-collar unionism is another. It is true, too, that those in positions of privilege are always reluctant to surrender their power, and are in situations of command which give them enormous leverage in the struggle between classes. So the whole experience of inequality under capitalism characteristically occurs within an ideological framework which is geared to the perpetuation of these inequalities by either denying their existence or by asserting that they are inevitable and essential. Yet the daily experience of alienation, instability and inequality repeatedly press forward collective demands for the redress of grievances which cannot, under capitalism, be permanently redressed; and as such this gives the Left a perennial base on which to build a mass movement.

This after all was what Marx said of capitalism a century ago. He certainly expected that the experience of 'class', of being a seller of one's labour power, would become the predominant experience of labour under capitalism. He anticipated that capitalism's inherent need to accumulate would be experienced by the working class as a process that constantly eroded any part of their life-cycle that was free from the discipline of work and industry. As all other forms of labour were destroyed, a proletariat would emerge whose unity, based in common industrial and social experience, would obliterate all other patterns of social cleavage, and render it immune to the ideological persuasions of the bourgeoisie. Marx argued that this working-class experience would be a source of industrial and political radicalism, as well as of autonomous class politics. He anticipated that this radicalism would be a response to the intensification of work and the persistent unemployment to which the declining rate of profit under capitalism would give rise, and to the deprivations and inequalities that would accompany the concentration of ownership and capital. Radicalism would be an expression of the proletariat's profound sense of alienation from a system of production which subordinated their interests and requirements as human beings to the imperatives of industrial and financial capital; and it would be reinforced by a growing opposition to the social consequences of the constant instability and social change endemic to capitalism.

Marx and the next generation of revolutionary socialists also believed that the working class under capitalism would be able to pursue their industrially and politically radical ends with ever greater impact; that the concentration of workers in ever larger productive units, and the inability of bourgeois ideologists to build effective legitimating structures, would leave workers free first to build collective institutions of self-defence (particularly trade unions) and eventually to create political institutions for socialist advance. Marx seems to have seen a kind of 'natural' connection between socialist ideas and working-class experience, and to have been convinced that there were sufficient incentives in its experience under capitalism to pull the working class into revolutionary socialist politics. It is this faith, that the working class will turn socialist, and will in the end come to see the need for revolutionary action, that has inspired successive generations of the revolutionary Left since Marx wrote.

The fit between Marx's expectations and actual events has been sufficiently close to make his writings relevant to at least a minority in each generation of the Left. If we examine the history of the working class in Europe and even in America over the last century, we find that it has been a major source of support for radical politics. It has created its own institutions of self-defence and collective advance, and those institutions have tended to press for greater equality in the distribution of wealth, income, ownership and power, education and status. And although there have always been voices speaking to and from within each national working class, arguing for hierarchy, inequality and racial or religious superiority, the predominant tone of working-class politics has so often been a socialist one. By this I mean that over the last hundred years the symbols, programme and rhetoric of very many working-class political movements and institutions have claimed some kind of socialist aim, and have in some way equated working-class emancipation with the creation of a socialist society.

But of course many of Marx's expectations have proved quite false. Many non-socialist organisations have sunk and maintained roots in the working class, both indigenously (craft unionism) and from outside (Conservatism, Christian Democracy, radical Liberalism). Many of the socialist symbols have become just that – part of the rule book or the party constitution, without immediate impact or significance. And the predominant form of socialism to win mass support in Western Europe has been reformist and social democratic, concerned to pursue 'socialist ends' within constitutionally sanctioned channels, and subject as a result to a long process of growing conservatism. Even Euro-Communism must be seen as an example of this. Most important of all for our purposes, the British working class has obviously not turned to revolutionary socialist politics.

The dominant political perspective amongst large sections of the British labour movement has been, and remains, 'Labourist'. By that I mean first that workers have taken the wage relationship under capitalism as unalterable, and have concentrated their industrial and political efforts on improving their lot within it. In addition, the belief has predominated that politics is about *parliamentary* action; and any widespread knowledge of, or interest in, extra-parliamentary forms of working-class political activity has been limited. Moreover, although the language of the British labour movement has been the language of 'class', there has rarely been any generalised sense of class as an antagonistic, as distinct from a defensive, community; and working-class political culture has rarely sustained anything other than a highly instrumental attitude to the institutions of the labour movement, either to trade unions or to the Labour Party. Trade unions and the Labour Party have been valued for what they could bring in terms of more money, better job security and greater degrees of job control within the existing system of wage labour. Only rarely can one find examples of any generalised ideological commitment to these institutions as representatives of a class community in struggle with a hostile capitalism. Instead high levels of trade union membership, and high levels of working-class Labour voting, have proved compatible with a generalised acceptance of ruling-class condemnations of union power and of Labour Party radicals; and this ideological/cultural subordination has given working-class industrial militancy a vulnerability to government appeals for moderation that has been all too evident after 1974. As Richard Hyman has observed:

The contradictions inherent in trade union consciousness are plainly revealed in the responses of workers to opinion surveys – which for all their distortions and over-simplifications cannot be dismissed altogether. The majority are often willing to criticise the unions for economic difficulties, blame workers for most strikes – which they regard as a major 'problem' –, support legal restrictions on the right to strike, and approve government curbs on pay increases. In this respect the views of most trade union members would not appear to differ radically from those of other sections of the population. Such findings follow naturally from the purely sectional perspectives of most organised workers in respect of their normal trade union activities: they are ready to accept the virtually universal condemnation, by press and politicians, of *other* workers'

271

disputes. Of course they do not endorse the dominant ideology in relation to their *own* industrial activity: but this activity is itself often transient, rarely resulting in any enduring revision of consciousness. There is very little evidence to support the romantic belief that participation in a major industrial struggle naturally generates an 'explosion of consciousness' with lasting consequences.[21]

What the Left faces in Britain is a classic case of the dominance of an entire capitalist culture. The British labour movement, led by the Labour Party, has long subordinated its perspectives to a ruling ethos, whose very strength and connection to the society's dominant institutions gives it an apparent neutrality that helps to obscure the class interests that it serves. That ethos is a complex one: partly composed of specifications of what constitutes legitimate political action (not least stressing the conventions of parliamentary politics and the rejection of the use of working class industrial power for political ends); partly made up of attitudes to wider social and economic processes (the 'naturalness' and neutrality of market forces, the possibility of 'a fair day's wage for a fair day's work', and the existence of a 'national interest'); and partly underpinned by generalised values that favour moderation, compromise, reasonableness, tradition, discipline and authority. To the degree that such specifications have come to predominate, to that degree also have the underprivileged accepted the legitimacy of their unequal universe, and sought its resolution in individual striving or within carefully limited institutional channels. And the strength of such a ruling culture should not be underrated. The forces sustaining it are considerable and pervasive. As F. Parkin has observed in an often quoted passage: 'Members of the underclass are continually exposed to the influence of dominant values by way of the educational system, newspapers, radio and television and the like. By virtue of the powerful institutional backing they receive these values are not readily negated by those lacking other sources of knowledge and information'.[22]

Nor should the dominance of such a ruling culture surprise us. It *is* difficult to see the connections between inequality, instability and capitalism. The strength of capitalism has always lain in the way in which its central processes have remained anonymous and hidden, managing to look both natural, neutral and unavoidable, divorced from the structures of privilege that they actually sustain. What could be more neutral than a market exchange between equals, more innocuous than the pursuit of self-interest, more accidental than the distribution of economic advantage and disadvantage in a competitive struggle? Yet the fit between working-class experience and the ruling culture is never total. There is always a 'space' which the Left has got to reach, an autonomous working-class subculture of mutualism and democracy which the Left has got to tap. To quote Richard Hyman again:

A wide range of studies has clearly documented the inconsistencies inherent in most workers' social attitudes. Typically, they do not question the dominant ideology when formulated in abstract and general form: it is precisely at the level of the overall political economy that the class which is the ruling material force of society is most manifestly also its ruling intellectual force. Yet in respect of their concrete and specific experience they fail to endorse the full implications of the dominant ideology, adopting cynical attitudes towards those in positions of authority, and engaging in actions (in the present context, going on strike) unacceptable to those who are wholeheartedly committed to the prevailing ideological perspective.[23]

It is in that space between class experience and the ruling ethos that Westergaard and Resler have located the existence of a counterculture of latent working-class protest, 'an ideology at half-cock – not a full-blown radical (let alone revolutionary) ideology because its elements are contradictory and lack the coherence implied in classical concepts of working class consciousness', a defensive ideology in which 'individualistic aspirations are linked with a sense of social injustice and of the exploitation characteristic of an unequal power situation'.[24] What characterises that ideology at the present time is its weakness: its ability to sustain day-to-day cooperation with capital alongside a latent class hostility; its only dim perception of the range and source of class inequality; and its political immobility caused by the absence of any clear belief that the situation is remediable or that a realistic alternative is available. Yet beneath the surface of industrial peace and the 'consensus' tapped by opinion surveys lie these untapped and ill-articulated resentments, 'of widespread indeed routine, popular distrust, of a common sense of grievance, a belief that the dice are loaded against ordinary workers, which involves at the very least a rudimentary diagnosis of power and a practical conception of conflicts of interest between classes'.[25] It is these resentments which the existing political parties cannot resolve and which the Left has to harness, educate and transform if a world scarred by capitalist inequality is ever to progress to a free and democratic socialism.

## III

When Marxists argue that capitalism must be transformed, the onus lies with them to say why, and with what it should be replaced. The

273

obligation is on them to argue four things convincingly: that effective reforms from within the existing set of property relationships are impossible; that as a result reformist politics are both bankrupt and a major obstacle to the achievement of socialist goals; that there is a socialist alternative to the capitalist way of running things; and that this can be achieved, given courage, determination and organisation. None of these points is easy to establish. The first and second are always challengeable by the many apologists for Labour Party failures, with their much used theses of 'the unripe time' and 'the one more push for the New Jerusalem'. The specification of the socialist alternative is not an area on which revolutionaries in Britain (outside the nineteenth-century anarchist groups) have ever spent much time; and the fourth of these propositions can never be proved without trying. But the arguments must be made. What socialists seek, after all (as indeed do so many well-intentioned liberals and social democrats), is only a society in which jobs are secure, in which work and living is meaningful, in which basic standards of provision and amenity are guaranteed to all, in which the full range of human potentialities can be developed and realised, and in which social justice and the dignity of men and women are the overriding criteria governing public and private life. However much socialists may disagree amongst themselves over specific programmes, and over questions of both strategy and tactics, they all more or less share the same ultimate goal of a society governed by the principle of 'from each according to his ability, to each according to his needs', a society in which the fact that people differ in ability, gender or race will not mean that they must differ in experience and rewards. That principle and that society has lost none of its attractiveness for all the defeats and compromises of socialist politics over the years.

Now there are many who would argue that such a society is impossible: that alienation is endemic to industrial production, that the lack of mass control is inevitable in large-scale organisations, and that social justice and a free society lie beyond the capacity of an imperfect human nature. Others have argued that, on the contrary, it can be (or indeed already has been/is being) achieved by a gradual and piecemeal sequence of changes. How often do we hear that *the* problem of capitalism is the anarchy of its markets, so that socialism is about planning and public ownership; or that *the* problem of capitalism is its inequality, so that socialism is about welfare provision and tax redistribution; or that *the* problem of capitalism is its élitism, such that the socialist answer has something to do with the sharing of industrial power by managers and unions in a new concordat with the democratic state. The argument of this analysis has been more scathing – that capitalism is both incompatible with the creation of a stable, just and equal society and at the same time not open to incremental change of a socialist kind. It is the law of value that gives capitalism its inherent instability, and necessitates its inequalities and exploitation. To remove the law of value, to still the dull imperatives of the market and to end for ever the silent domination of capital, requires the removal of an entire system of property relationships in which the pursuit of profit is the dominant motif, and its replacement by the active industrial, social and political self-government of working people. The view of socialism held by the revolutionary Left is, in this sense, a distinctive one. As one group of socialists has recently put it:

In Britain today the dominant popular conception of socialism – shared alike by its supporters and opponents – is a social democratic one. The core of this socialism is nationalisation plus the extension of the welfare state. If revolutionary politics is to make any headway this conception must be challenged and displaced. The basic aims of revolutionary socialism are the transformation of *production relations* (aiming at the abolition of the antagonistic relations of production which form the basis of the division into social classes) and popular self-administration (aiming at the conquest of State power by the working people, and the abolition of 'the State' as a form standing 'above Society').[26]

The socialist wager has always been that the destructive impact of prolonged capitalism on the capacities, self-confidence and ways of thinking of its working class can be rolled back and negated by the educational experience of the struggle for, and maintenance of, a socialist society. Socialism does not equal public ownership plus the National Health Service, important though the National Health Service is. To pursue that as socialism is to take the route to a corporatist capitalism, in which the existing set of antagonistic social relationships will continue to prevail behind a rhetoric of working-class advance. A socialist society will exist only when an entire working-class actively run their own industries and communities on democratic lines, consciously and articulately deciding for themselves the priorities of social production and welfare. Such a society will doubtless require new institutions, including the social ownership of the entire means of production, underpinned by an effective system of participatory democracy at factory and community level. It is that kind of society which alone can release the vast productive potential that capitalism's subordination of economic activity to private profit so criminally wastes. Such a socialist society will not be anarchic, without rules or discipline; nor will it be a paradise for the idle. On the contrary, only when men and women rule themselves can the true minimum of required social restraints be realised, and the productivity released to generate the surplus on which the old, the young and the infirm can be properly and securely sustained by the productive labour of others. If such a society still tolerates unemployment, large-scale poverty and major inequalities in its patterns of reward, then socialism will indeed have proved to be an empty vision. But it is because I believe that no society that is truly democratic will tolerate such injustices that socialism remains for me an active utopia; and it is because I believe that capitalism cannot exist without that injustice that its transformation remains an essential prerequisite to human progress. No society in which men and women consciously and repeatedly have to fix the priorities by which they regulate their lives could regularly leave the poor to starve and the ill to die so that the production of armaments can go on unhindered and the privileges of the few remain intact. Yet that is what capitalism does on a world scale and on a daily basis. The need for its removal becomes ever more evident.


## IV

The tragedy of the British Left is that it currently lacks any political vehicle through which to achieve that socialist transformation. There are many, of course, who see the Labour Party as such a vehicle, worth fighting for and within in order to bring that society about. I have argued by implication here and more explicitly elsewhere,[27] that such arguments are unconvincing. The Labour Party will not be transformed into an adequate socialist force; nor indeed will the Labour Left even qualify as such until (and unless) it toughens its economic and social analysis and widens its political strategy to contemplate the limits of parliamentarianism itself. The Labour Party is a coalition in which the right and centre are, and will remain, powerful; and one in which the left-wing analysis and leverage will continue to be crippled by the Tribunite failure to recognise the necessity for mass working-class action and for an effective international strategy of socialist advance. If the only barrier to socialism was the tenacity of a capitalist élite, then a Labour Party strategy geared to putting socialists in positions of power in existing state and industrial structures would indeed suffice. But since the barrier to socialism is capital itself, an appropriate political strategy has to do much more, and aim at nothing less than the entire replacement of a world system of property relationships. If such a thing is possible at all, it will require a social force as powerful as a self-confident and fully mobilised working class, which the parliamentary preoccupations of Tribunite MPs do nothing to create, and indeed which they hinder. It is easy to see the attraction of the Labour Left to aspiring socialists. Their activity is fully in the mainstream of the existing labour movement. Tribunite pressure *is* able to win small gains, and remains unchallenged by any more obviously effective revolutionary alternative. Nor can there be any doubting the sincerity and socialist aspirations of many Tribunite MPs. They seem genuinely to believe that an opportunity has been lost since 1974, and can be grasped again by renewed efforts. Yet their analysis is just as likely as not to culminate in the very corporatist alliance between the State and capital to which modern capitalism is inexorably moving. The Labour Left indeed march with the future. But that future is a capitalist, not a socialist one, and the Left's break with Tribunite preoccupations must therefore be total.

Nor is the present state of the revolutionary left very inspiring either. The Communist Party continues to carry too great an ideological baggage from its past, continues to be too preoccupied with defending and glorifying the horrors of post-Stalinist Russia, continues to be too internally undemocratic, and remains too committed to the very Left Labour alliance and political strategy that has proved so barren since 1974. Certain of the Trotskyist groups seem little better. Currently they are tiny and sectarian. Their organisational divisions still reflect by now obscure disputes within world Trotskyism in the late 1940s. To an outsider, the level of theoretical sophistication within the groups seems low, their published analyses of our present situation seem crude and unimpressive, their view of revolutionary politics all too often vague and insurrectionary, and their papers mistakenly vulgar and unsophisticated. Nonetheless it is the members of these organisations who, week by week, maintain a steadfast opposition to the backsliding of Labour politicians and national trade union leaders, and who constantly attempt to relate these struggles to the wider question of socialist transformation. It is from their ranks in the first instance that the much needed new grouping on the Left must come, if genuinely socialist politics are ever to 'take off' on any scale in the British labour movement. For that is certainly what is required – a 'moving on' in Ralph Miliband's words – 'the formation of a socialist party free from the manifold shortcomings of existing organisations and able to draw together people from such organisations as well as people who are now politically homeless'. It must be the function of that organisation to create a body of worker intellectuals capable of forming, spreading and sustaining a truly socialist alternative to the bankruptcy of Labourism, and in that way provide 'a credible and effective rallying point to help in the struggle against the marked and accelerating drift to the right in Britain'.[28]

The basis of that credibility must be an adequate analysis of the present crisis in Britain, situated firmly in a complex understanding of developments in world capitalism as a whole. There is after all an impressive pedigree for the assertion that 'without revolutionary theory there can be no revolutionary movement'[29]; and for the belief that since capitalism is not self-unmasking, it falls to the lot of the revolutionary party to educate the working class in the true nature of their position. Such an analysis must be complex, to match the complexities of the situation in which workers and their families find themselves. It must be sophisticated and self-confident, actively challenging the competing explanations of our present ills that are repeatedly offered by politicians and commentators outside the Marxist camp. *The Left must argue and convince its way into the minds of the British labour movement.* The time for empty slogans and easy chants, if it ever existed, has now well and truly gone.

The Labour Party's failure, at one level, has always been a deficiency of theory; and it is a deficiency of theory that the Marxist Left cannot afford to repeat. The Left currently has a plethora of complex analyses, all of which share (amid their differences) a common recognition that it is Marxism which alone is able, because of its scientific understanding of the logic of capitalist development, to provide the most appropriate theoretical apparatus within which to connect the specific manifestations of capitalist irrationality to a more general analysis of the overall development of capitalism as a world system. The importance of this theoretical debate within the Marxist Left cannot be overstressed, for a successful struggle for working-class support does not require a 'tailoring' of slogans and programmes to existing levels of consciousness. On the contrary,

effective intervention in the current industrial struggle necessitates an adequate general theory of capitalism and the transition to socialism; a theoretical analysis of the present disposition of the class struggle – the objectives of the ruling class, the role of the unions, and the state of working-class consciousness; and a set of strategies and tactics, of immediate and transitional demands, which are internally coherent and are explicitly related to the first two elements.[30]

The job of the revolutionary left is to link Marxist theory with working-class struggle, as *the* way of convincing a growing audience of both the viability and necessity of the socialist alternative; and to do that it must first educate itself in the complexities of the system that it would have the working class replace.

The Left's starting point, of course, must be the defence of basic working-class and trade union rights in the face of capitalism's attempt to offset its crisis of profitability at the working-class's expense. Opposition to incomes policy, demands for total job protection and opposition to the intensification of work routines, must be the basic bill of fare of socialist struggle, and the strengthening of autonomous rank and file organisation its first institutional goal. But such demands, though vital on the route to a socialist society, must not be confused with socialism. ' "Workers' policies" are not automatically socialist policies, and socialist policies don't arise out of the trade unions in a spontaneous way. Scientific socialism and revolutionary strategy develop alongside the class struggle and not out of it.'[31] What the Left has to build is a renewed *socialist culture*, by fighting on a broad front against the manifestations of capitalist cultural hegemony within the labour movement itself. The Left has to fight against nationalism, against racism, against sexism and against the culturally Philistine, as it links the immediate issues of working-class resistance to a wider and deepening analysis of capitalism.

The overriding political problem for the Revolutionary Left is *how* to make this connection between particular defensive struggles and the wider struggle against capitalism as a whole. Ernest Mandel has well argued that, left to itself, 'any success in the defensive struggle [must] remain only fragmentary and provisional. In the long run the logic of capital will reassert itself so long as we remain under the capitalist system.' It is the recognition of that logic (that working-class militancy *does* erode rates of capital accumulation) that constantly wears down the industrial militancy of a proletariat denied genuinely revolutionary socialist political leadership. Without such leadership, and without a generalised familiarity with a Marxist understanding of the contradictory nature of capitalist development, working people must in the end be vulnerable to the appeals of politicians for moderation and restraint. It requires a firm grasp of the exploitative nature of capitalism to be able to spot, and to refute, the slide in the argument so commonly used by those who govern us, from the valid recognition that working-class militancy *accentuates* the problems of capital accumulation to the false claim that it is the *cause* of those problems. Crisis and unemployment are organic to capitalism, as we have seen; and it is only if and when industrial militancy is buttressed by socialist political radicalism that the capacity of capitalism temporarily to transcend its crises at the expense of working people will finally be prevented. That is why, to follow Mandel further, 'any defensive combat must be integrated into an over-all anti-capitalist strategy that seeks to foster, by all possible means, a mobilisation of the working class around transitional demands directed against the fundamental causes of the evils from which the workers suffer.'[32]

Exactly what those transitional demands ought to be will doubtless continue to be a matter of dispute on the Left. Mandel's list includes public ownership under workers' control of any company laying off workers, and of all key credit institutions, as part of a struggle to create a network of democratically elected workers' committees through which to elaborate an economic plan that is genuinely reflective of the needs of the working population as a whole, and via which to arm the working class against any fascist counter-reaction. Certainly such a revolutionary strategy will need to stress the overriding lessons of this period of Labour Government. It will need constantly to emphasise the way in which even the democratic State is led by the logic of international capitalism to act as the agent of capital restructuring at the expense of the working class; and how as a result a socialist working class must resist State encroachment on already achieved levels of job security, job control and income levels, *in spite of* the fact that this will intensify the crisis by eroding still further already threatened rates of return on capital. Instead of drawing back in the face of the contradiction between working-class strength and national capitalist competitiveness, as Labour politicians and trade union leaders are prone to do, a socialist working class should instead go on to draw the lesson of the internationalisation of capital that has so dogged the economic strategy of this Labour Government. For if the experience of the Labour Government since 1974 tells us anything, it is that only *concerted international action between labour movements* can ever hope to counter the vast global power of capital, and prevent effective working-class resistance in one national capitalism merely speeding the international restructuring of capital towards more supine labour movements. Indeed its scale of operations is capitalism's ultimate source of strength, and the task it sets for its proletariats in an international capitalist crisis is truly enormous. But the scale of the problem must not prevent it from being faced; and the building of international ties must be a vital early component of any effective socialist strategy in the 1980s.

It seems to me that the way forward for the Socialist Left has to be an international one, however daunting that appears, and that the need now is to encourage the creation of a network of socialist militants within each major national and especially multinational company. For a socialist working class will need to create its own 'shadow' administrative structure within each multinational, to link factory to factory in one national context, and factories to factories across national boundaries. Only such a structure can give workers in any one section of a multinational concern any effective leverage against the company as a whole, and provide that vital linkage through which a sense of working-class international solidarity can be recrystallised. Even for workers based in nationally oriented companies this linkage with similar workers in competitor firms both at home and abroad is essential, to forge the real basis of a genuinely international labour movement. Socialist intellectuals have their role here too: to offer their skills to such an emerging movement and to provide it with the arguments, the languages, even the clerical assistance and fund raising which a viable labour movement requires but which hard-pressed industrial militants tend to lack both the time and the energy to generate for themselves.

In other words, the Left needs its own 'think tank' of a particular kind, its own intellectuals willing to put their time and effort at the service of working-class industrial and political struggle, to assist in the creation of a set of alternative proletarian institutions and a strong internationalist counter-culture of socialism. Indeed the creation of a new generation of worker intellectuals requires precisely such an alliance between workers and intellectuals; and the visible international-isation of capital and its obvious incapacity to maintain even existing living standards and employment levels will make that alliance both uniquely necessary and uniquely possible in the 1980s. Of course such a new party will face many difficult tasks in the creation of the conditions under which a transition to a democratic socialist society can take place. Its initial task must be to equip workers with the arguments and theories with which to resist the ideological onslaught of employers and politicians alike, and to share in the deprivations and comradeship of the struggles to defend and advance existing levels of working-class industrial and political power that will inevitably be precipitated by the deepening crisis of the 1980s. This alone will be an enormous task. So many of the conventional wisdoms of bourgeois society remain unchallenged even by socialist intellectuals; and the mass dissemination of socialist arguments has still to be begun in earnest. At the same time the Party will also have to act as a link between industrial struggles, and between industrial struggles and other middle-class protest groups – will have, that is, to link those fighting over the use to which the social surplus is put to those fighting about the conditions under which that surplus is generated – with the aim of creating a broad national coalition of classes. In addition, and at the same time, the party will have to act as a linkage between national struggles, constantly to feed into any particular industrial or social dispute both information and contacts that can illuminate the international nature of capitalist exploitation. So that in the end the Party can be the catalyst to the creation of a coalition of classes willing to go beyond the mere defence of working people and their families against the instabilities and deprivations of capitalism to assert instead their collective determination to administer the key institutions of industry and society in a genuinely democratic way.

Now of course the scale of these tasks is enough to fuel the arguments of those who would despair of their successful attainment, and who would instead offer either the Labour Party or a managed capitalism as easier and quicker routes to that same end. Yet surely the lesson of this study is that the Labour Party is not such a route; and that, left to itself, even a managed capitalism will only create greater degrees of unemployment and human degradation. This means both that an incremental movement to a civilised society is less and less likely to be available to reformers as the years pass; and that working-class resistance to growing unemployment, falling living standards and intensified work routines *will* come, whether the Left acts or not – to which the Left will have to make some kind of response. The thesis of this study is that if that response is of the traditional Labour Party kind, it will in the end fail to realise the aspirations of working-class militants and political radicals alike; and that if the working-class protests of the 1990s are to be effective the 1980s have to be spent establishing the international linkages between different labour movements which alone can offer some chance of creating a social force strong enough to replace capitalism.

I realise that the very pursuit of such an objective (to the degree that it looks likely to succeed) also increases the likelihood of a right-wing authoritarian response; the Left must be ready for that. But 'sabre rattling' of a Tribunite kind, as the anti-Benn hysteria of 1974 demonstrates all too clearly, will be enough to initiate a right-wing reaction if the crisis of British capitalism intensifies; and the job of the Left is to go beyond the rattling of sabres to use the next ten years quietly to build a labour movement strong enough to resist such a challenge if and when it comes. This is a possibility in Western Europe precisely because the existence of liberal democratic political institutions provides the political framework within which an *open* struggle for the loyalty of entire social classes can be waged. The socialist Left must value and defend those political institutions as it seeks to win that struggle. Indeed the equation of socialism with democracy is vital, for a socialist society that is not democratic is not worth having and a democracy that lacks a socialist base must become increasingly a sham. Yet the creation of a socialist working class, and a socialist counter-culture of ideas and institutions, will only be the product of a socialist party that is rich in its theoretical sophistication, democratic in its organisation, and courageous and combative in its style. Such a party has yet to be created. Its creation is *the* socialist task of the 1980s.

It would be dishonest, and ultimately self-defeating, to deny the magnitude of the problems which such an exercise has somehow to overcome. Socialists have to find a way of linking immediate issues to longer-term perspectives, and of linking national struggles to a wider internationalism. In Gramsci's words, we have to find a way through which 'the present [can] be welded to the future, so that while satisfying the urgent necessities of the one we may work effectively to create and anticipate the other.'[33] We have to find a way of uniting a working class within which capitalism has already sown the seeds of strong internal divisions; and of countering the powerful ideologies mobilised against us. We have to find a way of breaking with the legacy of our own past of previous revolutionary failures and degenerations; and in particular we have to find an effective way of countering the equation of socialism with Russian totalitarianism with which our opponents will seek to tar us. We have to clarify our attitude to parliamentary action, finding a balance between the parliamentary preoccupations of the Tribunite Left and the disdain of the parliamentary tactic so common in Trotskyist circles. We have to find a way of resolving theoretical differences in fraternal debate, as we establish that degree of organisational unity which alone can inspire confidence in a revolutionary alternative. We have to find ways of countering the alternative scenarios of racism, nationalism and corporatism that are actively canvassed among working people by our political opponents. We have to encourage the consolidation of autonomous working-class institutions, within which to resurrect a socialist culture and a confident proletariat ready and equipped to take over the reins of power in a complex industrial society. And we have to be prepared to anticipate and negate the degree of overt coercion that a revolutionary socialist movement can expect to encounter from the bourgeoisie and its state apparatus as our political strength grows.

This last problem at least is for the moment a distant one, Ireland apart. Given the revolutionary Left's weakness 'the imperative need remains to win the working class, before there can be any talk of winning power. The means of achieving this conquest, not of the institutions of the State but of the convictions of workers . . . are the prime agenda of any real socialist strategy today'.[34] The importance of that strategy lies in the fact that capitalism will not fall by itself. It will just go on creating inequality, instability and alienation until it is replaced; and it will continue to rely on social democratic and Euro-communist political parties to stabilise its social relationships, by exercising a disciplining hegemony over its working classes in the manner of this Labour Government. Yet neither Labour Parties nor capitalism will ever remove the question of socialism from the agenda of history. As Marx said so long ago, history remains on the side of the revolutionary proletariat. The task of this generation of Marxists, like the generations before it, is to be the catalyst that can show the way.

# References

(Place of publication London unless otherwise indicated.)

## Chapter 1 The Government's economic performance

1. *Labour's Programme 1973*, p. 7; and the Labour Party election manifesto ('*Labour's way out of the crisis*'), Feb. 1974, p. 14.
2. *Labour Party Annual Conference Report 1973*, p. 129.
3. Harold Wilson, *Democracy in Industry*, Labour Party, 1973, p. 7.
4. *Labour Weekly*, 8 Oct. 1971, p. 1.
5. The text is given in *Labour Weekly*, 2 Mar. 1973, p. 11.
6. The *Guardian*, 3 Oct. 1972, p. 10.
7. *Labour Weekly*, 23 Mar. 1973, p. 15.
8. The *Guardian*, 4 July 1972, p. 8.
9. *Labour Party Annual Conference Report 1973*, p. 166.
10. ibid., p. 167.
11. ibid., p. 164.
12. The *Guardian*, 3 Oct. 1973, p. 1.
13. Labour Party election manifesto, Feb. 1974, p. 1.
14. The *Guardian*, 5 Mar. 1974, p. 1.
15. *House of Commons Debates*, 5th ser., vol. 870, col. 45 (12 Mar. 1974).
16. The *Guardian*, 6 Sept. 1974, p. 1.
17. *Report of the Committee of Inquiry on Industrial Democracy* (Chairman: Lord Bullock), HMSO, 1977.
18. *Britain will win with Labour* (Labour Party election manifesto, Oct. 1974), p. 3.
19. *House of Commons Debates*, 5th ser., vol. 871, col. 278 (26 Mar. 1974).
20. ibid., col. 286 (26 Mar. 1974).
21. Labour Party election manifesto, Oct. 1974, introduction.
22. *House of Commons Debates*, 5th ser., vol. 871, col. 306–7 (26 Mar. 1974).
23. ibid., col. 295 (26 Mar. 1974).
24. ibid., col. 327 (26 Mar. 1974).
25. ibid., vol. 877, col. 1053 (22 July 1974).
26. ibid., vol. 890, col. 284 (15 Apr. 1975).
27. ibid., col. 288 (15 Apr. 1975).
28. ibid., col. 272–3 (15 Apr. 1975).
29. ibid., vol. 880, col. 84 (29 Oct. 1974).

30. ibid., vol. 890, col. 283 (15 Apr. 1975).
31. In his budget speech, April 1975.
32. The *Guardian*, 22 Jan. 1975, p. 1.
33. Peter Jay, in *The Times*, 31 Mar. 1977, p. 21.
34. *Labour Party Annual Conference Report 1976*, p. 188.
35. Harold Wilson, quoted in *The Times*, 30 Oct. 1974, p. 12.
36. The *Guardian*, 20 Feb., 1976, p. 18.
37. *House of Commons Debates*, 5th ser., vol. 890, col. 282–3 (15 Apr. 1975).
38. The *Guardian*, 23 July 1974, p. 6.
39. *The Times*, 13 Nov. 1974, p. 7.
40. *House of Commons Debates*, 5th ser., vol. 881, col. 256 (12 Nov. 1974).
41. ibid., col. 279 (12 Nov. 1974).
42. ibid., col. 271 (12 Nov. 1974).
43. ibid., col. 253 (12 Nov. 1974).
44. ibid., col. 276 (12 Nov. 1974).
45. *The Times*, 13 Nov. 1974, p. 16.
46. *House of Commons Debates*, 5th ser., vol. 890, col. 320 (15 Apr. 1975).
47. See note 44 to Chapter 2.
48. *The Times*, 15 Mar. 1977, p. 12.
49. The *Guardian*, 21 Aug. 1975, p. 4.
50. *House of Commons Debates*, 5th ser., vol. 909, col. 237 (6 Apr. 1976).
51. *The Times*, 16 Nov. 1976, p. 1.
52. ibid., 6 Nov. 1975, p. 1.
53. ibid., 3 Feb. 1977, p. 20.
54. ibid., 25 Sept. 1978, p. 1.
55. *Observer*, 2 Jan. 1977, p. 11.
56. *Financial Times*, 31 May 1979, p. 25.
57. *The Times*, 20 Feb. 1976, p. 14.
58. See *The Times*, 23 June 1976, p. 1 and 15 June 1976, p. 16.
59. *House of Commons Debates*, 5th ser., vol. 912, col. 912 (7 June 1976).
60. ibid., vol. 917, col. 42 (11 Oct. 1976).
61. *The Times*, 20 Oct. 1976, p. 19.
62. ibid., 1 Oct. 1976, p. 1.
63. ibid., 16 Dec. 1976, p. 7.
64. ibid.
65. *The Guardian*, 16 Dec. 1976, p. 6.
66. *House of Commons Debates*, 5th ser., vol. 890, col. 289 (15 Apr. 1975).
67. *The Times*, 11 Nov. 1976, p. 16.
68. The *Guardian*, 13 Jan. 1978, p. 4.
69. *The Times*, 7 Dec. 1977, p. 29.
70. ibid., 3 Oct. 1977, p. 19.
71. ibid., 19 May 1977, p. 23.
72. ibid., 27 Oct. 1977, p. 27.
73. ibid., 1 Nov. 1977, p. 21.
74. ibid., 26 Sept. 1977, p. V.
75. ibid., 9 Feb. 1978, p. 12.
76. ibid., 18 May 1978, p. 24.
77. ibid., 18 May 1978, p. 1.
78. ibid., 14 Oct. 1978, p. 19.
79. ibid., 26 Aug. 1978, p. 15.

80. The *Guardian*, 14 Dec. 1978, p. 18.
81. *Financial Times*, 21 Feb. 1979, p. 6.
82. *The Times*, 15 June 1978, p. 12.

## Chapter 2 The Labour Government and the trade unions

1. Unpublished paper in the author's possession.
2. On this, see P. Jenkins, *The Battle of Downing Street*, Charles Knight and Co. 1970; E. Heffer, *The Class Struggle in Parliament*, Gollancz 1973; R. H. S. Crossman, *The Diaries of a Cabinet Minister*, vol. I, Hamish Hamilton and Cape, 1977.
3. In an unpublished paper in the author's possession.
4. L. Minkin, 'The Labour Party has not been hijacked', *New Society,* 6 Oct. 1977, p. 8.
5. J. Elliott, *Conflict or Co-operation: the growth of industrial democracy*, Kogan Page, 1978, p. 27.
6. L. Minkin, op. cit., p. 7.
7. James Callaghan, Michael Foot and Sam Silkin, on 17 and 18 May 1977.
8. Denis Howell, Fred Mulley and Shirley Williams, at Grunwick, 19 May 1977.
9. *The Times*, 25 May 1977, p. 23; and Elliott, op. cit., pp. 273–7.
10. See Elliott, op. cit., p. 218.
11. The *Guardian*, 7 Mar. 1974, p. 15.
12. ibid., 29 Mar. 1974, p. 19.
13. ibid., 27 Mar. 1974, p. 28.
14. ibid.
15. ibid., 3 Apr. 1974, p. 5.
16. ibid., 5 June 1974, p. 26.
17. ibid., 4 Apr. 1974, p. 6.
18. ibid., 16 Apr. 1974, p. 28.
19. *Financial Times*, 13 May 1974, p. 6.
20. TUC, *Collective bargaining and the Social Contract*, p. 9.
21. ibid., p. 9.
22. The *Guardian*, 31 Aug. 1974, p. 1.
23. *Observer*, 8 Sept. 1974, p. 9.
24. The *Guardian*, 15. Oct. 1974, p. 1.
25. *Sunday Times*, 12 Jan. 1975, p. 6.
26. *The Times*, 23 Nov. 1974, p. 4.
27. The *Guardian*, 12 Dec. 1974, p. 30.
28. *The Times*, 22 Jan. 1975, p. 1.
29. ibid., 2 July 1975, p. 1.
30. *Sunday Times*, 29 June 1975, p. 2.
31. Jack Jones, to the TGWU conference, quoted in the *Observer*, 6 July 1975, p. 1.
32. *The Times*, 12 July 1975, p. 3.
33. *Observer*, 17 Aug. 1975, p. 1.
34. The *Guardian*, 4 Sept. 1975, p. 7.
35. *The Times*, 26 Sept. 1975, p. 16.

## References

36. *Labour Party Annual Conference Report 1975*, p. 164.
37. *The Times*, 26 Aug. 1976, p. 1.
38. ibid., 25 Aug. 1976, p. 1.
39. ibid., 1 Aug. 1977, p. 1.
40. Including Peter Jay (see *The Times*, 25 Sept. 1975, p. 14).
41. J. Hughes, 'A Rakes' Progress' in M. Barratt Brown, ed. *Full Employment: Priority*, Nottingham, Spokesman Books, 1978, p. 14.
42. ibid., p. 34.
43. *The Times*, 19 May 1977, p. 4.
44. ibid., 2 Feb. 1977, p. 5.
45. ibid., 15 May 1976, p. 3.
46. ibid., 18 June 1976, p. 2.
47. See, for example, *The Times*, 1 July 1977, p. 29.
48. *The Times*, 19 Feb. 1977, p. 1.
49. ibid., 25 Apr. 1977, p. 2.
50. ibid., 23 May 1977, p. 2.
51. ibid., 4 Apr. 1977, p. 1.
52. ibid., 31 Mar. 1977, p. 1.
53. ibid., 14 Apr. 1977, p. 1.
54. ibid., 11 Aug. 1977, p. 1.
55. ibid., 21 July 1977, p. 8.
56. ibid., 30 May 1978, p. 1; and BBC 'Panorama', 2 Oct. 1978.
57. *The Times*, 22 Feb. 1978, p. 23.
58. ibid., 3 Dec. 1977, p. 1.
59. ibid., 30 Dec. 1977, p. 1.
60. *Winning the Battle Against Inflation*, Cmnd 7393, HMSO, July 1978, p. 3.
61. Text given in *The Times*, 15 Nov. 1978, p. 4.
62. Quoted in M. Barratt Brown, op. cit., p. 78.
63. *The Times*, 26 July 1977, p. 1.
64. ibid., 27 July 1978, p. 1.
65. *Tribune*, 8 Sept. 1978, p. 6.
66. ibid.; see also chapter 7, pp. 265–7.
67. *The Times*, 16 June 1977, p. 1.
68. *The Times*, 5 Sept. 1978, p. 3.

## Chapter 3 The Industrial strategy of the Labour Government

1. *Labour's Programme for Britain*, 1972, pp. 7, 12.
2. ibid., p. 16.
3. ibid., p. 16 (my italics).
4. ibid., p. 13.
5. 'The National Enterprise Board: Labour's State holding company', Report of a Labour Party study group, The Labour Party, 1973, pp. 9, 12, 14, 21.
6. *Labour's Programme 1973*, p. 13.
7. *The Times*, 3 Oct. 1973, p. 5.
8. ibid., 4 July 1974, p. 23.

9. ibid., 15 June 1974, p. 19.
10. *The Times*, 20 June 1974, p. 1, and 20 May 1974, p. 1.
11. *The Regeneration of British Industry*, Cmnd 5710 (HMSO 1974), p. 2.
12. *The Times*, 1 Feb. 1975, p. 17.
13. The *Guardian*, 12 Feb. 1975, p. 17.
14. *The Times*, 17 Nov. 1975, p. 1.
15. ibid., 15 May 1974, p. 1.
16. ibid., 1 July 1974, p. 1.
17. ibid., 5 May 1976, p. 2, and 16 Nov. 1976, p. 1.
18. The *Guardian*, 3 Nov. 1975, p. 14.
19. *Financial Times*, 8 Aug. 1975, p. 14.
20. *The Times*, 24 Oct. 1977, p. 25.
21. *Labour's Programme 1973*, p. 29.
22. *The Times*, 7 Nov. 1975, p. 1.
23. *Labour's Programme 1973*, p. 23.
24. The *Guardian*, 23 Feb. 1977, p. 18.
25. *The Times*, 23 Nov. 1975, p. 23.
26. Eric Varley, quoted in *The Times*, 22 Oct. 1975, p. 25.
27. *The Times*, 2 Feb. 1978, p. 17.
28. *Tribune*, 27 Jan. 1978, p. 1.
29. The Labour Party election manifesto, October 1974, p. 10.
30. See, for example, *The Times*, 17 Nov. 1975, pp. 1, 19.
31. *The Times*, 2 Mar. 1976, p. 15.
32. ibid., 4 May 1977, p. 19.
33. 'A workers' inquiry into the motor industry', *Capital and Class* (2), Summer 1977, p. 103.
34. *Observer*, 8 Dec. 1974, p. 2.
35. *The Times*, 9 Feb. 1978, p. 21.
36. J. Harrison and B. Sutcliffe, 'Autopsy on British Leyland', *Bulletin of the Conference of Socialist Economists* 4(1), (Feb. 1975), p. 5.
37. 'A workers' inquiry into the motor industry', op. cit., p. 111.
38. 'British Leyland: the beginning of the end', Counter-Information Services *Anti-Report No. 5*, p. 1.
39. *Sunday Times*, 27 Apr. 1975, p. 62.
40. *House of Commons Debates*, 5th ser., vol. 890, col. 1746 (24 Apr. 1975), my italics.
41. *The Times*, 12 Feb. 1977, p. 17 and 15 Feb. 1977, p. 17.
42. ibid., 17 Oct. 1977, p. 19.
43. Derek Robinson, chairman of the Leyland's shop stewards' combine committee, quoted in *The Times*, 9 Feb. 1978, p. 21.
44. *The Times*, 6 Oct. 1976, p. 1.
45. The *Guardian*, 4 Jan. 1975, p. 1.
46. *House of Commons Debates*, 5th ser., vol. 927, col. 387, 390, 391 (2 March 1977).
47. CIS *Anti-Report*, op. cit. (38), p. 3.
48. 'A workers' inquiry into the motor industry', op. cit., p. 108.
49. *Labour's Programme 1973*, p. 31.
50. *The Times*, 19 Nov. 1977, p. 7.
51. ibid., 23 March 1978, p. 1.

## References

52. See D. Coates *The Labour Party and the Struggle for Socialism*, Cambridge University Press, 1975, p. 36.
53. *Report of the Labour Party Working Party on Industrial Democracy*, Labour Party, 1967, p. 10.
54. *Report of the Royal Commission on Trade Unions and Employers' Associations 1965–1968* (Chairman: Lord Donovan), HMSO 1968.
55. J. Elliott, *Conflict or Co-operation: the growth of industrial democracy*, Kogan Page, 1978, p. 211.
56. *Labour Party Annual Conference Report 1973*, p. 187.
57. Harold Wilson, *Democracy in Industry*, The Labour Party, 1973, p. 12.
58. *Labour's Programme 1973*, p. 27.
59. Labour Party election manifesto, February 1974, p. 10.
60. ibid., October 1974, p. 13.
61. Regulations published by the Department of Industry, quoted in *The Times*, 18 Aug. 1977, p. 15.
62. Elliott, op. cit., p. 238.
63. *The Times*, 3 Feb. 1977, p. 19.

## Chapter 4 The determinants of Labour politics

1. On this, see L. Minkin, *The Labour Party Conference*, Allen Lane, 1978, *passim*.
2. D. Steel, *The Times*, 21 Mar. 1977, p. 1.
3. D. Coates, *The Labour Party and the Struggle for Socialism*, Cambridge University Press, 1975, pp. 144–57.
4. *Labour Party Annual Conference Report 1975*, p. 228.
5. The *Guardian*, 18 Apr. 1977, p. 10.
6. *The Times*, 6 Aug. 1977, p. 1.
7. J. Haines, *The Politics of Power*, Hodder and Stoughton, 1977, p. 50.
8. It should be noted that recent historians of the CBI have stressed its limited impact on policy; see W. Grant and D. Marsh, *The C.B.I.*, Hodder and Stoughton, 1977.
9. J. Goldstein, 'The multinational corporation', in R. Miliband and J. Saville, eds, *The Socialist Register 1974*, Merlin, 1974, p. 281. For various positions in the debate on the relationship between multinational corporations and the nation state, see R. Murray, 'The internationalisation of capital and the nation state', *New Left Review* 67 (May–June 1971), pp. 84–109; and Bill Warren's reply in *New Left Review* 68 (July–Aug. 1971), pp. 83–8; both are reprinted in H. Radice, ed., *International Firms and Modern Imperialism*, Penguin, 1975.
10. The *Guardian*, 31 Jan. 1977, p. 16.
11. For further reading on the nature of the State in advanced capitalism, see below, p. 299.
12. K. Marx, *Capital*, Dent, 1972, I, xiv.
13. K. Marx, *The German Ideology*, Lawrence and Wishart, 1970, p. 57.
14. ibid., p. 59.
15. For an interesting recent discussion of this, see P. Anderson, *Passages from*

*Antiquity to Feudalism* and *Lineages of the Absolutist State*, both published by New Left Books, 1974.

16. Marx, *Capital*, Chicago, Charles Kerr, 1909, III, p. 211.
17. See in particular *Capital* I, pp. 138–9.
18. *The Communist Manifesto*, in K. Marx and F. Engels, *Selected Works*, Lawrence and Wishart, 1968, pp. 38 and 40.
19. D. Yaffe, 'Value and price in Marx's Capital', *Revolutionary Communist* (1), Jan. 1975, p. 45.
20. D. Yaffe, 'The Marxian theory of crisis, capital and the state', *Economy and Society* 2(2), (May 1973), pp. 203, 213.
21. ibid., p. 204.
22. For further reading, see below, p. 299.
23. K. Marx, *The Grundrisse*, Penguin, 1973, p. 414.
24. Quoted in Yaffe, 'Value and price in Marx's Capital', op. cit., p. 41.
25. P. Mattick, *Marx and Keynes*, Merlin, 1971, p. 64.
26. D. Yaffe, 'The Marxian theory of crisis, capital and the State', op. cit., p. 205.
27. See references to the work of Yaffe, Sweezy and Mattick in the suggestions for further reading.
28. Mattick, op. cit., pp. 129–30.
29. A. Crosland, *The Future of Socialism*, Cape, 1956; J. Strachey, *Modern Capitalism*, Gollancz, 1956; also A. Shonfield, *Modern Capitalism*, Oxford University Press, 1965; R. Dahrendorf, *Class and Class Conflict in Industrial Society*, Routledge and Kegan Paul, 1972; and C. Kerr, *et al.*, *Industrialism and Industrial Man*, Penguin, 1973.
30. Mattick, op. cit., p. viii.
31. On this, see E. Mandel, *Late Capitalism*, New Left Books, 1975, p. 170; and G. Minnerup, 'West Germany since the war', *New Left Review*, 99 (Sept.–Oct. 1976), p. 13.
32. D. Yaffe, 'The crisis of profitability: a critique of the Glyn-Sutcliffe thesis', *New Left Review* 80 (July–Aug. 1973), p. 48.
33. For a further discussion of this, see M. Itoh, 'The inflational crisis of capitalism', *Capital and Class* 4 (Spring 1978), pp. 1–11; and E. Mandel, *The Second Slump*, New Left Books, 1978.
34. A. Gamble and P. Walton, *Capitalism in Crisis: inflation and the State*, Macmillan, 1976, p. 165.
35. See H. Robinson, 'The downfall of the dollar', in R. Miliband and J. Saville, eds, *The Socialist Register 1973*, Merlin, 1973, pp. 397–450.
36. See A. Hone, 'The primary commodities boom', *New Left Review*, 81 (Sept.–Oct. 1973), pp. 83–92; and Mandel, *The Second Slump*, pp. 25–6.
37. For the figures on this, see P. Bullock and D. Yaffe, 'Inflation, the crisis and the post war boom', *Revolutionary Communist* 3/4 (Nov. 1975), p. 38.
38. For a study of car workers and their political attitudes prior to this, see J. Goldthorpe *et al.*, *The Affluent Worker*, Cambridge University Press, 1968/9.
39. B. Fine and L. Harris, 'Recent controversies in Marxist economic theory', in R. Miliband and J. Saville, eds, *The Socialist Register 1976*, Merlin, 1976, p. 171.
40. See Bill Warren, 'Capitalist planning and the State', *New Left Review*, 72 (Mar.–Apr. 1972), pp. 3–30.

## References

41. On this, see I. Gough, 'Productive and unproductive labour', *New Left Review* 76 (Nov.–Dec. 1972), pp. 41–72.
42. Gamble and Walton, op. cit., p. 173.
43. Bullock and Yaffe, op. cit., p. 32.
44. A. Glyn and B. Sutcliffe, *British Capitalism, Workers and the Profits Squeeze*, Penguin, 1972, p. 19.
45. Yaffe, 'The crisis of profitability . . . ', op. cit., p. 54.
46. Mandel, *Late Capitalism*, p. 179.
47. B. Rowthorn, 'Unions and the economy', in R. Blackburn and A. Cockburn, *The Incompatibles: trade unions and the consensus*, Penguin, 1965, pp. 211–12.
48. P. Bullock and D. Yaffe, op. cit., p. 41.
49. See Coates, op. cit., ch. 5.
50. Glyn and Sutcliffe, op. cit., p. 69.
51. The *Guardian*, 3 Oct. 1974, p. 18.
52. *The Times*, 21 Feb. 1977, p. 15.
53. The *Guardian*, 31 Jan. 1977, p. 14.
54. *The Times*, 3 May 1977, p. 17.
55. Between 1948 and 1970 employment in education grew by 173 per cent, in insurance, banking and finance by 126 per cent, and in professional services by 83 per cent. This compares with an overall increase in the total occupied population of 9.3 per cent, and a *fall* in employment in agriculture, forestry and fishing of 54 per cent, in railways of 54 per cent, in cotton of 42 per cent and in coal mining of 44 per cent.
56. See Yaffe, 'The crisis of profitability . . . ', op. cit., p. 55.
57. See Coates, op. cit., *passim*.
58. See Yaffe, 'The crisis of profitability . . . ', op. cit., p. 55.
59. See B. Fine and L. Harris, 'The British economy since March 1974' in the *Bulletin of the Conference of Socialist Economists*, 4(3), (Oct. 1975), p. 6.
60. J. Harrison, 'British capitalism in 1973 and 1974: the deepening crisis', *Bulletin of the Conference of Socialist Economists*, 3(1), (Spring 1974), pp. 55, 56.
61. Gamble and Walton, op. cit., p. 35.

# Chapter 5 The political power of trade unionism

1. S. E. Finer, 'The political power of organised labour', *Government and Opposition* 8(4), (1973), p. 391.
2. ibid., pp. 393 and 394.
3. F. Cairncross, 'Curbing the trade unions', *The Guardian*, 19 May 1975, p. 12.
4. P. Johnson, 'A brotherhood of national misery', *New Statesman*, 16 May 1975, p. 652.
5. C. Wright Mills, *The New Men of Power*, New York, Harcourt Brace, 1948, p. 8.
6. T. Lane, *The Union Makes Us Strong*, Arrow Books, 1974, p. 230.
7. T. Cliff, *The Crisis: Social Contract or Socialism*, Pluto Press, 1975, p. 114.

8. Lane, op. cit., p. 224.
9. Cliff, op. cit., p. 126.
10. L. Althusser, 'Ideology and ideological state apparatuses', in his *Lenin and Philosophy*, New Left Books, 1971, p. 127.
11. R. Hyman, 'Industrial conflict and the political economy', in R. Miliband and J. Saville, eds, *The Socialist Register 1973*, Merlin, 1973, p. 117.
12. T. Clarke, 'The raison d'être of trade unionism' in T. Clarke and L. Clements, eds, *Trade Unions Under Capitalism*, Fontana, 1977, p. 17.
13. For a fuller consideration of this, see R. Hyman and B. Fryer, 'Trade unions: sociology and political economy', in J. McKinlay, ed., *Processing People: cases in organisational behaviour*, Holt-Blond, 1974, pp. 150–214; and R. Hyman and I. Brough, *Social Values and Industrial Relations*, Oxford, Blackwell, 1975.
14. Hyman and Fryer, op. cit., p. 174.
15. For a fuller consideration of this, see the Glasgow University Media Group, *Bad News*, Routledge & Kegan Paul, 1976; and P. Beharrell and G. Philo, eds, *Trade Unions and the Media*, Macmillan, 1977.
16. V. L. Allen, *Militant Trade Unionism*, Merlin, 1966, p. 27.
17. *Labour Party Annual Conference Report 1976*, p. 188.
18. Hyman, op. cit., pp. 118–19.
19. Quoted in R. Hyman, *Marxism and the Sociology of Trade Unionism*, Pluto Press, 1971, p. 18.
20. *The Times*, 22 Aug. 1977, p. 5.
21. R. Miliband, *Parliamentary Socialism*, Merlin, 1961, p. 13.
22. Quoted in Allen, op. cit., p. 33.
23. *The Times*, 22 Aug. 1977, p. 5.
24. R. Collins, 'How the unions got enmeshed in massive joblessness', The *Guardian*, 22 Jan. 1976, p. 13.
25. L. Minkin, 'The Labour Party has not been hijacked', *New Society*, 6 Oct. 1978, p. 8.
26. Including D. Coates, *The Labour Party and the Struggle for Socialism*, Cambridge University Press, 1975, Chapter 8.
27. *The Times*, 22 Aug. 1977, p. 5.
28. ibid., 10 Feb. 1977, p. 21.
29. D. Yaffe, 'Trade unions and the State: the struggle against the social contract', *Revolutionary Communist* (7), (Nov. 1977), p. 25.
30. B. Fine, *Marx's Capital*, Macmillan, 1975, p. 60.
31. P. Anderson, 'The limits and possibilities of trade union action', in Clarke and Clements, p. 334.
32. See Althusser, op. cit., pp. 83–4 and 137; and R. Miliband and N. Poulantzas, 'The problem of the capitalist state', in R. Blackburn, ed., *Ideology in Social Science*, Fontana, 1972, pp. 238–64.

## Chapter 6 The weakness of the Labour Left

1. *Sunday Times*, 9 Oct. 1977, p. 3.
2. *The Times*, 10 Mar. 1978, p. 3.

# References

3. *The Times*, 4 Oct. 1976, p. 3 and 1 Dec. 1976, p. 4; and *Sunday Times*, 21 Nov. 1976, p. 1.
4. See his *What's Left of the Labour Party*, Sidgwick and Jackson, 1977.
5. See Coates, *The Labour Party and the Struggle for Socialism*, Chapter 7, for an earlier analysis.
6. For a full report, see M. Hatfield, *The House the Left Built*, Gollancz, 1978.
7. See L. Minkin, *The Labour Party Conference*, Allen Lane, 1978, Chapter 13.
8. Shirley Williams is one example. See her speech reported in full in The *Guardian*, 22 Jan. 1977, and the subsequent correspondence.
9. *Tribune*, 7 Mar. 1975, p. 5.
10. Full details of the five rights can be found in the *Sunday Times*, 11 May 1975, p. 8.
11. The *Guardian*, 20 Mar. 1975, p. 1.
12. Brian Sedgemore estimated that the deficit with the EEC cost 450,000 jobs in British manufacturing industry (*Tribune*, 16 May 1975, p. 1). Tony Benn's figures were similar (500,000 'with more to come'), *The Times*, 19 May 1975, p. 2.
13. *Tribune*, 14 Nov. 1975, p. 5.
14. ibid., 27 July 1974, p. 1.
15. ibid., 20 Dec. 1974, p. 6.
16. Neil Kinnock, MP, *Tribune*, 18 July 1975, p. 5.
17. *Sunday Times*, 22 Feb. 1976, p. 1.
18. *The Times*, 5 May 1976, p. 2, and 24 Feb. 1976, p. 1.
19. See Stephen Fay and Hugo Young, 'The day the £ nearly died', *Sunday Times*, 14, 21 and 28 May 1978.
20. NEC policy statement on banking and finance, quoted in *The Times*, 10 Sept. 1976, p. 12.
21. *Tribune* periodically denounced the export of British capital. See in particular the editions published 29 Aug. 1975, p. 13; 18 Mar. 1977, p. 2; and 19 Aug. 1977, p. 2.
22. See B. Sedgemore, *The How and Why of Socialism*, Nottingham, Spokesman Books, 1977, p. 17; and the interview with Adrian Ham (former special assistant to Denis Healey) in *Tribune*, 30 July 1976, p. 5.
23. *Tribune*, 8 Nov. 1974, p. 1.
24. ibid., 31 Jan. 1975, p. 5.
25. Sedgemore, op. cit., pp. 30, 31.
26. *Tribune*, 27 Apr. 1975, p. 2.
27. *The Labour Party and the Struggle for Socialism*, Chapter 7.
28. *The Times*, 3 Sept. 1977, p. 4.
29. ibid., 30 Apr. 1976, p. 1.
30. *Sunday Times*, 21 Dec. 1975, p. 32.
31. *The Times*, 24 Sept. 1976, p. 14.
32. Bob Cryer felt it necessary to defend his decision (*Tribune*, 17 Sept. 1976, p. 4).
33. *Sunday Times*, 29 Jan. 1978, p. 10.
34. ibid., 28 May 1978, p. 33.
35. The title of his book published by Quartet Books in 1975.
36. Stuart Holland, *Strategy for Socialism*, Nottingham, Spokesman Books, 1975 (pamphlet), pp. 18, 19.
37. See Sedgemore, op. cit., pp. 27–8.

38. Holland, *Strategy for Socialism*, pp. 27, 32.
39. ibid., pp. 43, 53, 66.
40. Coates, op. cit., Chapter 8.
41. Sedgemore, op. cit., pp. 36–7.
42. Holland, *The Socialist Challenge*, pp. 204, 234.
43. D. Marquand, 'Clause 4 rides again', *The Times Literary Supplement*, 26 Sept. 1975, p. 1095.
44. *The Times*, 8 Sept. 1976, p. 17.
45. M. Barratt Brown, 'Technological unemployment', in *Full Employment: priority*, Spokesman Books, 1978, pp. 86–7.
46. See B. Sedgemore, 'The socialist case for import controls', *Tribune*, 21 Nov. 1975, p. 1.
47. P. Bullock and D. Yaffe, 'Inflation, the crisis and the post-war boom', *Revolutionary Communist* 3/4 (Nov. 1975), p. 7.
48. A. Heath and J. Wood, 'The Labour Party, the E.E.C. and Ireland', *Revolutionary Communist* 2 (May 1975), p. 43.

## Chapter 7 The lessons of Labour in power

1. *Tribune*, 2 May 1975, p. 5.
2. *The Times*, 13 May 1978, p. 2.
3. L. Panitch, *Social Democracy and Industrial Militancy*, Cambridge University Press, 1976, pp. 235–6.
4. *The Times*, 16 July 1976, p. 6.
5. Panitch, op. cit., p. 236.
6. ibid., p. 235.
7. See J. Goldstein, 'The multinational corporation' in R. Miliband and J. Saville, eds. *The Socialist Register 1974*, Merlin, 1974, for a discussion of the problems presented to social democratic parties by the power of multinational corporations.
8. See B. Clarke, T. Humphris and C. James, *Reasonable Agenda*, Fabian pamphlet, 1977.
9. J. Westergaard and H. Resler, *Class in a Capitalist Society*, Heinemann, 1975, pp. 142–4.
10. See the references to the literature on state power under capitalism in the suggestions for further reading, p. 299.
11. For further documentation, see P. Townsend, 'An overview', in M. Barratt Brown, *Full Employment: priority*, Spokesman Books, 1978, p. 10.
12. Westergaard and Resler, op. cit., p. 87.
13. See J. Goldthorpe *et al.*, *The Affluent Worker*, Cambridge University Press, 1969, III, p. 60.
14. R. Miliband, quoted in R. Hyman, *Strikes*, Fontana, 1972, p. 87.
15. T. Clarke and L. Clements, *Trade Unions Under Capitalism*, Fontana, 1977, p. 13.
16. Westergaard and Resler, op. cit., p. 108.
17. F. Field, *Unequal Britain: a report on the cycle of inequality*, Arrow Books, 1973, p. 28.

## References

18. Westergaard and Resler, op. cit., p. 131.
19. ibid., pp. 141–2.
20. For an earlier statement, see D. Coates, 'Politicians and the sorcerer', in A. King, *Why is Britain becoming more difficult to govern?*, BBC, 1976, pp. 34–9.
21. R. Hyman, 'Industrial conflict and the political economy', in R. Miliband and J. Saville, eds, *The Socialist Register 1973*, p. 126.
22. F. Parkin, *Class Inequality and Political Order*, Paladin, 1971, p. 92.
23. Hyman, op. cit., p. 126.
24. J. Westergaard, 'The rediscovery of the cash nexus' in Miliband and Saville, eds, *The Socialist Register 1970*, p. 125.
25. Westergaard and Resler, op. cit., p. 403.
26. A. Cottrell *et al.*, 'Socialist strategy in capitalist restructuring' (paper to the Bradford CSE conference, July 1978), p. 5.
27. Coates, *The Labour Party and the Struggle for Socialism*, Chapter 8.
28. R. Miliband, 'Moving on', in R. Miliband and J. Saville, eds, *The Socialist Register 1976*, p. 140.
29. V. I. Lenin, *What is to be done*, Moscow, Progress Publishers, 1964, p. 25.
30. Hyman, op. cit., p. 130.
31. 'Our tasks and methods: the founding document of the R.C.G.', *Revolutionary Communist* (1), p. 9.
32. E. Mandel, *The Second Slump*, New Left Books, 1978, p. 207.
33. Quoted by D. Elson, 'Which Way "out of the ghetto"?' (unpublished paper to the CSE conference in Bradford, July 1978, p. 2).
34. P. Anderson, 'The antimonies of Antonio Gramsci', *New Left Review, 100*, (Nov. 1976–Jan. 1977), p. 78.

# Further reading

Inevitably many of the sources for a study such as this are relatively inaccessible to the general reader. The documents of the organisations themselves, and the back copies of appropriate newspapers and journals, are not easily available in local libraries. But some secondary sources have already been published. The policy-making process within the Labour Party after 1970 has been discussed by Lewis Minkin in his important study, *The Labour Party Conference* (Allen Lane, 1978), and by M. Hatfield, *The House The Left Built* (Gollancz, 1978). The debate on industrial democracy within the Party has been described by J. Elliott in his *Conflict or Co-operation: the growth of industrial democracy* (Kegan Paul, 1978); and the 1976 financial crisis was carefully documented by Stephen Fay and Hugo Young in 'The day the £ nearly died', *Sunday Times*, 14, 21 and 28 May 1978. The events surrounding the Lib–Lab pact have been described at length in A. Mitchie and S. Hoggart, *The Pact: the inside story of the Lib–Lab Government 1977–78* (Quartet Books, 1978). Counter Information Services published a pamphlet, *Paying for the Crisis*, which records the policy of the early years of the Labour Government, and this can be obtained from CIS, 9 Poland Street, London, W1; and D. McKie, Chris Cook and M. Philips have summarised the main events of the years after 1974 in their *Guardian/Quartet Guide to the Election* (Quartet Books, 1979). Joe Haines's *The Politics of Power* (Hodder and Stoughton, 1978) should also be consulted; the *British Journal of Industrial Relations* publish a chronicle of recent events in industrial relations and government economic policy in each edition of their journal; and *Keesing's Contemporary Archives* is also an invaluable source for the student of contemporary politics. Also, Ken Coates has edited an important collection of essays, *What Went Wrong?* (Nottingham, Spokesman Books), whose publication in September 1979 came too late for detailed consideration here, but which contains the views of leading academics and political activists on the left of the Labour Party.

On the Labour Party the classic study still remains R. Miliband, *Parliamentary Socialism* (Merlin, 1961); and this can usefully be supplemented by L. Panitch, *Social Democracy and Industrial Militancy* (Cambridge University Press, 1976), by D. Howell, *British Social Democracy* (Croom Helm, 1976) and by L. Minkin and P. Seyd, 'The British Labour Party', in W. Paterson and A. H. Thomas, eds, *Social Democratic Parties in Western Europe* (Croom Helm, 1977).

## Further reading

There is an extensive literature on trade union power and its limits. The most useful collection of writings is in T. Clarke and L. Clements, *Trade Unions Under Capitalism* (Fontana, 1977); and you might usefully read T. Lane, *The Union Makes Us Strong* (Arrow Books, 1974). Lewis Minkin has contributed important essays to this topic: in particular, 'The British Labour Party and the Trade Unions: crisis and compact', *Industrial and Labour Relations Review*, 28, no. 1 (October 1974); and 'The Labour Party has not been hijacked', *New Society*, 6 Oct. 1978. Richard Hyman's work is also valuable: in particular *Strikes* (Fontana, 1972); *Industrial Relations: a Marxist introduction* (Macmillan, 1975); 'Industrial conflict and the political economy', in R. Miliband and J. Saville, eds, *The Socialist Register 1973* (Merlin, 1973); *Marxism and the sociology of trade unionism* (Pluto, 1971); with B. Fryor, 'Trade unions: sociology and political economy', in J. McKinlay, ed., *Processing People* (Holt-Blond, 1974); and, with I. Bough, *Social Values and Industrial Relations* (Oxford, Basil Blackwell, 1975). V. L. Allen, *Militant Trade Unionism* (Merlin, 1966) is also important; as is the collection of essays edited by R. Blackburn and A. Cockburn, *The Incompatibles: trade unions and the consensus* (Penguin, 1965). The treatment of trade unions in the media is discussed in P. Beharrell and G. Philo, *Trade Unions and the Media* (Macmillan, 1977); and a lot of useful information on trade union membership and organisation can be found in R. Taylor, *The Fifth Estate* (Routledge, 1978). The general development of Government economic policy has been discussed in R. Guttman, 'State intervention and the economic crisis: the Labour Government's Economic policy 1974–75' in *Kapitalstate*, 1976. The background to the particular stage of government economy integration reached in the 1970s can be put together by reading S. Young and N. Lowe, *Intervention in the Mixed Economy* (Croom Helm, 1974); M. Shanks, *Planning and Politics: the British experience 1960–1976* (Allen and Unwin, 1977); and Alan Budd, *The Politics of Planning* (Fontana, 1978). Planning agreements have been discussed by L. Vance in 'Negotiating planning agreements' (W.E.A. *Studies for Trade Unionists*, 3, no. 9, 1977). The thesis that these are part of a drift to a corporate economy has been argued in R. E. Pahl and J. T. Winkler, 'The coming corporatism', *New Society*, 18 Oct. 1974, and criticised by J. Westergaard, 'Class inequality and corporatism', in A. Hunt, ed., *Class and Class Structure* (Lawrence and Wishart, 1977). Developments in the car industry have been documented more fully. See in particular H. Beynon, *Working For Ford* (Penguin, 1973), the two reports by Counter Information Services: *British Leyland, the Beginning of the End, Ford: an anti-report*, and *A workers enquiry into the car industry* (CSE Books, 1978).

On industrial democracy and the Labour Left, there are a number of important sources. Stuart Holland, *The Socialist Challenge* (Quartet Books, 1975) is essential reading; and its general themes are repeated in S. Holland, *Strategy for Socialism* (Nottingham, Spokesman Books, 1975) and B. Sedgemore, *The How and Why of Socialism* (Nottingham, Spokesman Books, 1977). G. Hodgson has recently defended Left Labourism in *Socialism and Parliamentary Democracy* (Nottingham, Spokesman Books, 1977). The publications of the Institute for Workers Control are also valuable, as is Richard Hyman's critique, 'Workers' control and revolutionary theory', in R. Miliband and J. Saville, eds, *The Socialist Register 1974* (Merlin, 1974). M. Barratt Brown, *Full Employment: Priority* (Nottingham, Spokesman Books, 1978) is a useful additional source. The problems surrounding Left Labourism are discussed in

R. Miliband, 'Moving on', in Miliband and Saville, eds, *The Socialist Register 1976* (Merlin, 1976) and in the subsequent discussion in *The Socialist Register 1977*. For a full critique of the Tribunite alternative economic strategy, see A. Glyn, *Capitalist Crisis: Tribune's "Alternative Strategy" or Socialist Plan* (Militant, 1979). J. Westergaard and H. Resler, *Class in a Capitalist Society* (Heinemann, 1975) is also essential reading.

The most difficult set of further readings are also the most important – those that explore the nature of the world system within which Labour Governments have to operate. Marx's *Capital* (3 volumes) is less daunting than many people sometimes fear, and this is particularly so when it is read in conjunction with one or more of the many commentaries that are now available: with M. Eldred and M. Roth, *A Guide to Marx's Capital* (CSE Books, 1978), E. Mandel, *Marxist Economic Theory* (Merlin, 1962); G. Kay, *Development and Underdevelopment: a Marxist analysis* (Macmillan, 1975); J. Harrison, *Marxist Economics for Socialists* (Pluto, 1978); B. Fine, *Marx's Capital* (Macmillan, 1975); or even E. Mandel, *The Formation of the Economic Thought of Karl Marx* (New Left Books, 1971).

On the particular nature of the postwar boom and its subsequent developments, see E. Mandel, *Late Capitalism* (New Left Books, 1975) and the same author's *The Second Slump* (New Left Books, 1978). Alternative explanations are offered in P. Baran and P. Sweezy, *Monopoly Capital* (Penguin, 1965) and the associated work by J. O'Connor, *The Fiscal Crisis of the State* (New York, St Martin's Press, 1973). Mandel is discussed critically by B. Rowthorn in *New Left Review 98*; and by implication by D. Yaffe, 'The Marxian theory of crisis, capital and the state', *Economy and Society* 2, no. 2 (May 1973) (which, in an amended form, reappears as part of P. Bullock and D. Yaffe, 'Inflation, the crisis and the post war boom', *Revolutionary Communist* 3/4 (Nov. 1975). Yaffe draws heavily on P. Mattick, *Marx and Keynes* (Merlin, 1971); and his dispute with 'neo-Ricardian' positions is made clear in B. Fine and L. Harris, 'Recent controversies in Marxist economic theory', in Miliband and Saville, eds, *The Socialist Register 1976* (Merlin, 1976), which has an extensive additional bibliography. For an earlier and quite distinct treatment of the British situation, see A. Glyn and B. Sutcliffe, *British Capitalism, workers and the profits squeeze* (Penguin, 1972); or the more eclectic study by A. Gamble and P. Walton, *Capitalism in Crisis: inflation and the State* (Macmillan, 1976). For a much more general survey of the impact of capitalism on the work process see H. Braverman, *Labour in Monopoly Capitalism* (New Left Books, 1974).

There is, finally, an extensive literature on the role of the State in advanced capitalism. R. Miliband, *The State in Capitalist Society* (Weidenfeld and Nicolson, 1968), is a useful start, together with N. Poulantzas, *Political Power and Social Classes* (New Left Books, 1973), and the exchange between them, 'The problem of the capitalist state' in R. Blackburn, *Ideology in Social Science* (Fontana, 1972). See also E. Leclau, 'The specificity of the political: the Miliband Poulantzas debate', *Economy and Society* 4, no. 1 (1975); and J. Holloway and S. Picciotto, *State and Capital: a Marxist debate* (Arnold, 1978).

# Index

miners' dispute, 8, 11, 59
Minkin, Lewis, ix, 55, 57
minimum lending rate, 48
monetarism, 52, 218–19, 236
money supply, 25, 40, 41, 189
monopolies, 87, 157, 175, 193, 243
multinational corporations, 87–9, 101–6,
    107, 145, 157, 182, 249, 262
Murphy, Sir Leslie, 114–15
Murray, Len, 60–3, 64–5, 68–9, 73–5, 84–5,
    211, 213, 215–16

National Economic Development
    Council, 35, 110–13, 139
National Enterprise Board, 6, 9, 11, 85,
    87–90, 92–3, 96–8, 102, 114–28, 142,
    148, 157, 234, 236, 258
National Executive Committee, 2, 53,
    86–7, 100, 229, 240
National Union of Journalists, 72
National Union of Miners, 62, 65, 74, 76,
    139, 212, 215
National Union of Railwaymen, 64
nationalisation, 6, 9, 88, 89, 92, 249, 250
North Sea Oil, 6, 18, 26
organic composition of capital, 170, 188,
    189, 197
Organisation for Economic Co-operation
    and Development, 21, 36, 181, 185
Organisation of Petroleum Exporting
    Countries, 161

Panitch, Leo, ix
Parkin, Frank, 272
parliamentary majority, 150
Pay Board, 59
pay paradox, 218
Peart, Lord, 80
pensions, 9, 13, 89
Peugeot-Citroën, 104
planning agreements, 6, 88, 92–4, 100–6,
    112, 148, 251
political agenda, 17, 178
post-war boom, 179–91
Poulantzas, Nicos, ix, 224
poverty, 84
Prentice, Reg, 63, 227
Price Commission, 109
price controls, 8, 9, 29, 87, 89, 106–10
private sector
    banks and, 249–50
    black list of, 75–6, 106–7
    cash problems in, 22
    Labour Government attitude to, 22,
        86–9, 98–9

state aid to, 47, 88–9, 103, 113, 121
productivity, 111
productivity agreements, 111
profits
    realisation of, 22
    crisis in, 193
    tendency of the rate to fall, 170–1, 172–3,
        197
protectionism, 247
public sector borrowing requirement, 44

referendum, 230–2
*Regeneration of British Industry, The*, 90–1,
    97, 100–1, 120
rents, 13
Resler, Henrietta, ix, 264, 267, 273
revolutionary socialists, 270, 273, 275, 277,
    278–83
Rodgers, William, 80
Rolls Royce 1971 Ltd., 93, 115–16
Ryder, Lord, 98, 114, 116
Ryder Report, 121–2

Scanlon, Hugh, 2, 67, 74, 85, 125
Scargill, Arthur, 223
*Scottish Daily Express*, 136
Scottish Labour Party, 151
Scottish National Party, 152
secondary picketing, 80–1
Sedgemore, Brian, 233, 236, 241
social contract, 4, 5, 23, 24, 59, 82–3
social justice, 14, 16
social spending, 24
social wage, 23, 30
socialism, 274–5
socialists, 274–5, 277, 278–83
socially necessary labour time, 167
South Africa, 57, 58
Spain, 57
state
    borrowing, 37, 44, 187–8
    control of industry, 86–94, 97–113,
        142–6, 243–7
    ideological apparatuses, 120, 206
    inflation and, 188–91
    spending, 24, 25, 26, 37, 39, 84, 183–8
Steedman, Ian, 171n
Steel, David, 153
sterling
    exchange rate of, 10, 12, 19–20, 32, 43,
        44, 49, 95
    crises in, 33, 36–7, 38–41, 64
Strachey, John, 177
strikes, 74, 79, 118, 123, 124–6, 196

# Index

subsidies
  food, 8, 13, 33, 37, 41, 82
  to industry, 23, 29, 39, 41, 69, 90, 100, 101, 102–6, 112, 184, 185, 186, 193
surplus value, 167, 185
Sutcliffe, Bob, ix, 191

taxation
  company, 22, 28
  personal, 14
  problems of, 24–5
Thomas, J.H., 213
Thompson, E.P., 259
toolroom workers, 74, 84, 123–4, 126
trade cycle, 180
trade unions
  contradictory role of, 206, 208, 219, 220, 224–6
  incomes policy and, 14, 59–80
  Labour Government and, 1, 2, 14, 29, 53–85, 197–8, 225–6
  power of, 16, 59, 70–1, 82–5, 202–26
  strategies for, 220–4
Trade Union and Labour Relations Act, 4, 8, 135
Trades Union Congress, 1, 8, 33–5, 60–2, 64–6, 68–70, 72, 75–9, 84–5, 101, 109, 133, 139–40, 156, 203, 216
Transport and General Workers Union, 60, 74, 215
Treasury, 42, 44, 64, 155–6, 235
Tribune, 229, 233
Tribunites, 227–56, 277
Trotsky, Leon, 211
Townsend, Peter, 70n

unemployment, 10, 17, 30–1, 33, 36, 46, 65, 68–71
unequal exchange, 167, 180

Union of Construction, Allied Trades and Technicians, 139
Union of Shop, Distributive and Allied Workers, 215
United States government, 39, 158
unproductive labour, 167–8, 186

value added tax, 27
value, law of, 170
Varley, Eric, 83, 98, 101, 123–6, 151
Vietnam war, 181
Villiers, Sir Charles, 35, 76

wage rates, 8, 11, 12, 32–3, 63, 66, 80
Walton, Paul, ix
wealth tax, 10, 258
West German capitalism, 158, 181
Westergaard, John, ix, 264, 267, 273
Whittaker, Derek, 125
Williams, Shirley, 8, 9, 71, 232
Wilson, Harold, 2, 5–6, 8, 10, 33, 35, 63, 64, 75, 89, 91, 104, 122, 125, 156, 236, 240
worker co-operatives, 136
working class
  attitudes to the Labour Party, 271–3
  militancy, 25, 33, 34, 43–4, 52, 67, 74, 79–81, 108, 146, 196, 225, 259
  political consciousness, 271–3
  strength, 183
World Bank, 182
world economy, 21, 179–91
world recession, 21
world trade, 21, 26, 27, 35–6, 42
World War II, 179
Wyatt, Woodrow, 228

Yaffe, David, ix, 196, 223
Young, Hugo, 242